IR35: Personal Service Companies

Second Edition

IR35: Personal Service Companies

Second Edition

Anne Redston

South Bar House
South Bar Street
Banbury
Oxfordshire OX16 9AB
United Kingdom
Telephone: +44 (0) 870 241 5726
Facsimile: +44 (0) 1295 819776
Part of the Wolters Kluwer Group

Disclaimer

This publication is sold on the understanding that the publisher is not engaged in rendering legal or accounting advice or other professional services. The publisher, its editors and any authors, consultants or general editors expressly disclaim all and any liability and responsibility to any person, whether a purchaser or reader of this publication or not, in respect of anything and of the consequences of anything, done or omitted to be done by any such person in reliance, whether wholly or partially, upon the whole or any part of the contents of this publication. While this publication is intended to provide accurate information in regard to the subject matter covered, readers entering into transactions on the basis of such information should seek the services of a competent professional adviser.

Legislative and other material

While copying in all statutory and other materials resides in the Crown or other relevant body, copyright in the remaining material in this publication is vested in the publisher.

The publisher advises that any statutory or other materials issued by the Crown or other relevant bodies and reproduced or quoted in this publication are not the authorised official versions of those statutory or other materials. In their preparation, however, the greatest care has been taken to ensure exact conformity with the law as enacted or other material as issued.

Crown copyright legislation is reproduced under the terms of Crown Copyright Policy Guidance issued by HMSO. Other Crown Copyright material is reproduced with the permission of the Controller of HMSO and the Queen's printer for Scotland.

Ownership of Trade Marks

Typeset in the UK by Mac Style Ltd, Scarborough, North Yorkshire
Printed by Bell & Bain, Glasgow

Contents

Acknowledgements

My thanks to those who read and commented on various chapters of this book. Without their considerable assistance *IR35 – Personal Service Companies* would have been easier to write but much less interesting. Any remaining mistakes or errors of judgement are my own. I particularly appreciated the help provided for the first edition by Martin Benson, Colin Davis, Nigel Eastaway, Roy Faichney, Malcolm Gammie, Peter Gravestock, David Heaton, David Maclean, Divya Malde, Julian Taylor, Sarah Walker and John Whiting; the second edition has particularly benefited from the comments of Tauqeer Bhatti, Kevin Miller, Emma Nelson and Peter Seedhouse. I'd also like to thank Lissa Allcock, John Newth, Keren Newth, Annette Morris and my husband David Earle, for his inimitable combination of technical knowledge and imperturable calm.

Anne Redston

March 2002

Table of cases

Table of statues

Table of statutory instruments

Table of EU legislation

Table of manuals and handbooks

Abbreviations

Inland Revenue Manuals

AP	Assessment Procedures
CGM	Capital Gains Manual
DMG	Decision Maker's Guide to Working Families Tax Credits
DTRM	Double Tax Relief Manual
ECM	Employer Compliance Manual
EH	Enquiry handbook
EPM	Employment Procedures Manual
ESM	Employment Status Manual
IM	Inspector's Manual
IH	Investigation Handbook
ITH	International Tax Handbook
NAG	National Audit Group Instructions
RG	Residence Guide
SAT1(1995)	The New Current Year Basis
SAT2	Self Assessment – The Legal Framework
SE	Schedule E Manual

Other Inland Revenue booklets

IR20	*Residents And Non-Residents – Liability To Tax In The UK*
IR56	*Employed or Self-employed*
IR175	*Supplying Services through a limited company or partnership*
COP 14	*Code of Practice into Company Tax Returns*

Other abbreviations

CA	Contributions Agency
CT	corporation tax
CTSA	Corporation Tax Self Assessment
CTC	childcare tax credit
DPTC	Disabled Persons Tax Credit
EBT	employee benefit trust
ESC	Extra Statutory Concession
EPP	Executive Pension Plan
FAQ	Frequently Asked Question (per Revenue website)
FCA (Gen) Regs	Family Credit Act General Regulations
FICO	Inland Revenue's Financial Intermediaries and Claims Office
FII	Franked Investment Income
FRS 12	Financial Reporting Standard 12
ILAs	Individual Learning Accounts

NICO	National Insurance Contributions Office
NMWA	National Minimum Wages Act
NRE	net relevant earnings
OECD	Organisation for Economic Co-operation and Development
PCG	Professional Contractors Group
PII	professional indemnity insurance
RIA	Regulatory Impact Assessment
SA	self-assessment system
SCO	Special Compliance Office
SLR	Student loan repayments
SSAS	Small Self Administered Scheme
TAS	Taxed Award Scheme
UEL	The upper earnings limit for National Insurance
WFTC	Working Families Tax Credit
WFPA	Welfare Reform and Pensions Act
WRAs	Working Rule Agreements

1 Introduction

IR35 is conceptually simple, but operationally complex. It involves income tax, corporation tax, National Insurance, and partnership tax. Special rules for self-assessment, subcontractors, residence and domicile all play minor roles. At its heart lie the status tests, distilled for over a century and laced with uncertainty.

The fact that IR35 is difficult is not unusual: anti-avoidance laws are often hard to understand. This usually doesn't matter, because they operate as 'Stop' signs in the statute book, warning taxpayers against taking certain routes. IR35 is different. It is not trying to prevent people using personal service companies, it is seeking to tax them effectively.

There is a simpler solution. If employees were no more heavily taxed than the self-employed, many anti-avoidance rules would fall away. If National Insurance was acknowledged as a tax, and levied fairly across the population, there would be no need for the personal services legislation.

In the Budget press release announcing IR35, the Chancellor said that it 'underlines the Government's commitment to achieving a tax system under which everyone pays their fair share'.

If we truly had a tax system where everyone paid 'their fair share', IR35 would not have been necessary. It was introduced because employees were seeking the same tax treatment as the self-employed. The true anomaly in the UK system is the unfair tax burden on employment, not the existence of personal service companies.

Many thousands of people – tax advisers, agencies, accountants, IT consultants, oil workers, media moguls and footballers – now have to understand these rules. Dawn Primarolo was optimistic that they would succeed. In the House of Commons debate on IR35, she declared:

> 'I do not believe that it is beyond the intellectual capacity of those IT consultants who are still protesting to get to grips with these rules.'(*Hansard* 3 May 2000, Col. 214).

This book is a response to Dawn's challenge. It aims to help those facing IR35 understand how it works. However, it comes with a health warning. This is new legislation, and will change and develop as the years progress. Some of its implications will have slipped by unnoticed; others may prompt speedy amendments. *IR35 – Personal Service Companies* is an initial assessment of the subject, not the last word.

2 Purpose and development of IR35

2.1 Introduction

Press Release IR35 was published in March 1999. It was headed 'Avoidance of tax in the provision of personal services', and was the very last Inland Revenue press release issued with the 1999 Budget papers. Since then it has developed into one of the most controversial tax changes ever proposed. This chapter explains why the rules were introduced, and considers how the legislation has evolved.

2.2 Background to IR35

2.2.1 The personal service company

The main shareholder of a personal service company (PSC) is also its director. Frequently he is its only shareholder and director, and there are no employees. Instead of working directly for clients, or taking up employment within other businesses, the individual operates via his company, which contracts with clients to supply the services of its director.

The service company invoices the client for the cost of supplying the director. The money received by the PSC is used to meet the expenses of the company, with the net profit paid out either as dividends on the director's shares, and/or as salary.

In the 1990s personal service companies became more common, partly as a result of changing employment patterns and partly because of the tax advantages, see Chapter 3.

2.2.2 Changing employment patterns

Under the traditional business model, individuals are recruited by employers, for whom they work for a period until moving on to join another organisation. This has changed, partly as a result of the recession of the late 1980s. Many skilled individuals were made redundant and, unable to find permanent employment elsewhere, began offering their services as consultants via their own service companies.

As the economy recovered, employers remained reluctant to increase head-count by taking on permanent staff. Instead, they used short-term contractors on a project-by-project basis. As each assignment ended, the workers were relocated or their contracts terminated. Service companies thus provided a flexible resource in a cost-conscious and ever-changing business environment.

In areas such as IT, companies did not want to recruit and retain expensive, immobile workforces for what were essentially short or medium-term projects. Once again, contract staff were the answer.

The increasing regulatory burden was a further reason why employers were reluctant to take on permanent staff. Using contractors allowed them to avoid, not only employer's National Insurance, but also arguments over unfair dismissal, maternity rights, and racial/sexual discrimination.

From the worker's point of view, the PSC route allows greater flexibility, increased control over the type and variety of work, and more power to negotiate rates of pay and other conditions. A company gives the appearance of more substance than a sole trader business, as well as offering the attraction of limited liability. From the client's perspective, service companies were seen to provide protection from the PAYE and NIC liabilities which might otherwise arise if a sole trader working for them was later recategorised as an employee.

Number of service companies

Not all contract staff have their own service companies. Some are employed directly by agencies who supply them to clients; others are taken on by employers directly, using fixed term contracts. But by the end of the millennium there were said to be roughly 66,000 personal service companies (WRPA, Regulatory Impact Assessment, para 15).

This was probably an under-estimate, since the projected income from IR35 increased from the original £475m in September 1999 (*IRPR* 23 September) to £900m in the Budget 2000 Red Book. This discrepancy was explained by Dawn Primarolo in the House of Commons as follows:

> '[For] our original assessments we estimated the number of companies that were using the loophole we described. We were challenged about this estimate, and ... I asked the Inland Revenue to assess thoroughly through our network the number of companies that appeared to be using that mechanism ... That is where the new £900m figure came from. In truth, the avoidance mechanism is being used far more extensively than we had anticipated.' (*Hansard* 3 May 2000, Col. 217)

Therefore, as at March 2000, government research suggested that around 125,000 companies would be brought within IR35, and there are of course others who remain outside the regime. This numerical estimate was broadly confirmed by the Revenue during the judicial review case (*R v CIR (oao Professional Contractors Group Ltd)* [2001] STC 629 – see **2.4**). They said that in 2000/01 there were between 90,000 and 120,000 PSCs; however they estimated the cost to the exchequer (if IR35 had not been implemented) at a much lower £350m. The reason for the discrepancy was not explained.

2.2.3 Growing government concerns

Proposals were brought forward in the early 1980s to close down the tax advantages of service companies, but these were rejected after widespread criticism. However in 1999 the concerns of the Department of Trade and Industry (DTI) and the Inland Revenue combined with those of the Labour Government to create a force for change.

The DTI saw service company arrangements as undermining the workers' employment protection. Budget Press Release IR35 expressed this as follows:

'Those who do participate (in the new arrangements) often have to pay a price in terms of loss of protection under employment law. They may find their terms and conditions altered – perhaps losing entitlement to sick pay or maternity leave. They may even lose their jobs without entitlement to notice or redundancy pay. They will usually have no right to any claim for unfair dismissal and may lose their entitlement to social security benefits through a failure to make adequate contributions.'

Ministers also worried that the use of service companies was unfair to the rest of the population who paid tax and NICs on their earnings in the traditional way. Dawn Primarolo, speaking in the IR35 debate on 3 May 2000, said:

'We want to stop people who are really the same as employees from dressing up their working arrangements by setting themselves up as a service company to avoid paying the correct levels of properly due tax and National Insurance ... Such avoidance is simply not fair to the rest of us, and we should deal with it.' (*Hansard* 3 May, Col. 212–3)

Mr Timms, speaking for the Government in the debate on the Welfare Reform and Pensions Bill on 3 November 1999, explained the financial consequences as follows:

'It is highly possible for a highly paid office worker earning perhaps £1,800 per week to pay no National Insurance contributions at all, while a nurse earning £300 a week pays £23.45 and her employer pays £26.53 in National Insurance … this is obviously not right and we are sorting it out.' (*Hansard*, Col. 404)

The Revenue for their part had been worried for some time about the rapid growth of personal service companies. The increasing artificiality of some arrangements convinced them that many service companies were being set up solely or mainly for tax avoidance purposes. In particular, they were concerned about the creation of composites, Friday to Monday companies, and the use of 'long-term temps'.

Composites

Composites or 'umbrella' companies are corporates whose shareholders/employees tend to have a skill in common. In a typical composite, a group of otherwise unconnected individuals form a company to supply services. Every shareholder has a different class of share, and the income each person generates pays the dividends on his own share class. In the late 1990s, when composites became commonplace, dividends were frequently paid monthly.

The Revenue saw composites as artificial structures formed largely to exploit the tax advantages of a PSC. Examples of composites unfavourably regarded by the Revenue included companies formed by train drivers and doctors' secretaries.

Friday to Monday companies

The tax and regulatory advantages of PSCs encouraged some employers to hive off parts of their work-force and re-engage them immediately as independent contractors each with their own service company. In some cases individuals were made redundant or given early retirement, only to return the following week as directors of a PSC. However their work, responsibilities and roles were substantially the same: what had changed was their employment rights and tax status.

The Friday to Monday problem was highlighted in IR35:

'There has for some time been general concern about the hiring of individuals through their own service companies so that they can exploit the fiscal advantages offered by a corporate structure. It is possible for someone to leave work as an employee on a Friday, only to return the following Monday to do exactly the same job as an indirectly engaged "consultant" paying substantially reduced tax and national insurance. The Government is going to bring forward legislation to tackle this sort of avoidance.'

The long-term temp

The Government also expressed concern about the 'long-term temp' – a person who worked in an organisation for some considerable time, but within the wrapper of the service company. In the House of Lords debate on the Welfare Reform and Pensions Act, Lord McIntosh of Haringey, for the government, said:

> 'Let us consider the case of two people sitting side by side in the computer department of a big company. One is an employee of the company, the other works for his own service company. They might both have been there for the same length of time; they are both part of the same team and work under the same team leader, doing the same type of work. It has been argued that because one worker has chosen to set up a service company he is somehow an entrepreneur and deserves to pay less tax and NIC ... I do not think his colleague at the next desk would agree.' (*Hansard* 13 October 1999, Col. 478)

The existence of large numbers of long-term temps thus reinforced the Government's conviction that it would be unfair to the rest of the working population if they turned a blind eye to service companies.

2.3 The legislative process

2.3.1 IR35

Press Release IR35 was issued on 9 March 1999. Apart from outlining the issue, and mentioning Friday to Monday companies, it gave few other details. However, it did say that:

> 'The proposed changes are aimed only at engagements with essential characteristics of employment. They should affect only those cases where these characteristics are disguised through use of an intermediary – such as a service company or partnership. There is no intention to redefine the existing boundary between employment and self-employment ... The Inland Revenue will over the next few months be working with representative bodies on aspects of the practical application of the new rules and on the production of guidance. Any groups interested in contributing to this process should write to ... Personal Tax Division.'

The tone of the press release, and its suggestion that all those with service companies were 'disguised employees' has been much criticised. Mr Justice Burton said:

'It appears to me wholly regrettable and unnecessary that such colourful language was used in the first press release … I am sure that there would have
still have been a vigorous resistance to the proposed legislation, however it
had been presented; but there might have been a good deal less resentment
and hostility had the government been less offensive in its approach.' *R v
CIR (oao Professional Contractors Group Ltd)* [2001] STC 629 – see **2.4**.

2.3.2 The April paper

The first sign of what the government was planning to do emerged in April,
when a paper was circulated to those bodies who had responded to the invi-
tation to contribute contained in the Press Release. The April paper was
heavily caveated, with the following warnings:

'This summary is for use as a basis for discussion but is not a consultation
document. This summary should not be taken as indicative of the form new
rules might eventually take and is not to be relied upon in individual circumstances where the underlying facts may differ.'

The proposals encompassed:

• All those who supply services through intermediaries, including companies,
  agencies and partnerships;

• Where the worker operates under the control of the client;

• As to the tasks undertaken or the manner in which they were controlled.

Where these conditions applied, the client was to deduct PAYE and NIC from
amounts invoiced by the intermediary. This obligation could however be
ignored if the client knew that 'substantially' all the monies related to the work
done were being paid on to the worker as salary, and were thus subjected to
PAYE and NIC in the intermediary. No definition was given of 'substantially'.

To make obtaining this information easier for the client, intermediaries could
register on a national database; registration would count as confirmation that
all relevant amounts would be paid on to the worker and subjected to PAYE
and NICs. Clients could thus access the database before paying an invoice in
order to find out whether they could pay it gross or whether they should first
deduct tax and NIC.

2.3.3 Problems with the April paper

These proposals were heavily criticised. In particular:

- The certification scheme was denounced as bureaucratic and burdensome;

- The crude 'control' test would catch many people who would have been regarded as self-employed if they had operated as a sole trader instead of via an intermediary;

- Anyone familiar with NIC and the NIRS2 computer system wondered how it would cope with miscellaneous receipts deducted from invoices and paid over by clients without any link to the workers' NI numbers;

- The extent to which expenses could be deducted (if at all) was unclear;

- Tax and NIC had to be deducted by the client in all cases where the invoiced amount was greater than the salary paid, even if the recipient was a non-shareholding employee who received a market rate salary;

- There were fears that the UK economy would be damaged by a collapse of the contracting market and by economic migration to more benevolent regimes such as the Netherlands.

Although the April proposals had initially been sent to a mere handful of people, word of their content began to spread. The Revenue finally received over 1,700 responses, most of them uncomplimentary. The proposals were condemned as oppressive, disproportionate and damaging to the economy.

2.3.4 The September Press Release

After considerable debate, a revised scheme was finally published in outline on 23 September. Under these new proposals, three features of the April scheme were dropped:

- The intermediary, not the client, became responsible for compliance with the legislation. The need for a certification scheme thus disappeared;

- An exemption was announced for 'genuine' employees of a PSC or partnership who were not shareholders or partners. A de minimis exemption was to be granted for small shareholders;

- The control test was replaced by a fairer version using the existing Schedule D/E divide. The individual worker would only be within the new rules if he would have been an employee of his client, had he not been operating within the 'wrapper' of a service company or partnership.

2.3.5 Tax legislation

Draft tax legislation was published in February 2000, and was then included as Schedule 12, Finance Act 2000. Although the Act did not become law until

July, the legislation took effect from the beginning of the 2000/01 fiscal year, by virtue of the Provisional Collection of Taxes Act 1968.

2.3.6 National Insurance legislation and regulations

National Insurance legislation cannot generally be backdated in the same way as tax. The Government thus introduced enabling clauses into the Welfare Reform and Pensions Bill, which was going through Parliament at the end of 1999. These provisions were broad-brush powers which allowed detailed regulations on personal service companies to be written later.

The legislation was introduced in the House of Lords, where it was fiercely debated. At one point the Bill was thrown out by the Upper House and returned to the Commons. However it succeeded in becoming law just before the end of the Parliamentary session.

Draft NIC regulations were subsequently published in February 2000; final regulations were laid on 13 March 2000 and came into force on 6 April.

2.3.7 Frequently Asked Questions (FAQs)

The Revenue faced considerable criticism for the way the consultation process had been handled, particularly in its initial stages. Partly as a reaction to this, and partly as an acknowledgement that many of their fiercest critics were from the IT industry, the Revenue used their website to ensure that those involved were kept informed as the legislation developed.

Particularly novel were the regular bulletins of Frequently Asked Questions on IR35 (FAQs), which covered everything from partnerships to composites, from overseas companies to travel expenses. This welcome development allowed the Revenue to deal with issues and uncertainties as they arose.

2.4 The Judicial Review

2.4.1 Outline

In autumn 2000 the Professional Contractors Group (PCG), an umbrella body comprised of 'knowledge-based workers' opposed to IR35, was granted leave to challenge the personal services legislation by way of judicial review. This took place in March 2001. However, when judgment was given on 2 April, Mr Justice Burton found for the government on all counts (*R v CIR (oao*

Professional Contractors Group Ltd) [2001] STC 629). Nevertheless, he made trenchant criticisms of Revenue guidance on IR35, which led to some changes being made in both the Employee Status Manual (ESM) and the Revenue's contract clearance process.

The PCG appealed the decision and the case was heard in December 2001 before Lord Justices Auld, Dyson and Walker. Judgment was given on 21 December, and was a victory for the Revenue (*Professional Contractors Group and others v CIR* [2001] EWCA/1945). Both the original judicial review and the appeal are discussed below.

2.4.2 Human Rights

The first point considered in the judicial review was whether IR35 was a breach of human rights. Article 1 Protocol 1 of the European Convention on Human Rights states that 'every natural or legal person is entitled to the peaceful enjoyment of his possessions'. This is, however, subject to the right of member states to 'control the use of property in accordance with the general interest [and] to secure the payment of taxes or other contributions'.

The PCG argued that the right to enjoy the benefit of a shareholding in a service company was a right of property, and that IR35 interfered with that right because:

- Little or no profit remains in the service company after the legislation has taken effect, and the value of the company and its shares is thus negligible; and

- The legislation is so uncertain in its impact that the 'enjoyment of the [contractors'] shareholding in the service companies and/or the very existence of the service companies are jeopardised'.

Both these arguments were examined separately.

Shareholding

Mr Justice Burton agreed with the PCG that IR35 reduced the value of the contractors' shareholding, but said that, under EU law 'it is in the first place for the national authorities to decide what kind of taxes or contributions are to be collected' *Svenska Managementgruppen AB v Sweden Application* [1985] 11036/84, 45 DR 211. Whilst there must be a balance between the demands of the general interest of the Community and the protection of the individual's fundamental rights, nevertheless the State has a wide power of appreciation in these areas and 'the Court will respect the Legislature's assessment in respect of such matters unless it is devoid of reasonable foundation' (*National and Provincial Building Society and Others v United Kingdom* [1997] 25 EHRR 127).

To be illegal, the High Court would thus have to hold that IR35 amounted to 'a de facto confiscation of some part of the taxpayer's possessions'. (*X v France* Application 9908/82, 32 DR 266 [1983]). Unsurprisingly, the judge did not consider that the personal service company legislation was 'even arguably' so severe as to be a breach of human rights under these principles.

Uncertainty

Mr Justice Burton agreed that there were areas of 'potential dispute' when considering the dividing line between the employed and the self-employed. However, he did not consider that:

> 'It offends against the concept of certainty for the common law of employ-
> ment to apply to a service contractor … any more than I conclude that it is
> contrary to Human Rights to apply such a law in an ordinary case to an
> individual.'

In other words, sole traders already have to cope with the grey area between employment and self-employment, and IR35 merely requires the same of contractors. The judge also pointed out that the concept of certainty 'allows for the possibility of the need of legal or accountancy advice', see *The Sunday Times v UK* [1979–80] 2 EHRR 245. Thus, if taxpayers need professional help before they can understand their tax position, this does not amount to a breach of human rights.

Conclusion

The judge in the High Court decided against the PCG, and the latter elected not to appeal this point.

2.4.3 Illegal state aid

High Court

The PCG argued that IR35 constituted illegal state aid to the personal service companies' larger competitors (known as 'bodyshops'), because the latter did not have the disadvantages of IR35. Mr Justice Burton broadly agreed with this, saying that:

'Companies unaffected by IR35 will have greater flexibility to arrange their tax affairs, to allocate tax between income tax and corporation tax, to defer tax liabilities, and to pay lesser salaries to those providing the services and higher dividends to shareholders, than service contractors.'

However, he said that this did not constitute state aid to the larger contractors, because state aid had to be specific, see for example *Italian Republic v Commission of the European Community* C-6/97 [1999] ECR 1–2981. He also cited the case of *Ecotrade SRL v Altiforni e Ferriere di Servola SpA* Case C–200/97 [1998] ECR 1–7907, where the court had distinguished 'between aids, which are selective in nature, and State measures of general application in the fields of taxation, social security, regulation of the economy and so on'.

IR35 was, said the judge, a general measure, intended to ensure compliance with the tax system generally. It was not targeted at any specific sector, even though many of those caught by it are from within the knowledge industry, and there was a resulting spin-off benefit to their larger competitors. He summarised the position as follows:

'This general measure did not have the object, and, in my judgment, also did not have the effect, of amounting to state aid to those competitors. Put another way, any consequence in respect of such competitors in certain sectors was an incidental side-effect.'

Court of Appeal

The Court of Appeal stated that 'the detriment imposed by IR35 can constitute aid only if it is to be seen as favouring other competing undertakings, in breach of the selectivity principle'. It was thus important to consider the relative position of those who were in competition with service companies caught by IR35.

Despite the fact that the High Court had found as a fact that the contractors were in competition with the bodyshops, the Court of Appeal emphasised that the relevant comparator for these purposes was the employees of the client. Lord Justice Walker said:

'Mr Barling has skilfully and determinedly argued that ... the relevant comparison is between a service company whose activities are caught by IR35 and a larger trading company, providing similar services, which is not caught. But ... I cannot accept that approach. Certainly the tax provisions of IR35 have to address the service company's liability to corporation tax, in order to avoid double taxation. But the aim of both the tax and the NIC provisions (an aim which they may be expected to achieve) is to ensure that individuals who ought to pay tax and NIC as employees cannot, by the assumption of a corporate structure, reduce and defer the liabilities imposed on employees by the United Kingdom's system of personal taxation.'

In addition, the judges reaffirmed that 'a mere propensity for a measure to favour one sector rather than another cannot amount to selectivity', and concluded by confirming the judgment of Mr Justice Burton, that IR35 was not a breach of the EU's state aid provisions.

2.4.4 Freedom of movement

High Court

The final PCG argument was that the legislation made the UK less attractive to those using personal service companies, and thus removed the incentive for them to come to, or stay within, the UK.

There is, of course, legislation similar to IR35 in other countries. In order to illustrate this point, the Revenue quoted from the Contractor UK website which advised:

'If your goal in going overseas is to escape IR35, the best plan is to ditch your UK company before you move overseas ... Not every country has historically been as laid back as the UK in allowing individuals to restructure themselves overnight and repackage their employment as a service from company to company!'

While this clearly caused some discomfiture to the complainants, the judge was correctly persuaded by Mr Barling, the PCG's Counsel, that restrictions elsewhere in the EU should not be taken into account when considering whether the legislation restricted freedom of movement. He also accepted that 'even minor breaches are contrary to Community Law'.

Three provisions of the EU treaty were thus considered. These covered freedom of movement for workers (Article 39), freedom of establishment (Article 43) and freedom to provide services in another member state without establishing oneself there (Article 49).

The judge carefully considered the extensive case law, concluding as follows:

'I am however just persuaded that the imposition of the tax regime by IR35, which is now less favourable than the previous welcoming tax regime, could be said to be an impediment to mobility, in the sense that a positive incentive for [those affected by IR35] to come or stay [in the UK] may now have been removed.'

In other words, there was what he called a 'marginal impediment' to freedom of movement. However, he went on to hold that this was insufficient to amount to a breach of either Article 39 or Article 43, although 'it is just arguable that there is a relevant restriction within Article 49'.

Court of Appeal

The Revenue argued that Mr Justice Burton was wrong to say that there was even a 'marginal impediment' to freedom of movement, and the Court of Appeal agreed. Lord Justice Walker said:

'IR35 cannot be regarded as discriminatory, either in the ordinary sense or under what the judge called dislocation. It does not provide a direct and demonstrable inhibition on the establishment of a business within the United Kingdom, or on the provision of services without establishment. Genuine self-employed activities will not be affected and a business of providing employee-like services will be taxed as if there was a real employment situation.'

2.4.5 Tax avoidance as a justification

High Court

Having held that IR35 may amount to a breach of Article 49, Mr Justice Burton then moved on to consider whether this breach could be justified. Justification is possible if there is a 'pressing reason of public interest', including 'the effectiveness of official supervision, the protection of public health, the fairness of commercial transactions and the defence of the consumer' (*Cassis de Dijon* 120/78 [1979] ECR 649).

Mr Barling argued that dealing with tax avoidance was not included under 'the effectiveness of official supervision'. He also raised the interesting point that, even if it were included, personal service companies did not constitute tax avoidance, but tax mitigation.

During the hearing Mr Justice Burton appeared to have some sympathy for this view, saying that 'adopting a corporate structure is better described as tax mitigation than tax avoidance. I see nothing to be critical of in people taking advantage of the laws.'

However, in his final judgment he moved away from this position, and accepted that IR35 was in fact aimed at tax avoidance. He then went on to say that, although the EU had ruled out tax avoidance as a justification in a number of earlier cases, these were all concerned with discrimination on the grounds of nationality. IR35 was not such a case, as it applied equally to UK nationals and those from overseas. There was thus no precedent for refusing the government's argument that 'combating tax avoidance and/or reducing a diminution in tax revenue' was justification for the breach, and he thus found in favour of the Revenue.

Court of Appeal

Because the Court of Appeal found in favour of the Revenue on state aid and freedom of movement, they did not need to consider the issue of justification, but did so for completeness. Lord Justice Walker reiterated Mr Justice Burton's view, saying that tax avoidance had not been rejected by the ECJ as a justification in all cases, but only where the measures against tax avoidance were discriminatory. In addition he said, in a passage which is sure to excite criticism from those affected by IR35, that:

> 'I note also that in paragraph 26 of *ICI v Colmer* the suggestion that the more artificial the tax avoidance which has to be countered the easier it may be to find justification. IR35 is aimed at relatively artificial avoidance since it counters only activities which are the provision, in the guise of self-employment (normally through a corporate vehicle), of employee-like services.'

2.4.6 Proportionality

High Court

The final point dealt with by Mr Justice Burton was proportionality. Even if the legislation was justified under EU law, it could be rejected if it were found to be disproportionate. A similar point on proportionality was considered as part of the PCG's Human Rights argument.

Proportionality has been defined in *Gebhard* C–55/94 [1995] 1 ECR 1–4165 as follows:

> 'National measures liable to hinder or make less attractive the exercise of fundamental freedoms guaranteed by the Treaty must ... not go beyond what is necessary.'

Mr Justice Burton found that IR35 was proportionate. He also said that it was not for him to 'canvass other possible methods of fiscal reform … it is not for me to enter into the political arena'.

Court of Appeal

Since the Court of Appeal had found in favour of the Revenue, there was no need for it to consider proportionality, but it was reviewed for completeness. Lord Justice Walker summarised the issue as follows:

> 'If the IR35 legislation had to be justified an essential part of the process of justification would be for the Revenue to show that its terms were appropriate and necessary to achieve its objectives; that whenever there was a choice between different measures which might be appropriate the least onerous had been chosen; and that the burdens imposed by the measures were not disproportionate to the aims pursued.'

This proved to be one of the most interesting issues raised during the Appeal. Lord Justice Walker said he wondered whether:

> 'It might not have been possible to bring forward measures which accorded some recognition to the existence of a sort of no-man's land between Schedule D and Schedule E, rather than insisting on the gulf which exists in theory (but not, always, in practice) between them. Such measures might still have contained robust sanctions against unacceptable tax avoidance.'

He also said that if there had been a need to consider proportionality, he would:

> 'Be inclined to think that the judge [in the High Court] did not go far enough in asking himself whether the IR35 measures were the least onerous which could be adopted in order to achieve their objective. In expressing that tentative view I am well aware of the difficulty of the task.'

These comments do suggest that the Court of Appeal judges considered that IR35 *is* disproportionate to the issue the government faced, but given that the Court of Appeal had rejected the PCG's fundamental challenges to EU law, proportionality was not an issue they had to consider.

2.4.7 Amendments to Revenue guidance

Although Mr Justice Burton dismissed all the PCG's arguments, he nevertheless pointed out a number of errors and weaknesses in the Revenue's approach to IR35. These are included as relevant through the rest of this book, but particularly important points are made at **7.3.4**, **7.4.7**, **7.6** and **7.7.1**.

Following the PCG case in March 2001, the Revenue acknowledged that it needed to make some improvements in the material it had published on IR35. A spokesperson was quoted as saying:

> 'We do accept that he has identified one or two examples … where we haven't been as operationally efficient as we should have been.' *Financial Times, 3 April 2001.*

2.5 Conclusion

The history of IR35 has been brief, but recent events have demonstrated the government's determination to retain this controversial and complex legislation despite fierce opposition.

3   Tax planning and IR35

3.1 General

Personal service companies became popular partly because of their tax advantages. But the more popular they became, the greater the loss of tax to the Treasury. It was this, combined with the fact that 'such avoidance is simply not fair to the rest of us' (Dawn Primarolo, *Hansard* 3 May 2000, Col. 213) which lay behind Ministers' determination to press ahead with IR35.

The main focus of the Government's attacks was on the use of dividends to avoid National Insurance, but service companies have other tax advantages. They include:

(a) Paying salaries to family members to absorb their tax allowances and lower rate bands;

(b) Utilising the corporate tax rules for expenses and capital allowances rather than the less generous reliefs available to employees;

(c) Maximising pension contributions in ways which are inaccessible to individuals;

(d) Obtaining a tax deduction against other income for interest on funds borrowed to invest in the business;

(e) Retaining surplus funds in the company to take advantage of the low corporate tax rates;

Access to a 10 per cent rate of capital gains tax on disposal of the company's shares.

This chapter explains some of the tax and National Insurance planning which lay behind the introduction of IR35. Personal service companies which fall wholly or partly outside the new legislation can still use these opportunities, as can small corporate businesses other than suppliers of personal services, see **4.2.1**. A number of pitfalls associated with these planning ideas, such as illegal dividends and the rules for directors' loans, are discussed at the end of the chapter.

Even where companies are caught by IR35, some tax advantages remain. Chapter 23 summarises those which survive, as well as highlighting others appropriate to the post-IR35 era.

3.2 Paying dividends rather than salary

3.2.1 Outline

One of the most significant tax planning opportunities for small companies arises from the combination of low tax rates on company profits (see **3.2.2**) and the absence of National Insurance on dividends (see **3.2.3**). Considerable savings can be made if most of the company's profits are paid out as dividends rather than as salary.

Two recent tax changes have further increased the advantages of this route. ACT was abolished with effect from 6 April 1999, and four weeks earlier the March 1999 Budget announced a reduction in the corporate tax rates for small businesses. It is no coincidence that the same budget gave birth to IR35.

3.2.2 Corporate tax rates

Salaries are deductible from profits and so reduce the corporate tax due, while dividends are paid out of post-tax profits. The rate of tax on company profits is thus a factor in deciding whether to pay salaries or dividends.

If tax on profits is higher than tax on salary, salary should be paid to reduce profits; if corporate taxes are low, but taxes on salary are high, it is better to pay the corporate tax and distribute the net profit as a dividend. There is of course a third factor, the relative taxation of dividends and salary, which is discussed at **3.2.3** below.

The salary versus dividend comparison is weighted in favour of dividends for small companies, because they are unlikely to pay tax at more than 20 per cent; some may also benefit from the 10 per cent starting rate.

In general, as the company becomes more profitable, the dividend route becomes less efficient. This is because corporate tax rates increase once profits exceed £300,000. Service companies with higher levels of profits should model their tax position under both the salary and the dividend routes in order to determine the optimum cut-off point.

Starting rate

The 10 per cent starting rate was introduced with effect from 6 April 2000 and was reduced to 0% from 6 April 2002. It applies only to the first £10,000 of profits, with a marginal calculation operating between £10,000 and £50,000 (s13AA ICTA 1988). The simplest way of calculating tax on profits between £10,000 and £50,000 is to establish a rate of tax for profits in the marginal band so as to arrive at the right tax charge overall. For 2001/02 this is 22.5 per cent; for 2002/03 it is 23.75 per cent.

The effect of the marginal calculation is to tax profits below £50,000 in such a way that when profits reach £50,000 *total* profits are taxed at the small companies' rate. It is sometimes mistakenly thought that there is a 10 per cent (or zero per cent) band, but this is not the case. The position is more complicated when the company has franked investment income.

Small companies' rate

The small companies' rate applies where profits do not exceed £300,000. The rate was 20 per cent until 2002/03 when it was reduced to 19 per cent. For profits between £300,000 and £1,500,000 a marginal rate applies. This has the effect of taxing total profits at somewhere between the small companies' rate and the full corporate rate of 30 per cent (s13 ICTA 1988).

As with the starting rate, the simplest way of dealing with this is to establish a tax rate for profits in the marginal band so as to get the correct answer overall. For 2001/02 this is 32.5 per cent, see Example 3A. Again, the position is more complicated when the company has franked investment income.

Example 3A

Tigger Limited's corporation tax profits for the accounting period ended 31 March 2002 are £350,000. Corporation tax payable is:

	£	Rate	£
Profit up to marginal band	300,000	20%	60,000
Excess	50,000	32.5%	16,250
Total tax			76,250
Tax rate	76,250/350,000	21.78%	

Other points

(a) The £10,000, £50,000, £300,000 and £1.5m limits are reduced pro-rata if there are associated companies. Thus, if there are two companies in the group, each limit will be halved (s13(3) and s13AA(4) ICTA 1988). Associated companies are defined in s416 ICTA 1988;

(b) The limits are reduced where the accounting period in question is less than 12 months (s13A(6) and s13AA(6) ICTA 1988);

(c) Accounting periods straddling 1 April are treated as two separate periods, one ending on 31 March and one beginning on 1 April (s86(3) FA 1994).

Exclusions from the reliefs

Neither the starting rate nor the small companies' rate is available (s13(1) ICTA 1988) for:

(a) Non-resident companies. However a non-discrimination clause in a double taxation agreement may allow the UK branch or agency of a non-resident company to access the starting rate or small companies' rate (*CCAB TR500* 10 March 1983);

(b) Housing investment trusts (s508A(1)(b) ICTA 1988);

(c) Close investment-holding companies. These are not defined in the legislation (s13A ICTA 1988), which instead says that all companies are close investment holding companies unless throughout the accounting period they exist wholly or mainly for one of the following:

    (i)   The carrying on of trade(s) on a commercial basis;
    (ii) Letting of property other than to connected persons;
    (iii) Holding shares in, administering, or lending money to a company which is not a close investment holding company.

For a situation where s13A might be applied in the context of a composite service company, see **23.4.4**.

3.2.3 National Insurance

The real benefits of paying dividends rather than salary derive from the fact that no National Insurance Contributions are due on dividends. Of the various tax advantages available to the service company, National Insurance avoidance was the main target of IR35. In the Revenue's first Frequently Asked Question (FAQ) 'What is IR35 about?' they said:

> 'Intermediaries such as service companies can be set up to provide the services of a single worker to a client in circumstances where, if it were not for the service company, the worker would be an employee of the client. The use of service companies in this way allows the client to make payments to the company rather than the individual, without deducting PAYE or NICs.

The worker can then take the money out of the service company in the form of dividends instead of salary. Dividends are not liable to NICs so the worker will pay less in NICs than either a conventional employee or a self-employed person. The Chancellor believes that avoidance of PAYE and NICs in this way needs to be tackled in the interests of fairness.'

In 1999 the government estimated that the use of dividends rather than salary by service companies was costing the Treasury £220m per year in lost National Insurance. It was expected that this amount would increase further as more people took advantage of the opportunity (WRPA, RIA para 14). In March 2000 further research indicated that the number of service companies 'using the loophole' was actually twice the original estimate (*Hansard* 3 May 2000, Col. 217). This would put the National Insurance loss up to £440m a year.

These savings come about because salary is subject to both employee and employer's NIC. Employee NIC is charged at 10 per cent on amounts between the employee's earnings threshold (£3,744 for 2001/02) and the upper earnings limit (£29,900 in 2001/02). Employer's NIC (at 11.9 per cent in 2001/02) is charged on all earnings above the employer's earning threshold (£4,535 in 2001/02). Since there is no cap on employer's NIC, its cost grows as salary increases.

The amount of NIC saved depends on the position of the individual, see Examples 3B and 3C below.

Taxation of dividends

Dividends received by an individual come with a 10 per cent tax credit. The dividend plus the tax credit constitute Franked Investment Income (FII). If the recipient is a non-taxpayer, the tax credit is not recoverable. FII received by a basic rate taxpayer is taxed at 10 per cent (the Schedule F lower rate) and thus the tax credit covers the liability.

Higher rate taxpayers pay tax on FII at 32.5 per cent, the 'Schedule F upper rate'. Taking into account the tax credit, this is equivalent to 25 per cent of the dividend.

Example 3B shows how this works, using a simple scenario where the director is already within the higher rate band, and including the employer's NIC saving.

Example 3B

Mike's company makes recordings of choral music. In the year to 31 March 2001 it has pre-tax profits of £10,000. Mike has other income which has brought him into the higher rate tax bracket; he has also paid the maximum Class 1 employee NIC liability. The company can either pay him salary or a dividend.

	Rate	£
Dividend		
CT profits		10,000
CT thereon	10.0%	(1,000)
Available to Mike		9,000
Dividend received		9,000
Add tax credit	1/9	1,000
		10,000
Tax thereon	25.0%	(3,250)
After tax income		6,750
Effective rate of tax	32.5%	
Bonus		
CT profits		10,000
Less bonus		(8,937)
Less employer's NIC		(1,063)
Profits subject to CT		0
Bonus received		8,937
Less income tax	40.0%	(3,575)
After tax income		5,362
Effective rate of tax	46.4%	

Example 3B shows that the use of dividends rather than salary can reduce the combined NIC and tax rate by 14 per cent where the shareholder/director is already within the 40 per cent tax bracket.

Where an individual is both a basic rate taxpayer and below the upper threshold for employee NICs, paying a dividend rather than salary produces an even more tax-efficient result. This is because:

(a) Profits in a small company are usually taxed at no more than 20 per cent (see **3.2.2**); when these profits are paid out as dividends they suffer no further tax when received by a basic rate taxpayer. This is in contrast to salary which would have been taxed at 22 per cent;

(b) By paying a dividend, both employer's NIC (as in Example 3C) and employee NIC are saved.

These advantages are demonstrated in Example 3C.

Example 3C

Bill is the sole shareholder in his woodcarving business. His company has taxable profits of £10,000, and he can choose either to receive all profits as a dividend, or as salary. He is a basic rate taxpayer, with £7,000 of other income. The calculation is the same as in Example 3B, apart from the final stage, the tax and NICs on Bill's salary.

	Rate	**£**
Dividend		
Corporation tax:		
Profits		10,000
Corporation tax	10%	(1,000)
Net profit paid as dividend		9,000
Income tax		
Basic rate tax payable		nil
Cash received		9,000
Effective rate of tax		10%
Bonus		
Profits before salary		10,000
Less salary		(8,937)
Less employer's NIC	11.9%	(1,063)
Profits subject to corporation tax		nil
Income tax		
Salary received		8,937
Employee's NIC	10%	(894)
Income tax	22%	(1,966)
Cash received		6,077
Effective rate of tax		39.2%

By paying a dividend Bill has reduced his combined tax and NICs rate from almost 40 per cent to a mere 10 per cent.

3.2.4 Other advantages of using dividends rather than salary

A number of other advantages arise from paying dividends rather than salary:

- Dividends provide a cash flow advantage, because tax on salary is deducted weekly or monthly under PAYE, whereas higher rate tax on a dividend is paid on 31 January following the fiscal year of receipt;

- Corporation tax is also paid later than PAYE, being due nine months and one day after the end of the company's accounting period (s59D TMA 1970);

- Abolition of ACT in 1999 further increased the cash flow benefits of dividends compared to salary.

3.3 Small salary payment

It is, however, not advisable for all profits to be paid out as a dividend. If no salary at all is paid, the individual will have no National Insurance Contributions record. As a result he will have no state pension, and will fail to qualify for contributory benefits such as statutory sick pay, see **22.5.2**.

Entitlement to contributory benefits can however be achieved without incurring either employer or employee NICs. For the year 2001/02 a salary of between £3,744 and £4,535 gives entitlement to benefits without suffering any National Insurance. Above £4,535, both employer and employee NICs become payable.

When calculating the salary to be paid, it may be necessary to consider minimum wage requirements, see **22.2**. For the payment of salaries to other family members, see **3.4** below.

Contributions to personal pensions and retirement annuities depend on the existence of net relevant earnings (NRE), essentially salary and taxable benefits. If salary and benefits are low, NRE will be low, and an individual's pension contributions will therefore be limited. This issue is discussed at **3.6** below, along with consideration of other forms of pension which do not depend on NRE.

A higher salary should be considered where the individual has allowable expenses, such as interest (see **3.7**), to deduct from his taxable income, as otherwise no tax relief may be obtained for the expense. This is because the tax credits on dividends are no longer repayable, see **3.10.2**.

3.4 Payments to family members

3.4.1 Outline

If the service company director has a spouse or partner whose taxable income is low, a salary from the company for administrative support provided will use up his or her available personal allowance and/or lower tax bands. Salary can also be paid to other family members in a similar position. However, the Revenue may challenge the deductibility of the salary paid, see **3.4.2** below.

It is also common for the spouse of the worker to own shares in the service company, so that dividends can be paid to the spouse from the company's profits. This provides another means of utilising the spouse's available personal allowance and/or lower tax bands. However the Revenue may seek to attack these arrangements under the settlements legislation, see **3.4.3** below.

3.4.2 Revenue attacks on salary payments

Care needs to be taken that the spouse/partner carries out sufficient work to justify the salary, see *Copeman v William Flood and Sons Ltd* [1940] 24 TC 53 and IM 1042. In *Copeman* the director of a family company employed his two children on salaries of £2,600 each. However the daughter drew only £70 of remuneration and the son £277. The Revenue contended successfully that only £350 in the case of the son and £78 in respect of the daughter had been paid for the purposes of the trade.

It was argued in the company's defence that directors have discretion to spend the company's money. However the judge said that:

> 'It may very well be that there are sums which are paid to the directors as remuneration for their services in accordance with the Articles of Association and in accordance with a resolution of the company, but it does not necessarily follow in the least that they are sums which are wholly and exclusively laid out for the purposes of the trade.'

If, following *Copeman*, the salary is disallowed in the company, there will be double taxation if the spouse/partner has already been taxed on the earnings received. For this reason the Revenue do not use the disallowance threat lightly, but where the salary paid is:

- Insufficient to attract a tax charge; or

- Appears to have been pitched so as to gain entitlement to benefits without payment of NIC; or

- The work done is hard to identify,

the Revenue may challenge the deduction (IM 1042).

In addition to the above, the Revenue may also seek to argue that the payment to family members is a settlement of monies on them, and thus effectively a payment into trust under Chapter IA Part XV ICTA 1988, see **3.4.3** below.

3.4.3 Revenue attacks on dividends

The Revenue sometimes seek to argue that shares held by family members are a settlement under Chapter IA Part XV ICTA 1988, and thus that the dividend income received should be reattributed to the worker. As stated at **3.4.2**, this point can also be made in respect of salary payments.

An example of how this legislation could apply to a service company is given in the Revenue's Settlements Manual at paragraph 4201:

'X is a consultant who sells his services at a daily rate plus expenses. He owns all the shares in a private family company through which he sells his services. The company receives all the income he generates. The company's only source of income is from work carried out by X. It has insufficient capital assets. X transfers his shares in the company to his wife by way of gift. His earnings in one year exceed £70,000 but he decides to draw only £40,000 salary. This leaves £30,000 profit for the company. The company then pays a dividend of £30,000 to Mrs X. The arrangement effectively transfers part of X's earnings to his wife. Under the Settlements legislation we would treat the dividend as the income of X.'

However, at least to date, the Revenue have been reluctant to litigate this point. This doubtless reflects the limitations of current case law:

(a) In *Young v Pearce and Young v Scrutton* [1996] STC 743, which was decided in the Revenue's favour, wives were given preference shares which had no voting rights and were only entitled to repayment at par value in a winding-up. These were held to be 'property which was wholly or substantially a right to income' (s660 ICTA 1988) and thus within the settlements legislation. However the same may not be true where ordinary shares are paid for by the spouse;

(b) In *Butler v Wildin* [1988] 61 TC 666, which the Revenue also won, the case concerned shares allotted and transferred to minor children, and this case can thus be distinguished from the normal service company situation.

However, there are some indications that the Revenue may now be prepared to seek to test the legislation in this area.

3.5 Expenses and capital allowances

3.5.1 Expenses

A company can deduct expenses from its taxable profits provided they are wholly and exclusively for the purposes of the business (s74(1)(a) ICTA 1988). Deductible expenses include items such as salary, training, travel, pension contributions and employer's National Insurance. The corporate tax rules for deductibility of expenses are far more generous than those available to employees, see **11.5**, although in some cases the worker who 'passes' IR35 may be entitled to home as office reliefs against his Schedule E income, see **11.11**.

Despite the requirement that the costs be 'exclusively' for the business, in practice apportionment is permitted, see IM 601e and *Taxation* 7 December 2001 pages 282ff. For instance, where a company is based in the home of the sole shareholder/director, it is normal for running costs such as light and heat to be split between business and private use. Car costs can also be apportioned.

3.5.2 Capital allowances

There are also tax reliefs for capital expenditure, again on a more generous basis than those available to employees, see **11.12**. The company can claim allowances if it 'has incurred capital expenditure on the provision of machinery or plant wholly and exclusively for the purposes of (its) trade' (s24 CAA 1990). Capital allowances can thus be claimed on computers, software, furniture and motor vehicles.

3.6 Pensions

3.6.1 General

The rules for pensions are complex, and a full discussion is outside the scope of this book. However, in assessing its options, the company should consider tax efficiency, administrative convenience, and the long term expectations of the directors.

Working through a personal service company allows access more tax-efficient pension vehicles that those available to individuals, including sole traders and partners. Many small companies use either a Small Self Administered Scheme (SSAS) or an Executive Pension Plan (EPP). Even where a personal pension vehicle is used, rather than a SSAS or an EPP, company contributions can achieve a useful NIC saving as compared to contributions made by an individual.

3.6.2 Tax advantages

Inland Revenue approved pension schemes have certain tax advantages:

- Contributions are deductible from profits for corporation tax purposes, and are free of NICs;

- No income tax or employee NICs are paid by the individual on any company contributions made;

- If contributions are made by an employee they are paid out of salary after deduction of both employer and employee NICs. They are, however, tax free and reduce the amount of income taxed at the individual's marginal rate;

- The pension fund itself is not taxed on either capital gains or income received. However, this advantage has been eroded since 2 July 1997 when pension funds were prevented from recovering the tax credit on UK dividends received;

- When the pension finally comes into payment, up to 25% of its value can be taken as a tax-free lump sum.

There are broadly speaking two types of UK approved schemes, personal pensions (**3.6.3**) and occupational schemes (**3.6.5**).

3.6.3 Personal pensions

A personal pension can be bought 'off the peg' from numerous financial institutions. Either the employer or the employee can make contributions. The administration involved is small.

Money saved in the personal pension is used on retirement to buy an annuity. There is also a drawdown option whereby the annuity can be deferred and income taken from the fund in the meantime.

Contributions to a personal pension are limited by:

- Net Relevant Earnings (NRE). This is broadly the individual's Schedule E salary plus any taxable benefits;

- Age at the beginning of the tax year. The older the individual, the higher the percentage of NRE that can be contributed. The figures are given in Table 3.1;

- The earnings cap. This sets a maximum NRE figure above which earnings cannot be taken into account for pension provision purposes. For 2001/02 it is £95,400.

Table 3.1 *NRE percentages for contributions to Personal Pension Schemes*

Age	Percentage
< 36	17.5
36 to 45	20
46 to 50	25
51 to 55	30
56 to 60	35
61 or more	40

Pension contributions should be made by the company rather than the individual. This is because a company contribution saves employer's NIC on the full amount of the contribution. Depending on the individual's pay level, it may also save employee NIC. If the contribution were made by the director or employee, he would receive tax relief but no NICs relief.

In small companies there is a tension between the desire to pay dividends instead of salary so as reduce the cost of NICs, and the need for NRE which provide the basis for pension contributions. If the workers are mostly remunerated by way of dividends, they are likely to have low NRE. They can, however, use the SSAS or EPP routes, see **3.6.5**. And from 2001 stakeholder schemes (**3.6.4** below) provide another solution.

3.6.4 Stakeholder schemes

Stakeholder schemes are similar to personal pensions, and were introduced from April 2001. They allow gross contributions up to £3,600, regardless of NRE. Contributions in excess of £3,600 must be supported by evidence of earnings, and are subject to the same limits as other personal pensions, see Table 3.1 above.

Stakeholder contributions above £3,600 which are supported by evidence of earnings can continue for four more years without any further evidence being required. Thus it may be possible to pay a significant salary level every fifth year, perhaps up to the earnings cap. This would create the maximum NRE for that year and establish entitlement to a high level of contributions over the next four years.

3.6.5 Occupational schemes

Occupational schemes can be either final salary or money purchase. Final salary schemes are more costly to administer than money purchase schemes, and have demanding regulatory requirements. They are thus usually not accessible to small businesses such as personal service companies, and are not discussed further in this chapter.

A money purchase (defined contribution) scheme is set up under trust. Employer contributions are not limited by the NRE rules, but are fully tax deductible as long as the funding of the scheme is only sufficient to allow the payment of employees' pensions at the maximum permitted level. This is two-thirds of the earnings cap (see **3.6.3**). For 2001/02 the maximum pension is thus £63,600. A company using a defined contribution scheme can thus frequently make higher contributions than would be permitted under the rules for personal pensions.

Employees may also make contributions, limited to 15 per cent of their net relevant earnings.

Two common forms of defined contribution schemes much used by service companies are the SSAS and the EPP.

Small Self-Administered Schemes

A SSAS can provide pension arrangements for up to eleven members. Unlike other occupational pension schemes, where investments in the sponsoring employer are limited to a maximum of 5 per cent of the pension fund, SSASs can operate almost as 'captive' funds, investing substantially in the sponsoring company. Significant tax planning opportunities are thus available.

Executive Pension Plans

EPPs provide benefits, usually to one member, by earmarking an policy purchased from an insurance company. The insurance company can loan back to the employer part of the assets held within the policy.

3.7 Interest relief

3.7.1 Outline

If the service company satisfies the definition of a close company, see **3.7.2**, and money is borrowed to invest in the company, tax relief may be available on the interest cost, see **3.7.3** below.

3.7.2 Close companies

Most personal service companies fit the definition of close companies found in s414 ICTA 1988. This is that the company is:

- Under the 'control' of five or fewer 'participators'; or

- Under the control of participators who are directors (ICTA 1988, s414(1)); or

- Five or fewer participators, or participators who are directors, together possess or are entitled to acquire such rights as would entitle them to receive the greater part of the assets available for distribution if the company was wound up.

A participator is a person who has a share or interest in the capital or income of the company and includes:

- Any person possessing, or entitled to acquire, share capital or voting rights;

- Any loan creditor;

- Any person possessing, or entitled to acquire, a right to receive, or to participate in, distributions or any amount payable by the company (in cash or in kind) to loan creditors by way of premium on redemption; and

- Any person entitled to ensure that present or future income or assets of the company will be applied directly or indirectly for his benefit.

A person has 'control' of a company

> 'If he exercises, or is able to exercise or is entitled to acquire, direct or indirect control over the company's affairs, and in particular, but without prejudice to the generality of the preceding words, if he possesses or is entitled to acquire the greater part of the share capital or issued share capital of the company or of the voting power in the company'

or if he is entitled to the greater part of the assets on its winding up (s416 ICTA 1988).

33

Most personal service companies fall within the definition because control is exercised by the shareholder/director who is clearly a 'participator', and by a small number of others, such as a spouse, partner, or other family members.

3.7.3 Deduction for loan interest

To succeed in obtaining a deduction, the company must be close throughout the accounting period, and must not be a close investment holding company (see **3.2.2**). In addition the shareholder must either:

- Have a 'material interest' in the company, which in this context means that he must own more than 5 per cent of the ordinary shares or be entitled to more than five per cent of the assets on a winding-up; or

- If the shareholding is less than five per cent, he must work for the greater part of his time in the management of the company or of an associated company.

In addition:

- The funds must be used either to buy shares in the company, or be lent to the close company for its business;

- The borrowing must be a loan, and not, for example, an overdraft or a credit card debt; and

- The interest paid must not exceed a commercial rate.

Care needs to be taken when an individual has both interest relief and receives most of his money as dividends, see **3.3**.

3.8 Retention of funds in the company

Because the rates of corporation tax suffered on the profits of small companies are lower than many individuals' marginal tax rates, see **3.2.2** above, money not required can be retained in the PSC. The company thus becomes a tax-efficient money box.

The surplus funds can then be invested, either in cash or in other assets, though this may affect the company's status for business asset taper relief purposes, see Sch A1, para 11 TCGA 1992; CG 17919–17920.

Alternatively, it can be loaned to the directors, shareholders or employees, but subject to the following constraints:

- A loan to a director cannot be more than £5,000 (s334 Companies Act 1985);

- If the loan is made other than to a director, it can exceed £5,000. However a cheap or interest free loan in excess of £5,000 is taxable under s160 ICTA 1988 unless it is a 'qualifying' loan, see ss353ff ICTA 1988;

- Care is also needed not to fall within the close company loan rules, see **3.10.4**.

3.9 Capital gains tax advantages

Shares in a service company are likely to be a business asset for taper relief purposes. Tax on the shares when sold can thus be as little as 10 per cent. The tax planning possibilities offered by the business asset taper are however outside the scope of this book, but it should be remembered that shares can only reflect the intrinsic worth of the business. A service company with minimal assets which simply sells the services of its only director is unlikely to have created transferable value. The existence of comprehensive anti-avoidance rules should also be noted.

3.10 Tax planning pitfalls

3.10.1 Introduction

In addition to the many tax advantages offered by the service company, there are a number of dangers. These include non-repayable tax credits, illegal dividends, and close company loan provisions. The risks of payments to a spouse are discussed at **3.4.2** and **3.4.3** above.

3.10.2 Non-repayable tax credits

Normally, when an expense reduces an individual's taxable income, he pays less tax. However, if he receives only dividends, this is no longer the case. From 6 April 1999, tax credits on dividends are not repayable.

Thus if the individual's taxable income consists entirely of dividends, and he also has deductions, such as interest (see **3.7**) to offset against his taxable income, there will be no repayment of the 10 per cent tax credit. If the individual has no other income against which the expense can be offset, the tax relief will be wasted. His salary payment may thus need to be adjusted in consequence, see **3.3**.

3.10.3 Illegal dividends

A dividend is only lawful if the company has sufficient distributable profits. If an interim distribution is made before the end of the financial year, it may exceed the profits later found to have been available. The company will thus have paid a dividend which is wholly or partly illegal (ss263–268 Companies Act 1985).

Illegal dividends are a particular risk for personal service companies, whose directors/shareholders commonly take quarterly or monthly distributions instead of salary. A check should thus be made before each withdrawal to see whether the dividend can legally be paid.

National Insurance implications

In February 1994 the Contributions Agency stated in a note to the ICAEW and other professional bodies that an unlawful dividend would be regarded as earnings for NIC purposes. However this view is questionable, since the fact that the dividend is illegal does not change its nature.

Loans to shareholders

Where an individual has received a dividend, and knows, or has reasonable grounds to believe, that it is illegal, the dividend is void for tax purposes. The company has not made a distribution as a matter of company law, and thus the dividend does not form part of the recipient's income for tax purposes. In other words, there has been no dividend and the cash still belongs to the company.

However, if the company is close (see **3.7.2**), a loan has been made to the shareholder, which may cause a tax charge to arise under s419(1) ICTA 1988. The rules for calculating the charge are given at **3.10.4**.

Relief will however be available under s419(4) ICTA 1988, if the dividend is repaid to the company within nine months of the company's year end. Repayment is also a requirement of s277 Companies Act 1985 when a dividend has been received by someone who knows or has reasonable grounds to believe that it is unlawful.

Innocent receipt

Where the shareholder had no knowledge of the illegality of the dividend and no reasonable grounds to believe it to be illegal, the above paragraphs do not apply.

However this situation is unlikely to apply to a PSC, where there is substantial identity between the directors and shareholders. The Revenue view is that 'when dealing with private companies controlled by directors who are shareholders, such a member ought to know the status of the dividend and it is our view that s277 Companies Act 1985 will apply in the majority of such cases' (CT 2007a:28).

Where it can be successfully argued that the shareholder did not know the dividend was illegal, the dividend does not have to be repaid. It will then remain a distribution under s209(2)(b) ICTA 1988. If such a shareholder then repaid the company (despite not being liable to do so) this would be a transfer of his own income and would not affect the higher rate position. In other words, if he repays the money to the company, he still pays tax on it.

3.10.4 Loans to participators

As discussed above, most personal service companies will be 'close' for tax purposes. One of the significant consequences of close company status is that if the company loans money to a participator (**3.7.2**), it may be required to pay tax equal to 25 per cent of the loan balance. The following rules apply:

- If the loan is repaid or written off *within* nine months of the end of the accounting period in which the loan was made, no tax is payable;

- If a loan is released, repaid or written off *after* nine months following the year end, the company can reclaim the tax charged, but it is only received by the company nine months after the end of the accounting period in which the loan, etc. was repaid, released or written off;

- If the amount is released or written off, it becomes taxable on the individual as if it were a dividend.

The effect of these provisions is to charge the company for the individual's use of the borrowed money, but only to the extent that he has not repaid the amounts within the permitted nine months following the end of the accounting period. A similar nine month period is granted to the Revenue if the tax has later to be repaid to the company. Example 3F shows how this works in practice.

Example 3F

Olive is the shareholder and director of Train, a company providing video services to the TV industry. It is a close company with a 31 March year end. Train loaned Olive £100,000 on 15 May 1999. On 20 August 2000, Olive repaid £70,000 and on 20 September 2001, Train wrote off the balance of the loan.

Olive borrowed the funds in the year 1999/00. She repaid £70,000 within nine months of the end of the company's 1999/00 accounting period, so this eliminates any close company charge on £70,000. The tax due on the balance is as follows:

Train

1.1.01   Corporation tax due of (£100,000 − £70,000) = £30,000 @ 25% = £7,500 (Note 1)

31.12.02 The company is due a repayment of £30,000 × 25% = £7,500 (Note 2)

Olive
Her taxable income for 2001/02 is increased by £30,000 + £3,333 = £33,333
This is subject to the Schedule F upper rate:

	£	Rate	£
Income	£33,333	32.5%	10,833
Less tax credit			3,333
Tax due			7,500

Notes
1. The loan outstanding at the end of March 2000 was £30,000. Tax is therefore due at 25 per cent on the normal payment date, nine months and one day after the end of the company's accounting period.
2. The loan was written off in September 2001. This is in the financial year ending 31 March 2002. Since tax has already become due, the repayment is not due until nine months after the end of the accounting period, namely on 31 December 2002.

The close company provisions can catch small companies unaware. For example, an overdrawn current account amounts to a loan for the purposes of these rules. See also **3.10.3** above on the implications of illegal dividends.

3.11 Agency legislation attack on PSCs?

3.11.1 Outline

It has been argued that the Revenue might seek to use the agency legislation (see **21.2.1**) against personal service companies which pass IR35. In the view of the author, this risk is overstated. The agency legislation should not apply in the normal situation where the worker is an employee and/or a director of the company, and he receives his money from the company either as salary or as dividends.

3.11.2 Section 134 ICTA 1988

The agency legislation says that where:

'(a) an individual ("the worker") renders or is under an obligation to render personal services to another person ("the client") and is subject to, or to the right of, supervision, direction or control as to the manner in which he renders those services; and

(b) the worker is supplied to the client by or through a third person ("the agency") and renders or is under an obligation to render those services under the terms of a contract between the worker and the agency ("the relevant contract"); and

(c) remuneration receivable under or in consequence of that contract would not, apart from this section, be chargeable to income tax under Schedule E,

then, for all the purposes of the Income Tax Acts, the services which the worker renders or is under an obligation to render to the client under that contract shall be treated as if they were the duties of an office or employment held by the worker, and all remuneration receivable under or in consequence of that contract shall be treated as emoluments of that office or employment and shall be assessable to income tax under Schedule E accordingly.' (s134 ICTA 1988)

It has thus been argued that a personal service company could be categorised as an agency under this legislation where:

- A personal service company supplies a worker to provide personal services to a client; and

- He is not remunerated by salary (chargeable under Schedule E) but via dividends.

The effect of this would be that the service company would have to deduct PAYE and NICs from all payments made to the worker.

However, this is to misread the legislation. Section 134 applies to 'remuneration' which is defined as 'every form of payment and all perquisites, benefits and profits whatsoever' with the exception that it 'does not include anything in respect of which he would not have been chargeable to tax under Schedule E if it had been receivable in connection with an office or employment held by [the worker]'.

Thus s134 cannot apply to dividends, which would not have been taxed under Schedule E but under Schedule F. That this is the case is reinforced by s20(2) ICTA 1988, which states that a dividend taxable under Sch F cannot be taxed under any other section of the Act.

Thus in the normal personal service company scenario, where a worker is paid either salary or dividends (or both), s134 cannot be used.

3.11.3 Consultancy fees

A personal service company can however fall within the agency rules when, instead of paying the worker a salary or a dividend, it remunerates him by 'consultancy fees'. This is the situation described in *Revenue Decision 4* (RD4):

> 'A limited company had been interposed in the contractual arrangements between a worker and an employment agency. Even though all the other circumstances were such that TA 1988 s134 would apply, the Revenue accepted that it was not necessary for the employment agency to operate PAYE. This was because the Revenue was satisfied that the contract with the employment agency for the worker's services was genuinely entered into by the company and not by the individual.
>
> The company then paid out fees to the worker and described them as "consultancy fees" claiming that they were not paid to the worker for acting as a director or employee of the company.
>
> The Revenue was able to recover PAYE from the company on the fees. This was because when it paid the worker, it was itself an agency within TA s134(1)(b).'

The same position is reflected in the Revenue Manual:

> 'If an office or a contract of employment between the individual and the "one-man" company cannot be established, the agency legislation will probably apply to the contract between the worker and that company. The terms of this contract will include at least an implied agreement by the worker to provide his or her services to the client through the company. Hence the company becomes an agency for the purposes of the agency legislation; that is, a third party through whom the worker is supplied to the client.' (ESM 2014)

Thus although the Revenue may use the agency legislation to attack service companies, the number of situations where this will occur are very limited.

4 Scope of personal services legislation

4.1 General

4.1.1 IR35 target constituency

IR35 is aimed at those who would have been employed by the client had they been engaged directly rather than via an intermediary. The Budget Press Release stated that:

> 'The proposed changes are aimed only at engagements with essential characteristics of employment. They should affect only those cases where these characteristics are disguised through use of an intermediary – such as a service company or partnership.'

This was reinforced by Dawn Primarolo in the IR 35 debate:

> 'Some people have chosen to use service companies because they do not fit the definition of self-employment, but still want to benefit from the tax breaks available for self-employment. They are really only employees who want a better deal from the tax system that than to which their status entitles them. Those people will be targeted by the new rules.' (*Hansard* 3 May 2000, Pt 24, Col. 214)

This chapter looks at the scope of the personal services legislation for both tax and National Insurance. The two sets of rules are similar, although not identical. Differences are commented on as appropriate throughout this book.

4.1.2 Sham companies

In the past the Revenue's only weapon against service companies was to argue that the arrangements were a 'sham'; that the company was simply a facade, designed to look as if real legal rights and obligations had been created between the company and the client, whereas in reality it was the individual who had contracted with the client. However, the Revenue rarely succeeded, and then usually only if the procedures and/or documentation were defective.

Post-IR35, service company arrangements can still be a 'sham'. If they are, and the contract is really between the individual and the client, the individual could be reclassified as an employee. IR35 would not be applicable, as it deals only with genuine arrangements under which a worker provides services via an intermediary.

However, it is unlikely that the Revenue will seek to argue this difficult point in the future. They will instead apply IR35 to all intermediaries where the worker would have been an employee had the services been supplied directly.

4.1.3 Legislation

The scope of the personal services rules is defined by Schedule 12, Finance Act 2000. This establishes that to be within the new rules for tax purposes there must be:

(a) An engagement for personal services provided on or after 6 April 2000;

(b) Where the services are provided to a business carried on by another person ('the client');

(c) And the worker would be regarded as an employee of the client but for the interposition of …

(d) … at least one intermediary between the worker and the client. The intermediary must meet certain defined conditions; and

(e) The worker either receives a payment or benefit from the intermediary which is not chargeable under Schedule E, or has the right to such a payment.

The same criteria are included in the parallel National Insurance regulations (SI 2000/727). They are discussed in more detail below.

4.2 Personal services provided on or after 6 April 2000

4.2.1 Personal services

The legislation only covers the provision of personal services. Engagements for the provision of goods, rather than for services, are completely outside these rules. Companies and partnerships involved in manufacturing, selling or distribution are thus not within the scope of IR35 (Sch 12, para 1(1)(a) FA 2000).

However, supplying goods does not of itself provide exemption from IR35. In addition to hiring out their own services to clients, some IT contractors have begun to supply small or occasional pieces of computer equipment to clients, believing that by supplying goods they have inoculated the company and prevented IR35 from applying. It is more probable that in this situation there are two supplies, of services and of goods, with the former being subject to IR35 if it meets the relevant conditions.

4.2.2 Provided on or after 6 April 2000

The legislation's start date was 6 April 2000. Engagements which were part-way through on that date are within IR35 in so far as the work carried out relates to the period after 6 April, see Sch 12, para 22 FA 2000.

Although generally the PSC rules are on a receipts basis (see **10.2**) an exception has been made for the commencement year. Money received before 6 April 2000, which relates to work done after that date, is brought into the calculation of deemed income for the year 2000/01. This was to prevent people accelerating cash receipts so that they fell into the previous fiscal year and so were received before the start of the new regime (Sch 12, para 22(2); SI 2000/727 reg 1(3)).

4.3 Provided to a business ...

4.3.1 Scope of definition

The legislation is limited to the provision of services 'for the purposes of a business carried on by another person' (Sch 12, para 1(1)(a) FA 2000). It thus excludes any contracts made by an intermediary with an individual on a personal basis. An example would be a gardener with a one-man company who spends two days a week in what might otherwise be regarded as a relevant engagement with a local family.

This exemption has been granted for the pragmatic reason that most of these contracts will in any event fall outside the PSC rules on other grounds, usually because the worker will meet the tests of self-employment set out at **4.4** below and Chapter 6.

However this is not invariably the case, and the exemption may then be turned to advantage. For example, the provision of domestic help by nannies, cooks and chauffeurs could be structured via a personal services company so as to fall outside of the new legislation. The PSC would have access to the tax planning advantages set out in Chapter 3, and the individual (or the client) could take this tax efficiency into account when agreeing payment terms.

Another example might be the provision of nursing services to a house-bound patient. Providing the contract was with the individual, and not, for example, with his insurance company or the local health authority, the engagement would fall outside the personal services rules.

The device would, however, not succeed where the cost of a chauffeur or nanny was reimbursed or paid for by the individual's employer, because the services would then be provided to the employer for the purposes of his business. Care should be taken with services that relate to rented properties, as the latter is likely to be a Schedule A business, see ESM 3129.

4.3.2 ... A business carried on by another person (the client)

For the legislation to be effective the worker must be supplying services 'for the purposes of a business carried on by another person ("the client")'. It has been argued that:

- The worker is providing services for the purposes of furthering his own business, not the business of another, and thus the legislation does not apply. However this interpretation begs the question, since if the worker is 'in business on his own account', he should pass the status tests and fall outside IR35 in any event;

- The client for whose business the worker is providing services is in fact the agency. This issue is explored in more detail at **23.3**.

4.4 The worker would be regarded as an employee of the client

It is necessary to consider whether, if the worker had contracted to supply personal services directly to the client, the contract between them would have been one of employment. In other words, would the worker have been regarded as an employee if there had been no intermediary?

In deciding whether the engagement would have the characteristics of employment it is necessary to look at the 'circumstances' under which the services are provided. This is defined in Sch 12, para 1(4) FA 2000 as including:

> 'The terms on which the services are provided, having regard to the terms of the contracts forming part of the arrangements under which the services were provided.'

The major point of reference is thus the contract or contracts under which the worker is providing services. Other surrounding facts may also be relevant –

for example, whether the worker has other clients and a business organisation. How this part of the legislation should be interpreted in the light of normal contract law is discussed in Chapter 5.

It is well known that there is no statutory definition of 'employment'. However, the question has come before the Courts on numerous occasions. The approach taken has been to identify factors which help determine whether a particular contract is a 'contract of service' (employment) or a 'contract for services' (self-employment), or possibly a third type of contract, see **6.4.3**. This may involve a review of whether mutuality of obligation subsists between the parties, see Chapter 5.

Typically the self-employed person has some or all of the following characteristics, which are discussed more fully in Chapters 6 and 7. He may have:

- greater control over his work than an employee;
- the right to send a substitute;
- some risk of making a loss if he does the job badly;
- the possibility of a profit if he works more efficiently;
- his own tools and equipment;
- no holiday or sick pay, and no notice period.

On the other hand, a typical employee is likely to provide his services personally, receive benefits such as holiday pay, take no financial risk and be subject to greater control and direction than a self-employed worker. There is also mutuality of obligation between himself and his employer, see Chapter 5.

4.5 Intermediaries

4.5.1 Introduction

For a worker to be within IR35 there must be at least one 'relevant' intermediary between the worker and the client. Commonly this is a company or partnership, but it could be an individual. The legislation lays down specific tests for each.

4.5.2 Company

A company is a relevant intermediary for the purposes of the legislation if either or both of the following applies:

- The worker has an interest in more than 5 per cent of the company (the 'material interest' test). In deciding whether he has more than 5 per cent it is also necessary to look at amounts held by his associates, such as family members and business partners. Both 'material interest' and 'associate' are discussed in more detail below; or

- A payment or benefit which is not chargeable under Schedule E is received or receivable by the worker from the intermediary, and this payment or benefit 'can reasonably be taken to represent remuneration for services provided by the worker to the client' (Sch 12, para 3 FA 2000).

It is enough for either of the tests to be satisfied. So a composite company made up of 100 workers, each with a 1 per cent shareholding, will fall outside the material interest test because each individual's shareholding is less than 5 per cent. But the payments from the client to the company have to reach the workers, and it is probable that this will be in a form which 'can reasonably be taken to represent remuneration', and if so, the individuals will be within IR35. This situation was described by Mr Justice Burton as one where 'the payment by the client is "traceable" through to a dividend' (*R v CIR (oao Professional Contractors Group Ltd)* [2001] STC 629, see **2.4**).

A number of 'IR35 avoidance schemes' have been marketed on the basis that they provide money to the worker in a form which cannot 'reasonably be taken to represent remuneration'. However, the phrase is so widely drawn that it is likely to allow most, if not all, such arrangements to be successfully challenged, see Chapter 23.

Associated companies

Companies are exempt from IR35 if the 'client' is an associated company as defined in s416 ICTA 1988 (Sch 12, paras 3(1) and 21(1) FA 2000). This is to prevent the rules applying where, for example, the owner/director of the holding company provides services to an underlying subsidiary, for which he received no specific remuneration. However, the subsidiary pays a dividend to the holding company and thence to the owner/director. Without this exemption, the holding company could be a relevant intermediary because:

- the director is a majority shareholder, and thus within the material interest test;

- he supplies personal services to another company (the subsidiary); and

- he receives a 'payment or other benefit not chargeable to tax under Schedule E' which could 'reasonably be taken to be remuneration' for the services provided to the subsidiary, namely the dividend (Sch 12, para 2(b)(i) FA 2000).

However, he has not provided any services to a third-party client, and thus should not be within the rules. Example 4A shows how the legislation would work, without this exemption.

Example 4A

John is the major shareholder of a small plc., Hips and Haws (H&H). H&H is a holding company with two trading subsidiaries, Band Ltd (B) and Count Ltd (C). B manufactures musical instruments, and C sells them. The structure of the group is as follows:

John is employed by H&H and his services are supplied to B Ltd and C Ltd by H&H. A management charge is made to the subsidiaries to cover the cost of his services. B and C pay their annual profits to H&H as dividends. In turn, H&H pays dividends its shareholder. Without the exemption in para 3(1), H&H would be an intermediary within IR35, and John would be subject to a deemed salary calculation. But John has supplied no third-party services; indeed the company's activities are manufacturing and selling, rather than providing personal services. It is thus appropriate that he should be removed from the scope of Schedule 12.

However, the group company exemption only applies if the both the 'intermediary' (H in Example 4A), and the 'client' (B or C) are under the control of the worker or the worker and another person (Sch 12, para 3(2) FA 2000).

This prevents the setting up of 'captive composites' where the client out-sources a department, gives the former employees shares in a company of which it is the majority shareholder, and pays them in dividends.

However, this restriction also means that the group exemption is not effective where the worker (together with another person) is not a majority share-holder in the holding company. Thus a director of H, with 10 per cent of the shares, who supplied services to B and C, could be caught by the PSC rules. This situation is shown in Example 3 at paragraph 3108 of the Revenue's Employment Status Manual:

'Ms M owns 60% of the shares in Holdco Ltd and Tradeco Ltd. Mr N and Mr O own a further 20% of the shares each. Ms M has control of both companies on her own. Therefore the conditions of liability will not be met with respect to her services. However, the exception will not apply to any services provided by Mr N and Mr O.'

There is however no reason why Mr N and Mr O should be brought within IR35 on first principles. This is a failing in the legislation and an amendment to the rules is needed.

It appears that, despite the ESM, the Revenue have accepted that this is the case. The Tax Law Rewrite project, in its proposed redraft of Schedule 12, says that:

> 'We propose to widen the definition of "associated company" … to include companies that are under the common control of the worker together with more than one other person. This is in accordance with Inland Revenue practice so represents a change to the law but not to policy. It is in the taxpayer's favour as it will allow more companies to escape the provisions of this Schedule.' [ED12 – *Draft Income Tax [Earnings and Pensions] Bill Part 2 Employment Income*]

Anyone affected by these provisions should thus refer to ED12 as proof that it is not Revenue policy to apply this part of the legislation; in due course such individuals will hopefully be able to rely on the rewritten legislation itself.

It is hoped that the matching regulation in the NICs legislation (SI 2000/727 reg 5(2)(a)) will be amended in parallel with the TLRC changes.

Material interest

Put simply, a person has a material interest in a company if he and his associates have any of the following:

(a) Control over more than 5 per cent of the share capital;

(b) Rights to receive more than 5 per cent of the dividends; or

(c) Rights to receive more than 5 per cent of the assets on a winding up.

The full definition (Sch12, para 3 FA 2000) is extremely detailed, in order to counter avoidance devices such as indirect holdings and the use of rights or entitlements. It states that a material interest is:

(a) Beneficial ownership of, or the ability to control, directly or through the medium of other companies or by any other indirect means, more than 5 per cent of the ordinary share capital of the company; or

(b) Possession of, or entitlement to acquire, rights entitling the holder to receive more than 5 per cent of any distributions that may be made by the company; or

(c) Where the company is a close company, possession of, or entitlement to acquire, rights that would in the event of the winding up of the company, or in any other circumstances, entitle the holder to receive more than 5 per cent of the assets that would then be available for distribution among the participators. For the definition of participator, see **3.7.2**.

In the context of a personal services company, the material interest test is met if:

- The worker, either alone or with associates, has a material interest in the intermediary; or

- An associate of the worker, either with or without other associates, has a material interest in the intermediary.

Associates

An individual's associates include any of the following (Sch 12, para 19 FA 2000):

- Relatives. These are the person's husband, wife, parent or remoter forbear, child or remoter issue, brother or sister. A man and a woman living together as husband and wife are treated as if they were married (Sch 12, para 21(4) FA 2000), and thus will count as 'husband' or 'wife' for these purposes. Revenue booklet IR175 simply says that 'family includes unmarried partners' but in fact unmarried partners of the same sex are not 'treated as if they were married'. A Conservative party amendment to extend this part of the legislation to gay couples was rejected by the House of Commons in June 2000;

- Business partners of the individual;

- The trustees of any trust settled by the individual, and also the trustees of any trust settled by relatives, whether or not they are still alive;

- The trustees of a trust which holds shares in the personal service company, if the individual has an interest in the trust. However there is an exemption for shares held in an employee benefit trust (EBT);

  EBTs hold shares in the company for the benefit of employees, for instance as part of an employee share option scheme (Sch 8, para 7(5) ICTA 1988). The exemption exists because an EBT may well hold more than 5 per cent of the company's shares, and thus all employees with an interest in the EBT would automatically and unfairly fall within the PSC rules. However the exemption does not apply to an individual who has held, at any time on or after 14 March 1989, a material interest in the company without taking account of the EBT shares, see Sch 12, para 19(4) FA 2000. For the use of EBTs in IR35 avoidance schemes, see **23.5**;

- The personal representatives of a deceased person, if the service company's shares are held in his estate and the individual is a beneficiary.

4.5.3 Partnerships

The inclusion of partnerships in the new rules was surprising, since, unlike a company, a partnership has no separate legal identity under UK law. The Revenue had previously argued that they could look through the partnership and recategorise an individual partner as an employee if he did not pass the status tests in respect of an engagement.

However, it is understood that the Revenue have received legal advice which indicates that where there is a contract between the client and the partnership, rather than between the client and the individual partner, it cannot be looked through in this way.

So a contract with a partnership would be effective in protecting a partner from recategorisation as Schedule E, even though the nature of his engagement clearly failed the status tests. Partnerships therefore had to be brought within the personal services legislation, if only to prevent them replacing companies as the new tax-efficient IR35 avoidance vehicle.

However, had the full PSC rules been applied to all partnerships providing personal services, the consequences for legitimate businesses would have been extreme. Fortunately, the Revenue accepted that this was unnecessary, and have limited the scope of the new rules. FAQ Partner 1 stated that the Revenue:

> 'Do not want the new rules to place unnecessary burdens on partnerships ... what they want to do is to distinguish between partnerships which can be used by a worker to control the form in which income from relevant engagements is passed on to him or her, and partnerships which are legitimate businesses but may occasionally second a partner to work for a client in circumstances which might otherwise be caught by our legislation.'

As a result, most genuine profit-sharing partnerships are excluded from IR35.

The ways in which partnerships can fall outside the rules, and what happens if they are caught, are discussed in Chapter 14.

It is worth noting that partnerships can be an intermediary, not only in respect of the partners, but also as regards employees of the partnership, see **14.4**.

4.5.4 Individuals

The legislation covers a third category of intermediary, the individual. Like partnerships, individuals have been included largely for anti-avoidance reasons. The purpose is to prevent a wife, say, contracting with a client company to provide her husband's IT services, and so avoiding the new rules. It is doubtful that such stratagems would in any event have been successful, even without the inclusion of individual intermediaries in the personal services legislation. The Revenue takes the same view, saying:

> 'It is unlikely in practice that you will come across the situation where there will be liability under the legislation where intermediary is an individual. Usually, in such circumstances, the worker will either be an employee of the individual, or the agency legislation will apply.' (ESM 3124)

If a worker's services are supplied via an individual, then that person is a relevant intermediary if the worker receives a payment or benefits, other than under Sch E, which can 'reasonably be taken to represent remuneration for services provided' (Sch 12, para 5 FA 2000). The rules are also operative where the payment or benefits are receivable rather than actually received.

For the application of the agency legislation referred to in ESM 3214, quoted above, see **3.11**.

4.5.5 More than one intermediary

It is possible for there to be more than one intermediary between the client and the worker – for example, a client might contract with a composite company which was in turn owned by an number of service companies. Alternatively, and more commonly, an agency could be interposed between the service company and the client.

Where there is more than one intermediary, it is necessary to establish whether they are all 'relevant' and thus within the scope of the legislation. To be 'relevant', an intermediary must have made a payment *directly* to the worker. Since agencies generally pay the service companies and not the workers, in most cases they will not be relevant intermediaries. Agencies are discussed further at **21.2**.

Where multiple intermediaries do fall within the PSC rules, then:

(a)   The legislation applies separately to each of them (Sch 12, para 14(3) FA 2000);

(b)   Where an amount is received by one intermediary and passed to a second, it is only included once in the deemed Schedule E calculation (Sch 12, para 15 FA 2000);

(c)   Each intermediary is jointly and severally liable for the worker's PAYE and NIC deductions in relation to engagements for which they were intermediaries (Sch 12, para 16 FA 2000). Concern has been expressed that this places an impossible burden on some intermediaries in the chain, as they may not know whether or to what extent the tax and NICs have been paid. However, since the legislation only applies to relevant intermediaries, they are in practice likely to be connected to each other and thus to know the true position. This therefore appears to be a problem which is more apparent than real.

4.6   Worker receives payment or benefit not within Schedule E

4.6.1   Interpretation

The worker is within the personal services legislation if:

(a)   A contract of employment would have existed between the worker and the client had there been no intermediary; and

(b)   The intermediary is 'relevant' within the meaning of the legislation; and

(c)   The worker receives from the intermediary a payment or benefit not chargeable to tax under Schedule E; or

(d)   He has rights *entitling* him to receive from the intermediary a payment or other benefit that is not chargeable under Schedule E (Sch 12, para 2(b) FA 2000).

Thus if the individual is, for example, paid in dividends, which are not chargeable under Schedule E, he is caught by (c) above; if he has the right (which has not been exercised) to receive a dividend, he is caught by (d).

The legislation extends the scope of the rule in order to minimise the chances of avoidance. The worker is still caught if:

- The payment or benefit is paid by a relevant intermediary to an associate of the worker, or the associate has rights which entitle him to the payment or benefit. This is to prevent the sums being diverted, say, to a spouse or family member. Associates are defined at **4.5.2**;

- The payment is made indirectly by the relevant intermediary, or the worker has a right to receive some indirect form of payment;

- 'Rights to receive a payment or benefit' includes an entitlement which is triggered 'in any circumstances'. Thus if, for instance, the worker could only access the money if the company was wound up, he would still be caught.

It has been argued that an employee with a 1 per cent shareholding, who is paid a normal salary under Schedule E, will be within the PSC rules because he has an entitlement to a dividend, i.e. a payment or benefit not within Schedule E. However this is not the case. To be within the personal services rules the payment or benefit must be from a relevant intermediary. In the case of a company, this means that either the worker must have a material interest, or he must receive a sum which can 'reasonably be taken to be remuneration' for services provided to the client (Sch 12, para 3(1)(b)(ii)). This will not be the position with dividends paid to 'normal' employees, as these are received as a result of their shareholding and not as remuneration for services to their client(s).

4.6.2 *De minimis* exemption

There is an exemption from the personal services tax rules where the relevant engagement forms a small part of a larger Schedule D business, see ESC A37 and paragraph 03001 of the Revenue's Schedule E Manual. These exemptions cover both self-employed individuals and partners and are set out in full at **14.3**.

For National Insurance purposes there is a statutory exemption for partners who receive small amounts of employment income, on a similar basis as for tax, see **14.3.4** (SI 2001/1004 reg 27).

4.7 Sole traders

An individual who does not operate via a company or partnership, but provides personal services as a sole trader, is not within IR35. Instead he is subject to the normal employment/self-employment tests set out above in Chapter 6.

If he fails these tests, so that he is categorised as an employee of the client rather than as a self-employed consultant, he will be within Schedule E. The client is liable for tax and NIC in respect of past payments, and may have difficulty recovering this from the individual. In other words the burden is normally on the client, rather than on the worker.

As a result, clients may increasingly require consultants to be engaged via their own service companies rather than as individuals. This gives the client protection from assessments to PAYE and NIC if the individual's status has been misjudged. The personal service rules may thus have the ironic consequence of increasing the number of service companies rather than reducing them, see **21.3.4**.

IR35 is also likely to cause an increased Revenue focus on status tests and the Schedule D/E divide, and this may impact sole traders as well as those with service companies and partnerships.

4.8 National Insurance

4.8.1 Legislation

Section 75 of the Welfare Reform and Pensions Act 1999 contains the primary National Insurance legislation. It requires the calculation of an 'attributable earnings' amount, which is then subject to employer's (and, if appropriate) employee's NIC.

The detailed regulations (SI 2000/727) are similar to the tax legislation, but there are divergences caused by the different structures of the tax and NICs systems. Two particular points which are fundamental to the operation of the NICs regulations on personal services are the annual earnings period and the aggregation of earnings rules.

4.8.2 Annual earnings period

For most employees, NIC is due as earnings are received, so that a monthly-paid employee has a monthly earnings period. The upper earnings limit is spread over these monthly payments, see Example 4B.

Example 4B

Desirée earns £4,000 a month and is employed as a dancer. She is not within the personal services regime. Her employee NICs are calculated as follows for the fiscal year 2001/02:

- the employee's earnings threshold (EET) at which employee NICs begin to be paid, is £4,535 or £378 per month;

- the upper limit (UEL), above which no employee NICs are payable, is £29,900 or £2,492 per month

- her monthly earnings subject to employee NICs are thus £2,114, being the difference between the lower and upper monthly limits;

- each month she pays NICs of £211 (2,114 × 10 per cent);

However, different rules apply for directors, who have an annual earnings period. As a result, earnings up to the EET are received free of NICs; they then pay NICs as earnings are received, until they reach the UEL.

The NIC regulations for personal services apply an annual earnings period to all those within the personal services regime, 'whether or not the worker is a director of the company for the year' (SI 2000/727 reg 6). It thus applies not only to service company directors, but to employees within the personal services rules. More controversially, it embraces partners to the extent that they have relevant engagements. Example 4C shows the effects.

Example 4C

In April 2001 Desirée sets up a personal service company and charges the theatre where she dances £5,000 a month. She pays herself a salary of £4,000. Her employee NICs position for 2002/03 is as follows, assuming the same rates and limits as in 2001/02:

1. In the first month she pays no employee NICs (4,000 < 4,535);

2. For the next month she pays employee NICs on £3,465 (4,000 − 535)

3. For the next five months she pays NICs on all her earnings at 10 per cent, at a cost of £400 per month;

4. In the eighth month £1,900 is subject to NICs, at a cost of £190, as she reaches the UEL;

5. For the remaining four months, no employee NICs are due;

6. There is no change to the payment of employer's NICs.

4.8.3 Aggregation of earnings

The annual earnings period does not apply only to the attributable earnings calculation. Other earnings 'paid to the worker by the intermediary in the year concerned, to or for the benefit of the worker in respect of employed earner's employment' must be aggregated with the result of the attributable earnings calculation, and the total assessed on the basis of an annual earnings period (SI 2000/727 reg 8(2)).

However the aggregation requirement only applies to earnings from the intermediary which relate to an employment. There is thus no requirement to aggregate the result of the deemed calculation with a partner's earnings from non-relevant engagements.

4.8.4 Interpreting the scope of the Act

A point of statutory construction has been raised in respect of the heading for s75 in the Welfare Reform and Pensions Act. The section is headed 'earnings of *workers* supplied by service companies'. This could be interpreted as suggesting that if a service company was not supplying 'workers' but merely 'services' it might fall outside the scope of the NIC rules.

The question of whether headings have any legal status, since they are not part of the legislation voted upon by parliament, was covered by Sir Rupert Cross in his classic work '*Statutory Interpretation*'. In his view, headings have parliamentary authority because they are included in the Bill and form part of the text entered on the Parliamentary roll. They are thus 'appropriately consulted to resolve an ambiguity in the text'.

He quotes in his support the ancient case of *Brett v Brett* [1826] 3 Add 210, during which Sir John Nicholl said that:

> 'To arrive at the true meaning of any particular phrase in a statute, that particular phrase is not to be viewed, detached from its context in statute: it is to be viewed in connection with its whole context – meaning by this as well the title and preamble as ... the enacting part of the statute.'

This approach was cited with approval in the more recent cases of *AG v Prince Ernest Augustus of Hanover* [1957] 1 All ER 49, and again in *DPP v Schildcamp* [1971] AC 1 23. This second case is of particular importance because of the House of Lords' conclusion that the scope of s332 Companies Act 1948 should be restricted by reference to its heading.

It would thus be possible to argue that the scope of the National Insurance Regulations could be similarly restricted by reference to the heading in the Welfare Reform and Pensions Act, so that they do not apply where 'services' rather than 'workers' were supplied. However, the Revenue would no doubt argue that this is mere sophistry, and that the meaning of the words is clear from their context within the rest of the legislation.

5 Hypothetical contracts and mutuality

5.1 Construction of the legislation

5.1.1 Tax

The personal services tax legislation applies where an individual provides personal services to a client:

> 'Under arrangements involving a third party (the intermediary) and the circumstances are such that, if the services were being provided under a contract directly between the client and the worker, the worker would be regarded for income tax purposes as an employee of his client.'(Sch 12, para 1(1) FA 2000)

The personal services legislation is thus based on a *hypothetical contract* directly between the client and the worker. It will apply if the 'circumstances are such that' the worker would be an employee of the client under this hypothetical contract. The circumstances:

> 'Include the terms on which services are provided, having regard to the terms of the contracts forming part of the arrangements under which the services are provided.'(Sch 12, para 1(4) FA 2000)

There are two important points of construction here. The first is that the actual contractual arrangements between the client and the intermediary, or between client, agent and intermediary, are simply aids which assist in constructing the hypothetical contract between the worker and the client; they do not determine the matter. This point was confirmed by Mr Justice Burton in *R v CIR (oao Professional Contractors Group Ltd)* [2001] STC 629, see **4.2**, when he advised that:

> 'The Revenue must bear in mind that under IR35 they are not considering an actual contract between the service company and the client, but imagining or constructing a notional contract which does not in fact exist.'

The second point of construction, which follows from the first, is that in interpreting this hypothetical contract, it is important to look at other factors in addition to the terms of the extant contracts. These might include:

- the number of other engagements taken on by the worker; and

- the extent of his business organisation.

This would reflect the assurances given in the House of Commons during the debates on the Welfare Reform and Pensions Bill in 1999, that these wider issues would be taken into account when the personal services legislation was drafted, see **6.6.4**.

5.1.2 National Insurance

The NICs regulations are similar to the tax legislation. They apply where a worker supplies personal services:

> 'Under arrangements involving an intermediary, and the circumstances are such that, had the arrangements taken the form of a contract between the worker and the client, the worker would be regarded for the purposes of Parts I to V of the Contributions and Benefits Act as employed in employed earner's employment by the client.' (SI 2000/727 reg 6).

The 'circumstances' are then commented on as follows:

> 'Any issue whether the circumstances are such as are mentioned in paragraph 1(c) is an issue relating to contributions that is prescribed for the purposes of section 8(1)(m) of the Social Security Contributions (Transfer of Functions, etc.) Act 1999 (decision by an officer of the Board.' (SI 2000/727 reg 6(4))

In plain English, this means that the Inland Revenue will decide what 'circumstances' should be taken into account, with a right of appeal to the Tax Commissioners. There is thus no danger that the 'circumstances' will be decided differently for NICs and tax. However, there are situations where a worker can be within IR35 for tax, but not for NICs and vice versa, see **12.7**.

5.1.3 Contracts with clients

Where a service company contracts directly with the client, the key question is the nature of the hypothetical contract between the worker and the client. Establishing whether this hypothetical contract is of service, or for services, and thus whether it falls inside or outside IR35 involves:

(a) Looking at all the 'circumstances', including but not limited to the written contract terms, see **5.1.1** above. In particular, the court may import other materials and patterns of behaviour in order to construct the hypothetical contract;

(b) Considering whether there is mutuality of obligation between the worker and the client, see **5.3** below; and if so

(c) Reviewing the status tests, see Chapter 6. In this context the perspective of the client, the other party to this contract, is of equal relevance to that of the worker.

5.1.4 Contracts with agencies

Both contracts need to be considered

Many service companies use agencies. Commonly the service company contracts with the agency, and the agency contracts with the end-user. When constructing the hypothetical contract between client and worker, the legislation requires that 'the terms of the *contracts* forming part of the arrangements' be considered. This suggests that the contracts between the service company and the agency, and that between the agency and the client, should both be taken into account in order to decide whether the engagement is caught by IR35. The Revenue have confirmed that they will ask to see both contracts, see FAQ Contract 2. This issue is discussed more fully in Chapter 23.

Problem 1: The agency contract cannot be accessed by the worker

In order to know whether he is inside or outside IR35, a worker must know the perspective of the client, who is the other party to the hypothetical contract. The agency/client contract is thus important. But in some cases neither the client nor the agency will make this available to the worker, for reasons of business confidentiality.

Where this happens, the worker has two options:

(a) Ask the client to provide a statement setting out the key terms, as suggested by the PCG Questionnaire, see **7.7.6**;

(b) Ask the Revenue to obtain the contract as part of a contract review, see **7.7.1**. If the client or agency will not cooperate with the Revenue, then the latter may be prepared to give an opinion based on the worker's understanding of the position. However, this may not be reliable, see **7.7.4**.

> If the contract is provided to the Revenue only on condition that the worker does not see it, he may not understand the Revenue decision as he has not seen the evidence on which it is based. The only way the individual can thus achieve certainty (other than by asking the client for his understanding of the key terms) is to ask for a formal decision, see **7.8**, and then challenge it in court. In this situation the Revenue would have to disclose the evidence on which they were relying.

Problem 2: The contracts contain different terms

It is inadvisable for a service company to enter into a contract with an agency if the contract with the end-user is on different terms. This is because conflicting terms make it more difficult to construct the hypothetical contract.

For example, if the clause between the agency and the service company allows the use of a substitute, while that between the client and the agency does not, would this clause have been contained within the hypothetical contract? If the client had no knowledge of the clause, and it had never been called upon, it would be difficult to maintain that it was a term of the hypothetical contract.

However, the converse is equally true: if the contract between the agency and the client contains terms of which the worker is unaware, and to which he does not work, such as a high degree of control and direction, these too are unlikely to be part of the hypothetical contract. The court will seek to establish what the real terms of the contract would have been had there been a contract directly between the worker and the client.

Again, the best course of action for the worker is to obtain a note from the client setting out the key terms, see **7.7.6**.

Does having an agent reduce the IR35 risk?

The view that the only contract which has to be considered for IR35 purposes is the one between the agent and the service company, is discussed at **23.2** and **23.3**. For the possibility that the use of an agent will make it more difficult to establish mutuality between the client and the worker under the hypothetical contract, see **5.9**.

5.2 Contractual arrangements

5.2.1 Outline

Having accepted that IR35 depends on a hypothetical contract, the terms of that contract will for the most part be deduced from:

- The actual contracts between worker and client, or those between worker/agency and agency/client; and

- Any other relevant circumstances.

Because IR35 does not depend only on the written contracts, some basic principles of contract law may be applied in a different way. What follows looks at how contracts involving questions of status are normally interpreted. It then suggests the approach which might be taken under the personal services legislation.

5.2.2 The contract is normally the starting point

When considering whether a worker is employed or self-employed, the court usually begins by looking at his contract. The National Insurance legislation makes this explicit. An individual is an employed earner if he is working under:

> 'Any contract of service or apprenticeship, whether written or oral and whether expressed or implied.' (ss2(1)(a), 122(1) SSCBA 1992)

Under general law, where there is a written contract, the parties' subsequent conduct is not admissible in construing what the contract means (*Hooper v British Railways Board* [1998] IRLR 517). See also the status case of *Chaplin v Australian Mutual Provident Society* [1978] 18 ALR 385, where Lord Fraser said:

> 'The first principle is that, subject to one exception, where there is a written contract between the parties whose relationship is in issue, a court is confined, in determining the nature of that relationship, to a consideration of the terms, express or implied, of that contract in the light of the circumstances surrounding the making of it, and it is not entitled to consider also the manner in which the parties subsequently acted in pursuance of such a contract. The one exception to that rule is that, where the subsequent conduct of the parties can be shown to have amounted to an agreed addition to, or modification of, the original written contract, such conduct may be considered and taken into account.'

This is, however, manifestly not the case when applying the personal services legislation. Here it is necessary to look at 'the terms on which the services were provided' and not simply the written contracts. These only form 'part of the arrangements under which the services are provided'. The court is thus unlikely to confine itself 'to a consideration of the terms' which are in the written contracts between the parties.

5.2.3 Implied terms, extensions and variations

A contract can be written, oral, or implied, and, if written, is likely to contain both express and implied terms. An express term is one which the parties specifically deal with and include in the contract. An implied term is a right or obligation which is left unexpressed. In the case of the hypothetical contract postulated by Schedule 12, there will be no distinction between express or implied terms – the terms of the hypothetical contract are those 'on which the services are provided' whether or not they are contained within the written contracts.

However, in constructing this hypothetical contract, one can presume that a court would start from the written contract and may be guided to some extent by existing practice concerning the addition of implied terms or other extensions.

Implied terms

Under normal contract law, an implied term is deemed to be inserted in a contract if:

- It represents the true intention of the parties as to what the terms of the contract should be. This is sometimes known as the 'officious bystander test', following McKinnon LJ He said that an implied term:

  'Is something so obvious that it goes without saying; so that, if the parties were making their bargain, an officious bystander were to suggest some express provision for it in their agreement, they would testily suppress him with a common, "Oh, of course"'. (*Shirlaw v Southern Foundries* [1926] 2 KB 206);

- It is customary in the particular business, or the usual and well-known practice of the employer. This must be 'reasonable, certain and notorious' (*Bond v CAV Ltd* [1983] IRLR 360);

- The contract will only work properly if the clause is included. In *Roberts v Toyota (GB)* [1980] EAT/614 it was held to be an implied term of the contract that a sales manager had to have a valid driving licence.

However, while the courts are cautious about adding terms to written contracts, they need have no such constraint when considering the personal services legislation. The rules for implied terms are thus likely to be taken as only the starting point for interpreting an IR35 hypothetical contract.

Extension of contract by other documents or practices

A contract can be extended by other documents or practices, such as Handbooks or Manuals, which set out how workers should behave. This may happen either expressly, or where it is indicated by the parties' conduct. In *Market Investigations* (see **5.6.5**) the 'Interviewers' Guide' was held to be incorporated into Mrs Irving's contract. The judge said:

'The instructions in the "Interviewers' Guide", after having been seen by the interviewer, are incorporated into the terms of any contract which the interviewer may thereafter make with the company to participate in a particular survey.'

This was of profound importance, because it was the level of control over Mrs Irving shown by the 'Interviewer's Guide' which determined her status as an employee.

However in *Grant v South-west Trains* [1998] IRLR 188, the court held that the company's equal opportunities policy was not incorporated into the worker's employment contract, and in any event, it could not override the express terms of the written contract. In the case of a hypothetical contract, there may be no such limitation. Secondary materials which are relevant to interpreting 'the arrangements under which the services are provided' may be taken into account (Sch 12, para 1(4) FA 2000).

Variation in a contract

Any variation in a contract should normally be agreed, either expressly or tacitly, by both parties. The court is generally reluctant to *imply* a variation to a contract:

'It is fairly difficult, in the ordinary way, to imply a variation of contract, and it is very necessary, if one is to do so, to have very solid facts which demonstrate that it was necessarily to give business efficacy to the contract.'
Horrigan v Lewisham London Borough Council [1978] EAT/15

This protection from the imposition of implied terms will be less likely to apply to the hypothetical contract which is being considered by the personal services legislation. The court will construct the contract from the written documents and from the behaviour of the parties.

5.2.4 Where there is ambiguity, the contract normally decides status

General law

If the status of the worker is ambiguous, a written agreement normally decides the matter. In *Massey v Crown Life Insurance Co* [1978] ICR 590, Lord Denning held that where the relationship of the parties:

'Is ambiguous and is capable of being one or the other, then the parties can remove that ambiguity, by the very agreement itself which they make with one another. The agreement itself then becomes the best material from which to gather the true legal relationship between them.'

Lawton J made a similar point in the same case:

'If in all the circumstances of the case, including the terms of the agreement, it is manifest that there was an intention to change status, then in my judgment there is no reason why the parties should not be allowed to make the change. In this case, there seems to have been a genuine intention to change the status, and I find that the status was changed ...

When I heard the facts of this case recounted by counsel on behalf of the appellant, I was ... suspicious. It seemed nothing more than a device to deceive the Inland Revenue in order to get a tax advantage. The industrial tribunal went into the facts and in the end came to the conclusion ... that there had been a genuine attempt to make an agreement changing the appellant's status, and they excluded illegality. If there was no illegality, and it was a genuine arrangement, there could be only one consequence under the terms of the contract: *the appellant changed his status*' (the author's italics).

This is often referred to as the 'tiebreaker' – if all other factors are neutral, or the employment status of the worker is ambiguous, the intentions of the parties decide the matter. This principle was also affirmed in *BSM (1257) Ltd v Secretary of State for Social Services* [1978] ICR 894, where it was held that unless it could be shown that there were provisions in the contract which were *inconsistent* with the label put upon the relationship, the label itself decides the status.

Personal services legislation

How the tiebreaker test is to be applied in the context of the personal services legislation is unclear. It is the contract between the client and the service company which contains the tiebreaker clause. There is only a hypothetical contract between the worker and the client.

A clause in the written contract stating that both sides are operating as independent third parties *might* be imported into the hypothetical contract, but this cannot be taken for granted. Since the written contract is between an intermediary, and either the client or an agency, it would be self-evident that there was no intention to create employment, but this would not necessarily be true of a hypothetical contract directly between the worker and the client.

In the recent case of *FS Consulting Limited v McCaul* [2001] SpC 305 the Special Commissioner said, when considering such a clause, that:

'It is significant that the contract was between the Appellant and Topper [the agent], whereas Regulation 6(1)(c) of the 2000 Regulations provides that it is the notional contract between … the worker and … the client which is relevant.'

However, it is arguable that a clause confirming the intention of the parties should normally be imported into the hypothetical contract, unless other factors which would contradict this assumption are present. The Revenue accept this, saying that:

'It should be assumed that there would have been mutual intention for self-employment when deciding whether IR35 applies. Although the intention of the parties may not have been expressed, bearing in mind that the engagement is with an intermediary rather than an individual you should assume that there was a mutual intention for a contract for services. Therefore in borderline cases the opinion should be that IR35 does not apply.' (ESM 3286)

If there is uncertainty about whether or not to use the existing 'tiebreaker' test, the principles of *Pepper v Hart* [1992] 65 TC 421 might be invoked. In the IR35 debate on the Welfare Reform and Pensions Act, Mr Timms confirmed for the government that 'the same criteria will be applied in the same way as they always have been in the past' (*Hansard* 3 November 1999, Col. 429). Thus it could be argued that Parliament intended that 'the intention of the parties' should continue to be the tiebreaker.

5.2.5 Reality differs from written contract

In the *BSM* case, the judge held that even where there is a written contract, it can be overruled if:

'There are provisions inconsistent with that relationship, or that in practice the relationship was other than that stated in the contract.'

This will even more clearly be the case under the personal services legislation, where the wider 'circumstances' have to be considered when determining the content of the hypothetical contract.

Examples of cases where the courts have overruled the written contract include *Young and Woods Ltd v West* [1980] IRLR 201, where a sheet metal worker purported to change his contract to one of self-employment. The Court of Appeal held that there was no difference between his working arrangements and those of the remaining Schedule E staff, and thus held on the facts that he had remained an employee. Similarly in *Withers v Flackwell*

Heath Football Supporters' Club [1981] IRLR 307, the Employment Appeals Tribunal held:

> 'That both parties put the label "self-employed" on their relationship is far from conclusive and is to be disregarded when the reality is that the label, and the fiscal consequences that flow from its use, are adopted simply for fiscal reasons.'

5.2.6 No formal contract

Where there is no formal contract, but other documents exist, the House of Lords have held that:

> 'It was open to the industrial tribunal to find, as a fact, that the parties did not intend the letters to be the sole record of their agreement but intended that it should be contained partly in the letters, partly in oral exchanges at the interviews or elsewhere and partly left to evolve by conduct as time went on.' (*Carmichael and Another v National Power* [1999] 4 AER 897)

Thus, where there is no formal contract, the court may look to a number of sources for the true nature of the contractual arrangement. In the case of the IR35 hypothetical contract the legislation indicates that sources other than the written contract will be considered as a matter of course.

However, *Carmichael* also confirmed that where both parties agree on the terms of the engagement, this will normally determine the matter:

> 'The evidence of a party as to what terms he understood to have been agreed is some evidence tending to show that those terms, in an objective sense, were agreed. Of course the tribunal may reject such evidence and conclude that the party misunderstood the effect of what was being said and done. But when both parties are agreed about what they understood their mutual obligations (or lack of them) to be, it is a strong thing to exclude their evidence from consideration.'

It is thought that the same would be true of a hypothetical contract – what the worker and the client both understand to be the substance of the arrangements between them will be very significant in determining its nature.

5.2.7 Summary

When a court considers employment status, it starts by looking at the contract between the individual and his engager. It may occasionally imply or extend the terms of the contract, or ask whether it has been subject to variation. In general, it relies on the written agreement rather than on the subsequent behaviour of the parties, unless a clear contradiction exists between the contract terms and the reality of the relationship.

When considering the IR35 hypothetical contract, less reliance is likely to be placed on the written agreements. These form only part of the 'circumstances' under which the services are delivered to the client. The courts may be more willing to imply terms, consider variations, and import external documents when constructing the hypothetical contract than when deciding a status question for an individual.

Workers within IR35 must thus have regard to the wider context in which they are delivering their services, and be aware that other elements, in addition to the written agreements, could be used to determine the hypothetical contract. This may sometimes be beneficial, see Mr Justice Burton's words quoted at **7.6**.

Nevertheless, written contracts remain the starting point, and remain of great significance. Chapter 9 looks at ways of amending both the written contracts and the delivery of services to clients, so that the hypothetical contract will be more likely to fall outside IR35.

Having explored the methodology of the personal services legislation, the next step is to consider the nature of the hypothetical contract. For it to be a contract of employment, there must first be mutuality of obligation.

5.3 Mutuality of obligation – Outline

5.3.1 Relevance

If there is no mutuality of obligation (familiarly known as MOO), there can be no contract of employment. This was confirmed by Lord Irvine in *Carmichael and Another v National Power* [1999] 4 AER 897, where he said that if there is no MOO, the workers' claim to be employed 'founders on the rock of absence of mutuality'.

This followed the earlier Court of Appeal case of *Nethermere (St Neots) Ltd v Gardner* [1984] ICR 612, in which Stephenson LJ said that 'there must be an irreducible minimum of obligation on each side to create contract of service'.

The importance of MOO lies in the fact that if there is insufficient mutuality for an employment to exist, the worker cannot be within IR35. In other words, if he overcomes the hurdle of mutuality, the other status tests do not have to be considered.

This chapter explains what is meant by mutuality, summarises the key points, reviews existing case law and finally applies that case law to IR35.

5.3.2 Meaning of mutuality of obligation

Before there can be either a contract of service, or a contract for services, the parties have to accept that they have obligations to each other. If they have not, there is no contract of any sort. In any dispute about employment or self-employment, the first step is to consider whether mutual obligations exist between the parties.

Mutuality of obligation in the context of an employment can be explained by saying that, as a minimum, there is a continuing obligation on the employee to provide his own work, and on the employer to provide work – or, if there is no work, at least to pay the employee. It is not enough simply to do work for which the engager is obliged to pay – this is equally true of a self-employed relationship with a client (see *Hewlett Packard v O'Murphy* [2001] EAT/612, **5.9.4**). The key is the continuing obligation.

In the recent case of *Clark v Oxfordshire Health Authority* [1997] EWCA 4792, see **5.5.3**, the judge commented that 'an obligation by the one party to accept and do work if offered, and an obligation on the other party to pay a retainer during such periods as work was *not* offered, would … be likely to suffice'. There is no such obligation in a contract for services.

The mutual obligations between employer and employee may go wider. In *Wickens v Champion Employment* [1984] ICR 365, the court held that the contract then under consideration lacked 'the necessary elements of continuity and care' which were characteristic of mutuality in a contract of service. This has recently evolved into an implied obligation of mutual trust and confidence, see *Malik v Bank of Credit and Commerce International* [1997] ICR 606 at **5.8**.

5.3.3 Examples

A simple example of no mutuality is an electrician who comes to repair a fault in a company's power supply. He does the job and leaves; there is no obligation on the company to provide continuing work or on the electrician to do it. However, an electrician who is employed by a utilities company has to turn up for work each day, and his company is obliged to provide work and pay him.

An individual can work for a business for years without establishing mutuality of obligation. A journalist who writes a weekly column to a newspaper each week, which the editor can accept or reject, and who is only paid for what is accepted, will be working under a series of small contracts for services, as no mutuality of obligation has been established.

5.3.4 Employment law and IR35

Most cases concerning mutuality of obligation have been employment law disputes. The point at issue has been whether the worker is an employee, and so entitled to claim various employment rights. The courts have thus considered, as a first step, what constitutes sufficient mutuality of obligation for an employment to exist.

This is clearly of interest in the context of tax law in general, and personal services in particular. It is no less relevant to the hypothetical contract between the personal services worker and his client than it has been to the real contractual arrangements between workers and clients examined by the courts over the years. This was reaffirmed by Mr Justice Burton in the judicial review case (*R v CIR (oao Professional Contractors Group Ltd*, [2001] STC 629):

'It has now recently been emphasised, by the House of Lords ... that the test adopted in *Nethermere (St Neots) Ltd v Gardner* [1984] ICR 612 CA by Stephenson LJ, of an "irreducible minimum of mutual obligation" is another central piece of guidance in the analysis of whether there is employment or self-employment.'

5.3.5 Case law and MOO

There are several different strands of case law which consider MOO, and these are further developed in the next part of this chapter. These include:

(a) Whether, over the course of time, mutuality can come into existence causing a self-employed relationship to be converted into one of employment (see **5.4**). In the context of IR35 this may be relevant for long-term engagements;

(b) Whether there is mutuality of obligations between the parties throughout a period during which an individual works intermittently for one engager, and not only when the individual was actually working for the engager. If this is the case a global contract of employment may exist which links individual assignments (see **5.5**). It would be unusual for the IR35 worker to be vulnerable under this heading, but the relevant cases nevertheless contain some important comments on the nature of mutuality;

(c) Whether mutuality of obligation subsists between the parties when an individual is actually working on an assignment, see **5.6**. This is the key area for IR35 workers;

(d) Whether it is possible explicitly to exclude MOO from an individual assignment which would otherwise be characterised as one of employment (see **5.7**). Because IR35 is based on a hypothetical contract, the concept of an explicit exclusion of mutuality may be less relevant, but the leading case is nevertheless interesting.

5.4 Gradual development of MOO

5.4.1 Introduction

There is case law to suggest that a relationship, which at inception has no mutuality, can evolve or 'harden' over time into a contract of service as a result of the continuing relationship between the parties. The two leading cases are *Nethermere (St Neots) Ltd v Gardiner* [1983] ICR 319 and *Airfix Footwear Ltd v Cope* [1978] ICR 1210.

5.4.2 *Airfix Footwear Ltd v Cope*

In *Airfix Footwear* Mrs Cope, an outworker, was provided with shoes to assemble at home. There was no obligation on Airfix to provide the work, nor on the worker to do it. The court however held that over time the relationship between the parties had hardened into one where mutual obligations existed. The judgment reads:

'Having considered all the facts, including the fact that for seven years, generally five days a week, this company had delivered 12 dozen pairs of heels each day to the applicant for her to work on, except when lesser quantities were available, they found that there had by conduct been established a continuing relationship, a continuing contract of employment.'

The decision that this continuing relationship was a contract of service, rather than one for services, was however finely balanced. The Tribunal held that:

'The terms of the relationship … were as consistent with that of master and servant as with employer and independent contractor.'

Furthermore, the decision might have gone the other way if Mrs Cope had been a skilled professional. The Industrial Tribunal, whose judgment was upheld by the EAT, said that:

'If she was not an employee she must have been an independent contractor … In any event, *unlike a highly skilled and pre-qualified technical person* she had no skill to offer in the open market. Such skill as she learned was derived entirely from her experience of working with the appellants. In short, she was not a person in business on her own account.' (the author's italics)

5.4.3 *(St Neots) Ltd v Gardiner*

In the case of *Nethermere (St Neots) Ltd v Gardiner* [1983] ICR 319, the Appeal Tribunal found, by a 2:1 majority, that they had sufficient evidence to suggest that the *Nethermere* position was similar to *Airfix*. In other words, the original lack of mutuality had been replaced by a continuing contract of service, and that:

'There was no reason why well-founded expectations of continuing home-work should not be hardened or refined into enforceable contracts by regular giving and taking of work over periods of a year or more.'

However, this decision was reached with some difficulty. One judge dissented, holding that the lack of mutuality meant that there was no binding contract. Stephenson LJ found that 'on the evidence there was just enough material to make a contract of service a reasonably possible inference in favour of the applicants', while Dillon LJ concluded, with considerable ambivalence:

'If it is permissible on the evidence to find that … a contract had been established between each applicant and the company, I see no necessity to conclude that that contract must have been a contract for services and not a contract of service.'

5.4.4 Conclusions

Thus, where there is no initial mutuality, regular working for one engager can 'harden' the relationship into one of employment. However, in the context of IR35, the following points should be noted:

(a) *Airfix Footwear* draws a distinction between labourers and skilled workers, and suggested that the same implied contract of employment might not apply to the latter;

(b) *Nethermere* was borderline, and cannot be regarded as a strong authority;

(c) In the subsequent case of *Hellyer Bros v McLeod* (see **5.5.2**) it was submitted, and appears to have been accepted by the judge, that:

> 'The process of inferential enquiry approved in *Airfix* … and the *Nethermere* case – by an examination in the course of dealing for the purposes of deducing whether there was a contractual relationship between the two sides and (if so) what its terms were – is necessarily precluded in a case like the present where the parties have stated in meticulous detail in a series of contracts precisely what the terms of their relationships are.'

In other words, even if there is a course of dealing over time, which might be interpreted as giving rise to an employment, this can normally be contradicted by a specific provision in the agreement between the parties.

In the case of a hypothetical contract envisaged by Schedule 12, FA 2000, the protection from 'inferential enquiry' given by such specific clauses is less certain. While it must be helpful to describe 'in meticulous detail' the relationship between the parties, and these details may be implied in the hypothetical contract, they may not be determinative, see **5.2** above.

Nevertheless, given the doubts expressed by the courts in both *Airfix* and *Nethermere*, and the distinction made between manual workers and those who are 'highly skilled and pre-qualified technical person[s]', it would be difficult to use either case as a basis for saying that a contractor who works regularly, or over a long period, for one engager has thereby created an employment relationship by 'the regular giving and taking of work'. The inclusion of specific terms in client contracts may also help protect the position.

5.5 Global or umbrella contracts

5.5.1 Introduction

In most cases where mutuality has been considered by the courts, the employment rights in question were only accessible if the individual had an employment which extended over some qualifying period. For example, for unfair dismissal purposes, an individual must prove continuous employment for a period of one year (previously two years).

In these decisions the judges are therefore not considering whether an employment contract exists when the individual *actually* works for the client. Instead, they are looking at whether there is an umbrella contract of employment which subsists even when the individual is not working. These cases are thus of less direct relevance to IR35, as most contractors have a succession of contracts with different engagers. They nevertheless contain useful comments on the nature and scope of mutuality.

Two of the cases on global contracts were heard almost simultaneously, *Boyd Line Ltd v Pitts* [1986] ICR 244 and *Hellyer Brothers Ltd v McLeod* [1986] ICR 122. These were followed by the more recent cases of *Clark v Oxfordshire Health Authority* [1997] EWCA 4792 and *Carmichael and Another v National Power* [1999] 4 AER 897.

5.5.2 *Boyd Line* and *Hellyer*

In *Boyd Line* a trawlerman was engaged on a voyage-by-voyage basis; between voyages he was not paid by his employers and drew unemployment benefit. However, it was held that there was 'a global contract covering the whole period of (his) employment' including the periods for which he was not in work.

In *Hellyer*, a very similar case heard a few days earlier, the court found the opposite: there was no overall global contract between the trawlermen and the employers. Once the voyage was over, the men were free to go, and 'the employers ... were never under the least obligation in law to provide work for anybody.'

The difference between the two cases is very fine: indeed in summing up the earlier *Boyd Line* case the judge said, with reference to the decision of the lower court:

> 'We feel it probable ... that we would have decided the matter differently from the Industrial Tribunal ... (but) there was in our judgment evidence on which they *could* have found as they did, that there was a global or umbrella contract.'

In short, of the two leading cases on the umbrella concept, one decided that there was no such contract, while the judges in the other suggested that they would have come to a similar decision (i.e. there was no global contract) had they been considering the issue as the court of first instance. However, because of the rules governing appeals, see **7.8.3**, there were insufficient grounds to reverse the earlier decision of the Industrial Tribunal.

5.5.3 *Clark v Oxfordshire Health Authority*

In the more recent case of *Clark v Oxfordshire Health Authority* [1997] EWCA 4792, the court looked in detail at whether a global contract existed. Mrs Clark was a 'bank nurse' and worked for the Health Authority from time to time, under a contract which provided many elements that suggested a continuing contract of employment. These included:

- grievance and disciplinary procedures;

- membership of the NHS superannuation scheme;

- a rate of pay which was described as 'on the scale of £10,700 and rising by annual increments to £12,390'; and

- the Conditions of Service for nurses known as the 'Whitney Council Conditions'.

Nevertheless, the Court of Appeal held that there was no global contract of employment and made the following points:

(a) The Authority was at no relevant time under any obligation to offer the applicant work, nor was she under any obligation to accept it;

(b) The mutual obligations required to found a global contract of employment need not necessarily and in every case consist of obligations to provide and perform work;

(c) An obligation by the one party to accept and do work if offered, and an obligation on the other party to pay a retainer during such periods as work was *not* offered, would ... be likely to suffice;

(d) However ... *some* mutuality of obligation is required to found a global contract of employment ... in the present case (the judge could) find no such mutuality subsisting during the periods when the applicant was not occupied in a 'single engagement'.

The question of whether Mrs Clark was an employee when she was actually carrying out nursing services for the Health Authority was remitted back to the Industrial Tribunal for consideration, and the results of this review are unreported.

5.5.4 *Carmichael v National Power*

In this case two female tour guides worked for National Power for several years on a 'casual as required basis'. They were paid a flat hourly rate, and worked as guides when they were (a) invited to do so, and (b) available. No disciplinary action was taken if the women chose not to work.

The women had been seeking a declaration that they were employees under an umbrella contract of service, which linked together the periods they actually worked. The House of Lords held that:

> 'The parties incurred no obligation to provide or accept [work], but at best assumed moral obligations of loyalty in a context where both recognised that the best interests of each other lay in being accommodating to the other.'

Lord Irvine held that the case 'founders on the rock of absence of mutuality', so underlining the importance of this concept to employment status.

It should be emphasised that the courts did not comment on whether the women were employed or self-employed during the individual 'ad hoc contracts of service or for services' which existed when they were actually carrying out the guiding duties.

5.5.5 Conclusions

These cases are interesting for the light they shed on the nature of the mutual obligations necessary to create a contract of service. In all the cases there appear to be no sanctions if the worker decides not to work, or the engager decides not to offer the work. In addition, Lord Irvine's comment indicating that mutuality is fundamental to employment is of relevance, as is the decision of the Court of Appeal in *Clark*:

> 'The mutual obligations required to found a global contract of employment need not necessarily and in every case consist of obligations to provide and perform work ... An obligation by the one party to accept and do work if offered, and an obligation on the other party to pay a retainer during such periods as work was *not* offered, would ... be likely to suffice.'

5.6 MOO and the single engagement

5.6.1 Importance

Mutuality has been most frequently examined in the context of global or umbrella arrangements, but it is also clearly of fundamental importance to single engagements.

This has recently been confirmed by the recent case of *Montgomery v Johnson Underwood* [2000] A1 2000/2085, see **5.6.4** below, where the Court of Appeal said specifically that the tribunal was wrong in law not to consider whether the irreducible minimum existed in the context of the specific assignment under consideration in *Montgomery*.

The tribunal in *Montgomery* had stated, following *Secretary of State for Employment v McMeechan* [1997] IRLR 353, that the absence of mutuality 'appears to us largely irrelevant to the specific engagement'. The Court of Appeal's view on *McMeechan* was as follows:

> 'If he [the judge in the McMeechan case] did intend to reduce the "crite-rion of mutual obligation" and by inference "control" as well to no more than matters to be weighed up with all the other factors, with great respect I disagree. More to the point I consider such as approach to be contrary to the *Ready Mixed Concrete* case itself (which, of course, would not have bound the Court of Appeal) but also to *Nethermere* and *Carmichael* in particular.'

The most important cases which consider MOO in the context of individual contracts are set out below. Three, *O'Kelly v Trusthouse Forte plc* [1983] 3 AER 456, *Specialeyes* (unreported, see *Taxation* 4 July 1991) and *Montgomery v Johnson Underwood* [2000] A1 2000/2085, all found that there was no mutu-ality between the parties and thus no contract of employment. In the fourth case, *Market Investigations Ltd v The Minister of Social Security* [1968] 2 QB 173 the opposite conclusion was reached.

5.6.2 *O'Kelly v Trusthouse Forte plc*

The facts of the case were as follows. The Grosvenor House Hotel in London engaged casual workers on a function by function basis. However a large number of these casual staff were so-called 'regular casuals', i.e., they were engaged to such an extent that some had no other work. The question at issue was whether they were employees of the hotel.

It was found that the casuals had the following characteristics of employment:

(a) They provided their services in return for remuneration for work actu-ally performed. They did not invest their own capital or stand to gain or lose from the commercial success of the functions organised by the ban-queting department;

(b) They performed their work under the direction and control of the 'employers';

(c) When the casual workers attended at functions they were part of the 'employers'' organisation, and for the purpose of ensuring the smooth running of the business they were represented in the staff consultation process;

(d) When working they were carrying on the business of the 'employers';

(e) Clothing and equipment were provided by the 'employers';

(f) They were paid weekly in arrears and under deduction of income tax and social security contributions;

(g) Their work was organised on the basis of a weekly rota and they required permission to take time off from rostered duties;

(h) There was a disciplinary and grievance procedure;

(i) There was holiday pay or an incentive bonus calculated by reference to past service.

In addition to the above, a number of factors were considered by the Tribunal to be 'not inconsistent' with employment status:

(j) They were paid for work actually performed and did not receive a regular wage or retainer. It was however held that the method of calculating entitlement to remuneration is not an essential aspect of the employment relationship;

(k) Casual workers were not remunerated on the same basis as permanent employees. They did not receive sick pay, were not included in the employers' staff pension scheme and did not receive the fringe benefits accorded to established employees. It was held that employers can, however, adopt different terms and conditions for different categories of employee;

(l) There were no regular or assured working hours. It is however not a requirement of employment that there should be 'normal working hours';

(m) Casual workers were not provided with written particulars of employment. There is a statutory obligation to furnish written particulars of employment to employees.

Of greater interest were the following, which were held to be *inconsistent* with a contract of employment:

(n) The engagement was terminable without notice on either side;

(o) The casuals had the right to decide whether or not to accept work, although whether or not it would be in their interest to exercise the right to refuse work is another matter;

(p) The 'employers' had no obligation to provide any work;

(q) It was the parties' view that the casual workers were independent contractors engaged under successive contracts for services;

(r) It was the recognised custom and practice of the industry that casual workers were engaged under a contract for services.

The Industrial Tribunal decided that, despite the fact that the engagements had many of the characteristics of employment, the absence of mutuality of obligation indicated by points (o) and (p) meant that there could not be a contract of service. They said that:

> 'It is freely recognised that the relationship of the (casuals) to the employers had many of the characteristics of a contract of service. In our view the one important ingredient which was missing was mutuality of obligation.'

As a result, the workers were self-employed. They were:

> 'In no different position than any independent contractor who offers his services for a particular purpose or event (e.g., a jobbing gardener or a day labourer) and it was by their choice that they made their services available to a single customer.'

The Tribunal did not think that the absence of the risk element which was usually present in self-employment was a concern:

> 'Where the commodity offered is the simple supply of semi-skilled labour for a specific occasion, or series of occasions, it is not to be expected that there would be a financial investment or participation in the profits or losses of the business.'

In summary, the House of Lords held that there was:

- no mutuality of obligation;
- no successive small contracts of employment;
- no overriding umbrella contract; and that
- the workers were self-employed.

Until recently the Revenue sought to follow the decision of the EAT, which held that the individual contracts were of service rather than that of the Court of Appeal which concluded that the workers were in business on their own account in respect of the individual engagements as well as for the overall 'global' contract, and thus overruled the EAT. This was an astonishing rejection of the UK's doctrine of precedent.

However, following representations, the Revenue reconsidered their commentary in this area and the March 2002 guidance is much more balanced. In a future review they may also want to consider rewording the case law summary at ESM 7100 which still reflects their earlier preference for the EAT decision.

In a later case, *Four Seasons (Inn on the Park) Ltd v Hamarat* [1985] EAT/369, a 'regular casual' waiter was held to be employed. The case was distinguished from *O'Kelly*, because there was mutuality of obligation. Waite J said in his summing up:

> 'The company treated themselves as being obliged to engage Mr Hamarat as
> a wine waiter whenever there was work for him to do, and Mr Hamarat
> treated himself as obliged to attend whenever he was asked to do so.'

The recent decision in *Quinn v Voteforce Associates* [2001] EAT/483 was similar to that of the House of Lords in *O'Kelly*. Miss Quinn was 'one of a pool of about 30 casual waitresses who could be called up as and when required. They were not obliged to do the work that was offered.' The judge held that:

> 'It is clear, on the facts of this case, that there was no mutuality of obligation:
> the company was not obliged to provide work for Miss Quinn; she was not
> obliged to perform the work if it was offered. It follows that there was here
> no contract of service.'

5.6.3 *Specialeyes (Optical Services) Ltd*

The case of *Specialeyes* (unreported, see *Taxation* 4 July 1991) also considers mutuality. In 1989 the government introduced charges for eye tests, and in response to this change, Specialeyes engaged opticians to carry out sight-testing in its branches. In addition to these 'locums', the company also employed its own opticians. Specialeyes treated the locum opticians as self-employed, and the Revenue challenged this.

The Special Commissioners found as follows:

(a) Specialeyes was not obliged to offer any of the opticians work, and the opticians were free to refuse engagements offered without penalty. They could also stipulate their own hours of availability, even though, in practice, many worked up to six days a week. There was thus no mutuality of obligation;

(b) The locum opticians took out their own insurance cover against mal-practice claims, whereas Specialeyes paid for the insurance of its employee opticians;

(c) The opticians were paid by a fixed fee for each test performed, and submitted a monthly invoice, whereas the employee opticians received a salary, sick and holiday pay, medical insurance and a company car;

(d) Although Specialeyes provided all major items of non-portable equipment, the opticians supplied their own retinoscopes and ophthalmoscopes;

(e) The company had very little control over the opticians' professional work;

(f) The opticians attended the branches only to perform sight tests and carried out no other duties;

(g) Although the company could not function without the opticians, this did not mean that the opticians were 'part and parcel' of Specialeyes' organisation;

(h) Some of the opticians had their own practices elsewhere.

The Commissioners held that:

- there was there no mutuality of obligation;
- there was no overriding contract of employment;
- there was not a succession of small Schedule E contracts;
- instead there was a series of separate contracts for services with the locum opticians, who were thus self-employed.

5.6.4 *Montgomery v Johnson Underwood*

The recent case of *Montgomery v Johnson Underwood Ltd* [2000] A1 2000/2085 is an agency case where the point at issue was whether Mrs Montgomery was employed either by:

(a) the agency which placed her with the client; or

(b) the client.

It was decided at the Employment Tribunal and confirmed by the EAT that she was not an employee of the client.

The Court of Appeal then decided she was not an employee of the agency, because the agency exercised insufficient control. It was also held that there was insufficient mutuality of obligation between the worker and the agency for there to be an employment. As discussed at **5.6.1** above, the Court of Appeal in this case was dismissive of the EAT's view that mutuality should not be considered when looking at single engagements.

The case is also interesting for its comments on agencies, see **5.12** below.

5.6.5 *Market Investigations*

The case of *Market Investigations Ltd v The Minister of Social Security* [1968] 2 QB 173 concerned a part-time interviewer for a market research company. The court held that despite there being no overall mutuality of obligation, a series of separate employment contracts were created when the interviewer, Mrs Irving, accepted the engagements. This was despite the fact that:

(a) She undertook a number of short engagements over a period of time;

(b) She was free to accept or reject the work offered;

(c) She could work as and when she chose and did not necessarily have to complete seven hours' work during one day, although the work had to be completed by a specified date;

(d) There was no sick pay, holidays or overtime;

(e) She was free to work as an interviewer for other companies, although she didn't in fact do so.

The reasons given for the court's decision were that:

(f) She was subject to substantial control as to the manner and content of her work, although the court did hold that she did 'within the limits of her Instructions, deploy a skill and personality';

(g) She could not send a substitute without the prior permission of the company;

(h) She was paid on a daily basis plus a meal allowance, but could neither increase this amount by her own efforts, nor make a loss;

(i) She did not provide her own tools or equipment.

The decisive factor was the high level of detailed control to which she was subject once she agreed to do the work, so that the court held that she was not in business on her own account, and must be an employee. Mutuality in the context of the specific engagement was not discussed specifically but was implied by the decision that she was an employee.

5.6.6 Conclusions

These decisions demonstrate that:

(a) There may be no MOO even where relationships continue over a considerable period of time, as in *Specialeyes* and *O'Kelly*. In both of these cases the relationship could be broken down into a succession of small contracts of self-employment;

(b) The use of an agent (as in *Montgomery*) may make it harder to establish mutuality. This is discussed further in **5.9** below;

(c) It may be possible to distinguish a knowledge-based contractor from the interviewer in *Market Investigations* on the basis of control. The level of control over professionals is characteristically less, see **6.4.4**.

5.7 Deliberately excluding MOO

5.7.1 *Stevedoring v Fuller*

In the recent case of *Stevedoring v Fuller* [2001] EWCA Civ 2001 the engagers deliberately tried to exclude mutuality of obligation so as not to create employment.

The individuals involved were dock workers who had been made redundant by the engager. The following year they were invited to apply to supply services to the company on:

> 'An ad hoc and casual basis. This means that ... there is no obligation on the part of the company to provide such work nor for you to accept any work so offered.'

The facts of the case were as follows:

> 'From January 1996 each of the Respondents worked for the Appellants ... "on many more days than not". They did not work for any other employer. They were engaged directly by the Appellants and were offered work before other casual labour which was engaged through an agency. A rota system ensured that those who said they were available for work but were not offered it were rewarded and that those who were offered work for which they were not available were penalised. The Appellants provided training and (in the third year) protective clothing for the Respondents who worked under their control and direction.'

In addition, the dock workers were paid under deduction of PAYE, although this was described in the agreement between the parties as being 'for administrative convenience only'. At both the Employment Tribunal and the EAT the dock workers were held to be employees. The courts held that, although the document setting out the arrangements between the parties 'expressly negative mutuality of obligation', it also contained implied terms as follows:

> 'From the ways in which the parties have in reality conducted themselves since the inception of the agreements ... that the (Appellants) will (i) offer the (Respondents) a reasonable amount of work as and when the work is available, and (ii) that they will offer the (Respondents) that work in priority to other casual workers ... In return the (Respondents) impliedly agree to make themselves available for work on at least a reasonable number of occasions when the work is offered to them.'

However, these decisions were overruled by the Court of Appeal, who held that, because the parties had expressly negatived mutuality of obligation, there was no contract *ab initio*, and 'If there was no contract, there was no contract and one could not be created by the implication of terms in this way.' Even if there was a contract, the terms could not be implied because they 'flatly contradict the express terms contained in the documents'. Specifically, the court held that:

> 'The rota, the provision of training and protective clothing and the regularity with which some (but not all) of the Respondents did casual work ... can be explained by the fact that the Respondents were performing a series of successive ad hoc contracts of service or services. We do not see anything which is inconsistent with the framework set out in the documents to which all parties subscribed.'

It was also impossible for the court to hold that the contract had been varied, because the conduct of the parties 'remained the same throughout'.

5.7.2 IR35 implications

This case shows that, in a normal status case, it is possible to exclude mutuality, and thus employment status, by clear terms agreed between the parties, even where conduct might lead to a different conclusion.

However, the same analysis is not necessarily applicable to the hypothetical contract which lies at the heart of IR35. A court would clearly take into account 'the terms on which the services are provided having regard to the terms of the contracts' but these are explicitly stated to form '*part* of the arrangements under which the services are provided'. (Sch 12, para 1(1)(c) FA 2000)

Thus, where the terms of the contracts between the client and the service company include a similar negativing of mutuality, this term would be a factor to be considered in constructing the hypothetical contract, but it is unlikely to be as decisive as in *Stevedoring*. Other elements of the 'arrangements' may have more weight.

The term will, however, be taken into account and might, together with other elements, take the relationship outside IR35. It is thus considered important to have such a clause in the contracts, see **9.2**.

5.8 Expanding MOO – trust, confidence and care

In addition to the well-established principle that there will be MOO if the client is obliged to offer work (or, if there is no work, a retainer) and the worker has then to accept the work which has been offered, mutuality has other characteristics.

In the case of *Wickens v Champion Employment* [1984] ICR 365 the court said that the individual was not employed, in part because:

> 'The relationship between the employers and the temporaries seems to us wholly to lack the *necessary elements of continuity, and care of the employer for the employee,* that one associates with a contract of service.' (the author's italics)

The case of *Malik v Bank of Credit and Commerce International* [1997] ICR 606 considered a claim by two employees that their reputation in the market place had been damaged by their employers, who were thus in breach of 'the implied mutual obligation of trust and confidence' owed as between an employer and an employee. Lord Birkenhead, in the House of Lords, agreed that:

> 'The bank was under an implied obligation to its employees not to conduct a dishonest or corrupt business. This implied obligation is no more than one particular aspect of the portmanteau, general obligation not to engage in conduct likely to undermine the trust and confidence required if the employment relationship is to continue in the manner the employment contract implicitly envisages.'

Lord Steyn said that:

86

'The employees do not rely on … an individualised term to be implied from the particular provisions of their employment contract considered against their specific contextual setting. Instead they relied on a standardised term implied by law – that is, *on a term which is said to be an incident of all contracts of employment*. Such implied terms operate as default rules. The parties are free to exclude or modify them.' (the author's italics)

He went on to say that the evolution of this concept was a fairly recent development, and quoted Lord Slynn of Hadley who referred to:

'The changes that have taken place in the employment and employee relationship, with far greater duties imposed on the employer [than] in the past, whether by statute or judicial decision, to care for the physical, financial and even psychological welfare of the employee.' *Spring v Guardian Assurance plc* [1995] 2 A.C 296

These views were affirmed by Lord Johnston sitting in the Employment Appeal Tribunal in the case of *Serco Limited v Matthew Blair and Others* [1998] EAT/345 unreported, see **5.9.3** below, where he referred to 'the very personal nature of [the employment contract], and the need for mutual trust and confidence as between employer and employee'. It was reiterated by the judge in *Express and Echo Publications Ltd v Tanton* [1999] IRLR 367, where he said that 'the law now recognises unambiguously that a contract of employment involves mutual trust and confidence'.

It is thus arguable that the parties' hypothetical contract must include the default term – mutual trust and confidence – if it is to be an employment relationship. Whether this is the case in a contractor–client scenario will have to be decided by the courts.

5.9 Use of agent

5.9.1 Outline

A succession of cases have considered the concept of mutuality of obligation between the worker and the client where an agency is involved. These strongly suggest that the use of an agency may make it difficult to establish mutuality of obligation between the client and the worker.

5.9.2 *Montgomery*

In *Montgomery*, see **5.6.4** above, Mrs Montgomery worked for O&K Limited through an agency, Johnson Underwood (JU). The existence of the agency was a key reason why the Employment Tribunal and the EAT decided that Mrs Montgomery could not be an employee of the client, O&K, despite saying that:

'If we were to look at the situation as a whole from the point of view of the average lay observer, then the "general impression" would vindicate the applicant's submission that she was employed by [the client].'

It was further decided that Mrs Montgomery was not an employee of JU, the agency, because 'the degree of control that JU had over Mrs Montgomery was not of a nature or degree to make JU her master'. A subsidiary point was that 'the mutual obligation was that JU provided work for Mrs Montgomery through its contract to provided services to O&K [and] she promised to do that work … was insufficient'.

However, Mr Justice Buckley did not dismiss the possibility that there could be sufficient mutuality in a relationship with an agency. He said:

'For my part I would accept that an offer of work by an agency, even at another's workplace, accepted by the individual for remuneration to be paid by the agency, could satisfy the requirement of mutual obligation. I put it no higher because it would be necessary to look at the circumstances carefully and realistically. It may, for example, be more difficult to find that necessary mutuality in a very short assignment as opposed to one which was or had become more permanent.'

In the recent case of *Hanbury v EDS* [2001] EAT/369, the court quoted with approval from *Montgomery*, and said that:

'The Employment Tribunal had no difficulty in concluding that the Applicant was not employed by either BSB [the agency] or EDS [the client] under a contract of service … there was no mutuality of obligation, either between the Applicant and BSB, or between the Applicant and EDS, regardless of the contractual position between those respective parties. That conclusion is plainly permissible.'

5.9.3 *Serco Limited v Matthew Blair*

The most interesting comments concerning the consequences of a tripartite worker/agency/client relationship were made by Lord Johnston sitting in the Edinburgh Employment Appeal Tribunal in the case of *Serco Limited v Matthew Blair and Others* [1998] EAT/345.

In *Serco* the workers were on the books of an employment agency who hired them out to the client (Serco Limited). Lord Johnston at the EAT said that the existence of the agency precluded the workers being employed by the client. He referred to:

> 'The very personal nature of [the employment contract], and the need for mutual trust and confidence as between employer and employee, which we do not consider can be created by the acts of a third party [the agency], even in conjunction with the workers, particularly where the third party [the agency] remains part of the operational scene.'

This important comment suggests that where there is an agency involved in the relationship between the worker and the client, this may prevent a contract of employment arising between the parties.

5.9.4 *Costain v Smith* and *Hewlett Packard v O'Murphy*

In the recent case of *Costain Building and Civil Engineering Ltd v Smith and Another* [2000] EAT/215 there was also an agency in the chain between the worker and the client. It was held that the individual was not an employee. He worked for the client 'because he was hired out by the agency and paid by them and not because of any contractual connection with (the client)'. The client had:

> 'Sought a site engineer for a temporary period and they went to the agency to supply them with a worker. They did not identify the applicant nor did they specifically request him. Indeed, the identity of the required site engineer was immaterial.'

In *Hewlett Packard v O'Murphy* [2001] EAT/612, the court followed *Costain*. Here the worker claimed employment rights from Hewlett Packard despite the fact that he used his own service company and worked via an agency. The EAT found that 'the work and payment are not in dispute but what was disputed was whether they arose by way of mutual obligation which they clearly did not'.

5.9.5 *Motorola Ltd v Davidson* and *Melville Craig Group Limited*

The case of *Motorola Ltd v Davidson* [2000] EAT/46 was heard after the *Serco* case and before *Costain*. It is an agency case in which it was found that the worker was an employee of the client. However, it was argued solely on the basis of control, and the key point made in *Serco* (and followed in *Costain*) that there was no contractual nexus between the worker and the client was not made. The outcome could have been different had this important point been addressed. The concluding words of Mr Justice Lindsay were:

'We must emphasise that we have concentrated upon "control". As to whether we would have concluded more widely ... we say nothing: Motorola chose to argue only as to the "control" component and we, too, have limited observations to that subject.'

Specifically the judge pointed out that he was not looking at the range of issues raised in *Serco*, which implies that he might have decided differently had he done so.

5.10 Practical conclusions and consequences

5.10.1 General

Some key factors emerge from this review of case law:

(a) There will be no mutuality if the client is free to refuse to offer work and the worker is free to refuse it, see for example *Carmichael* (**5.5.4**) and *Quinn* (**5.6.2**). In practice this may translate into an absence of sanctions (**5.10.2**) and a right of the client to withdraw the work without pay or compensation (**5.10.4**);

(b) The existence of an agency in the chain between the service company/worker and the client may make it harder for mutuality to arise, see **5.8** and **5.10.3**;

(c) The recent extension of MOO to include 'mutual trust and confidence' (**5.8**) may make it easier to defeat IR35 in a typical contractor scenario.

5.10.2 The presence or absence of sanctions

In seeking to determine whether there is mutuality of obligation, it is important to know whether there are any sanctions available to either side when the worker does not work when it is offered, or the engager does not provide it when available.

(a) In *Carmichael*, the House of Lords found it significant that 'Mrs Carmichael was not available for work on 17 occasions, nor Mrs Leese on eight. No suggestion of disciplining them arose. The objective inference is that when work was available they were free to undertake it or not as they chose';

(b) In *O'Kelly*, Ackner LJ said: 'The company of course expected the applicants to accept engagements rostered, but to suggest that a failure to accept amounted to a breach of contract is going too far. They were entitled to chose whether or not to attend, and however irritating it might have been to the company if faced with a refusal, it would have been quite unreal to conclude that either party would have thought it was a breach of contract';

(c) In *McMeechan v Secretary of State for Employment* [1997] IRLR 353 (**23.3.2**), where the worker was found to be an employee, he suffered deductions from wages for unsatisfactory timekeeping, thus confirming that there were sanctions and that these were applied;

(d) In *Stevedoring,* there was no obligation to provide or accept work, and there was no sanction for refusing to provide or accept work;

(e) In *Motorola,* one of the indicators against the relationship being one of employment was that Mr Davidson 'was in a position to choose for any reason or none not to work for Motorola, either on particular occasions or at all, if so inclined, without that being in any way on his part a breach of contract with Motorola. Such freedom [was] not given to Motorola's full time employees or, as a rule, to any employees'.

However the judge said this was 'more theoretical than real' because Mr Davidson was obliged, under his contract with the agency, to 'be present during the times ... required by [the agent]' and 'to afford [Motorola] faithful services of a standard such as would sustain a contract of employment'. The *Motorola* case was decided on limited grounds, but the judge's comment that the freedom to 'walk away' is an indicator of self-employment remains relevant;

(f) In the case of *WHPT Housing Association Ltd v Secretary of State for Social Services*, see **6.7.3**, Mr Lowe, an architect, worked regularly from 9.30 to 5.30, was paid on an hourly basis for his work and was supplied with all relevant equipment by the engager. However, he was held not to be an employee because he:

> 'At no time undertook any obligation to present himself for service at the associations' premises at any time; (nor) to provide a specific number of hours' service ... and that his principal obligation was to work as an architect during the hours of service which he chose to offer ... in consideration for which the association agreed to pay him £3 per hour'.

In other words, there was no mutuality of obligation between the parties and no contract of employment; Mr Lowe was under no obligation to work fixed hours and there was thus no sanction if he did not.

5.10.3 Presence of an agency

As has been discussed above at **5.9**, the existence of an agency between the client and the service company may prevent mutuality of obligations arising between the worker and the client.

5.10.4 Client under no obligation to provide work

One of the characteristics of mutuality is that the engager should be obliged to provide work for the individual (or pay him if there is no work), and the worker should be available for, and carry out, the work.

Thus a contract that allowed the client to send the worker home if there were no work, and not pay him during this period, would be more similar to *Carmichael* than to an employment contract. It would be possible to construct a contract along these lines, although the worker would have to consider the very real commercial risk.

It is also possible that if either or both parties have the right to quit without notice, there may be no mutuality. This means that either the worker is not obliged to give notice, so he can move to another job at any point, and/or the client can get rid of the worker without notice. In *Montgomery*, the worker, who was clearly found not to be an employee of the client, 'acknowledged that she was free to walk away from that job at any time she wanted to'. See also *Motorola* at **5.10.2**.

It is emphasised, however, that this is an area which needs further testing in the courts. See **9.2** for drafting of contracts.

5.11 Application to personal services workers

The key question for the personal service worker is whether, under the hypothetical contract with his client, there is mutuality of obligation between himself and his client. As discussed above, existing case law gives guidance as to the answer to this question. However, it must also be recognised that this is new ground. At the time of writing there is no case law on mutuality in the context of hypothetical contracts of employment, and the view of the courts can thus only be surmised.

However, Mr Justice Burton said, in the context of IR35:

> 'Of course there is in fact no contract between the client and the service contractor, and thus no obligation on either party owed to each other, but it must be significant, when applying the common law test, to consider whether, looking at the actual relationship, and a notional contract, between the client and the service contractor, any obligation would be owed by the client.' *R v CIR (oao Professional Contractors Group Ltd)* [2001] STC 629

This suggests that the judge thought that in most contractor scenarios, the worker may have obligations to the client, but the client may have none towards the worker. The judge's actual words when hearing the case were as follows:

'How do you arrive at an irreducible minimum of obligation from someone who doesn't employ you … when there isn't any obligation at all? What is the obligation of the employer, not the employee … the obligation (of the client) to pay the money is not enough.'

Clearly, there can be situations where there is mutuality of obligation between client and contract worker. For example, if a client asks a specific individual to work on a computer helpdesk for the foreseeable future, and the worker agrees he will do this, then mutuality probably does exist between the engager and the worker. Similarly, where a six-month project finishes early and the client is then obliged to find other work – and the individual is obliged to carry out this work – then mutuality almost certainly exists.

But the existence of MOO between contractor and client is not a foregone conclusion. Consider the following:

(a) Where there is a single engagement but the client can send the worker home if there is no work, there may not be the mutuality of obligation characteristic of an employment, see *Carmichael* and **5.10.4**;

(b) Where a PSC worker is supplied via an agency to carry out a short-term assignment for the client, does the existence of the agency prevent mutuality arising between the worker and the client? The cases of *Serco*, *Costain* and *Hewlett Packard v O'Murphy*, as well as the comments of the judge in *Montgomery*, suggest that this may be the case, see **5.9**;

(c) If there is no notice period in either direction, or only in one direction, there may be no mutuality of obligation, see **5.10.4**;

(d) Will the courts decide that the nature of contract work means that the hypothetical contract may sometimes lack 'the necessary elements of continuity and care' and 'trust and confidence' (see **5.8**) which have been held to be characteristic of mutuality in a contract of service?

(e) Where the written contracts state that there is no mutuality between the parties, this is not determinative as it might be in a normal status case, see *Hellyer* at **5.5.2** and *Stevedoring* at **5.7.1**. However, it may be persuasive.

(f) Where a worker does regular work for the client, as in *Nethermere* or *Airfix*, see **5.4**, would there be sufficient mutuality to create a global

hypothetical contract of employment? In the case of a professional supplying services, the case law suggests that it has to be doubtful.

What is needed is a court case that will explore when the mutuality of obligation characteristic of a contract of employment exists within the context of
IR35.

6 Employed or self-employed?

6.1 Introduction

The aim of the personal services legislation is to discover whether the individual would be regarded as an employee if he were working as an individual rather than via an intermediary. If the answer is yes, he will be within the scope of IR35.

In order to decide whether someone is within the personal services rules, it is necessary to establish the nature of the hypothetical contract between the parties, and whether any mutuality of obligation exists between them. If there is no mutuality, there can be no employment. This is discussed in Chapter 5.

This chapter examines the detailed status tests, and Chapter 7 looks at how the tests work in practice, in the context of cases which are similar to the position of the IR35 worker. Chapter 8 reviews the Revenue guidance on status and considers how a Revenue determination might be challenged in the courts. Chapter 9 suggests whether and to what extent changes could be made to working practices so that individuals may more easily meet the status tests.

As a final point, it should be noted that some workers are deemed to be employed for National Insurance purposes, and this deeming provision has priority over the status tests for NICs, but not for tax. How this interacts with the personal services legislation is discussed at **12.7.2**.

6.2 Development and scope of legislation

It was initially proposed that a worker should fall within the personal services legislation if he was operating under the control of the client, see **2.3.2**. However, the government subsequently moved away from this crude measure, and adopted instead the existing tests, see *IRPR*, 23 September 1999:

> 'The rules will rely on the *existing* tests which are currently used to determine the boundary between employment and self-employment for tax and National Insurance Contributions purposes, instead of the alternative test put forward originally. Using these more familiar tests will help understanding of the new rules and ensure they are targeted on the right people.'

Mr Timms, speaking for the government, made the same point in the House of Commons on 3 November 1999:

'The conventional distinction will be used to decide whether the new rules apply to service company workers. That means that the same criteria will be applied in the same way as they always have been in the past.' (*Hansard* Col. 429).

The personal service legislation does not refer to the status tests as such, but they are implied. The rules apply where:

'The circumstances are such that, if the services were provided under a contract directly between the client and the worker, the worker would be regarded for income tax purposes as an employee of the client.' (Sch 12, para 1(1)(c) FA 2000).

As discussed at **5.1**, the 'circumstances' include, but are not limited to, consideration of the terms in the contracts between the service company and the client, or those between the service company/agency and agency/client. Because the legislation looks at the wider circumstances and not only at the written contracts, elements other than the written terms must also be taken into account.

These can be assumed to include factors such as whether the worker has a business organisation and the number and variety of his other contracts. In other words, the personal services legislation will look at the wider status tests and not simply at either the contractual terms, or the conditions of a single engagement.

6.3 Status tests and checklists

6.3.1 General

When faced by several hundred tax, National Insurance and employment law cases, together with others involving compensation and damages, the idea of using a checklist to determine whether or not IR35 applies looks like a tempting short-cut. But it may lead to the wrong decision: Cooke J. said in *Market Investigations Ltd v Minister of Social Security* [1968] 3 All ER 732 that:

'No exhaustive list has been compiled and perhaps no exhaustive list can be compiled of considerations which are relevant in determining that question, nor can strict rules be laid down as to the relative weight which the various considerations should carry in particular cases.'

More recently, in *Hall v Lorimer*, Mummery J. commented:

'In order to decide whether a person carries on business on his own account, it is necessary to consider many different aspects of that person's work activity. This is not a mechanical exercise of running through items on a checklist to see whether they are present in, or absent from, a given situation. The object of the exercise is to paint a picture from the accumulation of detail.

The overall effect can only be appreciated by standing back from the detailed picture which has been painted, by viewing it from a distance and by making an informed, considered, qualitative appreciation of the whole. It is a matter of evaluation of the overall effect of the detail, which is not necessarily the same as the sum total of the individual details. Not all details are of equal weight or importance in any given situation. The details may also vary in importance from one situation to another.'

While accepting that checklists are inappropriate, nevertheless the Courts have, over the years, explained which details may be of greater relevance, and which are less important. This has led to the development of 'status tests' – measures against which an individual's employment or self-employment can be judged.

The status tests are not found in legislation, but have been developed over time as cases have been argued in the courts. They are not fixed, but change as society develops. As a result IR35 could be viewed as uniquely flexible, responding to change as commercial realities alter. Alternatively it could be seen as inherently uncertain, and inappropriate to self-assessment.

Like it or not, liability to tax under the new legislation depends largely on these status tests. It is therefore essential to understand how they work, as part of the process of deciding whether an individual is within or outside IR35.

6.3.2 The concept of 'employment' in the courts

Employment status is dependent on the same legal tests, whether one is considering employment law, tax law or compensation claims. The Revenue accept this:

'Whether or not an individual is engaged under a contract of employment is not just a NICs or tax matter. It is a question of general law. It is crucial to the determination of many rights and obligations in matters such as redundancy pay, employment protection, maternity rights, health and safety legislation, sick pay and the law of contract and tort.'(ESM 1010)

However, they are not always so clear. IR56 says that when considering employment law 'other considerations may also be relevant, so your position under employment law will not necessarily be the same as under tax and National Insurance law'. The ESM contains this unhelpful comment:

> 'We are not bound on the status of an individual simply on the basis that they have, for example, registered for VAT; made returns assuming self-employment; applied and been accepted to pay self-employed NICs, or *received a decision from an Employment Tribunal.*' (ESM 112, the author's italics)

Tribunals and courts considering employment or compensation claims may be similarly dismissive of the worker's position for income tax or social security purposes. However, this is often because the individual's status has either not been properly examined for tax/NICs, or because he falls within the special rules for agencies or construction workers. See for example *Lane v Shire Roofing Company (Oxford) Limited* [1995] IRLR 493, where the judge referred to 'the lump, where workmen are engaged only for their labour and are clearly employees whatever their tax status might be.'

With the advent of IR35, the line between employment and self-employment has become even more important: the numbers affected by the status tests have grown and the former 'safe haven' of the limited company has been stripped away. It is thus vital that the Revenue, the courts and the employment tribunals adopt a consistent approach.

If an individual is classified as employed or self-employed after proper review by any one of these bodies, the others should accept the consequences. This was made explicit as long ago as 1980 in *Young & Woods Ltd v West* [1980] IRLR 201. In this case a worker had been treated as self-employed both by his engager and the Revenue, but was found to be an employee by the Court of Appeal. The judge held that the Revenue had a statutory duty to reclaim the self-employed tax reliefs granted to the worker.

6.3.3 Hierarchy of status tests

There are over a dozen status tests, but they are not of equal importance. For the purposes of this chapter they have been divided as follows:

- The 'in business on your own account' test. This is an umbrella test, in the sense that if a worker can show that he is running his own business, he will be self-employed. However, in order to demonstrate that he *is* running a business he will need to satisfy other specific status tests;

- Status tests which are so fundamental that if a single one of them is present, the worker will not be an employee, see **6.5.1**;

- Important status tests, which give strong support to an argument that someone is self-employed, see **6.5.2**;

- Minor status tests, which are helpful and persuasive when taken in context, see **6.5.3**.

6.4 The 'in business on your own account' test

If a person is in business on his own account, he will be self-employed and outside IR35. However, the opposite is not necessarily true.

6.4.1 The self-employed business

The simplest way of deciding whether someone is employed or self-employed is to answer the question: is he in business on his own account? This was the conclusion reached by Cooke J. in *Market Investigations*, who said:

> '"Is the person who has engaged himself to perform these services performing them as a person in business on his own account?" If the answer to that question is "yes", then the contract is a contract for services (i.e., self-employment). If the answer is "no", then the contract is a contract of service (i.e., employment).'

The judge went on to say that the status issue can be decided 'by asking whether the party is carrying on the business, in the sense of carrying it on for himself or on his own behalf and not merely for a superior'. In other words, the business must be that of the personal services worker; it is not enough that he contributes his skills to the business of another.

This was reaffirmed in the recent Court of Appeal case of *Lane v Shire Roofing Company (Oxford) Limited* [1995] IRLR 493 where Lord Justice Henry said that 'the question is ... whose business was it? Was the workman carrying on his own business or was he carrying on that of his employer's?'

In the context of IR35, Mr Justice Burton stated that the same test applies, saying that:

> 'The question of whether the service contractor himself has, prior to that engagement, performed or is, simultaneously with that engagement, performing (an important contrast to the duty of fidelity ordinarily owed by an employee), or will subsequently, after the termination of that engagement, perform, services for others, and is to be construed as carrying on business on his own account, is and must be a central consideration.' *R v CIR (oao Professional Contractors Group Ltd)* [2001] STC 629

99

It is this question – *is the individual in business on his own account?* – which has been one of the key issues courts have attempted to answer as they weighed up the facts in each case. In so doing they have set out a number of detailed status tests which are discussed below.

6.4.2 Being in business is not a necessary condition for self-employment

It is however possible for a person to be neither an employee, nor in business on their own account. Cooke J. concluded his statement above with the following less well-known dicta:

> 'The application of the general test may be easier in a case where the person who engages himself to perform the services does so in the course of an already established business of his own; but *this factor is not decisive*, and a person who engages himself to perform services for another may well be an independent contractor *even though he has not entered into the contract in the course of an existing business carried on by him.*' (the author's italics)

The workers in the agency case of *Wickens v Champion Employment* [1984] ICR 365 were found not to be employees. The case had been appealed by Mrs Wickens who argued that it had been wrongly decided by the lower court because:

> 'There is no evidence that these temporary workers were self-employed, no evidence that they were carrying on any business of their own or were doing anything other than working as employees for the employers.'

Nolan J. said that this was true, but not significant:

> 'The test (of employment/self-employment) does not include as a necessary element the question of whether the individual carries on a separate business. If it did, then it would follow that a casual worker must always be employed under a contract of service unless he has his own business and *that, plainly, cannot be the law.*' (the author's italics)

These comments are extremely significant in the context of the personal services legislation. While it is undoubtedly easier to prove that a worker is not an employee if he is clearly self-employed and in business on his own account, it may be possible to fall outside of IR35 simply by demonstrating one would not have been an employee of the client had there been no intermediary.

6.4.3 A third way

A small number of cases suggest that there might be a third type of contract, which is neither a contract of employment, nor a contract for services. They thus provide further support for the view that it is not necessary for a worker to be in business in his own account in order not to be an employee.

In the case of *Construction Industry Training Board v Labour Force Ltd* [1970] 3 AER 220 Cooke J. further developed his thinking on types of contract. Instead of the two alternatives given in *Market Investigations* above, he said:

> 'I think there is much to be said for the view that, where A contracts with B to render services exclusively to C, the contract is not a contract for services, but a contract sui generis, a different type of contract from either of the familiar two.'

This approach was followed by the Employment Appeal Tribunal in *Ironmonger v Movefield Ltd* [1988] IRLR 461. They took 'the view that the contract in this case is one sui generis' and thus that the relationship between Mr Ironmonger and Movefield was neither one of employment nor of self-employment. The same view was taken in *Pertemps v Nixon* [1991] EAT/496.

All these cases involved three parties, the agency, the client and the individual, which is commonly the case with contractors who are considering whether they are caught by IR35.

The application of these decisions to the personal services legislation has still to be tested, but the hypothetical contract between the worker and the client is likely to displace the concept of a contract 'sui generis' in situations where there is a tripartite worker/agency/client relationship, see for example *FS Consulting Limited v McCaul* [2001] SpC 305.

6.4.4 The professional

In *Hall v Lorimer* [1993] 66 TC 349, see **8.2.1**, Lord Nolan looked at the 'business on own account' test in the case of a professional. While acknowledging that if a person is in business on his own account, he will be self-employed, he said that this was not a particularly useful test if the worker is a professional, such as a surgeon or a singer:

> 'The question, whether the individual is in business on his own account, though often helpful, may be of little assistance in the case of one carrying on a profession or vocation. A self-employed author working from home or

an actor or a singer may earn his living without any of the normal trappings of a business.

For my part, I would suggest there is much to be said in these cases for bearing in mind the traditional contrast between a servant and an independent contractor. The extent to which the individual is dependent upon, or independent of, a particular paymaster for the financial exploitation of his talents may well be significant.'

6.4.5 Conclusion

If a person is 'in business in their own account' they will be self-employed and outside IR35. However, although employment and self-employment tend to be regarded as two sides of the same coin, this is not always the approach of the courts. It may be that the person is neither an employee, nor in business on his own account. And if he is not an employee, he will not be within IR35.

6.5 Fundamental status tests

6.5.1 Introduction

In the hierarchy of status tests (**6.3.2** above) three are fundamental:

(a) Substitution;

(b) Significant financial risk; and

(c) The ability to hire others to do the work in question.

If any of these can be proved to exist, the worker will fall outside of IR35.

6.5.2 Right to send a substitute

If an individual does not have to do the job personally, but can send a substitute, he is not an employee. This is because personal service is an essential ingredient of employment. However, a substitution clause is not a magic wand – the right to send a replacement must be real.

In the employment law case of *Express and Echo Publications Ltd v Tanton* [1999] IRLR 367, which concerned a newspaper delivery driver, the judge held that:

'Where ... a person who works for another is not required to perform his services personally, then as a matter of law the relationship between the worker and the person for whom he works is not that of employee and employer ... The only judgment which (the Tribunal) could properly have reached was that this was a contract for services.'

This was despite the fact that Mr Tanton's job had other characteristics which would normally indicate employment. For example:

- He was controlled as to where he delivered the newspaper – the management of Express and Echo (E&E) told him the route he had to drive;

- The van he drove was supplied by E&E;

- He wore a uniform supplied by E&E;

- His remuneration was on a per journey basis, and fixed by E&E, not negotiated by Mr Tanton;

- He could not increase his earnings by doing more work.

Precedents for the importance of substitution can be found in the words of McKenna J. in *Ready Mixed Concrete (South East) Ltd v Minister of Pensions and National Insurance* [1968] 1 All ER 433. He said it was one of the touchstones of self-employment:

'Freedom to do a job either by one's own hands or another's is inconsistent with a contract of service, though a limited or occasional power of delegation may not be.'

In *McMenamin v Diggles* [1991] 64 TC 286, Mr Diggles was a barrister's clerk, who had changed his contractual arrangements so that he was no longer an employee but self-employed, although he still ran the affairs of the chambers as is required of a barrister's clerk. One of the key factors that led the court to hold that he was self-employed was that his contract required:

'The provision of the services of a full-time Head Clerk of not less than 10 years experience in that capacity *being either Mr. Diggles or some other Clerk with that qualification.*' (the author's italics)

The clause accepted

In all three cases mentioned above – *Express and Echo, McMenamin v Diggles* and *Ready Mixed Concrete* – there was no doubt that the worker had a right to send a substitute, and that the client accepted this right.

In *Diggles*, the barristers for whom the clerk worked included the substitution clause in the contract at the outset of the engagement, and the court was told that it had been one of the factors which encouraged Mr Diggles to move from employment to self-employment:

> 'Mr. Diggles was at first reluctant to make the change because he would lose the security of employment ... But he realised that self-employed status would have some advantages ... The right to put in a substitute as Head Clerk might also be useful if he were sick or, later on, if he should want to ease up as he approached retirement. On reflection he was content to accept the change.'

In *Express and Echo* the judge commented that:

> '[The] right for Mr Tanton to provide a substitute driver was utilised by him from time to time and exceptionally, throughout a period of six months whilst Mr Tanton was ill, Mr Tanton paying the substitute driver, though receiving remuneration from the appellant. Clause 3.3 [the substitution clause], as the chairman expressly found, is not a sham.'

The clause disregarded

However, a substitution clause was ignored in the case of *Global Plant Ltd v Secretary of State for Health & Social Security* [1971] 3 All ER 385. Mr Summers had previously been an employed driver with Global Plant Ltd, but in 1968 asked to change his status to a self-employed contractor, and the company agreed. The new arrangements included a right to send a substitute, although the court was sceptical. Lord Widgery appears to have decided that the right was not genuine, and concluded that Mr Summers was an employee, saying that:

> 'Although it is recorded that if he could not work himself it was open to him to send another substitute driver if he was qualified to do the work ... I have little doubt that the intention of the parties was that Mr Summers should continue to work exactly as he had before even though in terms his new bargain did not require him to do so.'

The clause was also disregarded in the recent employment law case of *MacFarlane and Skivington v Glasgow City Council* [2000] EAT/1277. Here the Tribunal distinguished the case from *Tanton* because:

- The individuals could only send a substitute if they were unable to attend in person; they did not have an absolute right to send a replacement;

- They could not send *anyone* suitable, but had to choose their substitute from the Council's register;

- The Council itself sometimes organised the replacement;

- The Council paid the substitutes, whereas in *Tanton* they were paid by the worker, see **9.3.4**;

- The right was 'limited,' see below.

The clause 'limited'

As quoted above, in *Ready Mixed Concrete* the judge said that:

> 'Freedom to do a job either by one's own hands or another's is inconsistent with a contract of service, *though a limited or occasional power of delegation may not be.*' (the author's italics)

This sentence, but without the final phrase, has been quoted with authority in a number of key decisions, including *Nethermere*. However, in *MacFarlane and Skivington v Glasgow City Council* (see above) the judge emphasised this reference to a 'limited or occasional power of delegation' and said that:

> 'Properly regarded, *Tanton* does not oblige the Tribunal to conclude that under a contract of service the individual has, always and in every event, however exceptional, personally to provide his services.'

He gave the following example of a situation where *Tanton* was not relevant:

> 'A case where a person clearly to be taken to be an employee – say a school-teacher employed by a local authority – might have in his or her contract a provision that if he or she was unable to take a class then he or she might arrange for another colleague from the local authority's common room in the school to take it for him or her. No-one, surely, could say that the presence of such a clause would deny the teacher the label, otherwise appropriate, of being an employee ... It is, at the lowest, improbable that Parliament would have intended that the employer-employee relationship could be so easily avoided.'

The distinction between the two cases was summarised as follows:

> '*Tanton* ... does not deal with a limited ability to delegate such as that in the case before us. *Tanton* was a case where the individual could at his own will perform his contract by sending along someone else. Our case, by contrast, is a case in which, in limited circumstances, it would not be a breach of the individual's contract if, the individual being unable to attend, she arranged for another person approved by the employer to attend in her place.'

While it should be remembered that *MacFarlane and Skivington* is an EAT case, and thus at a relatively low level in the courts, contractors should take heed of these warnings. For a substitution clause to be fully effective, a limited or occasional power of delegation may not be enough. This view finds some support in the recent Special Commissioner's case of *FS Consulting Limited v McCaul* [2001] SpC 305. Here the worker had a right to send a substitute, but 'that replacement had to be another consultant who had previously supplied consultancy services to [the client]'. For the Revenue's view of this 'limited right' distinction see **7.4.1**.

The clause is not implied

In *Hall v Lorimer* [1993] 66 TC 349 (see **8.2.1**), Mr Lorimer sent a substitute in six of the 580 engagements which he carried out during the period under review. Although the fact that he had sent a substitute on these six occasions indicated that those particular engagements were not employments, this did not mean that Mr Lorimer was necessarily self-employed in respect of the other contracts he undertook. Lord Nolan said that:

> 'Mr Goldsmith [Counsel for the Revenue] added, and I would agree, that [this] had no significant bearing on the proper classification of the other 574 engagements.'

So the court did not infer that there was a right of substitution in the other contracts, simply because in others it had demonstrably been shown to exist. Mr Lorimer, however, had 'no formal written conditions of engagement' with his clients. Otherwise, the court might have read across from the contracts where the right was exercised, to the other engagements when he had no need of a substitute. But this is to speculate, as the facts in *Lorimer* were otherwise.

Client's permission or approval

If the client's permission has to be obtained for a substitute, case law suggests that there is no *right* of substitution. In *Market Investigations* (see **5.6.5**) Mrs Irving, a market research interviewer, was held to be an employee. One of the terms of her contract was that:

> 'The Company do not allow interviewers to send a substitute without prior permission of the Company'. However, being able to send a substitute with the client's permission does not amount to a 'right'.

Saying that substitution is not a right if the client has to give permission is not, however, the same as saying that the worker should be able to send anyone at all. In *Ready Mixed Concrete* the worker 'was entitled to employ competent substitute drivers, but if the company were dissatisfied he was to provide another substitute'. In *Express and Echo* Mr Tanton's contract said that:

> 'In the event that the contractor provides a relief driver, the contractor must satisfy the company that such a relief driver is trained and is suitable to undertake the services.'

In both cases the individuals were found to be self-employed. It is thus acceptable for the client to have the right of veto, but not that his permission should be required before a substitute can be sent.

Indeed, even the Revenue now accept that 'even where an engager's right to refuse to accept an unsuitable substitute is not expressly stated in a contract, it would probably be implied into the arrangements by the Courts' (ESM 1054). In other words, a contract which did **not** have some restriction on the right of substitution would be held to be unreasonable. See **9.3.3** for examples of where the Revenue accept that the rejection of a substitute will not contaminate the right.

No right to send a substitute

If a worker does not have the right to send a substitute, this does not necessarily mean he is an employee. Other factors must be considered in order to decide his status. In *McManus v Griffiths* [1997] 70 TC 218, a case concerning a caterer in a golf club, Mrs McManus was held to be self-employed despite the fact that:

> 'The club was insisting on Mrs. McManus personally (and not by a substitute) providing the service save during suitable holiday periods.'

But there were sufficient other pointers towards self-employment to outweigh the lack of a substitution clause, notably the fact that she could hire her own staff and was capable of profiting from the management of the business.

Summary

The case law on substitution can thus be summarised as follows:

- If a substitution clause is genuine, the worker is self-employed;
- The court will test whether the clause is genuine, and if it is not, it will be ineffective;

107

- Where a substitution clause is present in some contracts but not others, it will not become an implied term of the remaining contracts (**5.2.3**), so explicit inclusion is recommended;

- The clause is ineffective if the client's permission has to be obtained, but this does not prevent the client from vetoing an unacceptable substitute;

- Lack of a substitution clause does not necessarily mean that the worker is an employee.

The Revenue view of substitution can be found at **7.4.1**, while possible changes to a worker's contractual arrangements so as to include such a clause are discussed at **9.3**.

6.5.3 Significant financial risk and opportunity to profit from sound management

Although frequently considered separately when status tests are analysed, the tests of taking on significant financial risk and the opportunity to profit from sound management are two sides of the same coin.

The identification of financial risk as a fundamental test of self-employment goes back to *Montreal Locomotive Works v Montreal and A.-G for Canada* [1947] 1 DLR 161. Lord Wright said that the simple control test was in need of replacement:

> 'It has been suggested that a fourfold test would in some cases be more appropriate, a complex involving (i) control; (ii) ownership of the tools; (iii) chance of profit; (iv) risk of loss.'

It was reiterated in *Market Investigations* and again in *Global Plant* where Lord Widgery held that:

> 'If a man agrees to perform an operation for a fixed sum and thus stands to lose if the work is delayed, and to profit if it is done quickly, that is the man who on the face of it appears to be an independent contractor working under a contract for services.'

In *Diggles*, one of the factors taken into account by the court in deciding that he was self-employed was that:

> 'Mr. Diggles submits a monthly account of clerking fees, plus VAT, to each member of chambers and this should be paid within 7 days. For one reason or another, however, he may be owed at any one time something between

£3,000 and £6,000 by a member of chambers. Since he has to meet all the expenses of employing staff out of his fees, as well as meeting some chambers' expenses for which he is entitled to be reimbursed, he may run into cash flow problems which he did not experience before October 1985. He estimates that he needs to hold about £15,000 of his own money available to fund his financial obligations under the agreement.'

Lower levels of risk

Where the level of risk is lower, but still present, the case is less conclusive. The risk factor will need to be considered along with others in order to decide the matter. This was the case in *Lorimer*, where financial risk was only part of the picture. The Special Commissioner held that Mr Lorimer:

'Bears his own financial risk which is greater than that of one who is an employee, accepting the risk of bad debts and outstanding invoices and of no or an insufficient number of engagements. He has the opportunity of profiting from being good at being a vision mixer. According to his reputation, so there will be a demand for his services for which he will be able to charge accordingly. The more efficient he is at running the business of providing his services, the greater is his prospect of profit.'

However, the risk of not finding work is insufficient to bring the worker into Schedule D. In the Privy Council case of *Lee Ting Sang v Chung Chi-Keung* [1990] 2 AC 374 (see **8.3.1**), Lord Griffiths said:

'The picture emerges of a skilled artisan earning his living by working for more than one employer as an employee and not as a small businessman venturing into business on his own account as an independent contractor with all its attendant risks. The applicant ran no risk whatever save that of being unable to find employment which is, of course, a risk faced by casual employees who move from one job to another ... '

No risk

A complete absence of financial risk was however held to be compatible with self-employment in *O'Kelly* (**5.6.2**), where other points supported a contract for services. The court held that:

'Where the commodity offered is the simple supply of semi-skilled labour for a specific occasion, or series of occasions, it is not to be expected that there would be a financial investment or participation in the profits or losses of the business.'

It is also interesting to note the decision in *Midland Sinfonia Concert Society Limited v The Secretary of State for Social Services* [1981] ICR 454, where the judge held that the 'test ... of the chance of profit or risk of loss seems ... not particularly appropriate' when considering the status of orchestral musicians.

Summary

The case law can be summarised as follows:

- If a worker bears significant financial risk, he will be self-employed;
- If the risk is lower, but still greater than that borne by an employee, it is an indicator of self-employment, but not conclusive in itself;
- If he can increase his earnings, but not make a loss, he may be self-employed, but other factors will need to be considered;
- The risk of not finding work is not an indicator of self-employment;
- It is possible to be self-employed even if there is no financial risk.

The Revenue view of financial risk can be found at **7.4.2**; possible changes to a worker's contractual arrangements are discussed at **9.4** and **9.7**.

6.5.4 Hiring of staff

One of the key elements of an employment contract is the requirement that the worker provides personal service, see **6.5.1**. An individual will be self-employed if, having agreed to perform a task, he is free to hire someone else to help him to carry it out.

In the Privy Council case of *Australian Mutual Provident Society v Chaplin and Another* [1978] 18 Australian Law Reports 385, Lord Fraser said that:

> 'Power of unlimited delegation is almost conclusive against the contract being a contract of service.'

One of the decisive points in Mr Diggle's favour was that his contract required him to provide:

> 'A Junior Clerk or Junior Clerks and other ancillary staff ... whose services may be reasonably necessary to enable the Head Clerk to render efficiently the Full Clerking Services.'

and he could show in court that:

'As from the same date and in accordance with the agreement Mr Diggles engaged Miss Magnall and Miss Barnes as Junior Clerks and he also engaged an assistant Mr Liam Mooney and occasional casual helpers. Miss Magnall (Mrs Garlick) left in June 1989 to have a child and was paid statutory maternity pay by Mr Diggles who engaged a new Junior Clerk Miss Helen Berkley with effect from 29 March 1989.' (*McMenamin v Diggles* [1991] 64 TC 286)

A contrasting case is *Andrews v King* [1991] 64 TC 332, where Andrews was engaged by a firm called Stanberrys as a gangmaster to select and transport men to pick and grade potatoes. At the end of each week, Stanberrys gave Andrews a cash sum, and he paid the workers. The Revenue argued that Andrews was in business on his own account, and thus it was his responsibility to deduct any necessary PAYE from the sums paid to the workers. The courts disagreed, holding that there was a distinction between mere selection and hiring:

'As to the question whether or not he hired his own helpers, he certainly selected them but he did not himself pay them any wages. He did not engage men, pay them and then provide a gang en bloc to Stanberrys in return for a fixed charge. Having selected his gang, they all went together to the place of work selected by Stanberrys and the total sum paid for the work by Stanberrys was a sum which all the members of the gang had agreed, not Mr Andrews by himself. The net proceeds, after deduction of petrol money were divided equally between them. In my judgment, it is impossible to call that "hiring helpers".'

Being unable to hire staff may be an indicator of employment: In the case of *Lee Ting Sang v Chung Chi-Keung*, see **8.3.1**, the worker was regarded as an employee partly on the grounds that:

'He did not hire his own helpers; this emerged with clarity in his evidence when he explained that he gave priority to [Chung Chi-Keung's] work and if asked by [Chung Chi-Keung] to do an urgent job he would tell those he was working for that they would have to employ someone else ... if he was an independent contractor in business on his own account, one would expect that he would attempt to keep both contracts by hiring others to fulfil the contract he had to leave.'

However, as with substitution, the inability to hire staff does not *necessarily* mean that an individual is an employee – Lorimer was in this position, see **6.6.2**, but was still held to be self-employed.

Conclusion

If the worker has a genuine right to hire helpers in order to carry out the contract with the client, he will be self-employed. Hiring helpers means taking responsibility for them, a point well made by the Revenue, see **7.4.4(c)**. Possible changes to a worker's contractual arrangements to include such a clause are discussed at **9.5**.

6.6 Important status tests

6.6.1 General

In the hierarchy of status tests (**6.3.2** above), some are fundamental (**6.5.1**) and others merely supportive (**6.7.1**). In the middle are a number of important tests, which give strong support to an argument that an individual is self-employed. These are:

(a) Provision of significant equipment;

(b) Control; and

(c) The length and number of engagements: factors personal to the worker.

Of these, the third is of vital importance to the professional with his own service company, see **6.6.4** below.

6.6.2 Provision of equipment

Significant equipment

Where a worker provides significant equipment which is essential to carry out the task, he is probably self-employed. In the case of *Humberstone v Northern Timber Mills* [1949] 79 CLR the owner driver of a truck was held to be self-employed on the basis that:

> 'The contract ... was to provide not merely his own labour but the use of heavy mechanised transport, driven by power, which he maintained and fuelled for the purpose. The most important part of the work to be performed by his own labour consisted in the operation of his own motor truck and the essential part of the service ... was to be done by his own property in his own possession and control.'

Small tools

Providing significant equipment can be distinguished from supplying 'small tools', following a US case concerning the status of men who unloaded coal from railway wagons into bins which was quoted with approval by McKenna J. in *Ready Mixed Concrete*:

'We cannot agree that the unloaders … were independent contractors. They provided only picks and shovels. They had no opportunity to gain or lose except from the work of their hands and these simple tools.' (*US v Silk* [1946] 331 US)

However this does not mean that the provision of only small tools is indicative of employment. McKenna J. went on to say:

'A contract obliges a labourer to work for a builder, providing some simple tools, and to accept the builder's control. Notwithstanding the obligation to provide the tools, the contract is one of service. That obligation is not inconsistent with the nature of a contract of service. *It is not a sufficiently important matter to affect the substance of the contract.*' (the author's italics)

Client's equipment

It has long been the case that the provision of major items of equipment by the engager does not mean that the worker is necessarily an employee. In *BSM(1257) Ltd v Secretary of State for Social Services* [1978] ICR 894, the driving instructor was found to be self-employed despite the fact that the car he drove was supplied by BSM.

This was, however, taken a step further in the *Lorimer* case. Here, the Revenue argued that Lorimer was an employee because:

'The studio company owns or procures the supply of the equipment. The production companies do not own such equipment, still less does Mr Lorimer. The equipment is an integral part of the studio complex.'

However, Lord Nolan disagreed with the Revenue interpretation, quoting with approval from the Special Commissioner's judgment as follows:

'It is said that Mr Lorimer provides no equipment (i.e., he has no tools), he provides no "work place" or "workshop" where the contract is to be performed, he provides no capital for the production, he hires no staff for it. No, he does not. But that is not his business.'

This was an important development. It means that where an individual is a professional, the fact that he provides no equipment is not relevant and should not be taken into account one way or the other.

Summary

In conclusion, where the equipment is major, the engagement is likely to be self-employment; but where it is minor, it is not a factor either way. Specifically, where the individual is providing skilled services, the absence of equipment provided by the worker is irrelevant, and other factors such as the number/length of engagements (**6.6.4**) and financial risk (**6.5.3**) need to be considered. The Revenue view of the provision of equipment can be found at **7.4.5**; a discussion of the issue in the context of a worker's contractual arrangements is at **9.8**.

6.6.3 Control

The level and type of control exercised by the engager over the worker has historically been a key factor in deciding whether the contract is one of employment. Rights of control were divided into control as to *how*, *when*, *where* or *what* is done. In *Ready Mixed Concrete*, McKenna J. held that:

> 'Control includes the power of deciding the thing to be done, the way in which it shall be done, the means to be employed in doing it, the time when, and the place where it shall be done. All these aspects of control must be considered in deciding whether the right exists in a sufficient degree to make one party the master and the other his servant. The right need not be unrestricted.'

However, more recently the courts have dealt increasingly with skilled workers and professional people, over whom control is necessarily more limited. As a result the control test has declined in importance, although it still remains a factor for consideration. In a 1995 case, Mr Justice Lightman summed up the current position by saying that:

> 'The lack of "control" ... does not have the significance today that it once may have had as the litmus test for a contract of employment. It is certainly not a universal litmus test, and its importance (and indeed relevance) must depend in particular on the role to be played by the "employee" in the "employer's" business.' (*Horner v Hasted* [1995] 67 TC 439)

Control as to when and where the engagement is carried out

If the engager can control *when* and *where* the worker does his work, the worker is more likely to be an employee. But there are exceptions either way:

In *Lorimer* (see **8.2.1**) the client could 'dictate the hours to be worked, where he shall work, the date he shall work. He has no discretion in these matters.' But Lorimer was nevertheless held to be self-employed.

In *Market Investigations* (see **5.6.5**), Mrs Irving could work 'as and when she chose and did not necessarily have to complete seven hours work during one day' and the engager had 'no right to alter the place or area within which (she) has agreed to work'. However, she was still held to be employed.

Control as to what is to be done during the engagement

If the engager can control *what* is to be done, this can indicate employment. In the old case of *Stagecraft Ltd v Minister of National Insurance* [1952] SC 288, the two comedians involved were 'controlled' by their producer as to what part they played, and were held to be employed earners for National Insurance purposes. Lord Thomson said:

> 'What I find of more significance is the fifth condition, where the "artiste agrees to play the part (or parts) assigned to him (or her) during the whole run of the production ... this points to a definite contract of employment to serve the management by making his gifts available to the management in ways which the management can dictate over a period of time.'

Control as to how the work is to be carried out

In the case of *Collins v Hertfordshire County Council* [1947] 1 AER 633 it was suggested that the distinguishing feature of a contract of service is that the master can not only order or require *what* is to be done but also *how* it shall be done. This test has gradually become more complex and sophisticated. The current position is summarised below.

If the engager can control how the worker is to do the work, there will generally be an employment, unless other significant factors point to self-employment

It remains the case that if the engager can tell the worker how to do the work, he is probably an employee: In *Market Investigations* (**5.3.3**), the company had the right to exercise 'very extensive [control] indeed' over the interviewer largely via the publication called the 'Interviewer's Guide'. This formed part of the contractual terms of engagement. Cooke J. said that 'the control was so extensive as to be entirely consistent with Mrs Irving's being employed under a contract of service'.

In the Privy Council case of *Narich Pty Ltd v Commissioner of Payroll Tax* [1984] ICR 286, the lecturers who conducted weight watchers classes were 'tied hand and foot' by the contract with regard to the manner of performing the work under it and were thus employees, despite having been engaged on a franchise basis as independent contractors.

If, however, other factors outweigh the engager's control over *how* the work is carried out, the contract may nevertheless be one of self-employment. In the Australian case of *Queensland Stations Pty v Federal Comr of Taxation* [1945] 70 CLR 539, a drover was engaged under a written contract to drive cattle to a destination. The contract provided that he should:

> 'Obey and carry out all lawful instructions and use the whole of his time, energy and ability in the careful driving of the stock, that he should provide at his own expense all men, plant, horses and rations required for the operation, and that he should be paid at a rate per head for each of the cattle safely delivered at the destination.'

He was held to be an independent contractor in a judgement which was quoted with approval in *Ready Mixed Concrete*:

> 'In considering the facts it is a mistake to treat as decisive a reservation of control over the manner in which the droving is performed and the cattle are handled. For instance, in the present case the circumstance that the drover agrees to obey and carry out all lawful instructions cannot outweigh the countervailing considerations which are found in the employment by him of servants of his own, the provision of horses, equipment, plant, rations, and a remuneration at a rate per head delivered.'

Where the engager cannot control how the work is carried out, the worker may be self-employed, but is not necessarily so

However, it is not necessarily the case that a worker will be self-employed simply because he can decide for himself how to do the work. In *Cassidy v Ministry of Health* [1951] 1 AER 574, the judge pointed out that the owners of a ship may have no power to tell a certified ship's master how to navigate, but they may still have employed him under what is clearly a contract of service.

A more recent example is the case of *Lee Ting Sang v Chung Chi-Keung* [1990] 2 AC 374 (see **8.3.1**), where a craftsman was held to be an employee despite the fact that he was not controlled as to how to do his work. The Privy Council said that:

> 'It is true that he was not supervised in his work, but this is not surprising, he was a skilled man and had been told the beams upon which he was to work and the depth to which they were to be cut and his work was measured to see that he achieved that result ... He was simply told what to do and left to get on with it as, for example, would a skilled turner on a lathe who was required to cut a piece of metal to certain dimensions.'

116

Control over how the work is done may be an unhelpful test where skilled professionals are concerned

In *Morren v Swinton & Pendlebury Borough Council* [1965] 2 All ER 349, Lord Parker introduced a new element when he commented that:

'When one is dealing with a professional man, or a man of some particular skill and experience, there can be no question of an employer telling him how to do the work; therefore the absence of control and direction in that sense can be of little, if any, use as a test.'

This was further developed in *Hall v Lorimer*, see **8.2.1**, when the Special Commissioner said:

'The Crown's representative suggests that the production company has extensive control over Mr Lorimer. It dictates the hours to be worked, where he shall work, the date he shall work. He has no discretion in these matters. The Crown's representative accepts that the production company has no control over Mr Lorimer's skill in performing his functions and that Mr Lorimer must use his judgement, but the scripts of scripted programmes indicate control is exercised through what I might call stage directions. The Crown's representative contrasts this with an independent contractor who supposedly would have a choice of views and exercise control himself over all other aspects of a vision mixer's function.

I cannot see that control of the kind adumbrated helps very much towards solving the problem. If you accept an engagement for your services as a vision mixer, you must be provided with details of date, time and place, and of the period of time you are likely to be required. If you are part of a team to produce a show, it is inevitable that someone must organise it. You must attend rehearsals if they are necessary. If you play in an orchestra, you must pay attention to the conductor. In the production of a play, you must pay attention to the stage directions or to the producer's directions. That applies to the leading actor and actress, but they do not for that reason become "employees". *The independent contractor posited by the Crown's representative could hardly exist in the context of the production of a programme in conjunction with other people.*' (the author's italics)

This suggests that if one is deciding whether a professional person is self-employed, the control test may be the wrong one to use.

Right of dismissal as evidence of control?

In the case of *Serco Limited v Matthew Blair and Others* (EAT/345/98 unreported, see **5.9.3**) the EAT held that where the agency, rather than the client, has the power to end the contract with the workers, then the client does not have the necessary control over the workers to be their employer.

This was taken a step further in *FS Consulting Limited v McCaul* [2001] SpC 305, where the Special Commissioner held that Mr Simpson was an employee partly because:

> 'In the performance of his work [he] was also subject to [the client's] control to the extent that the contract between the Appellant and [the agent] provided that it could be terminated immediately if [the client] terminated its agreement with [the agent] because of the incompetence, unsuitability or unprofessional conduct of Mr Simpson.'

However, this does not appear to be sustainable. Surely clients also dismiss the self-employed if they are incompetent, unsuitable or unprofessional?

It is thus arguable that the absence of a right of dismissal suggests a contract for services; however, in the view of the author, its presence is not proof of employment. Rights of dismissal are discussed in more detail at **6.7.4** below.

No control

Absence of control means that the worker is not an employee, following McKenna J. in *Ready Mixed Concrete*:

> 'An obligation to do work subject to the other party's control is a necessary, though not always a sufficient, condition of a contract of service.'

Mr Diggles' barrister made the same point:

> 'Mr Oliver, applying the control test which, although no longer regarded as decisive, remains relevant factor, says that Mr. Diggles was not under the control necessary for an employment. He had wide discretion as to the way in which he provided clerking services, with no fixed hours of work and no obligation to obey orders. He had to avoid breaches of the Bar code of conduct because he was supplying services to barristers who were bound by that code but that does not mean that he was controlled in the sense required for a contract of service.' (*McMenamin v Diggles* [1991] 64 TC 286)

Summary

One could thus summarise the case law position by saying that:

- If there is no right of control there will be no contract of employment;

- If a worker is controlled as to how, what, where, and when to do the work, he will almost certainly be an employee;

- If one or more of these elements is absent, he may be either an employee or self-employed, depending on other factors;

- If he is a professional, the control test may be useless as a determinant of status.

The Revenue view of control can be found at **7.4.6**; possible changes to a worker's contractual arrangements are discussed at **9.6**.

6.6.4 Length and number of engagements: factors personal to the worker

Many short engagements

When Lord Nolan rejected the control test in the case of *Lorimer*, see **6.6.3** above, he turned instead to the question of 'the extent to which the individual is dependent upon, or independent of, a particular paymaster for the financial exploitation of his talents'. This has been summarised as 'factors personal to the worker' because it involves looking beyond each individual contract towards considering the pattern of the worker's engagements.

In the period under review, Mr Lorimer had about 580 engagements, most of one or two days' duration. The Revenue argued that:

> 'Each and every one of Mr Lorimer's engagements must of necessity be a contract of employment. He is an employee of company A on a Monday, company L on Tuesday; he is out of work on Wednesday and Thursday; he is an employee of company C on Friday.'

This was rejected, even ridiculed, by the court. The fact that 'Mr Lorimer customarily worked for 20 or more production companies and that the vast majority of his assignments lasted only for a single day' was described by Lord Nolan in the Court of Appeal as 'the most outstanding feature' of the case, and was decisive in the judgment that he was self-employed.

A similar point was made in *McMenamin v Diggles* where the barrister pointed out for Mr Diggles that:

> 'A number of separate contracts indicates professional activity rather than employment: and ... Mr. Diggles had a separate contract with each member of the Chambers, about 20 in all.'

This may, however, be harder to apply in the case of the unskilled worker, see the case of *Lee Ting Sang v Chung Chi-Keung* [1990] 2 AC 374 discussed at **8.3.1**.

Mr Lorimer had numerous short engagements, and the Revenue have taken this as their model when applying this test, see **7.4.7**. However the courts may be less demanding, see the discussion of actors and the Equity contract at **8.5**.

Many short engagements and IR35

The personal services legislation appears at first sight to be drafted on the basis of single contracts rather than the whole picture of a worker's activity, because it requires that each '*engagement* to which this Schedule applies' be reviewed to see whether it should be classified as employment or self-employment (Sch 12, para 2(1) FA 2000).

However, the nature of the hypothetical contract between the worker and the client is determined by considering 'the circumstances' in which the services are provided, see **5.1**. Although the 'circumstances' include the terms of the contracts between the parties in respect of the individual engagement, other factors are also to be taken into account. One would expect these to include the number and variety of the worker's engagements.

This interpretation would be consistent with early government assurances. Mr Timms, speaking in the House of Commons on 3 November 1999 said:

> 'There is no intention of applying the rules in any different way. They are well established and well understood; they are flexible; *they take account of the whole pattern of a worker's engagement*, so that a skilled worker who works for many different clients can be treated as one who is self-employed.'

This has subsequently been developed in the Revenue's *Tax Bulletin 45* article (and confirmed in ESM 0520) as follows:

> 'In deciding a person's employment status it may sometimes be necessary to take into account factors which are personal to the worker and which have little to do with the terms of the particular engagement being considered. For example, if a skilled worker works for a number of clients throughout the year and has a business-like approach to obtaining his engagements (perhaps involving expenditure on office accommodation, office equipment, etc.) this will point towards self-employment.'

Long engagements

Where a worker has a single long engagement, this is indicative of employment. In the recent IR35 case of *FS Consulting Limited v McCaul* [2001] SpC

305, the Special Commissioner held that the worker was caught by the personal services legislation partly because 'the relationship between [the worker] and [the client] had some element of permanency as it lasted for two and a half years'.

However a long engagement with one client is not of itself conclusive evidence of employment – other status tests have to be considered. This is accepted by the Revenue, see *Tax Bulletin 45* and **7.4.8**.

Conclusion

The position can be summarised as follows:

- Where there are many short term engagements, and the worker is a skilled professional, he is likely to be self employed;

- Where the worker is unskilled or semi-skilled, the case may be harder to prove, and other supporting status tests, such as taking significant risk or supplying equipment, may be necessary in addition. However the workers in *O'Kelly* (**5.6.2**) were effectively day labourers, and the House of Lords ruled that they were self-employed;

- Where there is a single long engagement, this is indicative of employment but not conclusive.

6.7 Minor status tests

6.7.1 Summary

In addition to the fundamental status tests (**6.5.1**) and those which are important (**6.6.1**), there are others which are helpful in indicating whether an individual is an employee or in business on his own account. They include:

(a) Exclusivity;

(b) Terms of payment;

(c) Rights of dismissal;

(d) The intention of the parties;

(e) Business structure.

A sixth concept, whether the individual is 'part and parcel of the organisation' in which he works, is now regarded as of less use. Each of these is discussed below.

6.7.2 Exclusivity

Where a worker provides services to only one engager, and agrees not to provide his skills to anyone else, he is likely to be an employee.

However, this is not invariably so. In the recent employment law case of *Jowitt v London Symphony Orchestra Ltd* [1990] EAT 301, Mr Jowitt argued that he was an employee because he could not work for another orchestra. However, the Employment Appeals Tribunal held that there was no reason why a self-employed person should not say by agreement 'I will give my services to you (the employer or payer) for a given period of time'.

Conversely, if there is no exclusivity, and the worker can provide services for others, this does not necessarily mean that he is self-employed, particularly where the work is not full time. The judge in *Market Investigations*, holding that the worker was employed, said:

> 'Nor is there anything inconsistent with the existence of a contract of service in the fact that Mrs Irving was free to work for others during the relevant period. It is by no means a necessary incident of a contract of service that the servant is prohibited from serving any other employer.'

Having said this, one would normally expect to find that a self-employed person was free to work for others, and that the freedom of an employee was more restricted. Possible changes to a worker's contractual arrangements so as to include such a term are discussed at **9.13**.

6.7.3 Payment terms

The way a worker is paid is an indicator of his employment status, but is not decisive. There are two elements to the question of payment terms, the way in which 'pay' is delivered, and whether there are any other 'benefits'. The Revenue view of payment terms can be found at **7.4.9**; the extent to which it may be possible to change a worker's contractual arrangements is discussed at **9.9**.

Pay

While being paid a fixed sum on a project basis is typical of self-employment, being paid by the hour doesn't mean the worker is an employee. Accountants and lawyers, who are clearly self-employed, measure their time and bill their clients on an hourly basis or even by the six-minute unit.

In *O'Kelly* (**5.6.2**) the workers were paid for work actually performed, rather than receiving a fixed wage. The court held that 'the method of calculating entitlement to remuneration is not an essential aspect of the employment relationship'.

In *Lorimer* the judge said that charging method was less important than its underlying purpose:

> 'Many of the invoices, it is true, indicate the hours Mr Lorimer attended for the shooting session, but the object appears to me to be to provide the reason for the particular charge out rate.'

In the case of *WHPT Housing Association Ltd. v. Secretary of State for Social Services* [1981] ICR 737, Mr Lowe, an architect, was found to be self-employed, even though his arrangements with the engager had many of the characteristics of employment. These included the fact that he was supervised by the chief architect and had to attend the offices from 9.30 am to 5.30 pm (and his timekeeping was criticised). He was also supplied with all relevant equipment by the engager. One of the key reasons for him being found to be self-employed was that he was paid an hourly rate and only for the hours he actually worked; in contrast, none of the employees were paid an hourly rate. The judge said:

> 'The inescapable inference that I draw from [the] facts is that Mr Lowe, at no time, undertook any obligation to present himself for service at the association's premises at any time ... [nor] to provide a specific number of hours' service ... and that his principal obligation was to work as an architect during the hours of service which he chose to offer ... in consideration for which the association agreed to pay him £3 per hour.'

Thus where a personal service worker can move to a project basis and be paid accordingly, it will strengthen his case for self-employment (see also **9.4**). However, if this is not possible or desirable, retaining an hourly rate does not necessarily mean he is employed.

Benefits

Generally, the receipt of benefits is indicative of employment. However:

(a) Where a worker receives no benefits he is not necessarily self-employed, see *Stagecraft Ltd v Minister of National Insurance* [1952] SC 288;

(b) Conversely, some workers have been held to be self-employed, even though they receive some 'employee type' benefits, because of the strength of other factors. In the *O'Kelly* case discussed at **5.6.2**, the casual workers had a whole range of employee-type benefits but were held to be working under contracts for services.

Similarly, in the case of the actors McCowen and West, see **20.2.2**, they were held to be self-employed, despite the fact that their contracts had:

- Minimum rates of pay;

- Overtime, bank holiday and Sunday premiums;

- Agreed rates of touring and subsistence allowances;

- Holiday pay;

- Agreed disciplinary procedures.

6.7.4 Right of dismissal

Employees have a statutory right to a minimum period of notice, and their contracts will usually include a notice period, and perhaps a provision for payment in lieu of notice (PILON). The self-employed tend to be engaged until the task is finished, but can be dismissed if they breach their contract.

In *Morren v Swinton and Pendlebury Borough Council* [1965] 1 WLR 576 the judge compared the case of Mr Morren, who was held to be an employee, with that of another worker, Mr Kaufman, who was clearly self-employed:

> The respondents ... *had the right to dismiss him*, he was paid such matters as subsistence allowance and for holidays, national insurance contributions were paid in regard to him, and, in addition, *there was provision for one month's* notice. Pausing there, it seems to me that, looked at on those facts, the only possible inference is that he was engaged under a contract of service. How different is the contract with Mr Kaufman, who is not paid a subsistence allowance; nor is national insurance contribution provided in regard to him; and he is not entitled to holidays. Further, there is *no provision for termination of his services or service by notice.* (the author's italics)

The fact that the workers in the *O'Kelly* case could be dismissed without notice was one of the key facts which led the court to decide they were self-employed (**5.6.2**); the same was true in the recent employment law case of *Costain Building and Civil Engineering Ltd v Smith and Another* [2000] EAT/ICR 215. In the light of these precedents, the view expressed in *FS Consulting Limited v McCaul* [2001] SpC 305, that the right of a client to dismiss a worker for incompetence is evidence of employment is, in the view of this author, unsustainable.

In *Serco Limited v Matthew Blair and Others* (EAT/345/98, see **5.9.3**) it has been held that where the agency, and not the client, has the power to dismiss a worker, this may be evidence that the worker is not an employee of the client.

Where a worker has a notice period, but is claiming self-employment, some comfort can be taken from the words of the judge in *McManus v Griffiths* [1997] 70 TC 218:

> 'It is suggested on behalf of Mr and Mrs McManus that the three-month notice period is indicative of a contract for service rather than for services. I do not think that it is indicative of either. I regard the provision as neutral.'

Thus in conclusion, the lack of a notice period is indicative of self-employment, but its existence does not necessarily mean that the worker is employed. Possible changes to a worker's contractual arrangements so as to exclude such a clause are discussed at **9.14**.

6.7.5 Intention of the parties

The intention of the parties can be described as a 'tiebreaker'. If all other factors are evenly balanced, what the parties intend the worker's status to be will normally settle the matter. This was most clearly expressed in *Massey v Crown Life Insurance Co* [1978] ICR 590:

> 'It seems to me on the authorities that, when it is a situation which is in doubt or which is ambiguous, so that it can be brought under one relationship or the other, it is open to the parties by agreement to stipulate what the legal situation between them shall be.'

Similarly in *Global Plant* (**6.5.2**) Lord Widgery held that:

> 'One must not overlook that the intention of the parties was that the relationship should be that of an independent contractor, and although the parties cannot by intention make a transaction into something which it is not, yet it is recognised that such intention is a factor for consideration in these cases.'

However, it is unclear whether this test will be effective in the context of the hypothetical contract between the worker and the client, see **5.2.4**. Nevertheless, it is recommended that it be included in contracts, see **9.3**. Even if it is effective, it is of course not possible to metamorphose an employment relationship into self-employment simply by a change of label, see **5.2.5**.

The Revenue view of this issue can be found at **7.4.10**; they take the position that the tiebreaker still exists in an IR35 context, and that if other factors are equally balanced, the hypothetical contract will be one of self-employment.

6.7.6 Business structure

The existence of a 'business structure' is one of the factors which has been looked for when deciding whether someone is self-employed, see for example *Lorimer* **8.2.1**. However Cooke J. held that a business structure was not essential, see **6.4.2** above.

His dicta was followed in the Addison case (**20.5.2**) where the musicians playing for the orchestra were held to be self-employed although they had no demonstrable 'business structure'. They were 'pursuing his or her own profession as an instrumentalist, with an individual reputation' and this was enough.

However, in a corporation tax case Vinelott J. interpreted 'business structure' widely, so as to bring within it the musicians, Mr Lorimer, and many contractors:

> 'The business structure or entity or organisation may assume any of an almost infinite variety of shapes ... it may be represented by no more than the intangible elements constituting what is commonly called goodwill, that is, widespread or general reputation, habitual patronage by clients or customers and an organised method of serving their needs. At the other extreme it may consist in a great aggregate of buildings, machinery and plant all assembled and systematised as the material means by which an organised body of men produce and distribute commodities or perform services.' *RTZ Oil & Gas Ltd v Elliss* [1987] 61 TC 132

The Revenue view of business structure can be found at **7.4.11**; some practical recommendations are discussed at **9.12**.

6.7.7 Part and parcel of the organisation

The 'part and parcel of the organisation' concept was first put forward by Lord Denning in *Stevenson, Jordan & Harrison v MacDonald & Evans* [1952] RPC 10. Under this test, a worker will be an employee if he is integrated within the organisation where he works.

Cases where this concept was used with approval include *Cassidy v Minister of Health* [1951] 1 AER 574, where surgeons were held to be employees even though they were professionals providing a skill to the Health Service.

126

However the 'part and parcel' test has received short shrift from more recent judges. In *Ready Mixed Concrete* McKenna J. said that it:

> 'Raises more questions than I know how to answer. What is meant by being "part and parcel of an organisation"? Are all persons who answer this description servants? If only some are servants, what distinguishes them from the others if it is not their submission to orders?'

It was rejected in the Privy Council case of *Lee Ting Sang v Chung Chi-Keung* [1990] 2 AC 374 (**8.3.1**), with the judge warning that:

> 'In the building and construction industry the test may lead to the error of only considering those on the permanent staff as employed under a contract of service.'

In *Lorimer* (**8.2.1**), Lord Nolan felt that there was plenty of scope for people to become involved with an organisation without becoming part and parcel of it:

> 'Being one of a team to produce a programme does not, in my view, lead to the conclusion that, in Mr Lorimer's case, he is "part an parcel" of the organisation ... A violinist in an orchestra may be "part and parcel" of the orchestra for the performance being given but it does not follow that he is part and parcel of the organisation which runs or manages the orchestra.'

The Revenue appear to accept that the test is of limited use, see **7.4.12**. In summary, this is not a test about which personal service workers should be too concerned.

6.8 Overall summary

Before considering the status tests, the existence of mutuality of obligation should be established, see Chapter 5. When the status tests are examined, they should not be seen as equally important. The courts have clearly shown that if a contract includes a genuine right to substitution or to hire workers, the worker is self-employed. If he takes significant financial risk, he will also be outside IR35.

Other factors are less clear cut. The extent of control over the worker should be considered, but is unlikely to be significant in the case of a professional; the equipment test is inconclusive on its own unless major items are supplied by the worker; and other minor factors have to be weighed in the balance.

The status tests should not be seen in isolation. It is the whole pattern of the worker's engagements that need to be considered, and this may have the effect of allowing someone to fall outside IR35 when the individual engagement, considered alone, would not.

The following chapters look at recent case law on status, at the Revenue's interpretation of these tests, and what can be done to improve a worker's position.

7 Revenue view of employment status

7.1 Introduction

This chapter reviews the guidance given by the Inland Revenue on status, notably in *Tax Bulletins* 45 and 28, in booklets IR175 and IR56, and in the Revenue Manuals. It should be read against the background of:

- Chapter 5, which considers mutuality and the hypothetical contract which lies at the heart of the personal services legislation;

- Chapter 6, which reviews the status tests themselves; and

- Chapter 8, which looks at recent status cases.

If a worker wants to challenge the Revenue view as to whether he is caught by IR35, he is likely to need further advice, possibly from Counsel. The issue may eventually be decided by the Commissioners, and possibly the higher courts. Any such challenge will have repercussions for other workers, and could become a 'representative case'.

This chapter looks both at the Revenue's overall approach to the Schedule D/E divide, and at their published views on individual status tests. It also briefly considers the ground rules which apply when a case goes to court, and how to get the best out of the appeal system.

7.2 General

7.2.1 Overview

Status tests have always been relevant for the self-employed, and those engaging workers directly have long been aware of the fine line that divides a contract of service from one for services. IR35 has now increased the numbers of those affected by categorisation, and the Revenue has produced further and more focused guidance.

In many areas Revenue advice on status is clear and helpful. However, it is of necessity only an outline, and thus may be inappropriate when applied to borderline cases. The brevity of some of the guidance means there are omissions, and some of these are important. From time to time there is a certain colour to the advice which means that it does not do full justice to the case law.

Revenue advice on IR35 came in for some strong criticism from Mr Justice Burton in the judicial review. He said:

> 'It is essential that there is a sensitive and co-operative approach taken by such inspectors, and that the Revenue guidance is clear and helpful ... Revenue documentation ... has not always been either.'

The Revenue subsequently acknowledged that it needed to make some improvements to its guidance, see **2.4.7**, and a number of adjustments were made. The Employment Status Manual was then further amended in the March 2002 edition, and these changes have increased the objectivity and balance of the Manuals.

7.2.2 Leaflets and bulletins

IR56 – Employed or self-employed

Booklet IR56: *Employed or Self-employed* has been available for many years and provides outline guidance on the status tests. It is, however, too brief to be of much practical use, and can give the wrong impression, see for example **7.3.2** and **7.4.7** below. Judith Freedman, in her book *'Employed or Self-employed'* correctly points out that:

> 'In the Inland Revenue's own listings of leaflets it is stated of IR56 that "This can help you decide whether or not you are employed or self-employed, an area that causes a lot of confusion." IR56 would be unlikely to help much with that confusion in anything other than a reasonably clear case ... it is inadequate for those at the borderline – the very people who particularly need assistance.'

IR175 – Supplying services through a limited company or partnership

In May 2000 IR175, *Supplying Services through a limited company or partnership* was published. While providing some helpful and focused guidance, there are a number of difficulties. For example:

- It borrows from IR56 in many areas: both texts say 'if you can answer yes to the following questions, you would probably have been an employee of your client'. The problems with this approach are set out at **7.3.2** below;

- It advises that 'you will have to think about each contract individually'. But the overall pattern of an individual's work also needs to be considered, see **6.6.4** and **7.4.7**;

- It says that when an individual ceases to work through the intermediary before the end of the tax year, 'the deemed payment ... will be treated as having been made immediately before you stop'. This may not be the case, see **16.3.3**;

- In answer to the question 'What are my tax and NICs liabilities if I work overseas' the booklet says that 'your tax and NICs liabilities are the same as if you were employed directly by the overseas client. Further information on liability and the rules about residency can be found in Inland Revenue booklet IR120'. While IR120 is an admirable booklet, it contains not a single mention of IR35. The interaction of the personal service legislation with overseas issues is extremely complex area (see Chapters 17 and 18), and more appropriate Revenue guidance is needed;

- IR175 also says that a deemed payment 'can be paid as salary, but the rules do not require this to happen'. In view of the double taxation which occurs when the deemed payment is paid as salary (see **13.5.2**), this oblique reference is far from adequate: a more overt warning is necessary. This was addressed in the February 2001 Tax Bulletin, but no attempt was made to change this, or any of the other points listed above, when IR175 was revised and reissued in October 2001.

IR2003

This booklet summarises how to work out the deemed payment and includes a useful step by step guide; it also contains the answers to a number of key questions including the interaction of IR35 with corporation tax. In 2002 this booklet was included on the CD-Rom which is sent out as part of the Employer's pack.

Tax Bulletins

In April 1997 the recategorisation of subcontractors prompted an article in *Tax Bulletin 28* together with three useful worked examples, see **25.3**. *Tax Bulletin 45*, published in February 2000, looks at how the status tests affect personal service workers in general, and IT contractors in particular. Three more worked examples have been provided and are included at **25.2**.

Further helpful guidance on some areas of difficulty, including the procedure for obtaining Revenue opinions on contracts, was set out in *Tax Bulletin 51*, published in February 2001. Particularly welcome was the warning that paying the net deemed payment of salary could cause double taxation, see **13.5.2**, and the comments on in-year cessations, see **16.3.3**.

7.2.3 Inland Revenue Manuals

The most detailed guidance on status is that provided in the Revenue Manuals. These are available in every tax office, and are now accessible via the Revenue's website. Shortly after the introduction of IR35 a new Employment Status Manual (ESM) was published, made up of paragraphs extracted from the Schedule E Manual along with newly written sections such as those on service companies. A summary of key status cases was subsequently added.

It is this guidance which will be of greatest use both to practitioners and those affected by IR35. However, the length and complexity of the ESM is itself a demonstration of how difficult applying the status tests has become.

In using the Manual it should be noted that each status test is covered twice – once in summary form from ESM 500 onwards, and then a more detailed review from ESM 1000. Presumably this allows tax inspectors to save time by reading only the abridged version when dealing with more straightforward cases. But for non-Revenue users this double treatment is confusing, and it would be easier if the two were amalgamated into a single comprehensive summary.

It is no easy task to summarise employment status, and in some areas the Manual cannot be faulted. However, in others its perspective could be more balanced. These are commented on as appropriate through this chapter.

7.2.4 FAQs and other web-based assistance

As the IR35 debate developed, the Revenue used their website to good effect, publishing regular bulletins of Frequently Asked Questions (FAQs) on IR35. This allowed the Revenue to deal with issues and uncertainties as they arose, and bring issues quickly into the public domain.

The FAQs published to date were set out in the August 2000 issue of *Tax Bulletin*; however more have been issued subsequently and the FAQs have also been renumbered on two occasions. Superseded questions have now been archived, but they can still be accessed via the website.

The website also contains a very useful spreadsheet for working out the IR35 deemed payment. This is particularly helpful for those who wish to pay the right amount of salary during the year. However, it should be used with caution by those with non-standard arrangements, for example periods of non-residency or a commencement/cessation.

7.3 Overall approach

7.3.1 General

The Revenue accept that a person's status can only be decided by looking 'at the picture as a whole' rather than 'by adding up the number of factors pointing towards employment and comparing that result with the number pointing to self-employment' (*Tax Bulletin* 45), see **6.3.1**.

The Manual also acknowledges that the 'in business on your own account' test (see **6.4**) has its limitations:

> 'For example, it may not be particularly helpful when considering an engagement entered into by someone carrying on a profession or vocation. By way of illustration, actors or actresses may earn their living without any of the normal trappings of business – such as stock, premises, staff, etc. – yet for many engagements they are likely to be self-employed.
>
> In this type of situation it can help to consider in more detail the question of control and of other factors that may be present (for example, whether the individual is dependent upon or independent of a particular paymaster for the financial exploitation of his or her talents).' (ESM 0507)

7.3.2 Hierarchy of tests

Some factors are clearly more important than others, see **6.3.2**. Although the relative importance of each test can to some extent be inferred from the text of the Revenue commentaries, there is no overall guidance on which tests are decisive, and which merely supportive.

Booklet IR56 provides a glaring example of this. Under the heading: 'If you can answer "yes" to the following questions it will usually mean you are self-employed' the booklet correctly lists some of the key indicators of self-employment, including financial risk and the right to hire other workers to carry out the engagement. But it doesn't make it clear whether a worker has to answer 'yes' to all of these tests or just to some of them.

In reality if a worker met only *one* of the fundamental tests of self-employment (see **6.5.1**), such as the ability to hire workers to carry out the engagement, he would be self-employed. He could easily answer 'no' to the question:

> 'Do you provide the main items of equipment you need to do your job, not just the small tools many employees provide for themselves?'

and still be in business on his own account even if he provided no equipment at all, see **6.6.2**.

Unfortunately, the same approach has been borrowed for IR175, but with one further twist. The first question in IR175 is: *Do you work set hours, or a given number of hours, a week or a month?* This is not a test recognised by the courts as one which distinguishes the self-employed from employees. As another commentator has said:

> 'The Revenue knows contractors tend to work set hours so to state [that the existence of] set hours indicates that IR35 applies is to come at the issue backwards. It is a self-fulfilling prophesy but not one supported by case law.'
> David Smith in *Tolley's IR35 Defence Strategies*.

7.3.3 Employment as the default position

While accepting that booklet IR56 contains a mere six pages on the status tests, and acknowledges its limitations in its introduction, it does treat employment as the default position. On page 3 of IR56 it says that 'if you can answer "yes" to the following questions you will probably be employed'; on page 6 that if you can't answer 'yes' to the self-employed questions 'you will normally be an employee'.

In reality it would be possible for a person to answer 'yes' to at least four out of five 'employment' questions and 'no' to a number of the 'self-employed' questions and still be in business on his own account.

The *Tax Bulletin* is more balanced, stating:

> 'The role of the Revenue is to provide advice and guidance about the employment status resulting from a given set of circumstances, not to impose any particular status.'

This is reinforced by the opening words, in bold, of the Revenue's Employment Status Manual:

> **'The aim of employment status work is to ensure that the correct schedule of charge is applied and the correct class of NICs is paid. It is not to impose any particular status.'**

7.3.4 Mutuality of obligation

Mutuality is conspicuous by its absence from any easily available Revenue guidance: the *Tax Bulletins*, IR175, IR56 or the FAQs. The earlier version of the

Schedule E Manual opened its discussion on mutuality with words which are now notorious:

'The concept of "mutuality of obligation" is rarely of practical use when considering status for Income Tax purposes and it can easily confuse the issue. Do not consider it unless the engager or worker raises the subject.' (ESM 0154)

This approach was severely criticised by Mr Justice Burton in the course of the judicial review. He said that:

'It cannot be right for the Revenue simply to conclude, as it does in another such guidance document, ESM 0514, that "mutuality of obligation" is not a relevant issue: "Do not consider this factor when reviewing a work status, unless the engager or worker raises it." It has now recently been emphasised, by the House of Lords, in *Carmichael v National Power plc* [1999] 1 WLR 2042, that the test adopted in *Nethermere (St Neots) Ltd v Gardner* [1984] ICR 612 CA by Stephenson LJ, of an "irreducible minimum of mutual obligation" is another central piece of guidance in the analysis of whether there is employment or self-employment.'

As a result of this criticism, the Revenue significantly improved their guidance, saying that:

'There must be an irreducible minimum of mutual obligation for there to be a contract of service. That irreducible minimum is that the engager must be obliged to pay a wage or other remuneration, and that the worker must be obliged to provide his or her own work or skill ... In deciding whether an "umbrella" contract exists, the courts will consider whether there is an ongoing obligation on the part of the engager to provide work (or at least to pay the individual if no work is available) and an ongoing obligation to do work that is provided.' (ESM1071)

This picks up a number of important issues, but restricts the final two points (the obligation of the engager to offer work to the individual if that work is available and the obligation of the worker to carry out that work) to situations where there might be an umbrella contract. However, in *Montgomery* and *O'Kelly* the courts applied the same criteria to single engagements as to umbrella contracts, see **5.6**, and there is thus no justification for applying these points only to the latter.

ESM 0174 concludes by quoting the case of *Secretary of State for Employment v McMeechan* [1997] IRLR 353, which was decided very much on its own facts.

Nevertheless, the new guidance is a considerable improvement, and also refers more frequently to the leading decision of *Carmichael and Another v National Power*, see **5.5.4**, rather than relying on the much earlier cases of *Nethermere (St Neots) Ltd v Gardiner* [1983] ICR 319 and *Airfix Footwear Ltd v Cope* [1978] ICR 1210, see **5.4**.

7.4 Particular status tests

7.4.1 Substitution

The provision of personal service is the essence of employment, and the right of substitution is thus a fundamental status test. If it is possible to send a substitute, there can be no employment. The case law on substitution is discussed at **6.5.2**, and the practical implications of including a substitution clause in a contract at **9.3**.

Revenue guidance on substitution is contained within *Tax Bulletin 45* and at several places within the Employment Status Manual. However, there is a marked change of tone between the general discussion of status (mostly at ESM 1051ff) and the sections on contract clearance for IR35 purposes at ESM 3299 (see 'Testing the Right' below).

Substitute actually provided

The Revenue accept that where a substitute is actually provided, there cannot be an employment. In *Lorimer*, the Revenue's barrister, Mr Goldsmith, conceded that:

> 'Tax could not be charged under Sch E in respect of the profits made by Mr Lorimer on the six occasions when, with the consent of the production company concerned, he provided a substitute to carry out the work for which he had contracted. Mr Goldsmith accepted that in those cases Mr Lorimer could not be said to have earned his profit in the performance of a contract of service because in the result he was not paid for his own skill and labour.'

Right to provide a substitute

In *Tax Bulletin* 45 the Revenue confirm that:

> 'Personal service is an essential element of a contract of employment. A person who has the freedom to choose whether to do the job himself or hire

somebody else to do it for him, or who can hire someone else to provide substantial help is probably self-employed ... '

While not completely conceding the point that the worker cannot be an employee if there is a *right* to send a substitute (note the word 'probably' in the text), nevertheless the article indicates that the Revenue accept the view that the right of substitution is incompatible with employment.

This is confirmed with more confidence by paragraph 1054 of the ESM:

'*Express and Echo Publications Ltd v Ernest Tanton* (1999 IRLR 367) ... shows that where a worker does not have to perform the work personally, and can hire a substitute to carry out the work, that is inconsistent with employment and the worker will be self-employed regardless of other factors such as control, etc.'

What makes substitution a 'right'

The Revenue have set out a number of criteria which they say should be satisfied before there is a 'right' of substitution.

(a) The right of substitution has to relate to the work carried out for the client. *Tax Bulletin* 45 correctly says:

> 'A worker may choose to pay a helper to take phone messages and deal with invoicing and general book keeping work for the intermediary. But this would not be directly relevant when considering an engagement where the worker is engaged to lay bricks for a client.'

(b) The worker has to engage and pay the substitute. This is in line with the case law, see **9.3.4**.

(c) The client must not have 'an unreasonable right of veto' over the substitute (ESM 1052). At ESM 1054 the Manual goes further, and helpfully says that 'even where an engager's right to refuse to accept an unsuitable substitute is not expressly stated in a contract it would probably be implied into the arrangements by the Courts'. In other words, a contract which did **not** have some restriction on the right of substitution would be unreasonable. See **9.3.3** for examples of where the Revenue accept that the rejection of a substitute will not contaminate the right.

(d) Apart from a reasonable right of veto over unsatisfactory substitutes, the client's permission must not be a prerequisite, see FAQ Contract 5. In the view of the author, this is correct, see **9.3.3**, despite the words of Mr

Justice Burton in the judicial review (*R v CIR (oao Professional Contractors Group Ltd* [2001] STC 629), who said that:

> 'It would not be right to make an absolute statement, as the Revenue appears to do ... that the need to obtain the client's permission necessarily negates the existence of a right to substitution, and/or points to employment.'

> It may be, however, that the judge was referring to the right of veto discussed in (c).

(e) The Revenue then extend this requirement, saying that:

> 'A right of substitution is only likely to exist where the client does not mind, from one day to the next for the duration of the contract, who carries out the work, provided that whoever does so is suitably qualified and experienced.' (FAQ Contract 5 and ESM 3293)

This appears to the author to go too far, and be unsupported by the case law. In *Diggles,* see **6.5.2**, the barristers had engaged their Senior Clerk to provide 'Full Clerking Services' and although a substitute could be provided, the barristers (if asked) could reasonably have been expected to express a preference for Mr Diggles. Similarly, Mr Tanton (**6.5.2**) had been engaged as a driver, and although someone else stepped in when he was ill, this is not the same as saying the Express and Echo had no concern who did the job on a day-to-day basis.

'Limited' right

The fact that a limited or occasional power of delegation may not be enough to immunise the worker from IR35 is discussed at **6.5.2**. In the text of the Manual the Revenue say:

> 'If an engager has the right to refuse a substitute for any reason at all, this has the effect of enabling the engager to insist that the worker carry out the work personally. In that sort of situation the worker's right to supply a substitute is clearly more limited. Care needs to be taken to establish the true agreement. Why would a worker who genuinely wants the right to supply a substitute accept such a restriction of that right and why would an engager want anything more than a right to prevent an unsuitable person from carrying out the work? It may be that it is clear that a substitute would never be accepted because of the nature of the work and the substitution clause is a 'sham' inserted mainly with the intention of dressing up the contract as a contract for services.' (ESM 1054)

See also the Revenue summary of *MacFarlane and Skivington v Glasgow City Council* [2000] EAT/1277 at ESM 7220.

Testing the right

In the Manual's general discussion of substitution (i.e., that not specifically related to IR35 cases), the Revenue say they do not normally seek to test the right. They explain that because what is at issue is a *right* and not its exercise, 'disproving a claimed right of substitution can be difficult'. This leads the Manual to advise Inspectors that:

'Unless there is reason to doubt a claimed right of substitution it may normally be accepted at face value. If the claim later turns out to be untrue we will normally be able to rectify the matter later. Enquiries are more likely to be appropriate where other alleged terms are found to be false or a claimed right of substitution does not seem to make sense in relation to the contract.' (ESM 1056)

Where it is decided to investigate the substitution clause, the Inspector is reminded: 'Remember, if you are to ignore a claimed right of substitution it is for you to find the evidence that will show that the claimed right does not exist,' and 'you cannot assert that a right of substitution does not exist just because a substitute has never been provided'.

However, the Revenue approach to IR35 focuses more on the contractor providing the evidence. In April 2000 the following FAQ was published:

'*My contract specifies that I am allowed to hire a substitute. Will the Inland Revenue take this at face value? If not will I need to provide evidence to prove that this right is genuine?*'

The Inland Revenue will want to ensure that the right to send a substitute is a genuine right before it can be taken into account in deciding employment status ... [Where] the service company's contract is not with the client but with an agency, and there is a claimed right of substitution, the Inland Revenue would normally require a copy of the written contract between the agency and the client.

If you are unable to get access to that contract then you should ask the agency to send a copy to the Inland Revenue direct. If this is not possible you may be asked to provide alternative evidence. This could take the form of a letter from the client which confirms that it has agreed to your service company providing a substitute and that it does not matter which worker is provided on a day to day basis over the course of the contract.' (FAQ Contract 5)

The ESM paragraphs on substitution in the context of the contract clearance process reiterates the point on agency contracts, but goes further, saying:

> 'Many contracts submitted for written opinions contain clauses that appear to give a right of substitution. It seems likely that many of these clauses have only been inserted to try and break the requirement for personal service and change the contract from one of service to one for services. Normally a client requires the services of a particular worker and a substitute would not be acceptable *so there must be doubts about the validity of such clauses.*' (ESM 3293, the author's italics)

The contract clearance process is of course a customer service, see **7.7**, and it is not unreasonable for the Revenue to test the facts before they give a view on which the worker can rely.

However, if a contractor is investigated he should remember that legally the onus of proof is on the Revenue, not on the contractor. As stated above, the Manual warns Inspectors:

> 'Remember, if you are to ignore a claimed right of substitution *it is for you to find the evidence* that will show that the claimed right does not exist.' (the author's italics)

The ESM also sets out the questions an Inspector is likely to ask if he decides to challenge a substitution clause. These include the following:

- What documentary evidence is available? For example: letters exchanged before the contract is signed, job advertisements, bank accounts etc;

- Have there been circumstances in which you would expect a substitute to be provided, such as a domestic emergency, illness and holidays?

- Has a substitute ever been provided? If not, why not?

- If a substitute is used, who paid (or would pay)?

- Is there any evidence that a substitute has been rejected at any time? If so, why?

- Would the engager accept any substitute? If not, what restrictions are there?

- Are similar workers engaged on similar terms? If so, have they ever sent substitutes? If another similarly engaged worker has supplied a substitute, it rather suggests the claimed right is genuine;

- Is there evidence that any other terms in the agreement between the worker and the engager are a sham? If so, this may cast doubt on the credibility of the agreement as a whole. (ESM 1058).

Not being able to send a substitute

The Revenue accept that *not* being able to send a substitute does not mean that a worker is necessarily an employee:

'This factor does not necessarily work the other way. Where a worker has to undertake the work personally that does not mean the worker must be an employee. There are many examples (for example, in the professional field) where self-employed individuals have to undertake the work they have agreed themselves. The lack of a right to provide a substitute may be a pointer to employment but it is certainly not conclusive on its own.' (ESM 1053)

Engager refuses the substitute

If the client refuses to accept a substitute, this does not necessarily mean that the worker had no right to send one. The Manual provides a helpful example of another possibility:

'If you find that a worker ... wanted to send a substitute on one occasion but the engager refused to accept the substitute this would suggest a difference between the written term and the true agreement. The reason for the difference will be a question of fact. For example, it may be because the term is a sham. *Alternatively, the contractor may have failed to keep to his side of the contract and the worker has chosen not take action to enforce his rights.*' (ESM 1008 Example 2, the author's italics)

7.4.2 Risk

General

If a worker takes significant financial risk he will not be an employee, see **6.5.3**. This position is generally accepted by the Revenue:

'Individuals, who risk their own money by, for example, buying assets, bearing their running costs, paying for overheads and materials, are almost certainly self-employed. Employees do not usually need to risk their own capital.' (ESM 1031; there are similar words in *Tax Bulletin* 45)

Fixed price and overruns

Tax Bulletin 45 says that the Revenue would accept 'quoting a fixed price for a job, with the consequent risk of bearing the additional costs if the job overruns' as evidence of financial risk. This is expanded in the ESM to include correcting mistakes in the worker's own time and possibly at his own cost:

> 'Where a worker is required to put right mistakes or poor workmanship in the worker's own time, then this is a pointer towards self-employment. The pointer to self- employment will be increased where the worker must also supply replacement materials etc. For example, if a bricklayer has to re-build a wall and supply or pay for the cost of the mortar/bricks etc, this would be a stronger pointer to self-employment than if the engager supplied the replacement materials.' (ESM 512)

However, the Manual also suggests that Inspectors may wish to test the validity of such a clause:

> 'The written contract states that the worker will be liable for loss or damage caused by his own negligence. If in practice there has been no such loss or damage caused by the worker it is difficult to say whether the contractual term is genuine or not.' (ESM 1008)

However, just because a term in the contract has not been called upon does not allow the Revenue to say it is not genuine. In the case of an IR35 hypothetical contract, if both the client and the worker confirm that had there been loss or damage, the worker would have been responsible for making good, then this should be sufficient.

The Manual continues by advising Inspectors:

> 'If you find this situation in practice you should check whether any liability arose under this clause. If it did, who paid? If not the worker, why not? You should also check whether the worker carries appropriate insurance. If not, why not? If, in addition, the engager insures against this risk (at no cost to the worker) these two facts together would suggest (but not prove) the true position was different from that stated in the contract.'

This reinforces the need for contractors to have insurance, see **9.7.1**.

Training

Tax Bulletin 45 said that the Revenue accepted that where a skilled worker incurred significant amounts of expenditure on training to provide himself with a skill, he had thereby run a financial risk. The Bulletin said:

> 'This could be treated in the same way as investment in equipment to be used in a trade, as a pointer to self-employment, if there was a real risk that

the investment would not be recovered from income from future engagements.'

This useful comment finally found its way into the ESM in June 2001 (at paragraph 1031), but with two unhappy adjustments:

1. Expenditure on training was described as 'a lesser degree of risk' than purchasing plant and equipment. There was no such comment in TB45;

2. Secondly, the text in ESM 1031 read:

    'This can be treated as a *mild* pointer to self-employment *only* if there is a real risk that the investment would not be recovered from income from future engagements.' (the author's italics)

However, after representations, the March 2002 edition corrected the Manual so that ESM 1031 now repeats the guidance given in the Tax Bulletin.

Little or no risk

The Manual does accept that 'The absence of financial risk does not always mean the worker is an employee' (ESM 1031). However it goes on to say that:

'Nor does the absence of what would normally be regarded as a business organisation. Yet it is fair to say that workers without either are unlikely to be self-employed.'

However *Lorimer* (**8.2.1**) had only a rudimentary business structure and yet the judge held that a relatively low level of risk was sufficient for him to be self-employed:

'[He] bears his own financial risk which is greater than that of one who is an employee, accepting the risk of bad debts and outstanding invoices and of no or an insufficient number of engagements.'

This important part of the *Lorimer* case was ignored in the Revenue's 'fail' letter (ESM 3299, see **7.7.6** below), where it set out one of the reasons for categorising a worker as within IR35 as follows:

'The basis of payment (at an hourly rate by reference to a standard working week) means that there is little financial risk, *other than from invoicing.*' (the author's italics)

The possibility that a lower level of risk might be acceptable in an 'exceptional case' is mentioned in the Manual where it refers to the session musicians in

Addison and others v The London Philharmonic Orchestra Society Limited [1981] ICR 261 and *Midland Sinfonia Concert Society Limited v The Secretary of State for Social Services* [1981] ICR 454, see **20.5.2** and ESM 1031.

In these cases the musicians were held to be self-employed even though they 'did not risk their own capital in orchestral performances'. This was because 'they remained essentially freelance musicians pursuing their own professions as instrumentalists with individual reputations even when playing for an orchestra'. However, are these cases truly 'exceptional'? As discussed in **8.5**, could the same not apply to many IT professionals?

7.4.3 Profiting from sound management

If risk is one side of the coin, the opportunity to profit from sound management is the other, see **6.5.3**. The Revenue are clearly anxious to differentiate between employees (such as those paid by piecework) and the self-employed. At ESM 1035 they say:

> 'The Courts have concluded that a self-employed person often has an opportunity to profit from the sound management of the task. Of course an employee's income may also be related to his or her efforts or to other factors and so may not be regular or constant.
>
> An employee's income will depend on performance when paid by the piece. It could also depend on how long he or she works and that, in turn, could depend on outside factors such as the weather.
>
> It follows that the Courts interpret the opportunity to profit from sound management in a rather special way. What they have in mind is the worker who quotes a fixed price for a job and whose profit or loss depends on speed and efficiency and the capacity to reduce overheads and organise work effectively.'

This final paragraph is nothing more than evangelical exegesis. The courts do not 'interpret the opportunity to profit from sound management in a rather special [i.e., restricted] way'. The courts say that if you can profit from sound management you are more likely to be self-employed. Indeed, in *Lorimer* Nolan J. said that the worker's exploitation of his own reputation was sufficient to allow him to profit from sound management, see **8.2.2**. A similar point was made in the *Addison* case referred to at **7.4.2** above. People paid by the piece therefore pass this test – they can profit from sound management – but this alone may not be enough to make them self-employed.

7.4.4 Hiring staff

This is another fundamental status test, and if satisfied the worker will be self-employed, see **6.5.4**. Revenue guidance in this area is mixed:

(a) In IR56 they correctly distinguish between 'being free to hire people on terms of one's own choice to do the work which one has taken on, paying them out of one's own pocket,' which is characteristic of self-employment, and merely 'being authorised to delegate work or to engage others on behalf of one's employer';

(b) Similarly, in *Tax Bulletin 45* they rightly emphasise that the helper must be carrying out work which is intrinsic to the engagement, and not merely 'invoicing and general book keeping';

(c) In *Tax Bulletin 28* they warn that hiring others means that it is the worker's responsibility to decide on the employment status of those he has engaged:

> '*Are "gang masters" or "team leaders" employed or self-employed?*
>
> The answer depends on the precise terms of the agreements entered into by the various parties. The gang master or team leader, and the individual gang or team members, may all be employees of the contractor ... If, however, the gang master is responsible for engaging and paying the team members (out of his own all inclusive fee for delivering a particular task) he is almost certainly self-employed. The gang master or team leader would then have to decide if his men are employed by him, or self-employed.'

However, the ESM is much more cautious, to the extent of losing the plot. It says:

> 'A worker who hires an assistant is unlikely to be an employee. That is especially so where the nature of the work actually requires an assistant (for example, where installing or moving heavy objects is involved) and the worker is required to hire help at his or her own expense. On the other hand, a dairy may turn a blind eye to a milk roundsman deciding to hire a child as an assistant during the school holidays to "lighten the load". That would be rather different and would not inevitably mean that the milkman is self-employed.'

There is, however, nothing in the case law to suggest that the milkman's hiring of a child (one assumes within the provisions of the Children and Young Persons Act 1933) to 'lighten the load' would not be an indicator of self-employment. The Manual then continues:

'You do need to be sure that the work and payment involved make the hiring of an assistant a viable proposition. Where the worker is hourly paid it is unlikely the worker would pay someone else for "help" as such (the worker would still be working at the same remuneration but would effectively be voluntarily funding a helper out of their own pocket). And if the remuneration is low, is it possible to hire assistants? You should consider such claims critically.' (ESM 1059)

However, once again the argument is flawed: there is no reason why an hourly paid individual would not pay someone else for 'help' – most accountants do this. And a worker's claim to be self-employed will not be invalidated because he does not make a profit on the hiring – there may be all sorts of commercial reasons for hiring an assistant, such as the need to keep a client, meet a deadline or take a vacation. The Revenue have become overly defensive in this section of the Manual.

7.4.5 Provision of equipment

The March 2002 edition of the ESM has significantly improved Revenue guidance on the provision of equipment. ESM 511 previously began its discussion of this status test by saying: 'A genuine self-employed worker usually provides all necessary equipment to do the job,' and ESM 1061 had the similar phrase: 'A self-employed contractor generally provides his/her own equipment.'

These sentences have now been removed and replaced by more balanced guidance, including the important new sentence: 'Where the worker provides only minor items of equipment, he or she may or may not be self-employed.'(ESM 511)

Similarly, ESM 1009 Example 3 previously made the provision of only small tools the key test in reclassifying someone as an employee; it now ends by saying that in this situation the engagement 'may or may not be a contract of service depending on the other factors in the case'.

It is still possible to take issue with the first sentence of ESM 1061, which says: 'If the engager provides any necessary equipment, this fact will point towards the existence of a contract of employment,' and ESM 1062, which reads:

'In *Hall v Lorimer* a vision mixer was found to be self employed when the terms, conditions and facts surrounding his engagements were considered as a whole. This was despite the fact that the substantial and expensive equipment needed was provided by his engagers. Mummery J., in the High Court, considered that the provision of equipment by Lorimer's engagers undoubtedly pointed towards the existence of employment but this was not sufficient, by itself, to outweigh other pointers towards self-employment that were present in that particular case.' (ESM 1062)

In fact Lord Nolan in the Court of Appeal effectively overruled Mummery J.'s view that Lorimer's non-provision of equipment indicated employment. Lord Nolan accepted the Special Commissioner's view that it was *irrelevant* that Lorimer provided no equipment *because it was not his business to provide equipment,* see **6.6.2.**

Thus the Revenue conclusion that the provision of equipment by Lorimer's engagers 'undoubtedly pointed towards employment' and thus needed to be outweighed by other pointers towards self-employment is incorrect. It was not a factor either way, and thus did not need to be 'outweighed' by other factors pointing towards Schedule D.

The same could be said of an IT contractor providing specialist skills to a client with millions of pounds worth of computer equipment, or of an oil worker on a multi-million pound rig in the North Sea. It may be a require- ment of the task that a contractor works on the client's equipment – for example, installing a virus checker on a mainframe. Or he may be prevented from using his own equipment because of concerns about viruses, the need to protect commercial information, the demands of the Data Protection Act, or because he is working at a high security installation. None of these has any- thing to do with employment status, and treating the absence of own equip- ment as a significant status indicator is inappropriate.

7.4.6 Control

The control test is complex and has developed over time, see **6.6.3.** Although IR175 and the ESM's analysis of the status tests both begin with control, the Revenue agree that it has become less important in determining status, see ESM 1014. They are prepared to accept that:

'Whilst a high level of control is a strong pointer towards employment, it may not be conclusive on its own and should be considered in the light of all of the relevant factors and the overall picture.' (ESM 1015)

They also admit that Inspectors may find it difficult to prove that someone is an employee under this test:

'It is the right to exert control that is significant; not whether that right is exercised. In practice, the employer may rarely (or never) exercise this right;

particularly where the worker is a skilled individual used to working on his or her own initiative. It can be difficult to demonstrate both that a right exists and that there is actual control.' (ESM 1015)

Like other commentators, the Revenue divide their analysis of control into when, where, what and how, with additional paragraphs on the position of professional workers. These are considered in turn below.

Control as to when the engagement is carried out

The ESM quotes the unreported case of *Robin Hamilton v The Secretary of State for Social Services* in support of the view that 'the lack of a requirement to work specific hours usually has only marginal importance' (ESM 1021).

However, there is no mention of *WHPT Housing Association Ltd v Secretary of State for Social Services* [1981] ICR 737, see **6.7.3**, a reported case, where one of the key reasons for Mr Lowe being found to be self-employed was that he was paid an hourly rate and only for the hours he actually worked, in contrast to the company's employees who were paid a salary.

The approach of a later paragraph is, however, much more reasonable:

'Workers engaged under contracts for service may be subject to considerable restrictions where commercial pressures dictate. For example, if working on large sites where access is limited to normal working hours, the worker is not going to be able to work as and when he or she pleases. In such circumstances the limitations put on when the work can be carried out tells us nothing about the status of the individual and other factors will have to be considered.' (ESM 1021)

This is a particularly useful comment, as the requirement to work fixed hours on a client's site has proved to be one of the tests most heavily used by the Revenue when giving borderline IR35 opinions against the worker; where this occurs it may be worth drawing the attention of Status Inspectors to this paragraph in their Manual.

Control as to where the engagement is carried out

The ESM contrasts the two extremes:

'A requirement in a contract for a worker to work at a specified place is more characteristic of a contract of employment, than one of self-employment ...

Where a worker can carry out work wherever he wishes, the contract is more likely to be a contract for services.' (ESM 1019)

Where a contract requires services to be delivered at a specified location, the Manual uses *Stagecraft Ltd v Minister of National Insurance* [1952] SC 288 as support for classifying workers as employees; in fact the case turned on the ability of the engager to *move* an individual from one location to another.

However, the ESM also makes the very useful comment that 'where the nature of the work dictates where it should be carried out ... this factor is not likely to be of any significance in determining status'. This scenario is demonstrated at paragraph 1020 Example 3:

'Worker C is taken on as a cleaner. The contract requires Worker C to clean an office block 5 evenings each week. The nature of the work dictates where the work has to be carried out. Therefore this factor is of little relevance in determining status in this case.'

The Manual also warns that, while no control by the engager as to where the work has to be carried out is a pointer to self-employment, it is not sufficient on its own:

'Working practices are becoming more and more flexible and many employees now work from home. You should not accept that a worker is self-employed just because he or she does not work at the engager's premises. This is particularly true where the engager covers any expenses that the worker incurs as a result of working out of the office.' (ESM 1019)

Control as to what is to be done during the engagement

The ESM's summary of this area states that:

'If the worker contracts to complete a specific task and cannot be moved to another job, there is no control over what is done *and this factor becomes neutral.*' (ESM 1017, the author's italics)

In fact, of course, it becomes a positive indicator of self-employment, as is admitted later in the text – though the Revenue are quick to add that the engager might have control over another aspect of the work:

'Where, for example, a bricklayer is taken on to perform a number of specific tasks, the fact that there is no right of control over what the worker does is a pointer to self-employment but there might be a right over when the task is undertaken.'

The following Revenue examples demonstrate that a contract to complete a specific task precludes control over 'what' and thus points to self-employment:

'Painter B … contracts with the company to paint all of the offices on the third floor. The work is to be completed within three weeks. It is up to Painter B to decide what work he is going to do in order to fulfil this contract and the company cannot tell him to stop and paint another part of the building instead. In this case there is no control over what is to be done which points to self-employment.

Painter C … contracts with the company to paint all of the offices on the fourth floor. The work is to be completed within three weeks. Two weeks into the job the company asks him to paint part of the fifth floor, which Painter C agrees to do but for extra money.

Because the original contract was specifically to paint the fourth floor, the company did not have the right to instruct Painter C to carry out this additional work. Instead, Painter C has voluntarily agreed to undertake the additional work for an additional fee under a new and separate contract. The original contract to paint the fourth floor is still effective and he must complete that work within the agreed time scale. Again, the company has no control over what is to be done and the contractual arrangements point towards self-employment.' (ESM 1019 Examples 2 and 3)

Tax Bulletin 45, however, goes too far:

'A right to determine "what" work is carried out is a strong pointer to employment. It will normally be a feature whenever a client needs a worker to undertake whatever tasks are required at any particular time or where the worker is required to work as part of a co-ordinated team.'

The suggestion that the worker will be an employee if he is 'required to work as part of a co-ordinated team' runs counter to Lord Nolan's comment in *Lorimer* that 'if you are part of a team to produce a show, it is inevitable that someone must organise it … That applies to the leading actor and actress, but they do not for that reason become "employees".'

Control as to how the work is to be carried out

The Revenue summarise the position as follows:

'The presence of control over how work is done is a strong pointer towards employment. However, its absence is only likely to be a mild pointer towards self-employment. This is because many employees are experts in their particular fields with particular skills and specialist knowledge and are not subject to such control.' (ESM 1023)

However this paragraph also includes the helpful comment that where the engager has the right to review the work to ensure that it is 'to a satisfactory standard and subject to a final quality control check, this does not give the engager the right to control how the worker does the work. All that is happening is the engager is confirming that the contract has been complied with.'

In other words, this right to a qualitative check is **not** evidence that the client has control as to how the work is carried out.

No control

The Revenue accept that 'if there is no right of control it is unlikely that there will be an employment' (ESM 1015); the same point is made in *Tax Bulletin* 45. It would, however, be more correct to admit that if there is no control there **cannot** be an employment, see **6.6.3**.

Control over experts

Control is not a very useful test in the case of professionals, see **6.6.3**. In *Morren v Swinton & Pendlebury Borough Council* [1965] 2 All ER 349 Lord Parker said that:

> 'When one is dealing with a professional man, or a man of some particular skill and experience, ... the absence of control and direction ... can be of little, if any, use as a test.'

This was reiterated by the Special Commissioner in *Hall v Lorimer*, see **8.2.1**, and his assessment of the control test was approved by the judge in the Court of Appeal.

The Revenue stress that a professional can be an employee even if he is not subject to much control (ESM 1024), but do not point out the corollary: that the existence of control does not preclude the individual being self-employed, as in *Lorimer*. This is a very significant point, particularly in the context of IR35.

7.4.7 Number and variety of engagements

If one had to pinpoint a single reason why Mr Lorimer was held to be self-employed, it would be because of the number and variety of his engagements, see **6.6.4**. This is sometimes mentioned by the Revenue in conjunction with the need to have a business organisation. For example, *Tax Bulletin* 45 states:

'If a skilled worker works for a number of clients throughout the year, and has a business-like approach to obtaining his engagements (perhaps involving expenditure on office accommodation, office equipment etc.) this will point towards self-employment'

In *Lorimer* there was no connection between the number of clients and any expenditure on office accommodation or equipment, see **7.4.11** below, and linking the two can therefore be resisted.

IR175 similarly mentions that having a large number of clients can be an indicator of self-employment, but the point is highlighted in such a way as to suggest (perhaps unintentionally) a lack of Revenue enthusiasm for the concept:

'The number of clients you have **may** be relevant to the decision whether your work for each is as an employee, or as a self-employed person. If you have many different clients this **may** indicate self-employment, and be a factor that should be considered in addition to the actual details of each contract.'

More encouragingly, the number and variety of clients was the deciding factor in the Revenue's *Tax Bulletin* example Charlotte, see **25.2.4**, and in a similar situation one could thus expect the Revenue to agree that a worker was self-employed. ESM 1092 was rewritten for the March 2002 edition of the Manual and reinforces this point:

'Employment status may be affected by the way in which the worker generally carries on his occupation. In particular, the length of each engagement and the number of other persons for whom similar work is to be performed should be considered, and engagements need to be looked at in the context of the worker's exposure to bad debts and the amount spent on organising, obtaining or carrying out the work. In these circumstances many of the other factors that are normally associated with a contract for services may be absent ... Nevertheless, when looked at in the round, the personal factors which are present may be sufficient to make the contract a contract for services.'

The same point was endorsed by Mr Justice Burton in the judicial review:

'The question of whether the service contractor himself has, prior to that engagement, performed or is, simultaneously with that engagement, performing (an important contrast to the duty of fidelity ordinarily owed by an employee), or will subsequently, after the termination of that engagement, perform, services for others, and is to be construed as carrying on business on his own account, is and must be a central consideration.'

The position of a professional, such as an actress, who has a series of engagements and moves from one to the other is also relevant under this heading. The Revenue include the key case, *Davies v Braithwaite* [1933] 18 TC 198, in their summary at ESM 7024. However, curiously and in marked contrast to their summaries of other cases, they do not explain how it should be applied. The author's conclusions are given at **8.5.3**.

7.4.8 Regular, long, or exclusive engagements with the same client

Tax Bulletin 45 says that:

> 'Where this pattern of a number of different clients does not exist, but instead the worker is regularly engaged by the same client, this may indicate employment, see *Nethermere (St. Neots) Ltd v Gardiner* [1984] ICR 612'

However, the *Nethermere* case is not necessarily applicable to a professional working through a personal service company, see **5.4.3**. The Revenue may agree with this, because at the end of the article they appear to qualify their earlier general comments by saying that:

> 'Long periods working for one engager may be typical of an employment *but are not conclusive*. It is still necessary to consider all the terms and conditions of each engagement.' (the author's italics)

The March 2002 version of the ESM now makes the position even clearer:

> 'The length of a worker's contract is, of itself, a neutral factor in deciding whether a worker is an employee or self-employed. An individual could be engaged for a week's casual labour in a bar and be an employee despite the short term nature of the contract; another person may be engaged for a six month contract preparing a technical report on terms which amount to self-employment.' (ESM 0519)

> 'The length of engagement is neutral in determining the employment status. However, in general, the longer the engagement the more likely that it will be a contract of service and the shorter the engagement the less likely. This is not down to the length of the contract itself but because the other factors are more likely to indicate this to be the case. For example, the longer the engagement, more likely it is that the engager will want to, or need to, exert significant amounts of control over the worker ... the worker may become integrated into the engager's organisation ... the work may become less business-like and the personal factors are less likely to be significant.' (ESM 1075)

ESM 1105 comments on the linked area of providing exclusive services:

> 'The obligation to provide services exclusively for one master is a pointer towards employment. However, exclusive services clauses are not only found in contracts of employment. They may also appear in contracts for services. A self-employed individual running an agency for an insurance company may be precluded from selling any other company's policies. Similarly an author may agree to write for only one publisher.'

The most positive approach was that of the old Schedule E Manual, which advised Inspectors to be patient and not jump to conclusions:

> 'Bear in mind though that someone commencing in business may in practice work for the same engager under a series of separate contracts because he or she is unable to obtain contracts elsewhere. For example, a professional worker may start in business, set up an office and endeavour to obtain engagements in a particular field on a self-employed basis with a variety of engagers. If he or she continues in that vein but only manages to obtain work for part of the time through short-term contracts from one engager *the fact that only one engager is involved would not necessarily mean those engagements are employments.*' (SE 690, the author's italics)

This paragraph was omitted from the early editions of the new Employment Status Manual, but it was reinstated in the March 2002 version as ESM 1095. This is a welcome acknowledgement by the Revenue that it can, in practice, take time to establish a network of clients.

The March 2002 Manual also includes the following new passage which covers the opposite situation – where an individual moves from having a number of clients to working exclusively for one engager:

> 'An individual may have a number of short-term contracts with more than one engager which looked at individually would amount to employment but looked at together amount to self-employment. If that individual then begins to work virtually full-time for one engager, the series of separate contracts ... may ... be replaced by a contract of employment.
>
> On the other hand, the individual may start to work for just one engager because of better pay and conditions, ease of travel etc. But the underlying position may not change in that there is still a series of separate contracts. Where that happens the individual is likely to continue working under a series of contracts and to remain self-employed.' (ESM 1095)

This is a very important new addition to the Revenue guidance. For the first time they have acknowledged that there may be very good business reasons why an individual will extend a satisfactory contract, and have accepted that he can do so without necessarily changing his tax status.

As a final point, *Tax Bulletin* 45 includes a coded warning against splitting engagements into short periods in order to simulate a self-employed scenario:

'Where an engagement is covered by a series of short contracts, or an initial short contract subsequently extended for a longer period, *it is the length of the engagement* that is relevant, rather than the length of each contract.'

7.4.9 Payment terms

Pay

The guidance in the Manual here is to be preferred to that in *Tax Bulletin 45*. In the latter the Revenue comment:

'Employees tend to be paid a fixed wage or salary by the week or month and often qualify for additional payments such as overtime, long service bonus or profit share. Independent contractors, on the other hand, tend to be paid a fixed sum for a particular job. Payment "by the piece" (where the worker is paid according to the amount of work actually done) or by commission can be a feature of both employment and self-employment.'

This contrasts the self-employed on a project basis with the employee, but doesn't point out that independent contractors are also frequently paid by the hour, see **6.7.3**. The March 2002 edition of the Manual contains the more balanced comment:

'Care must be taken with this aspect as it is often inconclusive. There are many examples of employees who are paid by the piece or on the basis of commission and equally there are many self-employed individuals who charge by the hour or day. The hourly payment basis may, such as with many plumbers, accountants and lawyers, merely be a way of charging their time out and ascribing value to the work done. It is sometimes more helpful to see what underlies the method of payment.' (ESM 1041).

The final sentence echoes the decision in *Lorimer*, where it was said that payment by the hour was not necessarily indicative of employment:

'Many of the invoices, it is true, indicate the hours Mr Lorimer attended for the shooting session, but the object appears to me to be to provide the reason for the particular charge out rate.'

However the Manual then goes on to say:

> 'It is sometimes more helpful to see what underlies the method of payment. For example, does the hourly payment method enable the engager to exercise control over the worker? If he can, this is a strong pointer towards employment.'

This last comment takes the *Lorimer* decision that it is important to look at why an hourly rate is being charged, but instead of asking whether the purpose of the hourly rate is to justify the final bill, instead links it to control – and there is in fact no case law which suggests that paying by the hour is indicative of control. Many people pay their builders on an hourly basis, but have minimal control. Almost all accountants and lawyers are paid by the hour, but this does not mean they are employed by their clients.

Nevertheless, this version of the Manual is vastly better than the guidance which existed before March 2002, when the same passage read:

> 'It is often more helpful to see what underlies the method of payment. For example, it is reasonable to expect someone paying on the basis of the number of hours of attendance to exercise sufficient control to ensure value for money. Such control is indicative of employment.'

There is no suggestion anywhere in the case law that exercising sufficient control to obtain 'value for money' is in any sense a test of status. The new version of the Manual, while not perfect, is much to be preferred.

Benefits

The Manual and *Tax Bulletin* 45 make the same point:

> 'The absence of benefits such as sick pay, pension scheme membership, maternity rights, etc. in a short-term engagement will almost certainly be because they are inappropriate in such circumstances. Their absence may therefore be of little relevance in this type of situation and certainly will not inevitably lead to the conclusion that an employment does not exist.' (ESM 1075)

The opposite is also true, but passes without explicit comment – people can have benefits and yet still be self-employed, see **6.7.3**. The ESM does, however, warn Inspectors not to put the cart before the horse:

> 'The important point to remember though is that the presence or absence of these rights does not necessarily determine whether a worker is employed or

self-employed. On the contrary, it is the employment status (and the length of the contract) which determines whether the worker is entitled to many of these rights.' (ESM 1045)

Helpfully, the Manual points out that paid leave under the Working Time Regulations should be ignored when assessing status, see ESM 1046. Similarly, an entitlement to the Minimum Wage is 'unlikely to be a factor that will tip the balance to a contract of service' (ESM 1047).

7.4.10 Intention of the parties

The Revenue accept that the intention of the parties is the deciding factor if all other are equal, see **5.2.4** and *Tax Bulletin* 45:

'The intention can be decisive where the relationship is ambiguous and where the other factors are neutral.'

Helpfully, the Manual cites the unreported case of *WF and RK Swan (Hellenic) Ltd v The Secretary of State for Social Services* [1983] QBD, which found that tour couriers were independent contractors because this was the declared intention of the parties, and the other factors were equally balanced (ESM 1101). They also, correctly, warn against labelling a relationship as self-employed when the facts point in the opposite direction, see **5.2.5**.

In the context of the hypothetical contract, the Manual makes the very useful comment that:

'Where a case is borderline, mutuality of intention will remove any ambiguity about the employment status. As indicated in the examples of Gordon, Henry and Charlotte [see **25.3**], it should be assumed that there would have been mutual intention for self-employment when deciding whether IR35 applies. Although the intention of the parties may not have been expressed, bearing in mind that the engagement is with an intermediary rather than an individual you should assume that there was a mutual intention for a contract for services. Therefore in borderline cases the opinion should be that IR35 does not apply.' (ESM 3286)

7.4.11 Business organisation

In testing whether a worker should 'pass' the *Lorimer* business organisation test (**7.4.1**), the Revenue ask whether he:

'Has a business-like approach to obtaining and organising his/her engagements and incurs expenditure in this area of a type not normally associated with employment (for example provision of office accommodation, office equipment, etc.).' (ESM 1093)

This actually suggests rather more structure than was in place either for the session musicians (see **7.4.2**), or for Lorimer. The personal service worker should thus satisfy the requirements if he simply has a business bank account; takes bookings; confirms them; and keeps appropriate records. Lorimer did no more than this.

7.4.12 Part and parcel of the organisation

The ESM accepts that 'the Courts have played down the "part and parcel" test since it was first introduced and little reliance should be placed on it', see ESM 516 and **6.7.7**. This is reiterated in the longer discussion at ESM 1081, which says that 'this test is usually unhelpful when cases on the border are at issue'. In so far as it is relevant, the Manual explains that:

> 'Sometimes it is obvious that the worker is carrying on business outside and separate from the business of the engager. For example, a marketing expert who gives advice on specific problems from time to time in return for a fee, or a mechanic based outside the firm with a contract to maintain or repair the firm's equipment. In both cases the worker provides services for the firm and is not an integral part of it. Similarly, a building firm needs the services of plasterers but that alone does not make them part and parcel of the engager's business.' (ESM 516)

On the other hand:

> 'Where a worker is required to wear a firm's uniform, which is provided by the engager, or represents himself or herself to customers as a member of the engager's business then these are pointers to employment. This would also apply where a worker has management responsibilities for employees of the engager.'

These examples are both correct: uniforms and being part of the hierarchy are indicators of employment. However they are not definitive: Mr Tanton was self-employed even though he wore a uniform, see **6.5.2**. Although few contractors will have 'management responsibilities for employees of the engager', where they do they may still, like Lorimer, be doing so as part of the delivery of a professional skill to the organisation with which they have contracted.

7.4.13 Notice and termination

As discussed at **6.7.4** and **9.14**, this factor is inconclusive on its own. Lack of a notice period is indicative of self-employment, but its existence does not necessarily indicate employment. The Revenue accept this, see ESM 1085.

They do however focus on the negative – that the absence of a right of dismissal does not mean that the worker is necessarily self-employed – and quote Cooke J. in *Market Investigations Ltd v Minister of Social Security* [1968] 3 All ER 732 in their support. They overlook the more recent case in the other direction, *McManus v Griffiths* [1997] 70 TC 218, see **6.7.4**, where the judge held that the existence of a notice period was neutral.

7.5 Case studies

In *Tax Bulletin* 28 the Revenue included three worked examples of subcontractors: a general labourer classified as Schedule E, a plasterer who was held to be in business on his own account, and a bricklayer who was borderline, but marginally Schedule E, see **25.3**.

In *Tax Bulletin* 45 they followed the same model, with a further three case studies:

(a) Gordon, an IT consultant who works as part of the client's payroll team. Gordon would have been Schedule E had he worked directly for the client, and thus falls within the personal services rules, see **25.3.2**;

(b) Henry, a consultant engineer who would be classified as Schedule D, see **25.3.3**;

(c) Charlotte, who is borderline and just succeeds in falling outside IR35, see **25.3.4**.

These case studies can be found at Chapter 25, and demonstrate a practical and balanced approach to applying the status tests in the given situations.

7.6 Standard agency contracts

In *Tax Bulletin* 45 the Revenue commented on what they called 'standard contracts':

'The terms of contracts used by service company workers who obtain engagements through agencies tend to be of a standard form. Such contracts typically require the worker to work on the client's premises, use the client's equipment, work standard hours, be paid at an hourly rate and be subject to a high level of control. In such cases, the opinion of the Revenue about the engagement is likely to be that it would be employment.

Where a worker is engaged on this type of contract for a period of one month or more, and cannot demonstrate a recent history of work including engagements which have the characteristics of self-employment ... then we will say that the engagement would have been employment and therefore be covered by the new rules. Where the contract is for less than a month, then, although the engagement may still have been one of employment, the status position will be considered on a case by case basis.'

There were however two important exceptions:

- Where the standard contract forms part of a wider picture which, taken together, suggests self-employment, they accepted that in this situation the standard contract alone will not be decisive; and

- Where the engagement is *for a very short time* (as was the case in *Lorimer*) then the individual may be able to make a case for self-employment.

This advice on standard contracts was heavily criticised by Mr Justice Burton in the judicial review case:

'But, particularly given the fact that, at any rate at present, a contract on standard terms may or may not be imposed by an agency, or may be applicable not by reference to a particular assignment, but on an ongoing basis, and may actually bear no relationship to the (non-contractual) interface between the client and the service contractor, such documents can only form a part, albeit obviously an important part, of the picture. It is, in my judgment, inappropriate that there should be in the February Guidance ... that it is only where a contract in the agency's standard terms is for less than a month that the "status position will be considered on a case by case basis".' (*R v CIR (oao Professional Contractors Group Ltd)* [2001] STC 629)

Subsequently the Manual was updated with the addition of ESM 3284 which quotes from the above paragraph. However, despite using the judge's words, the Revenue does not draw the obvious conclusion that its earlier guidance was misleading. The wording of ESM 3287 almost exactly mirrors the *Tax Bulletin* 45:

'The terms of contracts used by service company workers who obtain engagements through agencies tend to be of a standard form. Such contracts typically require the worker to:

- work on the client's premises
- use the client's equipment
- work standard hours
- be paid at an hourly rate, and
- be subject to a right of control

In such cases, the opinion about the engagement is likely to be that it would be employment.'

Either the Revenue have merely paid lip-service to the judge's view, or else the retention of ESM 3287 reflects careless editing. It thus remains unclear whether the Revenue are, or are not, applying their original guidance on standard contracts – but anyone who considers that he has been subject to this standard treatment should be prepared to argue for individual 'case-by-case' treatment, as recommended by Mr Justice Burton.

7.7 Status reviews

7.7.1 Revenue commitment

The Revenue have for many years had a public commitment, set out in IR56, to provide guidance and, if requested, a written decision, on employment status. This opinion is given in line with the guidelines set out in Code of Practice 10 (COP 10).

This has now been extended by a more formal IR35 opinion process. As at June 2000, over 1,200 contracts had been submitted to the Revenue, and it was confirmed in the House of Commons that 53 per cent were found to be within IR35, and 47 per cent outside it (*Hansard*, 6 June 2000). This is encouraging, even allowing for the fact that the sample may be biased in favour of those who think they probably 'pass' IR35.

Following comments from Mr Justice Burton in the judicial review, the ESM now asks Inspectors to 'adopt a sensitive and co-operative approach' when carrying out this review work. They are reminded that they are providing a 'customer service' and not an enquiry into the taxpayer (ESM 3283). There has also been formal confirmation that seeking an opinion does not make a subsequent compliance review more likely, see FAQ Compliance 2.

7.7.2 Draft and framework contracts

In *Tax Bulletin* 45 the Revenue say categorically that 'an opinion will only be given on signed contracts and not on draft agreements'. At paragraph 129, the

161

ESM explains that requests for opinions on draft contracts present three main problems:

- If the Inspector decides that the worker is an employee, the worker may return with a succession of fresh proposals. There is a risk that the Revenue will be drawn into a time-consuming attempt to get the worker classed as self-employed;

- Only one party to a proposed arrangement may ask for the Revenue's opinion. But it takes two to make a contract and the Inspector may find later that the other person takes a different view about the facts;

- The terms of the proposed arrangement may not be the same as the reality when the work starts.

However, the Manual also indicates that an Inspector may be prepared to comment informally on hypothetical cases when he is satisfied that the parties genuinely need to find out in advance where they are likely to stand and provided all the following conditions are satisfied:

- The contract is in writing and either contains or is accompanied by sufficient detail to give the Revenue a reasonable understanding of what the job entails and how the worker is to go about it;

- The contract shows who is engaging the worker. Inspectors are advised not to deal with contracts drawn up 'without a particular business in mind';

- The contract is for a new business or a type of worker new to the business. When an 'employer' proposes to change the status of existing employees the Revenue will only comment when the changes have been implemented.

Any such advance opinion will be in writing and provisional; it can only be relied upon where the contract is 'fully acted upon in practice' and there are no 'oral or implied conditions' which were not made known to the Revenue. Unsurprisingly, the Inspector is not allowed to 'suggest how the contract might be altered to achieve the desired status' (ESM 129).

The same concern about unsigned contracts comes through in the section on framework documents and standard agreements:

> 'An accountant or agency may ask you to give an opinion on a standard contract to be used by a number of their clients. You should not agree to give an opinion in such circumstances. The opinion on a particular contract will depend upon the precise terms and conditions of the particular engagement in question and personal factors may also have to be taken into account.

You should also not give opinions on umbrella agreements. These are agreements that set out the terms and conditions that will apply at some future date should the two parties enter into a working relationship. They are not contracts in their own right. Any opinion will depend upon the actual contractual relationship when a binding agreement is entered into.' (ESM 3289)

There is, however, room for greater Revenue flexibility here. If the draft agreement has clear terms that take it outside IR35, there is no mischief in the Revenue confirming that this is the case. The terms can be overridden by other factors, particularly in the context of the IR35 hypothetical contract, but where this is not the case the worker (and perhaps in due course the client, from an employment law perspective, see **21.3**) can take comfort from the use of a standard 'pass' contract.

A similar point was made by Professor Freedman in her book *Employed and Self-employed:*

'The reluctance of the Inland Revenue to advise on hypothetical situations is understandable, but workers and their engagers need to know in advance how workers will be treated for tax purposes in order to cost contracts and agree fees.'

Mr Justice Burton also encouraged the Revenue to agree new standard contracts which would make it clear whether someone was inside or outside IR35. He said: 'Clearly some uncertainty could be resolved by the drafting, agreement and approval of a series of acceptable new standard forms.'

This is already the case with actors: an Equity contract is accepted as Schedule D by the Revenue, see **20.2.2** and **8.5.2**. However the Revenue have so far been reluctant to provide this help to others affected by the complexity of the case law.

7.7.3 Contract opinion paperwork

The paperwork required for obtaining an opinion was set out in the February 2001 *Tax Bulletin* and in FAQ General 4. It is also now possible to submit documents electronically, see the Revenue website and the 2002 Employer's pack.

To obtain an opinion the following should be sent to the Revenue:

(a) Copies of any contracts involved in the relationship;

(b) The worker's National Insurance number, the company's Inland Revenue reference number and the company's postcode. Workers in the TV and

Radio field should put 'TV' instead of the postcode. Workers in the film industry should replace postcode with 'FILM';

(c) Details of someone who can speak on behalf of the client, whom the Revenue can contact and also details of how they can speak to the worker;

(d) Any other information relevant to the particular engagement when submitting the contract. This might include, but not be limited to:

    (i) details of how the engagement was obtained and the recruitment procedure together with a copy of any adverts for the work in question;

    (ii) a description of the nature of the services to be performed together with any job or work specifications for the contract;

    (iii) copies of any tenders made by the intermediary;

    (iv) details of any additional contractual terms not included within the written contracts, whether oral, written or implied;

    (v) details of how and who allocates the work and the role the worker plays in the client's organisation i.e., does he/she work alone or as part of a team.

7.7.4 Revenue questions

Having received the information from the worker, the Revenue say that:

> 'We will often not be able to give you an opinion based solely on the contracts and may have to ask you for further information about the working relationship. This may mean that we will have to speak to the worker and to someone representing the client.' (*Tax Bulletin February 2001*)

This issue is explored in more detail by ESM 3292 (inserted in June 2001):

> 'Where a contract is submitted for a written opinion on whether it is covered by the legislation and:
>
> - some of the terms are ambiguous or unclear so you cannot provide an opinion; or
>
> - it does not appear to be comprehensive; or
>
> - you have doubts about one or more of the terms
>
> you will need to make further enquiries. The extent and nature of those enquiries will depend upon the particular case.
>
> For example, in some cases a telephone call to the worker may be sufficient to resolve a simple query. However, in others, you may need to make a more

extensive review which could include obtaining a copy of the contract between the client and the agency and talking to the various parties to the agreements in the relationship.

The extent of any enquiries will be very much a matter of personal judgement. However, where there is more than one intermediary to the relationship, for example an agency is involved, you may need to see a copy of the contract between the client and the agency in order to obtain a full appreciation of the arrangements and talk to a client contact. This will be important where you believe that a contract may have been framed in a particular way to avoid being caught by the legislation, for example with a substitution clause.'

If contact is made with the client, ESM 525 gives a summary of the questions which might be asked in order to establish the nature of the relationship. This section of the Manual has in some cases been used to write comprehensive and very demanding letters to clients. However this would seem to be in breach of Revenue guidelines:

'The notes below are intended to help you to establish the facts at an interview. They must not be issued to the engager, worker or adviser as a questionnaire to be completed. They are not an exhaustive list of issues to be considered in every case. Not all of the issues will apply in every case and some cases will call for further or different lines of questioning. They are intended as a source of ideas only and should therefore be used flexibly and thoughtfully … the preferred option is to ask general open questions which themselves lead to the answers on some of the issues listed below.'

Where an agency is involved, the guidance is further expanded by ESM 3295, which is one of the more bewildering sections of the Manual. The first four paragraphs take a fairly straightforward position:

'Before you can give an opinion on a contract, you may need to see a third party contract. This is most likely to be the case where the contract has been obtained through an agency. In such cases, as well as there being a contract between the service company and the agency there will be a contract between the agency and the client.

You may need to see the contract between the client and the agency where the service company contract does not appear to be comprehensive, is couched only in very general terms or you are concerned about some of the clauses in it. In the latter case this may be because you want to confirm the position regarding a right of substitution.

In such cases you should ask the worker to provide you with a copy of the contract between the third parties before giving an opinion. The service company will not be a party to the third party contract and may not have a copy of that contract, or access to a copy. If so then you should ask for the worker to arrange for a copy of the contract to be sent to you. Alternatively, you may ask for authority to approach the client or agency in order to obtain a copy of the contract.

Where the worker refuses to co-operate by arranging for a copy of the third party contract to be provided you should inform him or her that you will not be able to provide an opinion on the engagement.'

In other words, the agency contract is likely to be relevant as it provides the client's perspective on the hypothetical contract. If the worker refuses to approach the agent or client for a copy of the contract, then the Revenue cannot give an opinion, as only one side of the hypothetical contract has been made available.

However the following three paragraphs were added in June 2001, and harmonise poorly with the rest of the section:

'The third party contracts are what govern the relationship between the client and the agency. They are often lengthy commercial documents and many of the clauses will not be relevant to determining the employment status under IR35. Sight of the third party contract is, therefore, not always going to add much to the overall picture.

The worker does not normally have access to the third party agreement since he or she is not a party to it. If the service company defaults on its agreement, then the agency is liable to the client and not the worker. In order to protect the agency's interests you would expect any relevant terms and conditions to be reflected in the contract between the service company and the agency. For example, if the client wants to be able to control the worker and stipulates this in the agreement with the worker you would expect the agency would want to make sure this was included in the contract with the service company.

Whilst it is preferable to have a full picture of the full range of contracts it is not always essential to see the third party contract. If you are unable to obtain sight of the third party agreement then you should base any opinion on the information provided by the worker about what he/she understands to be the full terms and conditions of the working relationship.'

Some of the statements made here are surprisingly optimistic, albeit helpful to the contractors. It is unfortunately not the case that 'relevant terms and conditions [of the client/agency contract] are reflected in the contract between the service company and the agency' – in practice, there can be wide and worrying variations between the two.

However the main issues arising are as follows:

- Will the Revenue provide an opinion based only on the contractor's evidence, and without anything from the client, such as the contract with the agency? The answer appears to be no, if the worker is not co-operating with the Revenue, and yes, if the worker does his best, but cannot get the agency or client to provide their contract;

- Secondly, if an opinion is given without access to the client's perspective, can this be relied upon if subsequently the third party contract gives a different view? The Revenue have confirmed to the author that they will only be bound by this opinion if it reflects the reality of the arrangements. Any opinion provided without taking the client's perspective into account is thus of very limited use.

If neither the contractor nor the Revenue can obtain the third party contract, the contractor should seek other means of establishing the client's view of the relationship, see **7.7.5** below. This may, in any event, provide a better summary of the position than the agency contract, which may use standard terms, see **7.6.**

7.7.5 The PCG Questionnaire

One alternative way of obtaining Revenue clearance of a contract is to use the standard client confirmation letters available on the client section of the PCG website (http://www.pcgroup.org.uk). The use of a confirmation letter is designed to pre-empt any Revenue questions by asking the client to confirm the position in advance.

7.7.6 'Pass' and 'Fail' letters

The ESM sets out standard 'pass' and 'fail' letters, both for normal status cases and for those potentially within IR35. The standard letters for the former are at ESM 110 and ESM 111. In each there is a section inviting the Inspector to set out his reasoning. This is left open: 'Insert your explanation here setting out both the tax and NICs position. Your explanation can be as long as necessary.'

Until the March 2002 edition of the ESM, the IR35 letters were much more prescriptive, listing a number of factors which could have caused the engagement to pass or fail IR35 (ESM 3299 and ESM 3300). There were a number of problems with this approach:

1. Many of the points made in the 'fail' letter were not in fact decisive indicators of employment;

2. There was a risk that the template letter would tempt Revenue officials to short-cut the necessary study of the facts and the case law;

3. It also suggested a standard approach rather than encouraging the official to consider each application individually.

The revised 2002 edition of the Manual removed the lists of possible pass/fail reasons, so the Inspector is required to come to his own conclusion based on the facts. This is a major improvement and very much to be welcomed. It will however be interesting to see whether the old form standard 'pass' and 'fail' letters continue to be received by contractors despite the fact that they have been withdrawn from official Revenue guidance.

7.7.7 Relying on the opinion

The Revenue's opinion process came in for some robust criticism from Mr Justice Burton in the judicial review:

> 'In one case illustrated by the evidence, accountants on behalf of a service company had correspondence with the Inland Revenue, seeking guidance as to whether a contract which that company had entered into fell within the provisions of IR35. The result of the accountants' enquiry was that two different inspectors wrote, quite independently, to the accountants a month apart, without reference one to the other, giving entirely inconsistent answers: the one who gave the answer that IR35 would apply relied upon an entirely erroneous construction of the contract in question.'

If (as in this case) the Revenue give an opinion in the taxpayer's favour which is later found to be incorrect, can it be relied upon? If the requirements of Code of Practice 10 have been fulfilled, then the answer is yes for the past, but the position may be amended for the future, see ESM 112. COP10 states that: 'Apart from changes in the law, we will only withdraw a ruling if we discover that the information you gave us on application, or during subsequent correspondence, was either incorrect or incomplete.'

If the worker receives an opinion that he fails IR35, but this is later found to be wrong, is there any redress against the Revenue? Again, COP10 provides the answer. It says that:

> 'If someone wants to seek compensation in respect of incorrect advice we have given, then they must write to their local tax office, and:

- say why they were asking for advice;
- provide all relevant facts in an accurate format;
- show that they have actually received advice from us; which has led them to act in a manner determined solely by that advice; and
- suffered an actual financial loss (or a greater tax liability) as a consequence.' (see FAQ Compliance 5)

For example, an individual who would otherwise have received most of his income as dividends, but who suffered PAYE and NICs on a deemed income calculation following Revenue advice that he was within IR35, could argue that he had suffered a greater tax liability and NICs because of the Revenue's opinion.

7.7.8 Alternatives to seeking a Revenue view

The position is clear

The Revenue themselves suggest that many people will not need to seek an opinion. They say that:

> 'In most cases the question of whether a worker would have been an employee of the client if engaged directly will be obvious from a careful consideration of the terms and conditions under which the services are provided and the surrounding facts.' (ESM 3287)

Reasonable steps

The Revenue's IR35 penalty statement (**16.4.2**) states that if the service company in its capacity as employer:

> 'Acts prudently by taking all reasonable steps to understand and ensure that [its] intermediary service company or partnership meets its obligations under the service company legislation, no penalty will be imposed.'

The PCG sought to clarify what was meant by 'reasonable steps'. They consulted the Revenue before issuing a statement setting out that it means one or more of the following:

(a) Taking advice from a qualified professional such as a member of the Chartered Institute of Taxation, a Chartered Accountant, or a lawyer. If advice is taken from others, it is recommended that the individual satisfy himself that 'they have adequate experience of the tax and employment law relevant to IR35, and for your own protection you may also want to ensure that they have adequate Professional Indemnity Cover';

(b) Seeking Inland Revenue clearance, see **7.7.1ff**; or

(c) Satisfying yourself of your position by a review of the legislation and your own position. This would include

    (i) Familiarising yourself with the relevant legislation; and

    (ii) Reviewing guidance as to the main status tests and issues relating to employed and self-employed status; and

    (iii) Considering where you stand with regard to IR35 by looking at both your current contract(s) and your general business and personal circumstances;

    (iv) Documenting what your view is of your status and the key factors that lead you to this conclusion. The PCG advise that: 'This "self assessment" approach must be carried out objectively. Mere window dressing will of course be insufficient.'

7.8 Challenging the Revenue view

7.8.1 General

If the Revenue have given an opinion under **7.7** above, and the service company disagrees, then it can either:

- Satisfy itself of its view either by taking independent advice under option (a) of **7.7.8** above or by taking other reasonable steps under option (c). It is important to document the reasons for the position taken so that these can be deployed if the company is subject to a PAYE audit; or

- Take the matter to appeal.

If the latter route is chosen, the first step is to ask the Revenue for a formal decision under s8 Social Security Contributions (Transfer of Functions, etc) Act 1999, see SI 2000/727 reg 6(4).

Before a Section 8 decision is made, the opinion given to the service company will be reviewed by the Revenue's Personal Tax section, see ESM 3296. Assuming that they agree with the status inspector, the service company will then be sent a Notice of Decision (form DAA1) which may be accompanied by an explanatory letter.

The company will also receive 'A Guide to your Notice of Decision' (DAA2), which explains what action the company should take if it does not agree with the decision. The Guide contains an appeal form (form DAA3) which can be used to make an appeal. Once the formal decision is made and the notice is issued, the company has 30 days from the date of issue of the notice in which to appeal. Unless the parties come to a prior agreement the appeal will be heard by the General or Special Commissioners (*Tax Bulletin* June 1999).

As well as this formal determination route, an IR35 case may also reach the courts if the Revenue discover that a service company has been treating its worker(s) as outside IR35, but considers this to be incorrect. If the service company disagrees, and refuses to settle the liability, the Revenue may issue a determination under SI 1993/744 reg 49. The company can then appeal to the Commissioners.

It is recommended, before taking a case to the courts, that the service company obtain professional advice to ensure that:

- The strength of the worker's case is assessed;

- All available facts and arguments are mustered as soon as possible;

- No misleading facts or suggestions are made to the Revenue;

- The process is focused, so costs are kept to a minimum.

The first IR35 case to be reported, *Battersby v Campbell* [2001] SpC 287, see **8.6.2**, clearly demonstrates the consequences of going into the court room without sufficient preparation. In *Battersby* the taxpayer was unrepresented, and quoted no legal precedents in support of his argument that he was outside IR35. The Revenue, in contrast, cited 13 different cases.

7.8.2 Questions of law and fact

The courts have debated for some time whether employment status was a question of law, a question of fact, or a mixed question of both law and fact. This is important because it is only possible to appeal to a higher court on a question of law, not a question of fact.

The current view is that it is a matter of law, but that it involves matters of degree and fact which should be decided at the first stage of the legal process (*O'Kelly v Trusthouse Forte plc* [1983] 3 WLR 605, see **5.6.2**). In a tax case this first stage is the General or Special Commissioners, in an employment law case it is the Employment Tribunal.

Exceptionally, where the case turns on the true construction of a legal document, this will be a question of law which can be referred to a higher court, see *McManus v Griffiths* [1997] 70 TC 218 and *Davies v Presbyterian Church of Wales* [1986] AC 508. This is unlikely to be the case with a status issue under the personal services legislation, because Schedule 12, para 1(4) specifically provides that the written terms are only part of the 'circumstances' to be considered, see **5.1**.

The facts which are decided at the Commissioners cannot be interfered with by a higher court. Lord Griffiths in *Lee Ting Sang* (**8.3.1**) said that this was a pragmatic approach because of:

> 'The difficulty of devising a conclusive test to resolve the question, and the threat of the appellate courts being crushed by the weight of appeals if the many borderline cases were considered to be questions of law.'

7.8.3 Importance of agreeing the facts

Given the general proposition that determination of status involves matters of degree and fact which are decided by the court of first instance, it is vital that all relevant facts are put to the Commissioners. A higher court can only change the decision of the Commissioners if it can show that either:

- No reasonable Commissioner could have come to that decision on those facts; or

- The Commissioner made an error in the legal interpretation of those facts (*Edwards v Bairstow* [1956] AC 14 as applied by the Court of Appeal in *Nethermere (St Neots) Ltd v Gardner* [1984] IRLR 240, see **5.4.2**, and *McLeod v Hellyer Brothers Ltd* [1987] IRLR 232, see **5.5.2**.

In the *Lorimer* case, see **8.2.1**, the decision of the Special Commissioner that Lorimer was self-employed was upheld in the High Court and Court of Appeal. In the High Court Mummery J. said, commenting on the process:

> 'The Appellate Court will not interfere with the conclusion of the fact-finding tribunal where the decision as to the true nature of the taxpayer's arrangements comes within what has been described as the "band of possible reasonable decisions". The Appellate Court recognises that there are borderline or grey areas in which tribunals, properly instructed on the law and facts, can legitimately and reasonably arrive at different conclusions.'

This was put even more strongly by Lord Donaldson in the *O'Kelly* case, see **5.3.2**:

> 'The appellate court ... may well have a shrewd suspicion, or gut reaction, that it would have reached a different decision, but it must never forget that

this may be because it thinks that it would have found or weighed the facts differently. Unpalatable though it may be on occasion, it must loyally accept the conclusions of fact with which it is presented and, accepting those conclusions, it must be satisfied that there *must* have been a misdirection on a question of law before it can intervene.'

This serves to emphasise the vital importance of the first stage in the legal process, and the critical importance of the facts and arguments presented to the Commissioners. In the *Express and Echo* case discussed at **6.5.2** above, the judge said that further facts brought up on appeal should be ignored, despite the fact that Mr Tanton:

'Did not appreciate that there was such emphasis by the appellant on personal service by him as a requirement of a contract of employment, otherwise he would have given (further) evidence to the chairman at the Industrial Tribunal hearing. But no such evidence was given to the chairman, and … accordingly, that (further evidence) cannot help Mr Tanton.'

7.8.4 The legal process

It is beyond the scope of this book to explain either how best to argue a case before the courts, or the legal process which has to be followed as it progresses from the lower courts through the High Court and Court of Appeal to the House of Lords. However, before beginning a lengthy and expensive legal battle, it is worth bearing in mind the words of Lord Griffiths in *Lee Ting Sang* (**8.3.1**) that:

'There will be many borderline cases in which similarly instructed minds will come to different conclusions.'

In other words, the result in a difficult status case may go either way. One comfort to taxpayers is that the Revenue are in the same uncertain position. This is despite the confident words in their *Decision Maker's Guide to Working Families Tax Credits* at paragraph 22005 that:

'The decision maker decides whether a person is an employed or a self-employed earner. The decision maker should rarely have difficulty in deciding which category will apply.'

8 Status cases and IR35

8.1 Introduction

This chapter looks at a number of recent court decisions on status in the context of IR35, and gives some guidance on how they apply to personal services workers.

While some workers will clearly be self-employed, and others equally clearly employees, a third group occupies the grey area in the middle. In the immortal words of Mr. Justice Rowlatt, it is necessary 'to formulate some line of cleavage', so that those in the grey area are divided into Schedule D and Schedule E. This is no easy process, as Mummery J. commented:

> 'How narrow the line often is between, on the one hand, carrying on a business on one's own account with a succession of regular or casual clients and, on the other hand, being in a state of discontinuous employment with a succession of different employers. It is particularly difficult to draw the line in those cases where a person claims that his business consists of providing only his personal services and skill to another, valuable though those skills may be.' (*Hall v Lorimer* [1993] 66 TC 349, see **8.2.1**)

It may not always be the same line, since, although there are agreed status tests, their relative importance varies. In *Walls v Sinnett* [1986] 60 TC 150, Vinelott J. said:

> 'It is in my judgement, quite impossible in a field where a very large number of factors have to be weighed, to gain any real assistance by looking at the facts of another case and comparing them one by one to see what facts are common, what are different and what particular weight is given by another tribunal to the common facts. The facts as a whole must be looked at, and what may be compelling in one case in the light of all the facts may not be compelling in the context of another case.'

Thus, although it is possible and necessary to consider the status tests one by one, as was done in Chapter 6, it is also important to see them in context. This is because reviewing status tests is like any other analytic process. Dissecting five hundred football matches demonstrates what leads to glorious victory and what to ignominious defeat. Combing *Macbeth* for character, imagery, and concepts of celestial harmony explains why it is a dramatic success. But for real understanding, matches have to be played and plays watched. It is the same with case law: to appreciate how the different status tests work they must be seen in the context of an individual's situation.

This chapter reviews a number of recent court decisions and applies them specifically to IR35. It identifies some of the key factors which are relevant for personal services workers who are on the line between employment and self-employment.

8.2 Recent court decisions I: the professional

8.2.1 *Hall v Lorimer*

Hall v Lorimer [1993] 66 TC 349 was a milestone in the evolution of the status test. Ian Lorimer was a freelance professional in the TV industry, with no equipment and little business risk, who was held by the Courts to be self-employed. The reason the case is important for personal services workers is because Mr Lorimer passed few of the traditional status tests. The Revenue argued that he was an employee because he:

(a) Provided no equipment;

(b) Hired no staff;

(c) Ran no financial risk apart from the risk of bad debts and of being unable to find work;

(d) Had no responsibility for investment in or management of the programmes on which he was working;

(e) Had no control over the time, place or duration of each programme on which he worked; this was entirely in the hands of the production company.

Although Mr Lorimer was able to rebut some of these points to some degree – for instance, the court held that he ran greater financial risk than an employee – nevertheless they are in substance correct. He was however held to be self-employed, and the Revenue lost the case, despite having argued strongly that:

> 'All he is doing is contracting from time to time to put his work skills at the disposal of another for reward, that is not a business at all: it is the very essence of employment under a contract of service.'

Thus if the personal services worker's situation is substantially the same as that of Ian Lorimer, he too can make a case for self-employment. To succeed, he must show that he is selling a skill to a number of different clients, preferably for short periods; and that he has some rudimentary booking, invoicing and recording procedures.

8.2.2 Key factors leading to the decision

Skill is necessary, but not sufficient

Mr Lorimer was a vision mixer, and the court devoted some time to hearing what this involved:

> 'A vision mixer's function is skilled. A programme may be televised "live" or it may be rehearsed, recorded and shown as if it were live. A mixer has to have a sense of timing, a feeling for mood, anticipation, a feeling for music and dexterity in operating equipment. He is a type of editor. In a live show he has only one chance to get it right.'

However, merely being skilled is not enough to prevent classification as an employee, see *Cassidy v Ministry of Health* [1951] 1 AER 574 (**6.6.3**) where a surgeon was held to be employed by the health authority despite clearly being a highly specialist worker.

This principle that the skill alone is not enough was accepted in the *Lorimer* case. Lord Nolan said that:

> 'Mr Goldsmith (for the Revenue) submitted that the degree of skill involved in the work cannot alone be decisive. Again I agree. A brain surgeon may very well be an employee.'

Number and variety of clients

Mr Lorimer had numerous very short engagements with 22 active clients. Although in his first year 48 per cent of his engagements were with five companies, this percentage fell over the next three years as his business expanded and he developed a wider client base. Each engagement usually lasted one or two days, with the longest being for eight. The fact that he was 'independent of a particular paymaster for the financial exploitation of his talents' was found to be one of the main reasons why he was classified as Schedule D.

This confirms that when deciding whether a worker is employed or self-employed it is not simply a question of looking at a single contract, but the 'whole pattern' of his engagements. This is also true when deciding the nature of the hypothetical contract between worker and client which lies at the heart of the personal services legislation, see **5.1.1**.

Mutuality of obligation

The issue of mutuality of obligation was discussed at length in **5.3** above. Although mutuality was not a focus of the *Lorimer* case, it was agreed that:

> 'There (is no) question of an "umbrella" contract. Mr Lorimer can accept engagements or not as he wishes; similarly production companies are free to engage Mr Lorimer's services or not as they choose.'

The Revenue tried to argue for a succession of small employment contracts, see **5.3.3**, but this was rejected by the judge. Thus it is reasonable to conclude that the court considered there was insufficient mutuality of obligation between Mr Lorimer and his various clients for there to be a contract of employment.

Business structure

Mr Lorimer's business structure was rudimentary. In addition to having a business bank account:

> 'Bookings were usually made by telephone to his home, where he had an office, and were confirmed by letter which often stated the date, rate of pay, place of work and time. No formal written conditions were made. VAT was charged, Lorimer having registered for VAT from 1 February 1985.'

This was to held to be a reasonable business structure for certain types of self-employment. Lord Nolan said that 'a self-employed author working from home or an actor or a singer may earn his living without any of the normal trappings of a business'.

Financial risk

The Revenue tried to argue that Mr Lorimer's financial risk was inadequate, and thus indicative of employment. Their barrister said that:

> 'The risk he runs in not working for one production company under a long-term contract is that run by any employee who chooses to work on a casual basis. He runs the risk of being unable to find employment, of being unemployed and unpaid.'

However the court held that in fact he ran more risk than an employee. For example:

- He could and did lose money when a client became insolvent;

- Some clients were bad payers and made him wait up to three months before paying him.

However Mummery J., in the High Court, held that even this level of risk was not a necessary precondition for someone to be self-employed. Quoting *O'Kelly v Trusthouse Forte plc* [1983] 3 AER 456 (see **5.3.2**), he said that (the author's italics):

> 'The importance of that case is that the Court of Appeal held that it was quite possible for a fact-finding tribunal, properly instructed on the facts and the law, to conclude that a person was in business on his own account and not a party to a succession of contracts of employment *when all that he supplied was his own services, without providing any equipment or having any risk of loss of prospective profit.*'

Equipment

It was accepted by both sides in the case that:

> 'All of Mr Lorimer's work as a vision mixer is done at the studios owned or hired by the production company on equipment owned or supplied by the studio company ... Mr Lorimer does not provide or pay for any of the equipment which he uses in his work ... That equipment is complex and expensive and is provided by the studio company to the production company.'

The Revenue argued that the fact that he provided no equipment was one of the reasons why he was an employee, but the Special Commissioner (who was quoted with approval by Lord Nolan) gave this short shrift:

> 'It is said that Mr Lorimer provides no equipment (i.e., he has no tools), he provides no "work place" or "workshop" where the contract is to be performed, he provides no capital for the production, he hires no staff for it. No, he does not. But *that is not his business.*'

The judge was therefore saying that the provision of equipment or otherwise was irrelevant in deducing whether Mr Lorimer was employed or self-employed. His business was selling his skill – the fact that he had no equipment was immaterial. This is a very significant development for professionals, who commonly work on expensive equipment provided by their engagers.

Opportunity of profit

Not only could Mr Lorimer suffer greater losses than an employee, he could also make profits. The judge held that:

'He has the opportunity of profiting from being good at being a vision mixer. According to his reputation, so there will be a demand for his services for which he will be able to charge accordingly. The more efficient he is at running the business of providing his services, the greater is his prospect of profit.'

Expenses

Lord Nolan considered that the expenses Mr Lorimer incurred were 'quite different in nature and scale from those likely to be incurred by an employee', giving as an example the fact that:

'In the period from 1 February 1985 to 30 April 1986, his expenses, including the cost of running his car or otherwise travelling in the course of his work and of running his office from home, amounted to £9,250 against fees received of £32,875, though it may be that the figure for fees included some reimbursement of expenses.

Personal services workers might like to remember this when they review the expenses they can no longer deduct under the Schedule E rules – the very fact of having incurred the expense may itself be a small pointer towards self-employment! This point is in fact explicitly accepted in the Revenue's Employment Status Manual, see para 1093.

8.2.3 Conclusions

The key facts in the *Lorimer* decision are that:

(a) He was a skilled professional;

(b) He earned his living by working for a large number of different clients;

(c) There was no mutuality of obligation between him and his clients;

(d) His financial risk was slight, but more than that of an employee;

(e) He had a rudimentary business structure.

8.3 Recent court decisions II: the manual worker

8.3.1 *Lee Ting Sang v Chung Chi-Keung*

The 1990 Privy Council case of *Lee Ting Sang v Chung Chi-Keung* [1990] 2 AC 374 considered whether Mr Lee, a mason injured while chipping concrete on a building site, was an employee. Factors in favour of his self-employment were that he was a skilled artisan, his work was largely unsupervised and he worked for a number of different engagers.

However the Privy Council held he was employed because he:

(a) Provided no equipment, but used tools supplied by his engager;

(b) Hired no helpers;

(c) Had no responsibility for investment in, or management of, the work on the construction site;

(d) Did not price the job, which is normally a feature of a subcontractor with his own business;

(e) Was paid either a piece-work rate or a daily rate according to the nature of the work he was doing;

(f) Did not 'exercise any skill or judgement' but was 'simply told what to do and left to get on with it';

(g) Ran no financial risk, other than that of not finding work.

This sounds compelling, until one realises that Mr Lorimer also provided no equipment, hired no helpers and had no investment in the projects on which he worked, and that, like Mr Lorimer, Mr Lee worked for a succession of engagers. The differences between the two cases are set out below.

Opportunity of profit

Mr Lorimer could set his own rates and profit from his reputation, see **8.2.2**; Mr Lee, in contrast, was paid a rate set by the building contractor or sub-contractor for whom he worked.

Risk of loss

Although the Revenue argued that Mr Lorimer's risk of loss was insignificant, the court disagreed, see **8.2.2**. However, Mr Lee fell the other side of the line.

Lord Griffiths said that:

> 'The applicant ran no risk whatsoever save that of being unable to find employment, which is, of course, a risk faced by casual employees who move from one job to another.'

Skill and judgment

Although Mr Lee was described by the judge as 'a skilled artisan' his level of skill, in the context of the status tests, was apparently inadequate. The court held that:

> 'There was no question of his being called upon to exercise any skill or judgment as to which beams required chipping or as to the depths that they were to be cut. He was simply told what to do and left to get on with it as, for example, would a skilled turner on a lathe who was required to cut a piece of metal to certain dimensions.'

In *Lorimer*, Mr Goldsmith, the Revenue's barrister specifically distinguished the level and quality of skill exercised by the vision mixer with that of Mr Lee, saying that 'the work of Mr Lorimer, unlike that of Mr Lee Ting Sang, depended upon his own rare skill and judgement'.

Conclusion

On balance, the court in *Lee Ting Sang* found that:

> 'The picture emerges of a skilled artisan earning his living by working for more than one employer as an employee and not as a small businessman venturing into business on his own account as an independent contractor with all its attendant risks.'

This contrasts with the *Lorimer* case where the Special Commissioner said:

> 'I find that the activities of Mr Lorimer ... bear the hallmarks of a man who is in business on his own account and they outweigh substantially such factors as may be thought to militate against my conclusion that Mr Lorimer was in business on his own account.'

8.3.2 Relevance for personal services workers

The differences should be noted, because they were sufficient to make Mr Lee an employee and Mr Lorimer self-employed, despite the fact that they both worked on a number of short-term engagements for different clients:

(a) Mr Lorimer was a skilled professional, Mr Lee an artisan, and although described as 'skilled', worked at chipping concrete and sharpening chisels. The level of skill is clearly important factor in the dividing line between Schedule D and Schedule E;

(b) Although Mr Lorimer's financial risk was slight, it was greater than the simple risk of being unemployment. He could suffer bad debts as well as cash flow problems;

(c) Similarly, his opportunity for profit was greater than that of Mr Lee as he could set his rate to match his reputation, and could save money by working efficiently; Mr Lee's rate was set by his engager;

(d) Mr Lorimer had a rudimentary business structure which Mr Lee lacked.

8.3.3 Conclusion

The cases of *Lorimer* and *Lee Ting Sang* highlight the fact that the line between Schedule D and Schedule E is very fine. They also demonstrate that a professional, such as an IT contractor or journalist, may find it easier to cross the line and reach the safe haven of Schedule D than would a labour-only subcontractor with his own service company. The same point is made in *Tax Bulletin* 45, when the Revenue say that the number of engagements is a factor which:

> 'Will usually carry less weight in the case of an unskilled worker, where other factors such as the high level of control exercised by the contractor, are likely to be conclusive of employment.'

To be classified as Schedule D the unskilled worker is more likely to have to demonstrate other evidence of self-employment, such as greater risk, substitution, or the provision of significant equipment. The skilled worker has an inherently easier task.

8.4 Recent court decisions III: the special case

8.4.1 *Barnett v Brabyn*

Barnett v Brabyn [1996] 69 TC 133 contains elements which make it an attractive case to those seeking support in their arguments for self-employed status. However its facts are peculiar and those with personal services companies are advised not to rely upon it as a precedent.

Outline

Mr Barnett was a video technician working as an independent contractor with his father, who was one of two partners in a business called LTV. He filed tax returns on the basis that he was self-employed, and this was accepted by his Inspector.

However the Revenue subsequently discovered that Mr Barnett had not declared some of the money paid to him by LTV, and raised further assessments. Barnett argued that he was really an employee, and the tax liability was therefore not his, because PAYE and NIC should have been deducted by LTV. The court was made aware that he had fallen out with his father, and set up a business in competition with him.

The factors in favour of employment were that he:

(a) Was paid at an hourly rate, and had no realistic chance of making a loss;

(b) Continued to be paid when he was off sick and on holiday;

(c) Worked for no other business;

(d) Could not hire any workers without the consent of the partners;

(e) Operated entirely on the premises of the partnership and supplied no equipment;

(f) Provided no capital;

(g) Had no business bank account; and

(h) Did not submit invoices.

The factors in favour of self-employment were that:

(i) He chose his own hours of work;

(j) Both he and his father intended that he would be self-employed;

(k) Previous tax assessments had been made and accepted on a self-employed basis.

The judge held that he was self-employed, despite the number of factors which appeared to point to employment. The judge said that these 'might in an ordinary case carry some weight indicative of his status as an employee.' But he stressed the unusual facts in this case:

• Mr Barnett declined to give evidence in person, which meant that 'the findings of fact by the Commissioners are somewhat limited, and their decision had to be made on the basis of those limited findings';

- The significance of a number of the Schedule E factors 'must be very much affected by the family relationship between Mr Barnett and LTV'.

Whether the court was also affected by Mr Barnett's clear intention to avoid his own tax liability and transfer responsibility to his father, is not mentioned in the case report.

However, the judge clearly said that there were special facts in *Barnett v Brabyn*, and effectively warned against taking it as a precedent. It would thus be unwise for other taxpayers to do so.

Importance of **Barnett v Brabyn** *to personal services workers*

This case is important for two reasons. Firstly, it shows clearly that the facts and circumstances surrounding individual status tests are taken into account by the court, even to the extent of arriving at a decision which appears at odds with previous precedents.

Secondly, it reinforces the importance of looking at case law in context. Extracting status tests from individual cases is useful only up to a point, and beyond that point can be dangerously misleading.

8.5 Recent court decisions IV: the actors

8.5.1 McCowen and West

The background to the unreported case of McCowen and West is given at **20.2.2**. In 1989 the Revenue announced that it was recategorising actors who had standard Equity contracts as employees, with an amnesty for those who had been Schedule D for the previous three years (ESC A75). This blanket recategorisation was successfully challenged by Alec McCowen and Sam West in 1993, who convinced the Special Commissioners that they were self-employed.

Following this defeat the Revenue have now accepted that 'Schedule D assessment of a performer's/artist's earnings will normally be appropriate ... (they) will generally be assessable under Schedule D as a matter of law rather than concession' (IM 1810; ESM 4121–2).

8.5.2 Terms of the standard Equity contract

The following table shows relevant extracts from the Standard Equity Contract for West End theatres:

1.	Form of engagement	The Manager engages the Artist: • for the play entitled ...; • to rehearse and play the part of ....; • to perform in the chorus; • to perform in the chorus and to rehearse and play small parts as may be required by the manager; in addition to the above duties, to assist the Stage Management team.
2.	London runs and tours	The Artist agrees to perform at such theatres as the Manager shall require.
3.	Period of engagement	The engagement shall be one of the following: • For the period of rehearsal and run of the play, provided that the engagement can be terminated at or after the expiry of 12 months (15 months for musicals) by either party giving four weeks notice; the Manager shall give at least two weeks notice of termination of the run or pay the Artist at least two weeks salary in lieu of such notice; • For the period of rehearsal and thereafter until the engagement shall be terminated by either party giving to the other not less than four weeks written notice at any time after the Artist's first performance; • From (date) to (date), this period should not to be more than 12 months, or for the run of the production whichever shall be the shorter, provided that the Manager shall not give less than two weeks notice of the termination of the run.
4.	Opening date	The date rehearsals begin and the date the show opens.
5.	Rehearsal and performance salaries	This sets out the rehearsal salary and the performance salary, both of which are subject to Equity minima, and are before allowances.
6.	Payment of salary and NICs	The Artist's salary (unless based on a percentage of the gross receipts) shall be paid by cheque or BACS, or if mutually agreed, in cash, to reach the payee by the Friday of each week, provided that the Manager shall be entitled to recoup the appropriate portion of such salary for any rehearsals or performances on the ensuing Friday or Saturday from which the Artist shall have been absent.

		The Artist shall be given with every payment of salary an authentic pay advice slip countersigned by the Manager and stating the amount and nature of any deductions from salary. The slip shall constitute affirmation that the Manager intends to submit any sums due to the Inland Revenue or any other body from time to time authorised to accept such remittances.
7.	Touring allowance	If the Manager shall require the Artist to work beyond a radius of 15 miles from Charing Cross he shall pay the Artist a touring allowance.
8.	Number of performances	The Artist's salary shall cover not more than the following performances, Monday to Saturday – either eight per week if once nightly, or 12 per week if twice daily or nightly, and in any event not more than two performances per day.
9.	Understudies	This sets out the pay and other conditions if the contract is with an understudy and the understudy is called upon to stand in for the artist he or she is understudying.
10.	Manager's undertaking	The Manager confirms he is upholding various professional standards.
11.	Artist's undertaking	In accepting the Contract the Artist undertakes to perform the services required of him/her under this Contract in a diligent and competent manner, to play the parts as directed and not to insert or omit any words or business in the Artist's part not approved by the Manager and not deliberately to absent himself from any performance without the Manager's prior consent. He also undertakes to comply with the rules of any theatre at which he/she rehearses or performs and with all rules made by the Manager, in so far as they do not conflict with the terms of this Contract.
12.	Hairstyle	The Artist agrees to effect at the Manager's expense the following change to his/her hairstyle or the Artist shall not without the Manager's prior written consent change the style or colour of his/her hair after being auditioned or engaged.
13.	Agency	The Artist hereby authorises and requests the Manager to pay all moneys payable to him/her to his agent.

If the actor is operating via a limited company, the artist also gives a personal guarantee, stating that 'in consideration of the Manager entering into this Contract I hereby guarantee the compliance by X Limited of all its obligations under this Contract and I further guarantee personally to comply with all such obligations'.

8.5.3 Consideration of Equity contract terms

There are a number of surprising elements to the Equity contract. The first is that it includes none of the fundamental status tests identified in Chapter 6 – no substitution (the Manager supplies the understudies), no risk (the salary has to be paid), no hiring of others to help with the work.

The second is the extent of the Manager's control. He always has control over *how* (point 11) and *where* (point 2); he sometimes controls *what* (point 1) and *when* (point 8). The actor is not required to supply any equipment, is remunerated on a regular weekly basis and may even receive pay in lieu of notice (point 3). The engagement is likely to last a year and perhaps longer (point 3). When engaged via a service company, the personal nature of the arrangements is clear from the guarantee required.

If this contract were rewritten, substituting 'IT contractor' for 'actor', 'office' for 'theatre' and 'IT Manager' for 'Manager', would this pass the Revenue's IR35 clearance process? In the view of the author, it would not.

The question thus arises as to why the Special Commissioners decided McCowen and West (**20.2.2**) were self-employed? And why were the Revenue so convinced by the Commissioners' ruling that they did not appeal the case? One can only speculate, as the case is unreported. Some help can perhaps be gleaned from the much earlier decision of *Davies v Braithwaite* [1933] 18 TC 198, which also held that Miss Braithwaite, an actress, was within Schedule D rather than Schedule E.

The judge in *Davies v Braithwaite* said that he 'had to formulate some line of cleavage' between the two Schedules, and did so as follows:

> 'An employment as opposed to a mere engagement in the course of carrying on a profession, I do not think that is a very difficult term of distinction, though in general, perhaps it is a little difficult to apply to all cases, as every distinction is. But I would go further than that, and what I say is that it seems to me that where one finds a method of earning a livelihood which does not contemplate the obtaining of a post and staying in it, but essentially contemplates a series of engagements and moving from one to the

other – and in the case of an actor's or actress's life it certainly involves going from one to the other and not going on playing one part for the rest of his or her life, but in obtaining first one engagement and then another, and a whole series of them – then each of those engagements could not be considered an employment, but is a mere engagement in the course of exercising a profession, and every profession and every trade does involve the making of successive engagements and successive contracts and, in one sense of the word, employments.

In this case I think it is quite clear that Miss Braithwaite must fall under Schedule D because here she does not make a contract with a producer for a post. She makes a contract with a producer for the next thing she is going to do, and then with another producer, and then a third producer, and at any time she may make a record for a gramophone company or act for a film, if she likes. I think essentially whatever she does or whatever contracts she makes for the running of a play which may last a long time are nothing but incidents in the conduct of her professional career. Therefore, I think she is taxable under Schedule D.'

This case was quoted in *Hall v Lorimer*, and Lord Nolan in his final summing up said that the parallels drawn between Mr Lorimer and Miss Braithwaite were appropriate. He quoted with approval the following words of Pennycuick V-C in *Fall v Hitchen* [1972] 49 TC 433:

'I do not think that most people today would use the word 'post', which does not seem very apt to cover the countless instances of employment in the sense of a contract of service; but every word of that judgment is applicable as between the carrying on of a profession and an engagement in the course of carrying on that profession, on the one hand, and a contract of employment, on the other hand.'

Acting is one of the oldest professions, Information Technology one of the newest. But it is not unreasonable to see parallels. Many IT consultants have found:

'A method of earning a livelihood which does not contemplate the obtaining of a post and staying in it, but essentially contemplates a series of engagements and moving from one to the other ... in obtaining first one engagement and then another, and a whole series of them.'

8.5.4 TV and film workers

An interesting comparison can be drawn between actors and workers in the Film/TV industry. As explained at **20.11.2**, the Revenue send employers an annually updated list stating which types of 'behind camera' workers it considers to be self-employed. Many of those on the list who qualify as Schedule

D either supply substantial equipment or work on premises other than those provided by the engager. But in addition, a number of workers are classified as self-employed:

> 'Provided that they are engaged on a temporary, casual or freelance basis –
>
> - for a one-off production such as a feature film or a single drama or documentary, **or**
> - for less than nine months on a series or a specific strand of a programme.
>
> In exceptional circumstances the period of nine months may be extended if specific authority is sought from this office.'

Those within this category include most types of director and producer, choreographers, nurses, sculptors, scriptwriters, and publicists. In short, they are all skilled individuals exercising a profession, like Miss Braithwaite.

It thus appears that the Revenue do accept that the Miss Braithwaite model applies other than to actors, but it is equally clear that they do not accept that it is relevant, for example, to IT contractors. A representative case on this issue will have to succeed in the courts if the Miss Braithwaite principle is to be more widely accepted.

8.6 IR35 cases

8.6.1 General

At the time of writing a small number of IR35 cases have been taken to the General Commissioners, and all have been won by the Revenue. None of these have been reported.

Two cases were heard by the Special Commissioners: *Battersby v Campbell* [2001] SpC 287 and *FS Consulting Limited v McCaul* [2001] SpC 305, and the Revenue were successful on both occasions. However, the taxpayer represented himself in *Battersby*, and the barrister in *FS Consulting* did not focus on the traditional status tests. In addition, neither worker had a similar fact pattern to *Braithwaite* (see **8.5.3**), and neither was able to argue a lack of mutuality. Both cases are discussed below.

It is expected that more cases will come to court over the next two years, including one or more 'representative' cases, see **20.4.1**. It is hoped that these will explore both mutuality and *Braithwaite* as well as other status issues.

8.6.2 *Battersby*

Battersby v Campbell [2001] SpC 287 was the first IR35 case to come before the Special Commissioners. Unfortunately for those who were hoping for some useful guidance on the application of IR35 to those in the 'grey area' between Schedule D and Schedule E, the taxpayer was unrepresented and used no case law in his defence. This was in marked contrast to Revenue counsel, who supported his arguments by referring to 13 previous cases.

One of the taxpayer's main aims appears to have been to establish that 'people who supplied their services through service companies were not "tax fraudsters"'. While the Special Commissioner said she 'had much sympathy with these comments', she went on to say that IR35 had changed the rules and Battersby's company fell within the new legislation.

The reasons for this decision and that in *FS Consulting Limited v McCaul* [2001] SpC 305 are set out at **8.6.4**. The Special Commissioner in both cases was Dr Nuala Brice.

8.6.3 *FS Consulting*

Unlike *Battersby*, the contractor in *FS Consulting* was represented by a barrister. However, the latter appears to have given relatively little attention to the traditional status tests, but instead concentrated on the following arguments:

- Where an agency is involved, it is not necessary to look at the relationship between the client and the worker, but only at that between the agency and the worker;

- The aim of the legislation is to tax the worker as if the service company did not exist. If there had been no service company, the agency would have had to consider whether s134 ICTA 1988 applied (see **21.2.1**). However, because the individual was not controlled 'as to the manner' of his work, he would not have been within s134, and thus would not have been subject to the deduction of PAYE and NIC.

The first of these arguments was dismissed by the Commissioner, see **23.2**. The second was an idiosyncratic argument which ignored the exact words of the legislation. The Commissioner held that it was irrelevant because IR35 and the agency rules were 'both ... effective, and a decision can be reached on either or both regulations'.

The Commissioner then considered the various status tests and found that the taxpayer was caught by IR35. Her reasoning is set out at **8.6.4** below with comments.

8.6.4 Reasons for decisions

The Commissioner weighed up the various factors as set out in the table below. The column headed 'B' indicates that the point was made in the *Battersby* case, the column headed 'F' that it was raised in the *FS Consulting* case. The similarity of the points made suggests that this may become a template to be used by the Commissioners. The comments are those of the author.

In favour of employment	B	F	*Comments*
Provided his own work or skill (i.e., personal service)	✓	✓	Agreed, but subject to right of substitution, see Notes (a) and (b) below.
Worked a fixed working week with any absence to be agreed	✓	✓	Agreed, but not a significant factor in the case of a professional, see *Lorimer* case quoted at **8.2.1.**
He was part of a team made up (in part) of employees.	✓	✓	See *Lorimer* quoted at **6.6.3** where the judge said that being part of a team was not relevant.
The project manager (an employee) decided what and when it was to be done (i.e., control as to what and when).	?	✓	This is unclear in the *Battersby* decision; it may not be relevant, see *Lorimer* again.
In *Battersby* 'responsibility for the quality, quantity and performance of the services rested with [the client] at all times.' In *FS Consulting* the contract between the service company and the agency provided that the worker had to take all necessary instructions from the client and comply with its rules, regulations and procedures.	✓	✓	Agreed that this is some evidence of control but the phraseology in *FS Consulting* appears to have come from a standard contract, see **7.6.** Did the client require self-employed contractors to comply with rules, regulations and procedures too?
Mr Battersby 'was subject to [the client's] control in as	✓	✓	In *Serco Limited v Matthew Blair and Others* [1998] EAT/345

much as the contract provided it could be ended for incompetence or misconduct'.

'Mr Simpson was also subject to [the client]'s control to the extent that the contract between the Appellant and [the agent] provided that it could be terminated immediately if [the client] terminated its agreement with [the agency] because of the incompetence, unsuitability or unprofessional conduct of Mr Simpson.'

unreported) the court held that the fact that the agency, not the client, dismissed the workers was evidence that the client did not have sufficient control for there to be an employment between the worker and the client.

The lack of an ability to dismiss thus has been held to mean that there is insufficient control, but this is not the same as saying that the ability to dismiss equals control characteristic of employment. Surely any self-employed worker could be terminated without notice because of incompetence?

Did not hire his own workers.	✓	✓	Agreed that not being able to hire workers may be an indicator of employment, but it is not necessarily so, see **6.5.4**.
Did not provide his own equipment but worked on the client's equipment.	✓	✓	Agreed that this indicator of self-employment is not present, but the absence of this indicator does not mean he is an employee, see **6.6.2**.
Paid on an hourly basis.	✓	✓	This indicator does not mean he is an employee, see *Lorimer* again.
The relationship with the client had an element of permanency because it lasted seven years in the case of Mr Battersby and two and a half years for Mr Simpson.	✓	✓	A long engagement is a minor indicator of employment. However, self-employed people can have long projects, see **7.4.8**.
Never worked for more than one client at a time.	✓	✓	This is clearly the position for Mr Battersby, who only worked for one client. But Mr Simpson had the right to concurrent contracts – the judgment says that he 'was

			free, as a matter of contract, to undertake work for as many clients as he wished'.
Did not invest in any enterprise and did not bear any financial risk; had no opportunity of profit or risk of loss; all his invoices were paid.	✓	✓	The fact that all invoices were paid does not mean that there was no risk – the agency or the client could have gone bust, for example. See *Lorimer* for case law on this.
Was integrated into the structure of the client.	✓	✓	Case law indicates that this is largely irrelevant, see **6.7.7**.
In favour of self-employment			
Mr Battersby 'accepted the consequences of self-employment as he was unable to claim benefits when he was out of work'. However this was a consequence of choosing to work through a service company, and the IR35 legislation requires that the notional contract be considered – i.e., the actual arrangements and their practical consequences are to be ignored.	✓		This is a correct statement of the legal position, but remains one of the areas where the regime is unfair – the workers are taxed as employees of the client but cannot claim state or employee benefits.
Mr Simpson 'had the right to propose a replacement to substitute for [for himself] which replacement had to be another consultant who had previously supplied consultancy services to [the client] and had to be approved by [the client]. However the right of substitution was never used'.		✓	The fact that it had not been used is not relevant, see 6.5.2 and Notes (a) and (b) below.
The agreement was expressly not one of employment, but the Commissioner held that this was not conclusive, especially when considering a notional contract.	✓	✓	Agreed. However if all other factors are inconclusive, this is the balancing consideration – and if the other indicators had been correctly argued, this point might have become more important, see **5.2.4**.

The client was not obliged to pay the worker when he was on holiday or sick.	✓	✓	Agreed.
'In theory he did not enjoy job security with the client as [his] contract could be terminated on four weeks notice. However in practice he worked for [the client] for [several] years.'	✓	✓	This is a strange point – a notice period is normally treated as an indicator of employment, see **6.7.4**.
Not part of the management of the client and did not manage permanent employees.	✓	✓	Agreed.
There was very little direction and control as to how he carried out his work, but this is to be expected of a professional.		✓	Agreed, see **6.6.2**. This is not commented on in the *Battersby* decision.

Notes

(a) In *Battersby* the Revenue accepted that 'in theory the Appellant could have been substituted by another employee, in practice that had never been done'. It is unclear what is meant by 'substituted by another employee'; the fact that substitution had not occurred is not significant if a right existed, see **6.5.2**.

(b) In *FS Consulting* the Commissioner said: 'the Appellant had the right to propose a replacement to substitute for Mr Simpson, which replacement had to be another consultant who had previously supplied consultancy services to [the client]. However, the right of substitution was never used.' This appears to be a limited right of substitution, and the effect of this particular limitation could usefully have been further explored. See *MacFarlane and Skivington v Glasgow City Council* [2000] EAT/1277 discussed at **6.5.2**.

8.7 Other useful cases

8.7.1 Comparison of cases

Other status cases which are particularly useful for personal services workers are discussed in detail elsewhere in this book. They include:

- *Specialeyes*, see **5.6.3**;

- *Market Investigations*, see **5.6.5**;

- *O'Kelly*, see **5.6.2**.

The four cases, *Lorimer*, *Specialeyes*, *Lee Ting Sang* and *Market Investigations* all lie close to the Schedule E/Schedule D line. While bearing in mind the warning of Vinelott J. quoted at **8.1** above, it is nevertheless interesting to identify the factors which these four borderline cases have in common, and what differentiates Mr Lorimer and the Specialeyes opticians who were judged to be self-employed, from Mrs Irving and Lee Ting Sang, who were classified as employees. The table below summarises the key status tests and their application to each case:

	Lorimer	*Specialeyes*	*Lee Ting Sang*	*Market Investigations*
Mutuality of obligation	No	No	Yes	On an engagement by engagement basis, see **5.6.5**
Provision of equipment	No	Some	No	No
Hire own staff	No except substitutes	No	No	No
Financial risk	Some	Negligible	No	No
Provision of capital	No	No	No	No
Control over where	No	No	No	No
Control over when	No	Unclear	No	Yes
Control over how	Yes	Yes	No?	No
Other engagers?	Yes	Not in most cases	Yes, in series	Allowed but not taken up
Send a substitute	Sometimes?	Unclear	No	Only with permission

What this table shows is that:

- There was no mutuality of obligation (**5.3**) in either *Lorimer* or *Specialeyes*;

- Both Lorimer and the opticians had control over 'how' they carried out their work (**6.6.3**), and Mrs Irving and Mr Lee did not;

- In addition Mr Lorimer had greater financial risk than an employee, the occasional right to send a substitute, and numerous engagers. These are not points which were necessarily shared by the opticians, although some did have other clients.

8.8 Conclusion

Differences between the decided cases are very slight, and it is clear that IR35 will give rise to further decisions which may help to clarify the position. However, it should be remembered that Mr Lorimer had substitution, some financial risk, and numerous engagers, but still had to argue his case all the way to the Court of Appeal.

9 Changing the contractual relationship

9.1 Introduction

Contractual arrangements in the context of personal services are discussed in Chapter 5, along with a review of mutuality of obligation. Chapter 6 analyses the status tests which distinguish employees from the self-employed, and Chapter 7 comments on the Revenue view of status. This chapter considers the changes that could be made to individuals' contracts and working arrangements, so that they are more indicative of self-employment than employment.

Chapter 5 discusses the concept of the 'hypothetical contract' between the worker and the client which lies at the heart of IR35. In order to see if this hypothetical contract is one of employment, the 'circumstances' of the arrangements between the parties must be considered. It is not simply a question of considering the written contracts between worker and client, or worker and agency, but looking at other elements in his arrangements.

If a worker makes a fundamental change to his working practices and contractual arrangements, such as taking on significant risk or incorporating the right to send a substitute, he will be 'self-employed' and fall outside IR35, see **6.5.1**.

Workers who are on the borderline between Schedule E and Schedule D may be able to make less fundamental adjustments to their working practices which, when considered together with their existing arrangements, may make Schedule D classification more likely, see **6.6.4**.

One of the recommended changes is for the contracts to be for services to be supplied by the company and not for the supply of an individual worker. This is supportive of the position that personal services are not required by the client; it also reflects the view set out at **4.8.4**.

Before making any changes to contracts, it is important to remember that alterations made for tax reasons may have other consequences. Those entering into, or contemplating changes to, contractual arrangements as a result of IR35 are thus advised to take legal advice on the wider effects of any amendments, and also to consider their commercial implications. In addition, personal service workers should discuss any proposed changes with their agencies and clients. The client's acceptance is particularly important, see **5.1.3** and **5.1.4**.

The following paragraphs suggest some amendments which could be made to the 'arrangements'. They are examples only, and each worker's contractual arrangements are likely to need individual review. It is emphasised that it is not enough simply to change the written agreements; working practices must support the same interpretation. This is true to some extent in all status cases, but even more so in IR35, which emphasises the 'circumstances' of the hypothetical worker/client contract, see **5.1**.

In the sample clauses, 'the Company' is the service company, and the other party is generally the client. Similar clauses could be drafted in which one of the contracting parties was an agency, but see **5.1.4**.

9.2 Mutuality of obligation

If there is no mutuality between the worker and the client, then there will be no employment, see **5.3**. Because there is only a hypothetical contract between the two parties, the inclusion of an explicit non-mutuality clause in the contract between the service company and the client, or in the PSC/agency and agency/client contracts, does not of itself ensure that there is no mutuality (contrast *Stevedoring v Fuller* [2001] EWCA Civ 2001 where the clause was effective, see **5.7.1**). Instead, the wider terms on which the worker is providing his services will be examined, and whether or not there is mutuality will depend on the reality of the individual's working relationship with his client.

It is recommended that an explicit non-mutuality clause is nevertheless inserted in the written contracts, as these will be used by the courts to help them form a picture of the relationship between the worker and the client. A possible clause would be:

> 'The Client is under no obligation to offer work to the Company and the Company is under no obligation to accept any work which may be offered by the Client. Neither party wishes to create or imply any mutuality of obligation between themselves either in the course of, or between, any performance of Services.'

If the engager has the right to send the worker home without payment, then there may be no mutuality, see **5.10.4**. This sort of arrangement is common in the construction industry and the catering and restaurant trade, see *O'Kelly v Trusthouse Forte plc* [1983] 3 AER 456 at **5.6.2**.

9.3 Substitution clause

9.3.1 Introduction

If a contract contains a genuine substitution clause, the engagement cannot be an employment, see **6.5.2**. It thus falls outside the personal services rules. However, the Revenue warn against ineffective or sham clauses, see **7.4.1**.

A worker contemplating a substitution clause should consider the following:

9.3.2 Clause accepted by the client

To be genuine, a substitution clause must be accepted by the client. In practice many clients are resistant to such clauses, because the process of selecting a contractor can be lengthy, and involve both interviews and aptitude tests. Clients are often reluctant to surrender control over this selection process to the contractor himself. However, the client can reserve the right to reject a substitute, see **9.3.3**, and this may be helpful.

Where a clause exists, it may be challenged by the Revenue, see **7.4.1**. The worker should thus ensure that the client and any substitute would be prepared to support its authenticity, if necessary in court.

9.3.3 Appointment, permission and veto

It is the worker, not the agency or the client, who must have the right to appoint the substitute, see for example the recent case of *MacFarlane and Skivington v Glasgow City Council* [2000] EAT/1277 (see **6.5.2**). There will be no right of substitution if the client goes back to the agency and asks for another worker because their normal contractor is sick.

The clause should not make provision of a substitute dependent on the client's permission, see **6.5.2**. This doesn't, however, preclude the client vetoing a particular substitute if he cannot satisfactorily deliver according to the terms of the contract. The clause contained in the *Express and Echo* case, which was accepted as valid by the court, read as follows:

> 'In the event that the contractor provides a substitute, the contractor must satisfy the company that such a substitute is trained and is suitable to undertake the services.'

In the ESM the Revenue give the following guidance:

'A reasonable right to reject a substitute would include

- refusal because of the substitute's inability to do the work effectively or within a reasonable time span (especially where payment is by the hour);

- the substitute being a known trouble maker;

- other workers refusing to work with the individual.' (ESM 1054)

The substitution clause could include a warranty that the substitute will be able to meet the requirements of the engagement.

9.3.4 Responsibility for work and for payment

If a contract has a substitution clause, responsibility for delivering the work remains with the contractor. The substitute effectively 'stands in the shoes' of the worker, and the latter can thus be held liable by the client for any breach of contract caused by his replacement. If the substitute does the work badly, the contractor is liable; if he breaches the client's procedures, the contractor can be sued.

A substitution clause means that if the worker is sick, the client can require him to send a competent replacement. If no appropriate person can be found, the client may claim damages against the service company.

It is also the service company, not the client or agency, who has to pay the substitute. In *Express and Echo*, Mr Tanton was regarded by the Revenue as an employee and thus had PAYE and NIC deducted from his earnings, but nevertheless still paid his substitute. In *Ready Mixed Concrete* **6.5.2**, Mr Latimer, with other owner drivers, employed and paid a relief driver with the company's consent.

If the substitute is an individual, and not another service company, responsibility for deciding his tax status rests with the intermediary who signed the contract with the client.

9.3.5 Identifying the substitute

Although case law talks about the *right* to send a substitute, it is helpful if a replacement has actually been sent in practice, as this is demonstrable evidence that the right exists. Mr Lorimer (see **8.2.1**) and Mr Tanton (see **6.5.2**) clearly had real live substitutes who stood in for them when required. The existence of an identifiable person who would take the place of the contractor has persuasive force, if only to convince the court that the right was not a sham. However, the fact that no substitute has actually been sent does not of itself mean that the worker had no right to send one.

9.3.6 The client contract

Where the service company contracts with an agency, and the agency with the client, the Revenue warn that they will ask to see both contracts (FAQ Contract 2). This would be necessary in any event to determine the 'circumstances' of the hypothetical contract between the worker and the client, see **5.1.1**.

If the first has a substitution clause, but the second does not, the Revenue are likely to argue the clause is a sham. At the very least, there will be uncertainty about the terms of the hypothetical contract. In a court of law, this would make for a messy case. The contractor may avoid this problem by getting a statement from the client, see **7.7.5**; an alternative defence is suggested at ESM 1008 Example 2 quoted at **7.4.1**.

9.3.7 Use of alternates

A Schedule attached to the contract giving the names of a number of workers, all of whom could equally well deliver the contract, amounts to substitution. An appropriate clause might read as follows:

> 'The Client acknowledges that the engagement will be undertaken by one or more individuals provided by the Company and nominated in the Schedule attached to this Contract. The Company reserves the right to change or replace such individuals, provided the Client is satisfied that the proposed replacement possess the necessary skills and expertise to carry out the engagement.'

However, there is a risk that the court might hold that this right was too limited to immunise the worker from IR35, see **6.5.2**. In addition, the Schedule could be challenged as a sham if all but one of the named individuals were either unable or unwilling to carry out the contract on the terms agreed.

9.3.8 Conclusion

If a worker has a genuine right to send a substitute and the client accepts that right, the worker will not be within IR35. But there are commercial risks involved in engaging a replacement, including that of being sued because the work has been done badly, and the costs of remunerating the substitute out of the worker's own pocket.

9.4 Project-based work

9.4.1 General

As discussed at **6.5.3**, if a worker runs the risk of making a loss as well as a profit, he is almost certainly self-employed. A personal service worker who moves from an hourly basis to a project basis will have taken on significant risk. The Revenue accept this, saying that:

> 'Financial risk could also take the form of quoting a fixed price for a job, with the consequent risk of bearing the additional costs if the job overruns.' (*Tax Bulletin 45*)

In *Global Plant Ltd v Secretary of State for Health & Social Security* [1971] 3 All ER 385 Lord Widgery held that:

> 'If a man agrees to perform an operation for a fixed sum and thus stands to lose if the work is delayed, and to profit if it is done quickly, that is the man who on the face of it appears to be an independent contractor working under a contract for services.'

Points to note in moving from an hourly basis to a project basis are discussed below.

9.4.2 Clause has to be genuine

The change has to be genuine, so that a worker who operates as part of a client team, for instance on an IT helpdesk, is unlikely to be able to change his contract in this way. But a designer of websites, a cameraman, or a journalist, may all be able to estimate the time it will take them to complete a piece of work and quote on that basis.

A typical clause will identify the task to be completed and the agreed fee, including the timing of any instalment payments. Will there be a bonus if the project is completed earlier than scheduled, or a penalty if it is late?

9.4.3 There has to be real risk

The downside is that there is real risk. If the worker under-estimates, he will either have to finish the work in his own time or renegotiate the contract with the client; if he over-estimates, his profit will increase – and the client has to accept that. There may be cashflow issues, or unsatisfactory work which needs to be reperformed at no extra cost to the client. If an agency is involved, it will need to review the extent of its responsibility in a situation where the service company fails to meet its obligations.

9.4.4 Contract variations

Allowing changes to the content, timing or cost of the project gives flexibility, and permits further negotiation if the work proves more complex than expected. It is, however, recommended that any changes be agreed in writing by both parties. This helps prevent the contract from imperceptibly slipping back to an hourly basis. An appropriate clause might be:

'Either party may request in writing changes to the type and scope of the services or to any other aspect of the Contract. Any such request must be sufficiently detailed to enable the other party to assess the effect of the proposed change on the cost, delivery dates or any other aspect of the Contract. Both parties agree to discuss and, if appropriate, agree such changes. Until a change is agreed in writing and signed by both parties, each party will continue to act in accordance with the latest agreed written version of the Contract.'

9.4.5 Other characteristics

Other parts of the contract should be consistent with the fact that the work is on a project basis. For example, it should:

- Include appropriate commercial warranties between the contractor and the client, and vice versa;
- Clarify ownership where intellectual property has been created during the project;
- Specify any requirements as to confidentiality;
- Include insurance cover, see **11.10** and **9.7**;
- Provide for termination of the contract only if there has been a breach of its terms by either party, see **9.14**.

9.5 Hiring staff

If a worker can hire staff to carry out part of the work he has undertaken to do for the client, this is a strong indicator of self-employment, see **6.5.4**. This is because the essence of employment lies in the provision of personal services. For this test to be effective, the worker must be able to delegate part of the job to be carried out for the client: it is not enough to employ someone to carry out the bookkeeping or accounting in respect of an engagement.

Many of the same practical points here apply as in substitution, see **9.3** above:

- The client must know and consent to this term of the contract;

- The right to hire the helper must rest with the worker, not the agency;

- While what matters is the right to hire someone else to do the job, it is helpful, if challenged, to be able to identify a 'helper';

- If the client has to give 'permission' for the worker to hire a helper, a right is unlikely to exist, see **6.5.2**;

- The worker should be responsible for paying the helper.

An appropriate clause might be:

'The Company has the right to engage sub-contractors and other third parties to support it in fulfilling its obligations under this Contract. Any reference in this Contract to the Company's staff also includes reference to such sub-contractors or third parties. The Company is responsible for any third parties so engaged and remains liable to the Client in respect of any services provided by such third parties, subject to the other provisions of this Contract.'

9.6 Control

9.6.1 General

Every worker should review the control test, which is discussed in detail at **6.6.1**, and consider how it applies to them. It may be possible to argue, like Mr Lorimer, that it is irrelevant, see **6.6.3** and **6.6.4**. But not everyone will be in his position, and it would be naïve to think that simply because the judge said the control test was peripheral in that case, that it can always be ignored.

9.6.2 Control over the specialist

Clauses which make contractors sound like Victorian housemaids are unhelpful:

'The Consultant shall at all times faithfully and diligently perform all duties in connection with the provision of the services.'

A far better reflection of the service supplied by a specialist contractor would be:

'The Company warrants that it undertakes this engagement as a specialist and that its staff will dedicate the time, skill and care which it requires, and will carry out this engagement in a professional manner at all times.'

9.6.3 Control as to when, where and what

Where it is possible for the worker to retain control over his hours, the place where he carries out the work, and the detail of what he delivers, this will be helpful in arguing for self-employment, see **6.6.3**. A contract might include a clause suggesting a minimal degree of control, such as:

'The Company agrees to comply with all statutory obligations and codes of practice, and any rules or obligations in force at the premises where services are performed under this Contract to the extent that they are reasonably applicable.'

9.7 Financial risks

9.7.1 Insurance

Even where the self-employed do not operate on a project basis (see **9.4**), they normally protect themselves from the risk of being sued by taking out Professional Indemnity and Public Liability insurance. No doctor, accountant or lawyer would work without this sort of cover. In addition, the Revenue may use the absence of insurance as a negative when assessing the contractor's status, see **7.4.2**. An appropriate clause might be:

'The Company shall ensure the provision of adequate professional indemnity insurance, public liability insurance, and employers' liability insurance, and shall make a copy of the policies available on request.'

Or, more specifically:

'The Company warrants that it will maintain the following levels of insurance cover for the duration of the Contract and for six months thereafter: Employers liability, £x; public liability £x; product liability £x and professional indemnity £x.'

However insurance is a real cost, not a cosmetic adjustment to a contract, and it may be expensive. For the Schedule E treatment of such insurance if the worker fails the status tests, see **11.10**; for a general discussion of risk, see **6.5.3**.

9.7.2 Remedying defective work

In addition to PI and other insurance cover, the contractor can increase his level of risk by agreeing to take responsibility for defective work. A clause reflecting this obligation might read:

> 'The Company agrees to rectify any work notified to it by the Client as unsatisfactory, provided that such notification is received within 15 days following the progress report which relates to the unsatisfactory work.'

As with many of the other contractual changes discussed in this chapter, this clause has real financial consequences:

- The service company could be required to provide services without further payment in order to remedy work previously carried out;

- If an agency is a party to the contractual arrangements, it may become involved in any disagreement between the client and the service company concerning the extent or nature of any defects;

- If the company defaults on its contract and moves to take up an engagement elsewhere, the agency may be required, under its contract with the client, to supply a replacement worker without further cost. Although the agency would clearly have a cause of action against the service company, it may not be cost-effective to pursue the claim.

9.8 Providing own equipment

Lorimer established that providing equipment it is not an essential ingredient of self-employment, see **8.2.1**. However, supplying retinoscopes and ophthalmoscopes was helpful in the *Specialeyes* case, see **5.6.3**, and the musicians in the *Addison* and *Midland Sinfonia* cases, see **20.5.2**, owned their own instruments. It is also clear from the Revenue example *Henry*, see **25.2.3**, that Henry's extensive use of his own computer for his engineering consulting project was taken into account when deciding his Schedule D status.

Thus while not a necessary condition, the provision of equipment may be helpful. A clause might refer to this obliquely:

> 'The Company shall, when utilising any of its own equipment or intellectual property in carrying out the engagement, ensure that any security requirements reasonably required by the Client are complied with.'

If the worker is classified as Schedule E notwithstanding, there might be no tax relief on this capital expenditure, see **11.11**. A discussion of the provision of equipment in the context of the status tests is at **6.6.2**.

9.9 Pay and benefits

9.9.1 Holiday pay and benefits

Some contractors receive employee-type remuneration, such as paid holidays. This 'benefit' may even be imposed by the client – in some companies it is an internal audit requirement that all workers, including contractors, take a break from their job to minimise the risk of fraud.

Paid holidays are, however, characteristic of employment, and it would be preferable if the worker's contractual arrangements simply provided for a maximum continuous period of work. The 'holiday' would then follow automatically.

A number of companies have also recently offered share options (normally an employee-type benefit) to third parties such as distributors or contractors, in order to forge closer links between the workers and the company.

If share options, holiday pay, or other benefits are provided, there is a presumption of employment. This can be rebutted if, for example, there is no mutuality of obligation, as in the *O'Kelly* case, see **5.6.2**, or there are other indicators of self-employment, as in *McManus v Griffiths* [1997] 70 TC 218. See **6.7.3** for a general discussion of benefits in the context of status issues.

9.9.2 Hourly rates

Although payment on a project basis indicates self-employment, an hourly or daily rate doesn't necessarily mean that the worker is employed, see **6.7.3**.

Where work is charged on a time basis it should be properly invoiced by the service company, either to the agent or directly to the client, on headed paper, and appropriate records kept, see **9.12**.

The contractual clauses might be as follows:

> '*Fees and expenses* – The Company's fee has been set to reflect the time spent on the provision of the services, together with other factors such as the – complexity and urgency of the work, the level of risk inherent in the

engagement, and the utilisation of techniques, expertise and know-how previously developed by the Company.

Unless otherwise agreed, fees will be calculated on the basis of 8 working hours each day from Monday to Friday, excluding public holidays. Time worked in excess of 8 hours or on public holidays or at weekends will be charged on a pro-rata basis plus 15 per cent. In addition to the fees, the Client agrees to pay all travel, accommodation and subsistence costs and other reasonable expenses incurred by the Company in connection with the provision of the services.'

9.10 Intention of the parties

The intention of the parties is normally a tiebreaker clause, so that if all other factors are evenly balanced, what the parties intend the worker's status to be determines the issue. However, in the context of the personal services legislation it is uncertain whether the tiebreaker will be effective, see **5.2.4**. However, its inclusion can do no harm, and may be useful.

A clause stating that the company and client intend to contract as independent third parties should therefore be included, as follows:

'The relationship between the Company and the Client is one of independent suppliers, and nothing in this Contract shall be interpreted as constituting any joint venture, partnership or relationship of employer and employee, as between the parties.'

The contract should also more generally reflect the fact that it is between independent third parties, and thus should set out the obligations of the client to the company as well as those from the company to the client. Possible clauses include:

- 'The Client shall ensure that the Company is accorded sufficient access to any of the Client's premises, information, data or personnel, as is required for the Company to carry out the services to be supplied under the Contract;

- The Client will ensure that its staff, including senior management, are available to give such assistance as the Company reasonably requires in order to carry out the services under the Contract;

- The Client warrants that its staff have the necessary skills and experience to provide the Company with the support needed for the Company properly to fulfil its obligations under the Contract;

- The Client shall ensure that it has appropriate back up, security and virus checking procedures in place for any computer facilities it provides;

- The Client agrees at its own expense to provide to the Company all information that the Company reasonably requires for the proper performance of the Contract and in accordance with any timetable or other target for progress or completion agreed in writing between the parties;

- The Client shall, at its own expense, retain duplicate copies of all information provided to the Company and the Company shall have no liability for any loss or damage to the information provided by the Client, howsoever caused;

- The Client warrants that all information provided to the Company is accurate and not misleading in any material respect.'

9.11 Tax clauses

Existing contracts may contain clauses which make the service company responsible for PAYE and NIC, such as:

'The Company shall be responsible for making appropriate PAYE deductions for tax and NIC from the remuneration it pays to its staff and the Company agrees to indemnify the Client in respect of any claims or demands which may be made by the relevant authorities against the Company in respect of income or other tax relating to the provision of the services by the Company.'

It would be surprising to find this clause in a normal contract for services. An accountant's engagement letter does not say he will pay his own tax: his clients take this for granted. Such a clause would thus fall into the 'officious bystander' category of implied terms which do not need to be spelled out, see **5.2.3**. Putting a tax clause into the contract thus suggests that the parties are unclear about the worker's status.

Not only does it provide a marker for the Revenue, it is also unnecessary unless either:

- The contract is with an individual rather than with a service company or partnership. This is because the PAYE or NIC responsibility then legally rests with the client. In this case IR35 will not be in point, see **4.7**; or

- The service company is overseas, in which case the client may have some liability under the provisions of s203C ICTA 1988 and the corresponding NIC rules, see **19.4.1** and **21.3.2**.

9.12 Business structure

Although an absence of business structure is not fatal to a claim to be self-employed, see **6.7.6**, it is nevertheless recommended that a contractor should have at least a rudimentary business structure, as did Ian Lorimer, see **8.2.1**. Office equipment such as a fax, internet line, answering machine and mobile phone is helpful. Business stationery, including invoices with appropriate letterheads and business cards are also recommended.

If the services available are advertised, this too supports the argument that the service company is carrying on a business. The self-employed may advertise in trade journals, yellow pages or on the internet. However, the absence of advertising should not jeopardise Schedule D status: many self-employed people obtain all their work through agencies or by word of mouth.

9.13 Exclusivity

Where a worker provides services only to one engager, and agrees he will not provide his skills to anyone else, he is likely to be an employee, see **6.7.2**. Conversely, the freedom to work concurrently for a number of engagers is helpful in arguing for self-employment.

Contracts should thus include a clause giving the worker the right to provide services to others during the period of the engagement. It may be done obliquely, as:

> 'The Company confirms that other engagements undertaken during the period of this Contract will not give rise to a conflict of interest between the Company and its Client.'

Or more directly:

> 'This Contract will not restrict the Company from providing services to other Clients, providing only that the services to be provided under this Contract are not thereby restricted or impaired in any way.'

9.14 Termination and notice

The issue of termination is discussed at **6.7.4** and **5.10.4**. Some contracts also have a provision for a payment in lieu of notice (PILON). The latter is particularly unhelpful if the worker is trying to claim Schedule D status, as a PILON is clearly indicative of employment.

When reviewing the issue of termination, the commercial requirements of both client and worker should be considered, as well as the tax implications. A notice period will protect the client and give time for him to find a replacement worker and/or protect the worker from sudden termination of the agreement. Where a notice period is retained, reference can be made to the words of the judge in *McManus v Griffiths* [1997] 70 TC 218 quoted at **6.7.4**, which suggest that a notice period could be regarded as a neutral factor in determining questions of status.

9.15 Off-the-peg solutions

As an alternative to the painstaking and commercially risky task of contractual amendments, some contractors have been tempted by various 'off-the-peg' solutions, from employee benefit trusts to pre-packaged Schedule D contracts. These are discussed in Chapter 23.

10 Income and benefits from relevant engagements

10.1 Introduction

A deemed Schedule E calculation has to be carried out for all workers with relevant engagements, as does a National Insurance attributable earnings calculation (Sch 12, para 7 FA 2000; SI 2000/757 reg 7).

The deemed Schedule E and attributable earnings calculations are generally identical, but interactions with overseas tax and the NICs deeming provisions mean that it is sometimes possible to have a deemed Schedule E calculation but not an attributable earnings calculation, or vice versa, see **12.7.2**. For simplicity, the calculation is referred to throughout this book as 'deemed Schedule E', unless specific identification of one or the other is required.

The calculation is in nine steps, of which this chapter covers the first two. These establish the income received by the intermediary from relevant engagements, and payments and benefits received by the worker from the client or other third party. The chapter concludes by looking in detail at the benefits which might be included at Step Two, and how they should be taxed. Chapter 11 looks at Steps Three and Four, and the last five steps are discussed in Chapter 12.

10.2 Receipts basis

10.2.1 Comparison with normal rules for PAYE

The normal rule is that earnings of employees or directors are taxable (and subject to PAYE) on the earliest of the following occasions (s202B and 203A ICTA 1988):

(a) When *payment is made* of or on account of the emoluments;

(b) When a person becomes *entitled* to payment of, or on account of, the emoluments;

And if the worker is a director:

(c) When sums on account of emoluments are *credited to the director's current or loan account* by the company;

(d) If the amount of the emoluments for a period is determined before the period ends, the time *when the period ends*;

(e) If the amount of the emoluments for a period is not known until the amount is determined after the period has ended, the time *when the amount is determined.*

If these rules had been applied to income received by the service company, employees and directors within IR35 would have been subject to PAYE and NICs on amounts invoiced to the client but not yet received. In order to prevent this onerous result, the deemed Schedule E calculation is on a received basis for both tax and NIC.

The corollary also applies: if a prepayment is received in one fiscal year for work to be done in the next, it is included in the earlier year's deemed Schedule E calculation, although the related services have not yet been carried out (Sch 12, para 10(5)(a) FA 2000).

The intermediary thus needs to keep records on both a received and an accruals basis, so that the deemed Schedule E calculation as well as the corporation tax or partnership returns can be completed correctly.

10.2.2 Special rules for 2000/01

For the first year of the new rules there was an exception to the receipts basis. To prevent intermediaries accelerating receipts into 1999/00 for work to be done in 2000/01, the legislation says that 'payments or other benefits in respect of (services performed after 5 April 2000) shall be treated as if received in the tax year 2000/01' (Sch 12, para 22(2) FA 2000).

Also, in the first year it was sometimes necessary to apportion income received between pre-IR35 and post-IR35. The Revenue accept that 'provided any apportionment made seems reasonable, [the Inspector] should not spend a lot of time trying to establish detailed figures.' (ESM 3190)

10.2.3 Valuation of benefits

Where a benefit rather than cash has been provided, the date for it to be brought into the deemed Schedule E calculation is the date on which 'it is used or enjoyed' (Sch 12, para 10(5)(b) FA 2000).

The wording of this is likely to change following the Tax Law Rewrite's Exposure Draft 12 which proposes a technical amendment to this section.

This recognises that some benefits, such as company cars, are provided and enjoyed throughout a tax year, but the tax charge normally crystallises at the end of that period [*ED12 – Draft Income Tax [Earnings and Pensions] Bill Part 2 Employment Income*].

10.2.4 VAT

Where the company is registered for VAT, the amount to be brought into the deemed Schedule E computation is the net amount after VAT, see **13.10** and ESM 3160. For the treatment of VAT on expenses, see **11.3.9**.

10.2.5 Foreign currency

The receipts basis means that care is needed when dealing with foreign currency earnings.

- If an amount is invoiced in sterling, and the client agrees to pay in sterling net of any bank costs or foreign currency conversion costs, then the net amount received is included at Step One of the IR35 calculation;

- Where the client is invoiced in a foreign currency and pays in that currency, then the receipt for IR35 purposes is the net amount after conversion into sterling – so any FX losses or profits are automatically taken into account. However any extra costs, such as international transfer fees or commission charges, are not deductible from the receipt in Step One and would thus only obtain 'relief' within the 5 per cent allowance.

10.3 Apportionments of income

The intermediary may have to apportion income received from clients, either because more than one individual in the company has worked on the relevant engagement, and/or because the income relates both to relevant and other engagements. The legislation requires that this be done on a 'just and reasonable basis' (Sch 12, para 9 FA 2000). Revenue booklet IR175 – *Supplying services through a limited company or partnership* warns that:

> 'The Revenue will re-apportion any payment if it appears the company's or partnership's basis of apportionment is unreasonable. The company can appeal against the decision of the Inland Revenue.'

Appropriate management of the invoicing process can simplify this apportionment. Separate bills could be submitted for different types of work, or the invoice could split relevant engagement income from other work, and identify the person who performed the relevant engagement.

10.4 A single employment

The legislation says that the deemed Schedule E calculation should be carried out as if:

- The worker were employed by the intermediary; and

- The relevant engagements were undertaken in the course of performing the duties of that employment (Sch 12, para 11(2) FA 2000).

Thus, although there may be many engagements with different clients, all the contracts are considered together, as derived from a single employment with the intermediary, when carrying out the deemed Schedule E calculation.

However, the calculation itself assumes that the 'worker is employed by the client' (Sch 12, para 7 Steps Two to Four, FA 2000). The two concepts appear contradictory. Is the worker to be regarded as employed by the client, or by the intermediary? In particular, where a client provides a benefit to a personal service worker, is he:

- Acting as third party, because the worker is employed by the service company; or

- Acting as employer, because the worker is regarded as his employee?

The answer makes a difference in a number of areas, such as entertaining, travel, gifts and vouchers.

Paragraph 7 calculates the deemed Schedule E payment, and paragraph 11 deals with applying the Income Tax Acts in a wider sense. The author's view is that where paragraph 11 conflicts with paragraph 7, the former takes precedence. This also seems to be the approach taken by the Revenue, see **11.6.3**. However the position is not beyond doubt, and where it makes a difference this has been noted in the text.

10.5 Steps One and Two of the deemed Schedule E calculation

10.5.1 General

Step One brings together all payments and benefits which have been received by the *intermediary* in respect of relevant engagements. This is then reduced by 5 per cent, which represents a round sum expense allowance, see **11.2**.

Step One thus includes both cash paid by the client to the intermediary in settlement of invoices, and also 'benefits' received, such as reimbursed travel and subsistence expenses.

Step Two then adds into the calculation any payments and benefits received *by the worker* otherwise than from the intermediary, i.e., from a client or other third party. Not included in Step Two are:

(a) Payments/benefits received by the worker from the *intermediary*, see **10.5.2**;

(b) Payments/benefits received by the worker otherwise than from the intermediary which would not be *chargeable* if the worker were an employee of the client, see **10.5.3**;

(c) Payments/benefits received by the worker otherwise than from the intermediary which are *already taxable* under Schedule E, see **10.5.4**.

If the worker is an employee or director, payments or benefits received from a client are almost always already taxable under existing rules, because they will have been provided by reason of the worker's employment with the intermediary (s154(1) ICTA 1988).

Partners, however, do not have an employment, and thus benefits provided by the client cannot be by reason of the employment. Step Two is thus most commonly used to bring into tax payments or benefits received by a partner from a client. It will not normally be used in the more common situation where the payment or benefit is provided by the client to a service company director or worker.

Where a benefit is included in Step Two, it must be valued at its 'cash equivalent' (Sch 12, para 10(3)(b)). This is in line with the rules for employees. Specific requirements for the calculation of cash equivalents exist for some benefits, such as company cars, vans, accommodation and loans.

10.5.2 Payments/benefits received by the worker from the intermediary

A payment or benefit provided to the worker by the intermediary is not included in Step Two, because it is assumed to have been paid out of income received in Step One. To include it again would be double counting.

10.5.3 Payments/benefits received other than from the intermediary which are not taxable

Clearly it would be unfair to include payments or benefits received from the client in the deemed Schedule E calculation if these same amounts would not be taxed if the worker were employed directly.

Payments and benefits which escape tax do so either under a specific legislative provision, or by way of an Extra Statutory Concession (ESC). The Revenue have confirmed that they will use their care and management powers to extend the benefit of ESCs to workers within the personal service rules.

Payments and benefits excluded from tax either by legislation or concession include:

- Small loans, exempted from tax under s161 ICTA 1988;

- Personal incidental expenses, which are not 'regarded as emoluments of the office or employment for any purpose of Schedule E' providing they do not exceed £5 a night or £10 if overseas, see **11.7**;

- Training provided by the client, which are not included in 'emoluments of the employee from the office or employment', see **11.8**;

- Meals in the staff restaurant, which are not taxable by virtue of ESC A74, see **10.6.6(d)** below;

- Working Rule Agreement sums paid to the worker by the client, see **11.6.6**.

Where these amounts are received from the intermediary, or by arrangement with the intermediary, the position becomes more complex. These and other rules for allowable expenses are discussed further in Chapter 11.

10.5.4 Payments/benefits from a third party already within Schedule E

Payments or benefits which are received:

- From the client or other third party; and

- By the director or employee of a service company, or the employee of a partnership,

are usually provided by reason of the worker's employment with the intermediary. They are thus already taxable under Schedule E and are therefore not included within the deemed Schedule E calculation. They are also subject to NICs, see Table 10.1 below.

Not only are the benefits already taxable, but the reporting responsibility almost invariably attaches to the service company. This is because where a payment or benefit has been provided by a third party 'by arrangement with' the employer, it is the employer who has the P11D reporting obligations, not the client. (SI 1993/744 reg 46 and *SAT3(1995): Self Assessment – What it will mean for employers,* para 2.10.)

In a one-man company it is usually difficult (if not impossible) to argue that benefits provided to the worker by the client have not been arranged by the employer, because of the substantial identity between the 'employer' and the 'worker'.

The tax and NICs situation of the worker, the client and the intermediary in a range of different situations is examined at Table 10.1 below. The position differs depending on whether the payment is cash or a benefit, and whether it has been arranged or facilitated by the employer (i.e., the service company).

Table 10.1 *Tax and NICs on payments/benefits provided by client to an employee/director of an intermediary*

Item	By arrangement with worker?	Worker's tax position	Service company's tax position	Payer's tax position	NICs position
Business expenses	Yes	On P11D, claim under s198 ICTA	Include on P11D	No requirement	No requirement, see Note 7
Other cash, e.g., round sum allowance	Yes	Include on SA return, see Note 2	No requirement	Deduct PAYE, see Note 1	Service company's liability, see Note 3
Benefit e.g., use of car	Yes	On P11D	Include on P11D	No requirement, see Note 4	Service company's liability
Benefit	No	Include on SA return	No requirement	Provide details to worker, see Note 5	See Note 6
Hospitality e.g., gift or entertaining	No	See **10.6.6.**	See **10.6.6.**	See **10.6.6.**	See **10.6.6.**

Notes

1. Where a cash payment, such as a round sum allowance, is paid as a reward in connection with the employee's duties, the paying company has to deduct PAYE. This is because s203 ICTA 1988 states that:

   'On the making of any payment of, or on account of, any income assessable to income tax under Schedule E, income tax shall, subject to and in accordance with regulations made by the Board under this section, be deducted or repaid by *the person making the payment.*'

   In addition, under SI 1993/744 reg 2, an 'employer' is defined as 'any person paying emoluments'. In the context of a relevant engagement, the client will thus have to deduct and pay over PAYE. This is confirmed by FAQ Computation 11:

   'If a client makes payments to a worker in connection with duties being performed, either for direct reward, as a round sum expense allowance, or a specific reimbursement of travel which was not business travel, and the worker is an employee of another, the payments are assessable on the worker and the client should deduct tax through PAYE from payments to the worker.'

   There is a similar treatment when payments (other than reimbursed expenses) are made directly from the agency to the individual worker (as distinct from paying the service company), see FAQ Agency 4.

2. If the client does apply PAYE, it will normally be on BR basis (SI 1993/744 reg 28). The worker may thus need to pay further tax following completion of his self-assessment return. Third parties tend to inform the Revenue of such payments by letter, rather than formally completing a P60 and P35.

3. The client is however not liable for the NICs on these payments. The employer is always the secondary contributor, even when the payment is made by a third party. The service company therefore has to pay over the NICs in relation to any such receipts by the worker from the client (s7 SSCBA).

4. These benefits may have to be reported under s16 TMA, see **21.2.4** and **21.3.3**.

5. If, exceptionally, the rewards were not arranged by the employer, the third party must provide details of the benefit to the worker (SI 1993/744 reg 46AB and *SAT3(1995): Self Assessment – What it will mean for employers*, para 4.1). The value should be included on the individual's self-assessment return.

6. There is a Class 1A NICs liability on the intermediary for 2000/01 unless the third party volunteers to pay it; in subsequent years the liability is on the third party (s10ZA SSCBA 1992).

7. There are no NICs as long as the payment is to meet a 'specific and distinct' expense (SI 2001/1004 Sch 3(9)). Costs cannot be apportioned for NICs.

All of the above payments are taxed under existing Schedule E or NICs provisions by virtue of the worker's employment with the intermediary. Thus, although they are all paid by the client, none are taxed as part of the deemed Schedule E payment.

10.5.5 Interaction between IR35 and PAYE/P11D rules

Benefits are of course not only provided by the client to an employee or director of an intermediary, they can also be provided:

- By the intermediary to the worker; or
- By the client to a partner;
- By the client to the intermediary.

In each case the interactions between the normal PAYE/P11D provisions and the personal service rules is different. The various options are described in (a) to (d) below, and summarised in Table 10.2. The Table also shows what happens if the benefit, having been provided, is either taxable under existing provisions, or escapes tax by virtue of some concession, exemption or relief.

Benefits may be provided by:

(a) The intermediary, to the employee/director of a service company or to the employee of a partnership. These benefits are included on the individual's P11D and taxed under the normal rules. From 6 April 2000 they are also subject to Class 1A NICs, unless Class 1 already applies or there is some other exemption, see **12.3.3**. They are excluded from the deemed income calculation by Step Seven, because they are already taxable under normal rules, see **12.4**;

(b) The client, to the intermediary – such as a reimbursement of travel costs or phone bills. These amounts are included in Step One of the deemed income calculation, see **12.5.1**. They may then be excluded under Step Three, if they would have been deductible under the Schedule E rules, see **11.3**;

(c) The client, to the employee/director or a service company or to the employee of a partnership. These benefits will usually be included on the worker's P11D by the intermediary, because they will have been provided by arrangement with the employer, see **10.5.4** above. The worker may be able to claim tax relief under ss198ff ICTA, see **11.3.3**;

(d) The client, to a partner. These will be brought into the deemed Schedule E calculation under Step Two. Any relief for these costs is claimed in the partnership computation, not the deemed Schedule E computation, see **14.5.4** and **15.3.4**.

Table 10.2 *Personal service legislation and benefits provided*

Text Ref.	Provided by	Provided to	Include in deemed Sch E?	Remove from deemed Sch E if not taxable ?	Tax relief otherwise available?
(a)	Intermediary	Employee/ director	No	Yes, Step 7	Yes, under s198 on SA return
(b)	Client	Intermediary	Step 1	Step 3	No tax because item removed under Step 3
(c)	Client	Employee/ director	No	N/A	Yes, s198 on SA return
(d)	Client	Partner	Step 2	No	Yes, on partnership return

10.6 Common benefits

The nature of the contractual arrangements between most personal service workers and their clients means that benefits are not often provided. Risk areas include travel, subsistence, accommodation and phone costs. The temporary executive may receive a wider range of benefits, extending to private use of the company plane, a chauffeur and overseas trips.

An outline of the tax position for common benefits is given at **10.6.1–10.6.12** below. It concentrates on benefits provided by the client, either directly or by arrangement with the intermediary, rather than benefits provided by the intermediary.

10.6.1 Accommodation

There is no benefit charge if the accommodation satisfies the travel rules, see **11.6**. There is also an exemption for accommodation where the private use is 'not significant' (s155ZA ICTA 1988). In other situations its value must be ascertained in line with the rules set out in ss145 to 146 ICTA 1988.

There are a number of exemptions from this charge, which apply if the accommodation is:

- Necessary because of a special threat to the employee's security;
- Customarily provided for the better performance of the duties; or
- Necessarily provided for the proper performance of the duties.

As with most exemptions from the Schedule E charge, few people qualify. Examples of workers who might satisfy the 'customary' requirement are locum veterinary surgeons, if they are required to be on call outside normal hours, are in fact frequently called out and the accommodation is provided so that the vet can quickly access the place where he performs his duties (SE 11352). Another example would be a supply teacher in a boarding school who had pastoral responsibilities.

Directors do not qualify for any of these exemptions other than the first. Since a director of a service company will usually be taxed under the normal rules for Schedule E rather than under the deeming provision of IR35, because the benefit has been provided 'by arrangement with' the service company, see **10.5.4**, he will thus not have access to most of these exemptions. However if a worker is a partner, or an employee of a service company or partnership, he would potentially be eligible for these reliefs.

If a personal services worker considers that one of these exemptions does apply to him, he should discover whether the client has previously come to an arrangement with the local Inland Revenue Inspector in relation to the tax position of previous users of the accommodation.

10.6.2 Assets

The private use of company assets, such as a boat or aircraft, is chargeable as a benefit under s156 ICTA 1988, see Example 10A.

> **Example 10A**
>
> John is a partner in a small firm of accountants. A local company asks him to take up a position for six months as temporary finance director, and signs a contract with the partnership for his services. It is agreed between John and the partnership that the earnings from this engagement will not be included in the partnership profit pool but paid directly to John. The engagement is thus within the scope of the personal services rules, see **14.2.2**. John is allowed the use of the company yacht at weekends. This is a benefit provided by the client and must be included in his deemed Schedule E calculation at Step Two.
>
> If John had been operating via a service company, the benefit would have been included on his P11D, because it would have been 'by arrangement with' his employer, the service company, see **10.5.4**.

The benefit is on the 'annual value' of the asset, unless specific provisions exist to tax it separately. The 'annual value' is 20 per cent of the asset's market value when it is first used privately.

Some particular points to note are:

- The cost of the asset includes VAT, whether or not this can be recovered either by the client or by the service company (SP A7);

- The 20 per cent charge is replaced by the actual cost of hiring the asset if this is greater (s156(7) ICTA 1988);

- If the asset is used by more than one employee, or it is used partly for business, an apportionment is required (s156(2) ICTA 1988; SE 21625). It is assumed that apportionment would also be applied where an asset was used by more than one worker under the personal services rules;

- The NIC legislation does not accept the concept of apportioning a benefit between business and private use. Thus unless the cost is 'specific and distinct' (SI 2001/1004 Sch3(9)), or covered by an exemption, the full amount will be subject to Class 1A, see **11.4.2**. Where the item is included in the Step Two, as distinct from being on the P11D of a service company worker, then the tax rules rather than the NIC rules apply, see **12.3.3**. As a result apportionment may be permitted;

- If the asset is unavailable for part of the year, the benefit is reduced (s156(2) ICTA 1988);

- If ownership of an asset is transferred to the worker, there is only a benefit if the asset is transferred at less than its market value at the date of transfer. These rules are amended where there has been private use, see s156(4) ICTA 1988.

There are two useful exemptions from this charge:

(a) Computers provided by the client for the worker's private use. These are not taxable as long as the annual value is £500 or less (s156A ICTA 1988);

(b) Any assets where the private use is 'not significant' (s155ZA(3) ICTA 1988). This would cover the use of telephones, photocopiers and fax machines, as well as computers provided for work which do not fall within the s156A exemption. Unsurprisingly, this relief does not extend to the private use of aeroplanes, boats or cars, even if private use is not significant.

10.6.3 Cars

Where a personal service worker has been provided with a car by a client, he will be able to escape the scale charge if either:

• All travel in the car would have been allowable cost under the travel rules, so there is no private use, see **11.6**; or

• The car is a pool car, see below.

Some problems which may arise when the worker is provided with a car by the client include:

Hire cars

A hire car provided by the client is still a 'company car' for tax purposes. The fact that it has not come from the client's own fleet is irrelevant.

Pool cars

Pool cars are not taxable, as long as the strict conditions in ss159 and 159AB ICTA 1988 are complied with. These are that:

(a) The car is available to, and actually used by, more than one employee (or worker within the personal services rules), and is not ordinarily used by any one of them to the exclusion of the others;

(b) The car is not normally kept overnight on or in the vicinity of the residence of any of the employees/workers except while it is being kept on premises occupied by the client. The Revenue have a rule of thumb that a car is not regarded as 'normally kept overnight' at employees' homes if the total number of nights on which it is taken home – for whatever reason – is less than 60 per cent of the total number of nights in the period under review (IR Booklet 480). However they also warn that: 'If a car or van is taken home often enough to approach the 60 per cent limit – though without breaking it – it is unlikely that all the home to work journeys will satisfy the "merely incidental" test' (SE 23803);

(c) Any private use of the car by any of the employees or workers is merely incidental to its business use, see Example 10B.

Example 10B

Stephen has his own personal service company specialising in computer game theory. He is working away from his home in Bath on a relevant engagement in Manchester, which is expected to exceed two years. He is provided with a car by the client so he can travel between different offices in the Manchester area. In the evenings he uses the car to drive to his favourite vegetarian restaurant in the centre of the city. This is merely incidental to the business use, and there is no benefit.

However one weekend he obtains the client's permission to use the car to visit his father in Devon. This is private use, and as a result the car is not a pool car and has to be included on his P11D, see SP2/96.

Cars provided in succession

Where a worker has been supplied with a number of cars in the course of a tax year, perhaps by different clients, he should treat them as if they had been sequentially provided by a single employer (Sch 12, para 11(2) FA 2000). This has the following consequences:

(a) If a car is available for only part of the fiscal year, the tax charge can be reduced. Thus if a contractor is provided with a car by one client for a month, and two weeks later another car by a different client for ten months, his benefit charge will be reduced to reflect the period when he had no car. The same would apply if a client made available two different cars on separate occasions;

(b) However, where the worker is given the use of the same car and there is a gap when it was not provided, there is no reduction in the benefit unless the car has been unavailable for at least 30 consecutive days. Unavailable means that the car itself cannot be accessed; it is not enough that the driver cannot drive for the period, for example because of illness or a driving ban (Sch 6, paras 6 and 9 ICTA 1988);

This could impact on contractors who are at a client for one week a month, and are always given the use of the same car. Because the gap would not be 30 days, there would be no reduction in the car benefit. It would thus be possible for a contractor to have several cars which were technically available for use, because they were each provided by different clients for part of a month. The benefit cost would then be unacceptably high;

(c) When the car is available for periods of less than a year, the normal reduction for business mileage in excess of either 2,500 or 18,000 miles a year is also pro-rated, so that a car used for six months will have a reduced benefit cost if the contractor drives 1,250 or 9,000 miles;

(d) The business mileage rules are also applied on a per car basis, and thus if the car is changed part way through the year, the mileage must be calculated for each car, see SE 23304 and *Henwood v Clarke* (1997) STC 789. This is likely to be an area of particular difficulty for personal service workers;

(e) However the business mileage problems at (c) and (d) above will fall away from April 2002 with the introduction of the new emissions basis for the taxation of company cars.

10.6.4 Chauffeur

Interim executives working through a personal service company may be supplied with a chauffeur. Where the chauffeur is only used for business journeys, or to and from a 'temporary workplace' under the travel rules, see **11.6**, there will be no benefit.

Where there is 'private use', provision of a chauffeur is taxable. The benefit charge is based on the relevant proportion of the chauffeur's wages, including waiting time, overtime, pension contributions, and NIC costs. The tax exposure is thus significant, but can be reduced if the chauffeur does other jobs for the client, see Example 10C.

Example 10C

Maeve has her own personal service company and is acting Chairperson of a major plc. She is given the use of a chauffeur, who picks her up from her home in Wolverhampton every morning and drives her to the client's offices in Birmingham. She has been in this role for three years.

Her journeys from home to work are private mileage because a three-year assignment is outside the travel rules. Provision of the chauffeur is thus taxable. His costs total £30,000 per year, but it is estimated that only 20 per cent of this relates to the Chairperson. The benefit to be included on Maeve's P11D is thus £6,000.

When a temporary executive has the use of chauffeur it may be possible to argue that it should not be taxable, based on the 'merely incidental' part of the pool car test, see **10.6.3** above. SP2/96 discusses the situation where:

- The car is also used by others;

- It is not kept at the individual's home overnight; and

- A chauffeur is needed because the individual needs to work on his confidential papers in the car.

10.6.5 Conferences

A personal services worker may attend a conference, such as an overseas sales convention, organised by the client. This may be work-related training provided by the client, and thus not taxable, see **11.8.2**. Otherwise it is likely to be a benefit unless wholly, exclusively and necessarily in the performance of the duties.

The Revenue may not accept that a conference was necessary if the individual himself decided to go (*Owen v Burden* [1971] 47 TC 476). Workers should therefore ensure that they are 'instructed' to attend, and do not simply self-authorise their own attendance. There is likely to be an extra cost if the individual's spouse or partner accompanies the worker, subject to the exemptions provided by ESC A4.

Most clients with such events will have already discussed the tax treatment of attendees with their local district, and the worker should seek to discover what has been agreed.

10.6.6 Entertaining

This is an area when the liability to tax depends on whether paragraph 7 or paragraph 11 of Schedule 12 has priority, see **10.4**.

If paragraph 7 has priority, the worker will be taxed as if he were an employee of the client. Entertaining provided by an individual's employer is a benefit and included either in Step Two, if the worker is a partner, or otherwise on the worker's P11D.

However, if paragraph 11 has priority, which is more likely, the entertaining will have been provided by a third party. The following text has been written on the assumption that paragraph 11 has priority, but it should be noted that the position is unclear.

There is an exemption for employees provided with entertainment by third parties, where:

(a) The person providing the benefit is neither his employer nor a person connected with his employer;

(b) Neither his employer nor a person connected with his employer has directly or indirectly procured its provision; and

(c) It is not provided either in recognition of particular services which have been performed by the employee in the course of his employment or in anticipation of particular services which are to be so performed by him (s555(7) ICTA 1988).

However, personal services workers are unlikely to satisfy the above exemption, either because the entertaining:

• Normally falls outside (b) because the provision has been procured by the intermediary as part of the working arrangements; or

• Falls outside (c) because it has been provided by the client 'in recognition of particular services'; or

• Has been provided 'by arrangement with' the employer and thus is included on the employee/director's P11D on first principles, see **10.5.4**.

However, where the hospitality does meet the above tests, it will not be taxed.

The client will normally disallow these amounts as entertaining (or mistakenly include contractors in the firm's PSA, see **10.7** below). However, the amounts will generally be taxed again in the hands of the personal services worker. This was the case before IR35, as most entertaining provided by clients for personal service workers already falls outside the exemption in s555(7). While this double taxation is unwelcome, it is not a problem created by the new legislation.

The worker is likely to have practical problems establishing the value of the benefit to include on the P11D or in Step Two of the deemed income calculation. If the amounts are taxable, he should obtain details from the client in time to complete his calculation. He should also have regard to the defences listed below.

Defences

(a) The Revenue have accepted that some entertaining may be 'trivial' – for instance where a personal services worker joins a meal out with employees. They have indicated that this practice of ignoring trivial benefits would not however be appropriate if the functions were regular in nature or likely to involve significant costs per head, or were entered into chiefly for the personal services workers. They have suggested that this issue can only be resolved on a case by case basis, and recommended that any worker who is unsure about his position should consult his Inspector;

(b) An argument can be mounted that some meetings over a meal are necessarily incurred – the Revenue Manual (ECM 13029) suggests that this may be the case where, for example, the extension of a service contract is being discussed, or workers are detained beyond their normal hours for a briefing from head office;

(c) Where the personal services worker is entitled to tax-free subsistence under the travel rules, see **11.6.5**, the cost of the entertaining can be reduced by the amount of subsistence, or eliminated altogether, see NAG 5.130;

(d) There is an exemption for annual 'staff functions' under ESC A70 for amounts up to £75 per head. A contractor who moves from client to client may attend a number of such functions, each of which may be tax-free for the employees. However, as the worker is deemed to be employed by his service company (Sch 12, para 11(2) FA 2000) he is limited to £75 worth of staff parties per year. The Concession warns that:

> 'Where the cost of the entertainment is more than £75 per head, tax will be payable on the full amount assessable under the relevant charging provision. Where there is more than one annual function and their total cost per head exceeds £75, the functions that total £75 or less will not be taxed. Any other functions will be taxed in full.';

(e) Relief is also available under ESC A74 for free or subsidised meals provided for employees on the business premises, or in any canteen where meals are provided for the staff generally, or on the use of any ticket or token to obtain such meals, if:

- The meals are provided on a reasonable scale; and

- Either all employees may obtain free or subsidised meals on a reasonable scale, whether on the employer's premises or elsewhere, or the employer provides free or subsidised meal vouchers for staff for whom meals are not provided.

It is understood that the Revenue will apply this concession to personal service workers in the same way as it applies to the client's staff.

10.6.7 Fuel

Where fuel has been provided by the client for private use in a company car for any part of the tax year, the full-scale charge is applicable, unless the car itself was not provided for part of the year, see **10.6.3** above. There is no reduction in the benefit charge because only a small amount of private fuel has been provided. These rules may change from 2003/04.

Home to work travel is however not 'private mileage' if it falls within the travel rules, see **11.6**. If the engagement is not covered by the travel rules, however, care is needed. A small error, such as occasional reimbursements of fuel when a worker is called to the office out of hours, can give rise to a considerable tax bill.

10.6.8 Gifts

A gift provided by a client may escape tax if:

- It is either provided on personal grounds (for example, a wedding present) or as a mark of personal esteem (SE 01460); or

- It falls within ESC A70. This exempts small gifts in kind provided by third parties of up to £150 per annum. However this concession is not available if the gift is 'made either in recognition of the performance of particular services in the course of the employment or in anticipation of particular services which are to be performed'. This may apply to some gifts provided by a client to PSC workers.

10.6.9 Loans

Loans are an unlikely benefit, though it is possible that long term contractors might be given a season ticket advance on the same terms as employees. Temporary executives may succeed in obtaining more substantial loans.

If the client does lend money to the worker, and there is either no interest or the rate is below the Revenue's official rate, a benefit will arise unless:

- The loan is no more than £5,000 at any point in the tax year (s161 ICTA 1988); or

- It is a 'qualifying loan', such as to invest in a partnership (s160(1C) ICTA 1988); or

- The client's business is the lending of money, and the loan is on the same terms as is available to members of the public (s161(1A) ICTA 1988).

If the loan is written off, the amount becomes taxable on the worker, even if the contract has already terminated, see s160(3) ICTA 1988.

10.6.10 Relocations

Some personal service workers may have their relocation costs reimbursed by the client. This will not be a benefit as long as:

- Only 'eligible' relocation expenses are paid; and

- The total cost is not more than £8,000 (Sch 11A, ICTA 1988).

10.6.11 Telephones

If the mobile phone is *provided by the client* it will not be taxable, even if it is used for private calls. However, with the exception of evidenced business calls, the following are a benefit:

- Reimbursement of the worker's home telephone bills; or

- Mobile phone charges relating to the worker's own phone; or

- Phone vouchers provided by the employer.

Line rental is generally a benefit unless the line meets the wholly, exclusively and necessarily requirement, see *Lucas v Cattell* [1972] 48 TC 353. This test will be met, for example, if workers can show that it is genuinely part of their duties to deal with emergencies, such as an IT worker on call to deal with computer crashes. In such cases the Revenue allows the same proportion of the rental charge as the business use of the telephone is to the overall use (ECM 13044).

10.6.12 Travel and subsistence

Travel and subsistence costs are dealt with at **11.6**.

10.7 PAYE Settlement Agreements and Taxed Award Schemes

The client may use a PAYE Settlement Agreement (PSA) to meet the cost of some employee benefits. For instance, if the staff go on a day trip to Paris, the employer may calculate the tax and NIC and pay this over to the Revenue on a grossed up basis (s206A ICTA 1988).

However a PSA is not yet available where the benefit is provided for a third party, although this may that however be possible in the future, see the Revenue's consultation document, *Simplifying National Insurance Contributions for Employers*, issued on 7 June 2000.

However, third parties have long been able to use the Taxed Award Scheme (TAS) for tax. Since April 2000, the TAS can also be used to cover the NICs liability in relation to benefits and non-cash vouchers provided to third parties.

A client with a large number of personal services workers could thus use a TAS to pay the tax and NICs on benefits provided. However, appropriate communication is needed, particularly if the client has a fluctuating contractor workforce. The PSC workers might otherwise be unaware of the TAS and include the benefit in their own deemed income calculation or on their P11Ds.

11 Expenses included in deemed payment

11.1 Introduction

IR35 aims to tax the worker broadly as if his relevant engagements were an employment. As a result, the Schedule E reliefs for both expenses and capital allowances are applicable, rather than the more generous Schedule D legislation.

Step Three of the calculation gives relief on a Schedule E basis for expenses borne by the intermediary; Step Four deducts capital allowances on assets owned by the intermediary.

Under Step One of the calculation, the worker can also claim an additional expense allowance equal to 5 per cent of income received from relevant engagements.

11.2 The 5 per cent allowance

11.2.1 General

When carrying out the deemed Schedule E calculation, income received from relevant engagements is first reduced by 5 per cent (Sch 12, para 7 Step One FA 2000). Points to note include:

- It is immaterial whether the individual has been paid his earnings during the year as salary, or whether they are subject to a deemed Schedule E calculation: the 5 per cent deduction is identical because it is based on the relevant income received by the intermediary;

- The deduction is available only against income received by the *intermediary*. There is no 5 per cent deduction available against amounts paid directly to the worker by the client. It is thus more tax efficient for expenses to be reimbursed to the intermediary rather than being paid directly to the worker. For example, it is better for travel costs to be reimbursed to the service company than for the worker to be provided with the use of a car.

11.2.2 What does the 5 per cent deduction cover?

The Revenue's first FAQ on expenses explains that:

'Service companies will be able to claim a flat rate deduction of 5% of the gross fees receivable for any relevant engagements. This 5% deduction is not available to employees but will be allowed for service companies to enable them to meet the additional costs of providing their services in this particular way.'

Because the tax relief for expenses under the Schedule E legislation is somewhat limited, a number of unavoidable expenses will be suffered by the intermediary for which no explicit deduction is available in the deemed Schedule E calculation. The 5 per cent allowance gives relief for some or all of these costs, which include:

- Secretarial support;

- Accountancy and tax advice fees;

- The costs of seeking contracts;

- Computer equipment if not eligible for capital allowances, see **11.12** below;

- Postage and stationery;

- Training costs, see **11.8** below;

- Employer's and public liability insurance, see **11.10** below;

- Use of home as office in most cases, see **11.11** below;

- Bank and overdraft interest;

- Hire purchase payments, except in relation to vehicles used on business before 2002/03, see **11.6.8** and **11.6.9** below.

11.2.3 Interaction with corporation tax

Although in general an intermediary's actual expenses are likely to exceed the available tax reliefs, the opposite may also occur. The Revenue have confirmed that 'There will be no requirement to demonstrate expenditure: the 5 per cent deduction will be allowed in all cases.' (FAQ Expenses 2)

If the actual expenses are less than the 5 per cent allowed in the deemed Schedule E computation, some profits could remain within the charge to corporation tax, see Example 11A.

Example 11A

Jill, whose personal service company specialises in nursing services, has £70,000 of relevant income. A friend does her books and tax computation for £400 a year. She has no other expenses. Her year end is 5 April.

Her tax position for 2001/02 is as follows:

Deemed Schedule E calculation

	Notes	£
Relevant income		70,000
5% deduction		(3,500)
		66,500
NICs	1	(6,590)
Deemed Schedule E payment		59,910

Corporation tax	£
Income	70,000
Expenses	(400)
Deemed salary	(59,910)
Employer's NIC	(6,590)
CT profits	3,100
CT payable at 10%	310

Notes
NIC calculated as $(66,500 - 4,535) \times (11.9/111.9) = £6,590$, see **12.5.2**.

If the 5 per cent allowance has not been fully utilised by actual expenditure, a salary could be paid to a family member who has insufficient taxable income to utilise his personal allowance, in exchange for administrative help. This will both ensure that no residual profit is taxed in the company, and the relative will receive the money free of tax and NICs. However, the Revenue may challenge the payment, see **3.4**.

11.3 Expenses in the deemed Schedule E calculation

11.3.1 Step Three

Step Three allows relief for:

> 'The amount of any expenses met in that year by the intermediary, that would have been deductible from the emoluments of the employment if the

worker had been employed by the client and the expenses had been met by the worker out of those emoluments.' (Sch 12, para 7 Step 3 FA 2000)

The expenses which are allowable under the Schedule E rules for employees are discussed at **11.4** below. For what is meant by 'deductible from the emoluments of the employment if the worker had been employed by the client and the expenses had been met by the worker out of those emoluments', see **11.3.7**.

11.3.2 Cash basis

The expense is deductible when the cost is borne by the intermediary, not when the liability arises. As with income in Step One, see **10.2**, the deduction for expenses is thus on a cash rather than an accruals basis. This was clearly explained in FAQ Archive 10:

> 'How do I apportion the expenses when working out the deemed payment where a contract straddles the end of the tax year?
>
> When working out the deemed payment, relief should be given for all allowable expenses met by the intermediary in the tax year, in respect of relevant engagements, as set out at Step 3. Relief for the expense should be given by reference to the date when the intermediary meets the liability. This is the date when the bill is paid. There should therefore be no need to apportion any expenses.
>
> For example, an intermediary has a relevant engagement that runs from 1 January to 30 June 2001, during which the worker is required to work at a temporary workplace. In the course of this engagement the worker stays in bed and breakfast accommodation. The bill is settled on a monthly basis in arrears, with 14 days to pay. At the end of March a bill for £400 is issued which the intermediary pays on 12 April. The liability was met in the tax year 2001/02. Therefore, relief for the expense will be given when working out the deemed payment payable.'

11.3.3 Costs incurred by the employee/director rather than the intermediary

Since the deduction in Step Three is for expenses met by the intermediary, costs incurred directly by the worker do not come into the deemed Schedule E calculation. If these are allowable under the Schedule E rules, they can be claimed directly by the individual director or employee in his self-assessment form under ss198ff ICTA 1988. This puts workers in the same position as employees who bear the cost of allowable expenses in the course of their employment (Sch 12, para 11(4)(b) FA 2000). For partners, see **11.3.4** below, and for amounts covered by a dispensation, see **11.3.8**.

However, it is not efficient for the worker to bear the costs and claim s198 relief. This is because, although he can claim tax relief on the expense, he will not obtain NICs relief. If the amounts are met by the intermediary, they are taken out of the calculation at Step Three and so reduce the deemed payment. This saves both employer's and (sometimes) employee's NICs. Costs should therefore be borne by the intermediary, rather than by the worker.

Where a worker bears the expenses initially, but reclaims the amounts from the intermediary as business costs, see **11.3.7**.

11.3.4 Partners

Employees and directors have always been within the Schedule E rules, and thus should be more familiar with their requirements. Partnerships are brought within the rules by IR35, and may have a steeper learning curve.

Where partners initially bear costs relating to a relevant engagement themselves, they should ensure that these amounts are met by the partnership for the same reason as employees and directors – it will reduce the NIC on the deemed payment. If this does not happen, the partner should ensure that the amounts are claimed in the partnership computation. This is because there is no equivalent to s198 ICTA for partners, so tax relief cannot be claimed on the individual's own self-assessment return, see **15.3.4**. However, it should be noted that relief is only available in the partnership computation for expenses borne personally if the cost would have been allowable under the rules for Schedule E, see **11.3.6** below (Sch 12, para 18(3) FA 2000).

11.3.5 Apportioned costs

Although IR35 has a specific provision concerning apportionment of income, see **10.3**, there is no equivalent for costs. The legislation (Sch 12, para 9 FA 2000) requires that income be apportioned on a 'just and reasonable basis', and a similar approach can be taken for costs.

A cost may be apportioned because:

(a) It is partly for the purposes of the business and partly private. If a deduction is to be allowed for an apportioned cost in the Schedule E calculation, then 'a definite part or proportion' of the expense must meet the tests set out in ss198ff ICTA 1988 (IM 601e); or

(b) It relates partly to relevant engagements and partly to other work.

Although the NICs regulations do not recognise the concept of an apportioned expense, the tax rules take priority here, see SI 2000/727 reg 7 Step Three.

11.3.6 Expense disallowances

A practical question is the extent to which expenses disallowed in the deemed Schedule E calculation can be claimed in the corporation tax or partnership computation.

Partnership computation

A partnership can only deduct expenses relating to relevant income if they either meet the Schedule E tests or are within the 5 per cent allowance. It is thus not possible to offset 'surplus' expenses against other Schedule D income. (Sch 12, para 18(3) FA 2000.) A separate rule also prevents the Schedule E deemed payment from creating a loss (Sch 12, para 18(2) FA 2000), see **14.6.3**.

Corporation tax computation

No such explicit provision operates in the case of the corporation tax computation, so normal rules are followed. In some cases it is clear that an amount disallowed for Schedule E will be allowed for corporation tax. Examples include:

- Costs of accountancy and tax advice to calculate the deemed Schedule E amount, because the obligation to make the deemed payment is on the intermediary, not the individual;
- Filing costs relating to the company;
- Expenses of seeking contracts;
- Genuine costs of administrative assistance.

In other cases, even though there is no specific legal requirement to disallow excess costs as there is with partnerships, the deemed income calculation may focus attention on expenses which have previously been accepted as allowable by the Revenue.

For example, where part of the running costs of the home have been claimed as allowable for corporation tax, and the company's business is now seen to consist entirely of relevant engagements, the Inspector may question whether the deduction is justified – what work is actually being done at home and how much time does it take? Such questions could even lead into an enquiry into previous years. Care should thus be taken when completing the corporation tax computation.

11.3.7 Met by the intermediary

For an amount to be deductible under Step Three, it must have been 'met by the intermediary'. In earlier versions of the ESM this was interpreted by the Revenue as follows:

> '"Met" means only those expenses incurred and paid for by the intermediary. It does not include expenses that the worker meets personally and for which he or she is then reimbursed by the intermediary.' (ESM 3162 and 3168)

However this was not a view supported by case law. In *Cyril Lord Carpets Ltd v Schofield*, CA(NI) 1966, 42 TC 637, a case about capital expenditure funded by government grants, Lord MacDermott said:

> 'In common parlance a liability which has been discharged may be "met" by a payment no less than a liability which has not been discharged. In its natural signification the word connotes something set against or opposed to something else, and in pecuniary transactions it is, I think, as aptly used of a payment to be set against the cost of a debt discharged as it is of the payment made in actually discharging the debt. A, for example, flies to London from Belfast to give a lecture at the request of B. A pays for his ticket as he gets it and has therefore both incurred and paid for that expenditure. Later, B insists on paying A the amount of his expenditure. In doing so B has surely "met" the expenditure incurred as plainly as would have been the case if A had travelled on credit and B had paid the fare to the carrier.'

The Revenue have now accepted that 'met by the intermediary' includes 'paid for by the worker and reimbursed by the intermediary'. On 15 March 2002 they announced changes to the legislation making this explicit: new paragraph 7A has been inserted in the tax legislation, and a similar change has been made to the NICs regulations.

In practice the question of what is meant by 'met' was likely to be important only in a few situations, such as where the service company has a dispensation, see **11.3.8**. This is because expenditure not deductible at Step Three will usually be removed from the deemed income calculation at Step Seven, see **12.4**.

11.3.8 'Amounts which would have been deductible'

Step Three only allows an amount to be removed from the calculation if it has been met by the intermediary and it:

> 'Would have been deductible from the emoluments of the employment if the worker had been employed by the client and the expenses had been met by the worker out of those emoluments.' (Sch 12, para 7 Step 3 FA 2000)

This wording looks problematic in three areas:

- Personal Incidental Expenses (PIEs). These 'shall not be regarded as emoluments of the office or employment for any purpose of Schedule E' (s200A ICTA 1988) and are thus not deductible from the emoluments. This issue is discussed at **11.7**;

- Authorised mileage rates paid after April 2002. These are also specifically exempted from tax, see s197D ICTA 1988. This is covered at **11.6.9**;

- Dispensations. Where an employer receives a dispensation for expenses, the legislation disapplies the taxing statutes on those expenses or benefits. Section 166(1) ICTA 1988 states that when a dispensation has been granted 'nothing in this Chapter applies to those payments, or to the provision of those benefits or facilities'.

  Amounts covered by a dispensation are however covered by Step Three, because *if* the worker had met the expenses out of his own emoluments (i.e., they had not been dispensed) then he would have been able to claim relief for these costs under s198 ICTA 1988.

11.3.9 VAT on expenses

There is nothing in the legislation about VAT on expenses, and no guidance was given in either the first edition of the ESM or the FAQs. In an article in *Taxation*, 29 March 2001, Mark Morton said that 'the Revenue has confirmed that expense figures should be included in this calculation inclusive of VAT'.

This was presumably on the basis that Step Three deducts 'expenses ... that would have been deductible from the emoluments of the employment if the worker had been employed by the client and the expenses had been met by the worker out of those emoluments'. Had the worker been employed by the client, the amount he would have deducted from his emoluments would have been the gross expense, including any VAT.

However, when the ESM was reissued later in 2001, it included the sentence 'Where the intermediary is registered for VAT, use the net expenditure exclusive of any VAT' (ESM 3163). The pragmatic reason for this change of heart is clear – income is included in the deemed Schedule E on a net of VAT basis, so allowing expenses to be deducted gross would give an unexpected benefit to the taxpayer.

Does the legislation require that expenses be deducted net, or was the Revenue's original view correct? Step Three begins by saying 'Deduct the amount of any expense met in that year by the intermediary ... ' It could be argued that only the net expense is truly 'met' by the intermediary and thus the revised view is correct. However the point is not beyond doubt.

11.4 Schedule E expenses

11.4.1 Tax

The general Schedule E expenses rule is set out in s198(1) ICTA 1988. It allows deductions for expenses which have been 'wholly, exclusively and necessarily incurred in the performance of the duties of the employment'. The reliefs for travel and subsistence are more generous, only requiring that costs be 'necessarily incurred in the performance of the duties'(s198(1A) and Sch 12A ICTA 1988), see **11.6**.

Relief is also available under the Schedule E rules for:

- Personal incidental expenses, see **11.7**;

- Work-related training provided by clients or agents, see **11.8**;

- Expenditure on professional fees and subscriptions, see **11.9**;

- Indemnity insurance payments, see **11.10**; and

- Agents' fees paid by entertainers, see **20.2.4**.

11.4.2 National Insurance

Allowable expenses are deductible at Step Three of the attributable earnings calculation. Although the NIC rules for allowable expenses are not identical to those for tax, where they differ, it is the tax rules which are used (SI 2000/727 reg 7 Step Three).

This is intended to be a simplification, as if this were not the case, the calculation would have to be performed twice – once for NICs and once for tax. However, simplicity is elusive in the context of IR35. When one turns to Step Seven (**12.4**), which allows a deduction for amounts already subject to tax and NICs, the tax calculation gives relief only for amounts subject to tax; the attributable earnings calculation gives relief for amounts subject to NICs.

The implications of this become clear when one considers childcare provided by the intermediary. Childcare is normally subject to tax but exempt from NICs (SI 1979/591 Sch 3). It is not deducted at Step Three because it is not an allowable expense for tax; it is deducted at Step Seven for tax because it is subject to tax; however it can only be removed from the parallel attributable earnings calculation at Step Seven if it is a benefit 'in respect of which Class 1A contributions are payable'. This interpretation has been confirmed by the Revenue, see accountingweb 28 June 2001.

The effect of this is twofold:

- It brings childcare into IR35 for NICs even though it would have not be subject to NICs had the worker been employed by the client;

- The service company has to carry out two calculations, one for NICs and one for tax.

This is clearly a nonsense and needs revision.

11.5 The general rule: s198(1)

Meeting the 'wholly, exclusively and necessarily in the performance of the duties test' is extremely difficult. These words have been described as:

> 'Notoriously rigid, narrow and restricted in their operation. An expenditure may be "necessary" for the holder of an office without being necessary to him in the performance of the duties of that office; it may be necessary in the performance of those duties without being exclusively referable to those duties; it may perhaps be both necessarily and exclusively, but still not wholly so referable. The words are indeed stringent and exacting; compliance with each and every one of them is obligatory if the benefit of the Rule is to be claimed successfully. They are, to my mind, deceptive words in the sense that when examined they are found to come to nearly nothing at all.'
> (*Lomax v Newton* [1953] 34 TC 558)

The s198 test refers to 'the holder' of the job, and it is thus based on the requirements of the duties rather than those of the specific individual carrying out the engagement. To satisfy the rule the expenditure must be necessary to each and every person who might perform those duties. See for example the words of Donovan L.J.:

> 'The test is not whether the employer imposes the expense but whether the duties do, in the sense that, irrespective of what the employer may prescribe, the duties cannot be performed without incurring the particular outlay.'
> (*Brown v Bullock* [1961] 40 TC 1)

However this does not mean that every holder of the job would have to incur the same amount of expense. The Revenue confirm that:

> 'This test relates to the nature of the expense and not to the amount. For example, a business trip may be made by train, car or bus. As long as the trip is necessary it does not matter that the various modes of transport have different costs. If the whole of the expense is of a type that is necessarily incurred you should not attempt to restrict the deduction to the minimum that could have been incurred.' (SE 31645)

The expense must be incurred in actually performing the duties. The Revenue have summarised this as follows:

> 'It is not enough for the expense to be relevant to the job, or to be incurred in connection with the duties of the job. Nor is it enough if the expense only puts the employee in a position to start work or keeps the employee qualified to do the work.' (SE 31650)

The cost must also be 'wholly and exclusively' incurred, although apportionment is possible 'if a definite part or proportion of that expense can properly be attributed wholly and exclusively to the performance of the duties' (SE 31661). This principle was established by the cases *Hillyer v Leeke* 51 TC 90 and *Woodcock v CIR* 51 TC 698, even though these judgments went against the taxpayers. If, for example, an aircraft is used partly for business and partly privately, its costs can be split between those which are allowable for Schedule E and those relating to the private use.

However, where the expenditure serves two or more purposes at the same time, one of which is not to do with the performance of the duties, nothing can be claimed. An example is the cost of ordinary clothing. In *Ward v Dunn* [1979] 52 TC 517 a surveyor had his arguments rejected:

> 'When Mr Dunn purchases a suit he purchases it, maybe partly with a view to going round the sites but, at any rate, partly with a view to wearing it in the ordinary course as one wears clothing for comfort and for covering one's nakedness. Similarly, when he has clothing cleaned it is cleaned, doubtless

partly as a result of what happens on the construction sites, but also so that he may wear clean clothing and not dirty clothing. Similarly, when it is repaired as a result of damage which it has sustained when he has visited sites, it is repaired so that he may wear clothes which hang together, not clothes which are in rags ... The mere fact that that clothing is his ordinary clothing makes it, in my view, completely impossible for it to be said that the money which he is now claiming is money which is "wholly" expended by him in the performance of his duties.'

Section 198 is thus much less generous than the comparable section for expenses incurred by a company or a partnership under Schedule D, which merely requires costs to be 'wholly and exclusively for the purposes of the business' (s74(1)(a) ICTA 1988). As a result, many costs for which tax relief was available before IR35 was introduced will no longer obtain relief – at least not in the deemed Schedule E calculation. Relief will still be due in the corporation tax computation, but this may simply create a loss, see **13.7**.

Examples of expenses allowable under s198 include:

(a) Protective clothing worn as a matter of physical necessity because of the nature of the job, such as oil workers' overalls, see SE 32474;

(b) Clothing which is recognisably a uniform. The Revenue do not accept that an item of clothing is 'uniform' if it can be worn away from the workplace without its identity as uniform being obvious. The inclusion of a prominent and permanently fixed company logo on the clothing is usually required, see SE 32475;

(c) Books which have to be purchased by the worker in order to carry out the job, such as computer manuals necessary to operate equipment. But this is a difficult test to meet, see SE 32435.

11.6 Travel and subsistence expenses

11.6.1 General

The legislation for travel expenses (s198(1A) and Sch 12A ICTA 1988) is less stringent than the general rule. Instead of a requirement that costs be 'wholly, exclusively and necessarily incurred in the performance of the duties', travel expenses only have to be 'necessarily incurred in the performance of the duties'. Thus if a worker has to travel to Perpignan for a business meeting, the fact that he spends a few days beforehand cycling in the Pyrenees will not make his return trip to France inadmissible.

'Travel' includes any associated subsistence and other incidental costs such as car parking. Since many personal service workers have contracts which entitle them to travel and subsistence on top of a daily rate, it is important that these amounts fall as far as possible within the reliefs offered by the legislation.

The rules are complex, and explored at length in Inland Revenue booklet 490 (IR 490). The following summarises the key points relevant to those within the personal service rules.

11.6.2 Legislation

Section 198(1A) ICTA 1988 defines allowable travel expenses as follows:

(a) 'Amounts necessarily expended on travelling in the performance of the duties of the office or employment.' This covers journeys where the travelling itself is part of the duties, such as where the worker is a long distance lorry driver, and also trips between one place of business and another, such as between two offices of the same employer; and

(b) Other expenses of travelling which 'are attributable to the necessary attendance at any place ... in the performance of the duties of the office or employment, which are not expenses of ordinary commuting or private travel'.

This gives relief for journeys to carry out necessary duties of the relevant engagement, such as travelling from home to meet a customer of the client. However, there is no tax relief when the journey is 'ordinary commuting' or 'private travel'.

11.6.3 Ordinary commuting

A journey counts as 'ordinary commuting' if it is travel between home and a permanent workplace (Sch 12A, para 2 ICTA 1988). However, travel to and from a *temporary* workplace is tax free. So too is any associated subsistence and accommodation. Thus for the personal service worker to gain relief for his travel and subsistence, he has to show that the client's office is a temporary workplace.

For a workplace to be 'temporary' either of the following tests must be satisfied:

(a) The duties of the employment are not performed to a significant extent at that place. 'A significant extent' is generally interpreted by the Revenue to mean more than 40 per cent (IR 490 para 3.12);

(b) The engagement is expected to, and actually does, last for two years or less.

This second relief – the two-year rule – does not apply if the engagement comprises 'all or almost all of the period for which the employee is likely to hold the employment' (Sch 12A, para 5 ICTA 1988).

Initially this gave rise to fears that contractors would be unable to claim for travel to clients' sites, because if they were deemed to be employees of the client for tax purposes (Sch 12, para 7 Step 3 FA 2000), each engagement would be 'all or almost all of the period for which the employee is likely to hold the employment'.

However, Schedule 12, paragraph 11(2) FA 2000 states that the worker's 'employment' is with his own company, and this would indicate that travel to clients will not therefore comprise 'all or almost all' of his employment.

There is a clear legislative tension between the two paragraphs that was resolved by statements from the Revenue and the Minister. In FAQ Expenses 4 the Revenue said:

> 'A computer contractor provides services through a limited company; has a series of contracts with different clients around the country; and regularly travels from home to work at the premises of the company's clients.

> Provided the contractor does not expect to spend more than 40% of his or her working time at any one site, he or she is entitled to a deduction for all journeys from home to the client's premises. If he or she does spend more than 40% of his time at a single site, but the engagement is both expected to, and actually does, last for no more than 2 years, a deduction for travel costs will also be available.'

Subsequently, similar confirmation was given by Dawn Primarolo in the House of Commons debate on the Finance Bill, see *Hansard* 6 June 2000.

The TLRC, in their rewritten draft legislation on employment income, have proposed amending the legislation to clarify the position. Interestingly, they also state that current regime for travel expenses is in fact concessional:

> 'One of the categories of expenses that has caused most difficulty in calculating the deemed payment is travel expenses. Entitlement to travel expenses depends on whether or not a workplace is "temporary" and where the worker is based over the course of the employment. It is Inland Revenue practice to look at the travel deductions that would have been available during the combined period of all the relevant engagements as if they

represented a period of continuous employment with the intermediary. Paragraph 8 represents a proposed rewrite change to put this practice on a legislative footing. It is a change to the law but not to policy. It is in the tax-payer's favour.' (*ED12 – Draft Income Tax [Earnings and Pensions] Bill Part 2 Employment Income*)

Two-year test

If at some point during the two year period it becomes likely that the engagement will be extended beyond the two-year point, travel and subsistence becomes taxable from that date. Great care is therefore needed when negotiating and communicating extensions to engagements.

The two-year test is applied from the start date of the contract. An engagement which began on 6 July 1999 would have failed the two-year test if it was either expected to, or actually did, continue after 5 July 2001. This is true whether or not the relevant engagement was being carried out by a worker in a company (who was already within the travel rules) or by a partner, coming into the rules for the first time. The 6 April 2000 date, which marked the start of the new personal services regime, does not affect this in any way. The important factor is the start date of the engagement.

The following Examples 11B to 11J, adapted from IR 490, illustrate the various scenarios. The particularly harsh treatment in Example 11D should be noted, along with the fact that a period of work can remain continuous even where there is a break in attendance, see Example 11F.

Example 11B

Doris has set up her own personal service company based at her home in Warrington supplying secretarial services. Warrington is thus her permanent workplace. She is obtains a relevant engagement at an office in Wigan for 18 months. Relief is available for the full cost of Doris's travel between home and the temporary workplace in Wigan.

Example 11C

Duncan obtains a relevant engagement working full-time at a factory for 28 months. There is no relief for the cost of travel to and from the workplace, because his attendance there is known from the outset to be for more than 24 months, so the workplace is a permanent workplace. His home to work travel is therefore ordinary commuting for which no relief is available.

Example 11D

Dymphna's relevant engagement requires her full-time attendance at a workplace for 28 months but the posting is unexpectedly ended after 18 months. No relief is available for the cost of travel between her home and the workplace, because her attendance was expected to exceed 24 months (though in fact it does not). The workplace is therefore a permanent workplace and the

Example 11E

Earl has a relevant full-time engagement at a workplace for 18 months. After 10 months the posting is extended to 28 months. Relief is available for the full cost of travel to and from the workplace during the first 10 months (while his attendance was expected to be for less than 24 months) but not after that (once his attendance was expected to exceed 24 months).

Example 11F

Ernest is a subcontractor with his own service company. He obtains a relevant engagement to work full-time on a construction project which is expected to last for six years. Each time Ernest gets close to having worked on the site for nearly two years his employer moves him to another workplace for a week before returning him to the long-term project site.

Despite these moves, Ernest is spending a significant amount of his working time (more than 40 per cent) at one site and the period during which he is doing so is greater than 24 months. So Ernest is not entitled to relief for his travel from home to the site, see IR 490 paragraph 3.15 and Sch 12A, para 5(2)

40 per cent test

The two-year test is in the legislation (Sch 12A, para 5(1)(a) ICTA 1988), whereas the 40 per cent test is Revenue practice. Examples 11G and 11H show how it is applied:

> **Example 11G**
>
> Emily is a partner in a veterinary practice on the south coast. She obtains a relevant engagement under which she is required to supervise a seal sanctuary in Morecambe for one day each month. She has done this for five years. Although Emily goes to Morecambe for more than 24 months she does not spend more than 40 per cent of her working time there and she retains a permanent workplace on the south coast. So she is entitled to relief for her travel from home to Morecambe.

> **Example 11H**
>
> Ferdinand is a computer expert who provides his services via a personal service company. He is the company's only employee. Each year the company has around 15 contracts with different clients around the country to supply Ferdinand's services. He regularly travels from home to work at the premises of the company's clients. Provided he does not expect to spend more than 40 per cent of his working time for more than 24 months at any one site he is entitled to relief for all his journeys from home to the clients' premises.

Substantial effect test

Where a change in location 'does not have ... any substantial effect on the employee's journey, or expenses of travelling, to and from the place where the duties fall to be performed' then the two year period will be measured from the beginning of the earlier contract (Sch 12A, para 5(3) ICTA 1988).

This means that if a worker has an engagement with a client for 18 months, and then moves to a second contract in the next street, there is no 'substantial effect' on either the journey or the expenses of travelling. If the total time expected to be spent at both engagements taken together is more than two years, no tax relief will be available from the date on which the worker agrees to take up the second contract. Considerable care is thus needed when selecting engagements.

The substantial effect test can be difficult to apply. However the Revenue have confirmed that:

> 'Where a change in location has a significant effect on the journey an employee has to make to get to work and, in particular, the cost of the journey to work, the new location is a new workplace even if it is close to the old workplace.' (IR 490 5.8)

Example 11J demonstrates how the Revenue will interpret the rule:

Example 11J

Justin is a subcontractor with his own service company and obtains a relevant engagement working on a major bridge construction project. To begin with he works on the north shore but he is then transferred to work on the south shore. Crossing the river is inconvenient (which is why a new bridge is needed), and it takes Justin longer to travel to the south shore and costs much more than it did to travel to the north shore. The north and south shores could be described as a single construction site and, as the crow flies, they are not far apart. However, Justin's move from the north to the south shore has had a significant effect on his journey to work (and, in particular, the cost of that journey) so his workplace has changed for tax purposes.

Cessation of business

As explained above, the travel reliefs operate if the engagement does not comprise 'all or almost all' of the period for which the worker was employed. Since the worker is regarded as employed by his service company, this restriction will only become an issue if the employment is terminated following a single long engagement, or following an engagement which took up almost all of the period for which the worker operated via the intermediary, see Example 11K.

Example 11K

Chris was employed as a teacher trainer by a language school in London, but was made redundant in order to reduce headcount. However, the school quickly found they could not meet their commitments to students, and suggested he form his own service company. Chris worked for the language school for two years, and claimed over £1,000 a year on travel costs. In June 2000 he decided to close down the company to concentrate on writing novels. As he had only one engagement which comprised 'all or almost all' of the period for which he held the engagement, his travel costs could be disallowed.

Some workers may be able to take advantage of the practice set out in Revenue booklet 490 at paragraph 3.18:

> 'The Inland Revenue will not normally use this rule to deny relief for travel to a workplace which is the final posting for someone whose contract of employment has lasted for at least 5 years.'

11.6.4 Private travel

This is travel between either:

- The employee's home and a place that is not his workplace; or

- Between two places neither of which is his workplace.

The legislation here is stating the obvious – there is no tax relief for a private journey, such as between home and the football ground, or between the football ground and the pub.

11.6.5 Accommodation and subsistence

If business travel is allowable, so too is any associated accommodation or subsistence, see Example 11L.

Example 11L

Michael is required to spend three months working at the site of one of his clients. He travels to the site every Monday morning, stays in a hotel close to the temporary workplace and travels home late every Friday evening, eating dinner on the way. During the week he takes some of his meals in the hotel and others at a nearby restaurant. The cost of the accommodation and all the *meals are part of the cost of his business travel.*

However some expenditure which may be incurred during a business journey is not attributable to that travel. Private telephone calls, newspapers and laundry, for example, are 'essentially personal in nature and do not, therefore, qualify for relief as integral parts of the cost of business travel' (IR 490 5.8). Where the worker stays overnight, some limited relief is available, see **11.7** below.

11.6.6 Working rule agreements

Working rule agreements (WRAs) are collective agreements drawn up between representatives of employers and trade unions. They generally cover travel, accommodation and subsistence and are normally payable to specific groups of employees within the construction and allied industries.

The Inland Revenue and the Contributions Agency are not a party to these agreements but have accepted that certain WRA allowances paid for daily travel and lodging should not be taxed or subjected to NIC. This is broadly on the basis that the workers would otherwise be able to claim a deduction for the expenses under s198(1A) ICTA 1988, although the Revenue have indicated that:

> 'It now seems likely that many such expenses payments might not be deductible under the general expenses rule, with the result that the tax treatment of WRAs is, at least in part, concessionary.' *(Employee Travel and Subsistence Consultative Document,* May 1996, para 5.3.1)

The modified tax procedures are negotiated nationally and apply only where the client adopts the terms and conditions of the relevant WRA. However the client does not have to be a member of the relevant employers' federation, nor do workers have to belong to the union negotiating the allowances, for these procedures to operate (*IRPR* 13 February 1981).

It is understood that WRA amounts received by workers who are within the personal service rules should be treated in the same way as those received by ordinary employees. Thus, where (as is normal) the WRA is paid to the worker, it will not be brought into the deemed Schedule E payment, because it is not chargeable to tax, see **10.5.3**. However, if it were paid to the intermediary, it would be brought into the calculation under Step One. Only the actual costs met by the intermediary would then be deductible under Step Three, and this may be less advantageous.

11.6.7 Planning for travel costs

Workers can maximise their tax reliefs for travel and subsistence as follows:

(a) Costs should be met by the intermediary rather than being paid directly to the worker by the client, see **11.3.3** above;

(b) If the worker undertakes a series of short engagements, each of which satisfy the travel rules, he can claim home to work travel in each case, irrespective of whether the cost is reimbursed by the client. So a worker who lives in Brighton and has an 18-month contract in London, whose home to work travel costs are met by his service company, can reduce his deemed Schedule E income by this amount;

(c) Engagements at a single location which require both more than 40 per cent of the worker's time and are expected to last for more than two years, should either be avoided, or priced accordingly;

(d) Extreme care should be taken when negotiating an extension to a contract beyond the two year point, because the costs become taxable from the point when it is *expected* to exceed two years;

(e) It is possible to have a contract at a single location for more than two years, if it does not take up more than 40 per cent of the worker's time;

(f) Where a worker has an engagement with a client which requires him to work at a number of different sites, it is the *sites* which must be considered for the purposes of the travel rules, not the contract. So a single contract can extend for more than two years if the worker's location changes during the period, and he is within the travel rules in respect of each location;

(g) A new engagement should be a reasonable distance from the last, so as not to fall within the 'substantial effect' rule discussed at **11.6.3** above.

Additional tax reliefs may be available if the engagement is abroad, see **17.10.2**, or if the worker is from overseas, see **17.12.4**.

11.6.8 Vehicle running costs and business mileage – before 2002/03

Until April 2002 a worker with a *company* car, motorbike or bicycle could be paid the Revenue's authorised mileage rates for business travel, see FAQ Expenses 11. Alternatively, if he *owned* a car, motor bike or cycle and used it in the performance of a relevant engagement he could either:

- Claim mileage costs from the company, based on the Revenue's authorised mileage rates (FAQ Expenses 8); or

- Deduct the proportion of his total costs which related to his business use. This was calculated as the appropriate proportion (based on mileage) of the actual running costs of the vehicle including road fund licence, insurance, servicing and maintenance, annual subscriptions to breakdown/recovery services and the consideration, if any, for hire of the car under a hire purchase agreement. It also included the actual cost of fuel consumed for business mileage, but did not include deprecation (IM 710). He could also claim capital allowances, see **11.12** below.

Where the worker was reimbursed by the client at a rate lower than he could claim under either the Revenue's authorised mileage rates, or the more detailed calculation method, the difference could be deducted as an allowable travel cost.

However, where *excess* amounts were reimbursed to the intermediary, the full amount was brought into the calculation at Step One, with only the allowable amount being deductible at Step Three. Where excess amounts were reimbursed directly to the worker, they were taxable under the normal Schedule E rules, see **10.5.4.**

For non-IR35 workers, there was a difference between the tax and NIC treatment of authorised mileage rates. This was thought to be because the Revenue believed that the two-tier system of mileage rates required for tax is not practicable for NICs:

> 'In practice, as long as reimbursed travelling expenses do no more than cover the full cost of business travel there will be no liability for NICs. Only where travel payments are made over and above the full cost of business travel will there be a liability for NICs.' (IR 490 para 6.4)

However, this difference was irrelevant in the context of the deemed payment. This is because the attributable earning calculation uses the same expense rules as for tax, see **11.4.2** (SI 2000/727, para 7).

11.6.9 Vehicle running costs and business mileage – from 2002/03 onwards

From April 2002 authorised mileage rates become statutory (ss197AD–197AH ICTA 1988); the option to make a claim based on actual costs has been abolished and capital allowances are no longer permitted.

However the IR35 legislation as originally enacted was not compatible with ss197AD–197AH ICTA 1988 and amendments to the former were announced on 15 March 2002. These inserted new paragraph 7B into the tax legislation, and similar changes were made to the NICs regulations.

The result of these changes is that an individual within IR35 can obtain tax and NICs relief on authorised mileage rates paid to him by the intermediary. Where the intermediary does not pay the worker, the latter can make a claim for relief in his self-assessment form. This gives him relief for tax but not for NICs; it is therefore more efficient if the worker is paid the authorised mileage amounts by his intermediary.

11.7 Personal Incidental Expenses (PIEs)

Contractors often incur incidental expenses, such as laundry, personal phone calls and newspapers, when staying away from home. These do not form part of the individual's allowable subsistence costs, see **11.6.5.** Instead, there is limited relief for these expenses under s200A ICTA 1988.

This allows the worker to incur up to £5 per night (£10 outside the UK) if he is away on business overnight. This can be by reimbursement or claimed as an allowance. Particular note should be taken of the following:

- If the payment is more than £5, the whole amount is taxable and subject to NIC;

- If an employee stays away for several nights consecutively, the total allowance is £5 multiplied by the number of nights away. For example, where an employee stays away for four nights and claims £5 on the first night, £5 on the second, £6 on the third and £4 on the fourth, he is within the exemption because the total does not exceed £20. Where the number of nights is not consecutive, no averaging is allowed.

Where PIEs are paid to the worker by the client they are not brought into the calculation under Steps One or Two, see **10.5.3**. Thus the correct tax-free status is achieved.

However, a PIE received by the intermediary is brought into the calculation at Step One, but not removed by either Steps Three or Seven – because under the wording of s200A they are not to be 'regarded as emoluments of the office or employment for any purpose of Schedule E'. They are thus specifically exempted from tax rather than being a deduction from earnings (as required by Step Three) or being 'chargeable' (as required by Step Seven). The Inland Revenue have suggested that payment be made to the worker by the client to avoid problems with this part of the legislation.

Where a service company has not been aware of this point, it is hoped that the Revenue will nevertheless give the relief. If this does not happen, the taxpayer could argue that leaving the PIE within the deemed Schedule E calculation means that it has been treated as an emolument for the purposes of Schedule E, and this contradicts s200A ICTA 1988. A review of *Hansard* should indicate that the latter is to be preferred here over Schedule 12: there was clearly no intention when IR35 was introduced that personal service company workers would have to pay tax on PIEs.

11.8 Training

11.8.1 Training paid for by the worker

Normally no deduction will be given under s198(1) ICTA 1988 for training paid for by a worker within the personal service rules no matter how closely related it is to his job. This is because the expense is not incurred 'in performance of' the duties, see *Blackwell v Mills* [1945] 26 TC 468; *Humbles v Brooks* [1962] 40 TC 500 and *Parikh v Sleeman* [1990] 63 TC 75.

11.8.2 Training paid for by the client or agency

Training provided by the client

Relief for employees' training paid for by the client is available under s200B ICTA 1988. This covers 'work-related' training, defined as 'any training course or other activity which is designed to impart, instil, improve or reinforce any knowledge, skills, or personal qualities' which:

- Are, or are likely to prove, useful to the worker when performing his duties in relation to the client or the agency which provided the training; or

- Will qualify (or better qualify) the worker to undertake the relevant engagement, or to participate in charitable or voluntary activities arising through the engagement.

There is no restriction on the way the training is delivered. Self-tuition packages, computer based training, distance learning, work experience, work placement or informal teach-ins are all acceptable, along with more formal classroom based methods. It does not matter whether training is delivered internally or externally, or on a part-time or full-time basis, see SE 01220.

However, training provided for recreational reasons or to reward the worker is excluded from relief under s200C ICTA 1988.

Training provided by the agency

Under s200D ICTA relief is extended to training provided by someone other than the employer, where relief would have been granted had the training been provided by the employer. The Revenue have confirmed that this relief will cover training provided by the agency. In FAQ Expenses 6 they say that 'Any training provided by clients or agencies will not count as a taxable benefit, and no tax charge will arise.'

11.8.3 Limits of relief

During the consultation on IR35, it was proposed that relief should be available in the deemed Schedule E computation for training carried out by the service company, as well for as that paid for by the client or agency. These representations were rejected by Dawn Primarolo, the Paymaster General, on 2 December 1999. She said that:

> 'There have been suggestions, especially from IT and engineering consult-ants, that expenses for "work related training" should be an allowable deduction in the calculation of the minimum amount of tax and National Insurance Contributions that workers with service companies should pay, if their engagements meet the accepted definition of employment. Our inten-tion is that workers in service companies should be in the same position as employees with regard to what help they can get with training they pay for themselves … No deduction for training is therefore appropriate for service companies in calculating the minimum salary for tax and NIC purposes.
>
> I announced, on 23 September, that a 5% flat rate deduction for expenses would be allowed on top of all the other expenses … It is for the service company to decide how best to use the 5% deduction and that choice could be to provide for the worker's training needs.'

The Revenue have subsequently confirmed that:

> 'The deductions allowable … are based on those available to employees. Employees cannot generally get tax relief for money they spend on their own training, either while they are employed or in between jobs, and no deduc-tion will be allowed for service companies in calculating the minimum salary for tax and NIC purposes. However, the 5% allowance for general expenses is available to cover such expenses as training costs.' (FAQ Expenses 6)

11.8.4 Individual learning accounts (ILAs)

The Budget which announced IR35 also launched individual learning accounts (ILAs):

> 'Contributions made by employers into ILAs held by their employees will qualify for a deduction from taxable profits and will be tax and national insurance contributions free in the hands of their employees, provided employers contribute to the ILAs of their lowest paid workers on similar terms. ILAs will provide a 20% discount for everyone, on eligible training costs of up to £500 a year.'

The benefits of the ILA were mentioned by Dawn Primarolo when she rejected service company workers' plea for a more generous training deduc-tion. She said that:

> 'ILAs will introduce a range of discounts and grants for eligible learning. Anyone, including a service company worker, will be able to open an ILA.'

The legislation implementing the ILA was subsequently incorporated as new ss200E to 200H ICTA 1988. Thus an employer was able to make a contribution into an employee's ILA without the employee suffering any tax or NICs. The employer also received a deduction for the contribution against his corporation tax charge. However, the Revenue confirmed that if a contribution has been made into an ILA by the service company, this contribution will not be an allowable deduction in the deemed Schedule E calculation.

ILAs were suspended in the autumn of 2001 because of widespread fraud, and the government announced in the pre-budget review that they were going to introduce a replacement relief for employees' training. At the time of writing it remains to be seen whether this new provision will be accessible to those caught by IR35.

11.8.5 Indicator of self-employment

Some small compensation was provided for service company workers who spend their own money (or that of the service company) on training. The Revenue's February 2000 *Tax Bulletin*, analysing the status tests, said:

> 'Another example of a financial risk is where a skilled worker incurs significant amounts of expenditure on training to provide himself with a skill which he uses in subsequent engagements. This can be treated in the same way as investment in equipment to be used in a trade, as a pointer to self-employment, if there is a real risk that the investment would not be recovered from income from future engagements.'

11.9 Professional subscriptions

Employees can obtain tax relief for fees and subscriptions paid to professional bodies such as the Institute of Chartered Accountants and the Chartered Institute of Taxation. A list of approved organisations is available from the Revenue.

Subscriptions are commonly paid directly by employees and deducted on their self-assessment returns. In the case of a personal service worker it is more tax efficient for them to be paid by the service company or partnership on the worker's behalf, as this will reduce the relevant income subject to NICs, see **11.3.3** above.

11.10 Insurance

Professional indemnity insurance (PII) protects the worker from being sued for negligence by clients. Tax relief is available for PII under s201AA ICTA 1988, and amounts paid to settle claims against the worker are also allowable.

Where the PII cost has been met by the intermediary it is deductible at Step Three. Again, it is more efficient for this route to be taken rather than the worker claiming a deduction on his SA return. However there is no similar tax relief for either:

(a) Public liability insurance, which protects the worker against legal liability if he accidentally causes damage or loss to someone else's property, such as a computer owned by a client. Public liability insurance also covers accidental injury caused by the worker to another person on the client's premises; or

(b) Employers' liability insurance, which protects employers against claims for injury or illness brought by employees. It is a statutory requirement – the Employers' Liability (Compulsory Insurance) Act 1998 requires employers to maintain a minimum cover of £5m. Many personal service workers don't take out this type of policy because they are the company's only employee. It is nevertheless a legal obligation, because there is both an employer (the company) and an employee (the worker).

Employer's and public liability insurance costs can therefore only be relieved as part of the 5 per cent allowance, see **11.2**.

11.11 Home as office costs

Contractors have traditionally claimed part of the costs of heating, lighting and furnishing their homes on the grounds that their company is based there. These expenses are only allowable against their Schedule E earnings if they meet the stringent s198 ICTA test, see **11.5**. The Revenue summarise the position as follows:

> 'It is not enough that there should be a contractual obligation to work from home. It is not enough that there should actually be work at home. What is required is something more; that the nature of the employment itself must necessarily include an obligation to work at home.' (SE 32770)

They accept that these tests are satisfied in the case of certain workers, namely insurance agents, midwives, university lecturers, examiners, councillors and ministers of religion, see SE 32775. In the case of service companies, Inspectors are advised that:

> 'You should only accept that substantive duties are carried out at home where the company has a trade or business that goes beyond servicing individual client contracts and where that additional trade or business is serviced from home. For example a computer consultant may service individual client contracts that involve installing software but may also design, develop and market software from home as part of the company's business. That additional activity may be part of the substantive duties of the employment.' (SE 32800)

This passage is not written in the context of the hypothetical contract of employment with the client, but relates to the worker's actual employment with his own company. Where a worker has the sort of business described in SE 32800, the likelihood is that he would fall outside IR35 in any event. He would thus be able to deduct home as office costs under the normal rules for corporation tax, see **3.5.1**. However, this paragraph of the Revenue Manual shows that a deduction from the worker's Schedule E income is also possible, and may be more advantageous.

11.12 Capital allowances

11.12.1 Step Four

Step Four gives relief for capital allowances:

> 'In respect of expenditure incurred by the intermediary that could have been claimed by the worker under section 27 of the Capital Allowances Act 1990 if the worker had been employed by the client and had incurred the expenditure.'

Points to note include the following:

(a) To be deductible at Step Four the expenditure has to be incurred by the intermediary, not the worker;

(b) If the cost is incurred by the individual, allowances must be claimed on his self-assessment return, or the partnership return (**15.3.4**). They cannot be deducted at Step Four;

(c) It is preferable for assets to be owned by the intermediary, because the allowances deducted in Step Four reduce the deemed Schedule E amount and thus the NICs payable. If the assets are owned directly, there is tax relief but no NICs relief;

(d) The assets have to satisfy the narrower Schedule E rules for claiming capital allowances, discussed at **11.12.2** below, as follows:

- Assets which have been 'necessarily provided for use in the performance of the duties' (s27(2)(a) CAA 1990); or
- Before 2002/03, cars, motorbikes, and cycles used in the performance of the duties (s27(2A) CAA 1990). These rules changed from April 2002, see **11.6.9**, so that capital allowance claims are no longer permitted;

(e) Where an asset is accepted as within s27, the allowances will be subject to apportionment if the equipment is also used for private purposes (s79 CAA 1990);

(f) Step Four is a computational provision to allow the correct calculation of the deemed Schedule E income. It does not move title to the allowances from the company to the worker, or prevent the personal service company or partnership from claiming capital allowances under the normal rules for corporation tax or Schedule D.

11.12.2 Assets generally

Capital allowances deductions in the Schedule E computation are likely to be a major bone of contention between service company workers and their Inspectors. The Revenue view is as follows:

> 'A deduction will only be given for capital allowances in working out the deemed payment where the plant or machinery is necessarily provided for use in the performance of the duties of the relevant engagement. This is a strict test and means that relief will only be given where the duties of the engagement meant that the (service) company had to provide the equipment in question. If the company purchases the equipment out of choice then no deduction will be given.
>
> For example, where an IT contractor is required to use the client's computer equipment then no relief will be due for expenditure on computers owned by the service company. Neither will any relief be due where the client makes all the equipment necessary to do a job available but the worker uses his or her own computers, out of choice.' (FAQ Expenses 8)

In general, the Revenue are dismissive of claims by employees that their home computers are 'necessary'. They say that:

> 'Most employees will not be able to satisfy the statutory test for capital allowances in Section 27(2) CAA 1990 in relation to the purchase of computers, word processors and their peripherals. Even if they can show that such equipment is essential for their duties, it will normally be the case that the

employer will supply what is needed. It is not enough for the taxpayer to claim that what the employer provides or will provide is inadequate.' (SE 36730)

A gleam of hope appears in the Schedule E Manual, where Inspectors are advised as follows:

'If the expense is substantial, it would be reasonable to expect the contract of employment to include a specific reference to the requirement to incur it. If there is nothing explicit in the contract, find out whether the employee has approached the employer to provide the item, or to reimburse its cost, and, if so, with what response. If the employer is not prepared to bear the cost and advances the view that the expense is not considered necessary this will clearly weaken the taxpayer's claim, though without being entirely conclusive.' (SE 36560)

It might be thought from the above that if the contract between the service company and the client requires the service company to supply certain computer hardware, then the allowances can be claimed. However, this alone is not enough, as the capital allowance test is an objective one: what the job requires, not what the client and worker agree should be provided. The Revenue may also check with clients whether the expenditure was in fact 'necessary':

'You may also need to investigate whether other workers with similar duties have also incurred the same sort of expense and if not, how they manage to perform their duties.'(SE 36560)

11.12.3 Cars, motorbikes and bicycles

The rules for capital allowances on cars, motorbikes and bicycles have changed from 6 April 2002; the authorised mileage rates now include an element for the capital cost and any loan interest relating to the purchase of the vehicle, see **11.6.9**.

Before that date it was possible to claim:

- Capital allowances. The 'necessary' test was disapplied in the case of a 'mechanically propelled road vehicle or a bicycle' (s27(2A) CAA 1990), and allowances were due providing the asset was used 'in the performance of the duties'. This was not a difficult test to meet, although if there was private use only part of the cost was allowed;

- Interest, where the vehicle was purchased by a loan (s359 ICTA 1988). This was in addition to any amounts claimed under the capital allowances regime or using the authorised mileage rates. If the car was hired, a proportion of the hire charge was allowed (s35(2) CAA 1990).

12 Completing the deemed Schedule E calculation

12. 1 Introduction

The deemed Schedule E calculation begins with the income received by the intermediary in the fiscal year (Steps One and Two, see Chapter 10). Any allowable expenses and capital allowances are then deducted (Steps Three and Four, see Chapter 11). This chapter deals with the remaining five steps necessary to arrive at the result in Step Nine. These are deductions for:

- Pension contributions paid by the employer;

- NIC paid on salary and benefits;

- Amounts taxed under Schedule E otherwise than via this calculation; and

- NIC due on the deemed Schedule E payment.

The chapter also looks at what happens where a worker has attributable earnings for NIC, but no deemed Schedule E, or vice versa.

12.2 Step Five

12.2.1 General

Step Five gives relief for pension contributions made by the employer in the fiscal year. The various pension options open to a personal service company are discussed at **3.6**. Note that payments into Retirement Annuity Policies (RAPs) are not eligible for relief in the deemed income or attributable earnings calculation; payments must be into either occupational pensions or personal pensions.

Three particularly important issues within the context of the deemed income calculation are:

- The availability of NIC relief on the pension contribution, see **12.2.2**;

- The timing of payments, see **12.2.3**; and

- The calculation of net relevant earnings, see **12.2.4**.

12.2.2 NIC relief

It is recommended that pension contributions are made by the company rather than by the individual in order to obtain relief from employer's NIC. Contributions made by the individual will reduce only the tax due, and not the NIC.

However, using pension contributions to reduce the NIC cost is not possible for partners. Step Five of the deemed Schedule E calculation gives a deduction for 'any contributions made in that year for the benefit of the worker by the intermediary' if they:

(a) Are made to a scheme approved under Chapter 1 (retirement benefit schemes) or Chapter IV (personal pensions) of Part XIV of the Income and Corporation Taxes Act 1988; and

(b) Would not have been chargeable to income tax if they had been made 'by an employer for the benefit of an employee' (Sch 12, para 7 FA 2000).

Although it would appear at first sight as if this allowed partnerships to pay contributions into the personal pension schemes of their partners, there is no mechanism for this to happen under the relevant sections of Chapter IV – see for example s643 ICTA 1988. This is also the Revenue view, see note (3) to Example 14A.

Thus where partners fall within the deemed Schedule E calculation, they cannot reduce the deemed Schedule E amount by having their pension contribution paid by the intermediary. The NIC they suffer will therefore be higher than that of workers in a PSC who otherwise have the same income and expenses.

12.2.3 Timing of payments

Pension contributions are deductible under Step Five if they have been paid in the fiscal year to which the deemed payment relates. So a contribution paid *in* 2000/01 will be allowed in that year's earnings calculation, but a payment *based on* the deemed Schedule E amount and made after the year end will be deductible only against the following year's deemed payment. How to calculate the maximum in-year payment is discussed at **12.2.5**.

Although individuals can use the carry-back rules to pay pension contributions based on the previous year's net relevant earnings (s641 and s641A ICTA 1988), this option is not open to employers. Any employer contribution must be made, and the cheque cleared, by 5 April.

12.2.4 Net relevant earnings (NRE)

The deemed Schedule E payment counts as relevant earnings, see **3.6.3**, for the purposes of making pension contributions (Sch 12, para 11(7) FA 2000). Table 3.1 gives the percentages of net relevant earnings (NRE) which can be paid into a pension.

Interestingly, *any* pension contribution within the individual's NRE percentage can be deducted at Step Six. There is no requirement that the contributions be limited to a percentage of the deemed salary. Therefore where a worker is 50 per cent within IR35 and 50 per cent outside, the intermediary could pay a pension contribution reflecting the individual's total NRE and not simply those from his IR35 work, and deduct the full amount in the deemed income calculation.

12.2.5 Calculating the maximum contribution

Where the pension contribution depends on NRE derived from the deemed Schedule E amount, the calculation can be complex:

- Since the deemed payment will in practice be calculated after the end of the fiscal year, advance planning is needed if the pension contribution is to be deductible in the same fiscal year as the earnings are deemed to be paid;

- The pension contribution is deducted in arriving at the deemed Schedule E payment, but it is also a percentage of the payment. Since grossing up is also required for the employer's NIC, an algebraic formula or computer spreadsheet is required if the maximum contribution is to be paid, see Example 12A.

> **Example 12A**
>
> Emma's PSC provides services to the video and TV industry. In the year to 5 April 2002 she has £30,000 of relevant earnings after deducting the 5 per cent allowance and her Schedule E expenses. She is 40 years old and so can make a pension contribution of 20 per cent. She has also paid herself a salary of £10,000.
>
> To calculate her maximum pension contribution on the deemed Schedule E payment, and ignoring that on the salary already paid, the algebra is as follows:
>
> $\times = (N - ax) \times (100/[100+y])$
>
> Where:
>
> 'x' is the deemed Schedule E amount;
> 'N' is the result of all Steps except Five, Eight and Nine;
> 'a' is the maximum contribution payable under the Net Relevant Earnings rules; and
> 'y' is the Employer's NIC rate for the year.
>
> In this case the calculation is: $\times = (20,000 - 0.2x) \times (100/111.9) = 15,163$
>
> This gives the following result:
>
> | | £ |
> |---|---:|
> | Steps One to Four, Step Seven: (30,000 − 10,000) | 20,000 |
> | Step Five: Pension contribution (15,163 × 20%) | (3,033) |
> | Step Eight: Employer's NIC (15,163 × 11.9%) | (1,804) |
> | Deemed Schedule E payment (calculated) | 15,163 |

This calculation demonstrates the mechanism, but in reality the use of a spreadsheet is strongly advised, particularly where the worker is seeking to identify and pay the maximum contributions for the tax year. Specifically:

- Where there are no other Schedule E earnings, the calculation needs to take the employer's NIC threshold into account;

- Where, as in Example 12A, other salary had been paid, this could also be used as the basis for a pension contribution by the employer. This would change both the NICs paid under Step Eight and also the deduction for pensions in Step Five.

12.2.6 Stakeholder pensions, SSASs and EPPs

Stakeholder pensions have broken the link between pension payments and net relevant earnings for contributions of no more than £3,600 gross, see **3.6.4**. Contributions of more than £3,600 must be supported by net relevant earnings. However, this higher amount can continue to be paid for five years without any need for further NRE calculations (s646 ICTA 1988). Use of this higher amount may enable the pension contribution calculation to be simplified, although it could of course remain desirable to base the pension payment on actual NRE if this is higher.

In practice many of those who are making serious provision for their retirement are using a SSAS or an EPP, see **3.6.5**. Since these types of pension do not depend on NRE, the problem caused by the deemed payment is reduced.

12.2.7 Over-contributions

There is no relief for contributions made which are later refunded (Sch 12, para 7 Step Five FA 2000). Thus if the calculation is incorrect, and the deemed Schedule E earnings are lower than estimated before the end of the year, excess contributions will have been paid.

These will then be refunded to the employer by the pension fund because they are unsupported by net relevant earnings. The deemed Schedule E payment will thus have to be recalculated because of the refunded amount; this in turn will further reduce the NRE for the year, so creating a vicious circle.

12.3 Step Six

12.3.1 General

Step Six gives a deduction for any employer's NIC already paid for that tax year in respect of the worker. This covers both Class 1 NIC on salary paid to the worker in the year, and Class 1A on benefits provided, see **12.3.2** and **12.3.3** below.

Step Six refers to NIC paid 'for' the year, not 'in' the year. Class 1A NICs relating to a tax year which are paid on 19 July following the end of the tax year are therefore still deductible in the deemed income calculation.

12.3.2 Class 1 NICs

Class 1 is payable on salary and some benefits, including:

- Loans written off by the employer;
- Many vouchers;

- Tax paid by the employer to cover the employee's liability;

- Tradeable assets;

- Payment of the employee's personal costs, such as household bills.

Both employees and employers pay Class 1 NICs, but employees only pay to the extent that their earnings fall between the Employee's Earnings Threshold (EET) and the Upper Earnings Limit (UEL). The maximum employee NICs payable in 2001/02 is £2,535. Employer's Class 1 NICs are payable above the Employer's Earnings Threshold, and have no upper limit. Only employer's NICs are deductible in the deemed Schedule E calculation.

Class 1 NICs are due on the 19th day of the month following receipt by the worker of the payment or benefit, and the total for the year must be included on Forms P14 and P35, see **16.2.3**.

12.3.3 Class 1A NICs

Since 6 April 2000, Class 1A NICs have been due on all benefits unless *either* Class 1 already applies, *or* the benefit is:

- Covered by a dispensation;

- Included in a PAYE settlement agreement;

- Provided to employees (other than directors) earning less than £8,500. A deemed Schedule E payment is included in calculating whether the earnings meet the £8,500 threshold (Sch 12, para 11(3)(b) FA 2000);

- A reimbursed expense which is wholly for business; or

- Shares or options. In some cases these will already be subject to a Class 1 NIC charge.

Class 1A is due both on benefits provided by the service company and those provided by the client which were by arrangement with the service company, see **10.5.4**.

Class 1A has to be paid over by 19 July following the end of the tax year, two weeks after the submission deadline for the P11D form on which the Class 1A is based. However, if the deemed payment is delayed until this deadline, there will be interest on the overdue PAYE and NICs, see **16.4.2**. If interest is to be avoided, the service company will need to calculate the Class 1A NICs by 19 April rather than by 19 July. For penalties generally, see Chapter 16.

12.4 Step Seven

12.4.1 General

Step Seven gives relief for:

> 'Any payments or other benefits received in that year by the worker from the intermediary, in respect of which the worker is chargeable to income tax under Schedule E.'

This covers both salary paid and benefits provided to the worker in the same tax year. These are discussed in more detail at **12.4.2** and **12.4.3** below. Salary and benefits cannot be provided to partners, so this step is redundant if the worker is a partner. For the anomalous position concerning the provision of childcare, see **11.4.2**.

The Step Seven deduction is granted on the basis that the intermediary has used the income from relevant engagements to provide either salary or benefits to the worker. Since both the latter will be taxed in any event under the normal rules for PAYE and P11Ds, they are excluded from the deemed income calculation to prevent double taxation.

There is no attempt to link salary or benefits paid to the worker with relevant income received, so that if salary was paid in, say, June, but relevant income was not received until September, the salary would still be deductible in Step Seven.

If, following Step Seven, the answer to the calculation is nil or negative, the legislation says that 'there is no deemed Schedule E payment'. If the answer is positive, the calculation continues with Step Eight.

12.4.2 Salary

A deduction is only available for salary *paid* in the tax year. The amount of salary on which tax and NICs have been deducted (and which is thus shown on the P60) may therefore not be the same as the salary to be removed from the deemed income calculation under Step Seven. This is because, under the normal rules for PAYE, salary is taxable on the earliest of a number of events, including receipt, entitlement and crediting in the company's books (s203A ICTA 1988, see **10.2**).

Where a director has received a credit to his loan account, this counts as 'payment' of salary under s203A, and there is a liability to PAYE. However, for deemed income purposes, the credit will only be a 'payment' if the director has *unfettered* access to the sum in the loan account, see *Garforth v Newsmith Stainless Ltd* [1978] 52 TC 522. In a one-man company, it is likely that the director will be free to draw on his loan account and this problem is thus more theoretical than real.

12.4.3 Benefits

The worker can receive a benefit by four routes, of which only those in (a) below are deducted in Step Seven. A benefit can be provided:

(a) By the intermediary;

(b) By the client by reason of the worker's employment with the intermediary, and arranged or facilitated by the intermediary;

(c) By the client by reason of the worker's employment, not arranged or facilitated by the intermediary;

(d) By the client or third party, not by reason of the employment.

These are discussed in turn below.

Benefits provided by the intermediary

Benefits provided to the worker by the intermediary are deducted in Step Seven. They are included on the individual's P11D for the tax year and reported on his self-assessment form.

Benefits provided by reason of employment, facilitated by intermediary

Benefits provided:

• By the client or other third party;

• By reason of the employment;

• Which have been arranged or facilitated by the service company

are taxed under the normal rules for Schedule E, see **10.5.4**. They are thus not brought into the deemed Schedule E calculation either:

(a) In Step One, because they have not been received by the intermediary, but by the worker; or

(b) In Step Two, because they are otherwise chargeable to income tax under Schedule E.

Since they have not been included in the calculation in the first place, they are not excluded at Step Seven. They will, however, be included on the P11D, since the intermediary must report benefits which it has facilitated. They will then be taxed via self-assessment or a coding adjustment.

Benefits provided by the client by reason of the employment, which have not been facilitated by the intermediary

As discussed at **10.5.4**, most benefits provided by the client to the worker will have been facilitated by the service company, because of the substantial identity between employer and worker. Where, exceptionally, the benefit has not been facilitated by the employer, the client or other third party is responsible for passing details of the benefit directly to the worker, see **10.5.4**. The details should then be included on his self assessment form, see **15.3.4**.

Benefits provided by third party, not by reason of the employment

Benefits provided other than by reason of the employment are brought into the calculation at Step Two. Partners who fall within the personal services legislation are the most likely to be in this situation – they do not have an employment. The legislation does not deem them to be employees, but merely requires them to complete the deemed Schedule E calculation, see **10.5.3**.

Since partners are not taxed under the normal rules for Schedule E, there can be no deduction at Step Seven.

12.4.4 P11Ds

The P11D thus includes:

- Benefits which are removed from the calculation at Step Seven, because they are provided by the intermediary; and

- Benefits which are not included in the deemed income calculation at all, because they are provided by the client to the worker, and facilitated by the intermediary, see **12.4.3**.

It is thus important that the P11D is not blindly followed when identifying amounts to be removed from the deemed Schedule E calculation.

The deadline for completion of P11Ds is 6 July following the end of the tax year. If personal service companies take advantage of this two month period, they will be unable to finalise their deemed Schedule E calculation until after that date, so incurring an interest charge, see **16.5**.

12.4.5 Interaction with Step Three

Step Three gives relief for:

> 'The amount of expenses met in that year by the intermediary, which would have been deductible from the emoluments of the employment if the worker had been employed by the client and the expenses had been met by the employer out of those emoluments.'

These amounts include allowable travel and subsistence, PII cover, and other costs which meet the 'wholly, exclusively and necessarily' test, see **11.4**.

However, most of these amounts are technically 'chargeable' on the worker – the legislation simply allows them to escape assessment if an appropriate claim is made. They would thus also be deductible under Step Seven, which gives relief for all amounts 'in respect of which the worker is chargeable to income tax under Schedule E.' To prevent a double deduction, the legislation prevents any amounts which were deducted in Step Three from being relieved again under Step Seven (Sch 12, para 7 Step 7(b) FA 2000).

The Step Three deduction is broader than that in Step Seven, which does not allow relief if an amount was not 'chargeable'. Amounts which cannot be deducted under Step Seven include PIEs, see **11.7**, and amounts included within a dispensation, see **11.3.8**. From 2002/03, authorised mileage rates and passenger payments (which are exempt from tax under s197AD and 197AE TA 1988) are deemed to be chargeable (Sch 12, para 7B(3) FA 2000).

12.5 Step Eight

12.5.1 Class 1 charge

The deemed Schedule E payment is itself subject to Class 1 NICs. Although both income and benefits may be included within the calculation, there is mercifully no attempt to separate the NIC into Class 1 and Class 1A (SI 2000/727 reg 8(1)).

The service company is, of course, subject to Class 1A in respect of any benefits provided to the worker by the intermediary, but these benefits will have been deducted at Step Seven, and the NICs at Step Six, in arriving at the amount of attributable earnings, see **12.3** and **12.4** above.

12.5.2 Calculation of NIC due

Step Eight deducts the employer's NIC on the deemed payment. This is of course itself dependent on the deemed payment, and is thus calculated by a formula, see Example 12B.

Example 12B

David has a personal service company supplying tax services. Most of his work falls outside Schedule 12, FA 2000. However in July 2001 he takes up a relevant engagement for three days a week assisting the Inland Revenue. His company charges out his services at £2,000 a month, and David pays himself a salary of £1,000 a month. He has allowable travel expenses of £537 reimbursed by the service company.

	Notes	£
Step One: Income received		18,000
5% allowance		(900)
Step Three: Allowable expenses		(537)
Step Six: Employer's NIC on salary paid	1	(531)
Step Seven: Salary paid		(9,000)
Income after expenses, salary and NIC on salary		7,032
Step Eight: NIC on deemed payment	2	(748)
Deemed Schedule E payment		6,284

Notes

1. $(9,000 - 4,535) \times 11.9\% = 531$

2. $7,032 \times (11.9/111.9) = 748$

However this formula only works where the individual has other earnings which utilise the Class 1 NIC-free band (£4,535 in 2001/02). However, this is not invariably the case, and never applies to partners, who receive no actual salary, only deemed salary. In these situations the NIC-free band must be taken into account in Step Eight, see Example 12C:

> **Example 12C**
>
> In 2002/03 David doesn't pay himself a salary, but uses his other income to pay himself in dividends. After deducting expenses his relevant income is £15,000 before deducting employer's NICs. The 2001/02 NIC bands and rates have been retained for comparative purposes.
>
> | | £ |
> |---|---:|
> | Income after expenses | 15,000 |
> | NIC: (15,000 − 4,535) × (11.9/111.9) | (1,113) |
> | Deemed Schedule E payment | 13,887 |

For the further complexities in the calculation where the worker wants to calculate his pensions contribution, see **12.2.6**; for interaction with Class 2 and Class 4 NICs on partnership income, see **14.7.1**.

12.6 Step Nine

Step Nine states simply that 'the result is the amount of the deemed Schedule E payment'. This is then subject to PAYE tax and, if appropriate, employee NICs in addition to the employer NICs which have been deducted in the deemed income calculation.

12.7 Attributable earnings but no deemed Schedule E, or vice versa

In general a worker will either be within IR35, and thus liable for both Schedule E and NIC, or outside, and liable for neither. However, this is not always the case. Problem areas include overseas interactions (**12.7.1**); the National Insurance deeming rules (**12.7.2**); some divers (**20.6.2**) and the treatment of childcare (**11.4.2**). Worked examples of a worker within IR35 for NICs but not tax, and vice versa, are given at **18.5**.

12.7.1 Overseas interactions

Where a personal services worker carries out a relevant engagement overseas, he may be non-resident for tax, and thus have no deemed Schedule E calculation, see Chapter 17. However, he may remain within the UK NIC regime, and so have an attributable earnings calculation.

The opposite is also possible: an overseas worker can be UK resident for tax, but not be an employed earner for NICs. These situations are discussed in more detail in Chapter 18.

12.7.2 National Insurance deeming rules

There are also a number of specialised occupations which are deemed to be employments for NICs, but not for tax. Although a worker may be self-employed under the status tests at Chapter 6, this status may be over-ridden for National Insurance by various deeming provisions. The Social Security and Benefits Act 1992 says at s2(b) that:

> 'Regulations may provide ... for a person in employment of any prescribed description to be treated, for the purposes of this Act, as falling within one or other of the categories of earner defined ... above, notwithstanding that he would not fall within that category apart from the regulations.'

The personal services legislation applies, for National Insurance purposes, if:

> 'The circumstances are such that, had the arrangements taken the form of a contract between the worker and the client, the worker would be regarded for the purposes of Parts I to V of the Contributions and Benefits Act as employed in employed earner's employment by the client.' (SI 2000/727 reg 6(1)(c))

If the NIC provisions would have deemed a worker to be an employed earner had he been operating as an individual, then he will also be an employed earner under IR35. So an actor who is self-employed under the status tests can nevertheless be deemed an employed earner for NICs. If he was operating via a service company he would have an attributable earnings calculation but no Schedule E payment. In other words, he works through Steps One to Nine (Chapters 10 to 12), and pays NICs on the result, but not PAYE.

Examples of workers who are deemed to be employed earners for NICs include:

(a) Teachers and lecturers, see **20.9.2**;

(b) Actors and entertainers, see **20.2.2**;

(c) Office cleaners and cleaners of telephone apparatus;

(d) A person employed by his or her spouse. This is unlikely to have any effect on service company workers as any payments to the worker's spouse will be made by the company. The spouse will thus be an employee of the service company and already subject to NICs.

In addition directors are within the IR35 legislation for NICs, but only within the tax legislation if there is a hypothetical contract of employment between them and their client in addition to the hypothetical contract in respect of the office they hold as a director. This is discussed more fully at **20.3.2**.

A deeming provision also exists under which examiners are treated as self-employed for NICs if the whole of the work is performed under a contract of less than 12 months (SI 1978/1689 Sch I and II). However, they are employed for tax purposes: the Revenue have said that if an examiner disputes this, they are prepared to take the case to the Commissioners (ESM 4152). Examiners are therefore liable to pay Class 2 NICs but, if taxable under Schedule E, there will be no Class 4 NICs liability, see ESM 4150.

13 Corporation tax, dividends and VAT

13.1 Introduction

A personal service company that has a deemed salary calculation is not thereby absolved from the requirement to carry out a corporation tax computation. It is and remains a company, and thus within the scope of corporation tax. Similarly, the fact that the income is deemed to be the salary of the worker does not take supplies made by the company outside the scope of VAT.

There are however significant differences between the corporation tax rules and those for Schedule E. Different provisions govern expenses, the timing of receipts, and capital allowances. The taxation of personal services brings both sets of rules together. This chapter looks at some of the resulting complexities.

One key issue is the timing of relief for the deemed payment, which can only be deducted in the accounting period when it is 'treated as made'. If the company has an accounting year end other than 5 April, excess tax can arise which may not be relieved, see **13.3** below.

When seeking to understand the interaction between the two taxes, it may be helpful to remember that IR35 is anti-avoidance legislation. It aims to encourage those within the personal services rules to pay themselves their relevant income as salary through the year. If they do, they will have no deemed Schedule E payment. However, there are likely to be no profits available for distribution, and may even be a loss for corporation tax purposes, see **13.7**.

Where sufficient salary is not paid during the year, the Schedule E calculation deems an amount of income to be subject to PAYE and NIC. However, once the tax and National Insurance have been paid to the Revenue, the balance cannot simply be paid tax free to the individual. In other words, the tax and NIC does not frank a subsequent salary payment. If the net Schedule E amount is paid to the worker, he will be regarded as having received further salary which will itself be subject to tax and NIC, see **13.5.2** below.

If the worker wants to extract the taxed money from the company without suffering further tax, he can only do so as a dividend, see **13.6**. This is because relieving provisions prevent double taxation if the money is withdrawn in this way.

13.2 General

13.2.1 Deductibility for corporation tax purposes

The full deemed payment (i.e., before employee NICs and PAYE) is deductible for corporation tax purposes, as are the employer NICs, see Sch 12, para 17(1) FA 2000. However these amounts are only deductible for the accounting period in which they are treated as made, see **13.3** below. For the accounts treatment, see **13.11**; for corporation tax relief on expenses disallowed for IR35, see **11.3.6**.

13.2.2 Recognition of income

Corporation tax basis

Corporation tax computations are based on the accounts, and income is thus taxed on an accruals basis. This is required by both legislation and case law:

- Section 42(2) FA 1998 requires that computations be calculated on 'an accounting basis which gives a true and fair view, subject to any adjustment required or authorised by law in computing profits for those purposes'. This 'true and fair view' applies to both self-employed individuals and companies, since corporation tax follows income tax principles (s9 ICTA 1988);

- Case law similarly requires that computations follow recognised accounting principles, see for example *Herbert Smith v Honour* [1999] STC 173; *Gallagher v Jones* [1993] 66 TC 77; *Revenue Press Release* 137, issued 20 July 1999.

For corporation tax purposes, income is therefore included if it has been earned in the period, even if it has not been received, subject to any relief for bad debts.

Deemed Schedule E basis

In contrast, the deemed Schedule E amount is based on income *received* in the fiscal year, see **10.2** (Sch 12, para 7 FA 2000), and deductions are only available for expenses actually paid, see **11.3.2**. It is therefore important that the company's records are capable of analysis on both a received and accrued basis so that both the CT computation and the deemed Schedule E payment can be correctly calculated.

13.3 Accounting year end other than 5 April

The deemed payment and any related employer NICs are only deductible for the accounting period in which it is treated as made (Sch 12, para 17(2) FA 2000). As a result, year ends other than 5 April can cause double taxation which may never be relieved. Accounting periods ending on 31 March give the worst result. This problem, and some possible solutions, are explored below, using a series of worked examples.

Example 13A

Sarah has her own personal service company supplying advice to government ministers. The company's accounting period ends on 31 March. It receives £50,000 in the year to 2000/01 in relation to a relevant engagement for the Chancellor of the Exchequer. Corporation tax allowable expenses are £8,000; none of these are deductible for Schedule E. Income received in the fiscal year equals that accrued in the accounting period to 31 March. She pays herself no salary or dividends.

In 2001/02 the facts are identical; for ease of comparison NIC thresholds and rates are assumed to be the same as in 2000/01.

Year ended 31 March 2001: Corporation tax position

	Notes	£	£
Income			50,000
Expenses	1		(8,000)
Net profit			42,000
Tax at 10%	1,000		
Tax at 22.5%	2	7,200	
Tax due			(8,200)
Net profits			33,800

5 April 2001: Deemed Schedule E payment

		Notes	£
Step One	– relevant income		50,000
	– Less 5%		(2,500)
			47,500
Step Eight	– NICs	3	(4,688)
Step Nine	– the deemed payment		42,812

Notes

1 No relief is received for the deemed payment relating to this period as it has not been paid by 31 March.

---

2 The marginal tax on profits between £10,000 and £50,000 is calculated at 22.5 per cent, see **3.2.2**

3 NICs on the deemed payment calculated as $(47,500 - 4,385) \times (12.2/112.2)$, see **12.5.2**.

In the tax year 2000/01, Sarah pays tax on £42,812, and her company pays tax on £42,000, making £82,812. However the total income received is only £50,000, and this reduces to £42,000 on a CT basis once expenses are deducted, and to £47,500 on a PSC basis.

The problem is not solved in 2001/02, when the deemed Schedule E amount is the same, and therefore Sarah pays further income tax on £42,812, and the company carries back a loss of £5,500.

Year ended 31 March 2002: Corporation tax

	£
Income	50,000
Deemed Schedule E payment	(42,812)
Employer's NICs paid	(4,688)
Expenses	(8,000)
Net loss c/back against previous year	(5,500)

Year ended 31 March 2001: Corporation tax (revised)

	£	£
Income		50,000
Expenses		(8,000)
Net profit		42,000
Loss carried back		(5,500)
		36,500
Tax at 10%	1,000	
Tax at 22.5%	5,963	
Tax due		(6,963)
Net profits		29,537

After the loss carried back, Sarah pays tax on £42,812 in the tax year 2000/01. This means that an excess of £31,812 has been subject to tax when compared to the amount required to be taxed under the deemed Schedule E calculation.

This results from the fact that the deemed payment is deductible only in the period of account in which it is paid, rather than the one to which it relates.

13.4 Possible solutions to accounting year end date problem

13.4.1 Summary

Possible solutions to the problem examined in **13.3** above include:

(a) Treating 31 March and 5 April as identical. However this is not permitted by the Revenue, see **13.4.2**;

(b) Allowing a corporation tax deduction for the deemed Schedule E payment in the same way as a deduction is allowed for an actual salary payment. This has been rejected by the Revenue, see **13.4.3**;

(c) Providing for actual salary equal to the deemed Schedule E amount, see **13.4.4**. This is effective if certain conditions are met, but otherwise it may force the payment of further salary, which is then subject to tax and NICs;

(d) Claiming a loss, see **13.4.5**;

(e) Changing the accounting year end to 5 April, see **13.4.6**;

(f) Paying the relevant income (net of allowable deductions) as salary before 5 April, so that the deemed Schedule E payment is de minimis, see **13.5**.

Of these, (e) and (f) are both realistic options, with (d) as a 'backstop' for companies who were initially unaware of how the rules worked. Option (c) works in some limited scenarios.

13.4.2 31 March deemed to be 5 April?

For personal tax, the Revenue operate a concession whereby 5 April and 31 March are treated as interchangeable. This means that self-employed individuals who make up accounts to either date are treated as if they were on the fiscal year basis, see for example the article on self-assessment in *Tax Bulletin 10*, February 1994 and paragraph 1.98 *SAT1 (1995)*.

However, this concession does not apply for corporation tax purposes. If it were to be applied to personal service companies, the accounting date problem would disappear, at least for 31 March year ends. It would nevertheless remain to a greater or lesser extent for other accounting periods. However, the Revenue have not agreed to extend the concession to those affected by the deemed payment regime.

13.4.3 Provision for deemed payment?

One solution would be to provide for the deemed payment in the accounts, and allow this to be deducted for corporation tax purposes. This was raised with the Revenue, but the idea was rejected, see FAQ Computation 3:

> 'The deemed payment is a balancing item, to make up any shortfall in salary paid during the tax year. It will not therefore be possible to attribute any part of that amount to amounts provided for in a particular period. Service companies will still be able to make provision for actual salary payments made within nine months of the end of the accounting period. But the deemed payment can only be treated as a deduction in the corporation tax computation for the accounting period in which it is deemed to be paid.'

Such a provision might in any event not be allowable in the accounts, as it does not sit easily with the requirements of Financial Reporting Standard 12.

13.4.4 Provision for actual payment

A possible solution to the accounting date problem is for an amount equal to the deemed Schedule E payment to be provided, not as a deemed salary, but as actual salary. This ensures that relief is available in the appropriate accounting period, and so avoids the large overpayment of tax which may otherwise arise in year one (see Example 13A).

However, a deduction is only available in the Schedule E calculation for salary actually paid (Sch 12, para 7, Step Seven, FA 2000). Thus for this solution to work:

(a) The amount provided (for example, as a credit to the director's loan account) must be a sum on which the individual can freely draw, see *Garforth v Newsmith Stainless Ltd* [1978] 52 TC 522 and **12.4.2**; and

(b) The provision must be made by the end of the tax year, and tax and NICs thus paid over by 19 April following; and

(c) For the amount provided to be deductible for corporation tax it must be paid out as actual salary within nine months of the year end (s43 FA 1989).

Where provisions do not meet criteria (a) and (b), they will have no effect on the deemed Schedule E amount for that year; where they do not meet (c), the amount will not reduce corporation taxable profits.

Where the provision does not meet the requirements of (a) and (b), but payment of salary is subsequently made in order to satisfy (c), further tax and

NIC will be due on this actual salary, in addition to the tax paid on the deemed Schedule E amount, see **13.5.2**. While the provision has been effective in reducing the large corporation tax overpayment in year one, it has caused PAYE and NICs to be paid twice on what is effectively the same income. In this situation it therefore does not remove the problem, but simply transfers it from corporation tax to income tax.

13.4.5 Claiming a loss

If the accounting year end date problem is identified in year two, it is possible to pay the second year's earnings as actual salary in the year (see **13.5** below) so that there is no deemed income under IR35. This causes a loss to arise in year two, because both the deemed Schedule E calculation for year one and the actual salary for year two are both deductible against a single year's profits. The excess loss can then be carried back against the first year's profits.

Example 13B

Sarah decides to take up permanent employment with the Cabinet Office. She therefore resigns from her company on 31 March 2003. Her resignation causes the deemed payment to be accelerated, so it occurs on 31 March, see **16.3.1**.

Her income and expenses for the year to 31 March 2003 are the same as in the previous two years, and for simplicity the employer's NIC rate is assumed to remain at 12.2 per cent for all years.

Corporation tax position 2002/03

	£
Income	50,000
Deemed Schedule E payment for 2001/02	(42,812)
Employer's NICs paid for 2001/02	(4,688)
Deemed Schedule E payment for 2002/03	(42,812)
Employer's NICs paid for 2002/03	(4,688)
Expenses for 2002/03	(8,000)
Net loss available	(53,000)
Carried back to 2000/01	36,500
Loss unrelieved	(16,500)

The loss unrelieved is made up of the difference between the expenses allowable for corporation tax (£8,000) and those deductible in the deemed Schedule E calculation (£2,500), making £5,500 a year, or £16,500 over the three-year period.

If more time has passed, use can be made of the terminal loss provisions. On cessation of a business, trading losses can be carried back against the profits of the last three years of trading, under s393A ICTA 1988. The benefits of this can be seen by extending the worked example of Sarah, at Example 13A above.

Example 13B shows that Sarah can carry back the loss on termination against the profits arising in 2000/01 (s393A(2A) ICTA 1988). However, had she continued with her company for longer than three years, she would have been unable to make use of this carry back provision and would have suffered excessive taxation.

Making a terminal loss claim has thus succeeded in capturing the tax relief on the earlier deemed payment. However, it is far from ideal in cashflow terms and should thus be regarded as a 'rescue' alternative for companies who did not appreciate how the personal services rules interacted with those for corporation tax. For a practical implication of ceasing business, see **16.3.3**.

13.4.6 Change of accounting date to 5 April

A better solution is to change the accounting date to 5 April. This allows relief in the year for the deemed payment, and protects the intermediary from the over-payment scenario shown in **13.3** above. Even where efforts are made to ensure that the relevant income is paid out as salary, so that the deemed payment is small or negligible, see **13.5.3** below, a 5 April accounting date is a useful back-stop against underpayments. Example 13C shows how it would work.

Example 13C

If Sarah had changed her accounting date to 5 April, the results would be as follows, if all other facts were the same:

Year ended 5 Aril 2001: Corporation tax position

	£
Income	50,000
Deemed Schedule E payment	(42,812)
Employer's NICs paid	(4,688)
Expenses	(8,000)
Net loss c/forward	(5,500)

The same loss will arise each year, as it is the difference between the allowable expenses for corporation tax and those deductible in the Schedule E deemed calculation. For a discussion of corporation tax losses, see **13.7** below.

Other consequences of changing the accounting date

Changing the accounting date has other effects:

(a) Shortening the accounting period may defer corporation tax on other (non PSC) profits which occur after the new date;

(b) Similarly the extension of an accounting period may accelerate relief for losses. However, many PSCs will struggle to find a use for the losses created, see **13.7.2** below;

(c) A company must to notify the Registrar of Companies, using form 225(1) or 225(2), if it proposes to alter the accounting date (s225 Companies Act 1985). However this is not necessary if the new accounting date is not more than seven days before or after the existing date (ss223(2) and (3) Companies Act 1985). Thus a company with a 31 March year end can move to 5 April without needing to notify the Registrar;

(d) There are restrictions on the number of times a company may extend its accounting period other than under the seven day rule above;

(e) Following a change in date, care is needed with respect to the timing of claims and elections.

13.5 Withdrawal of funds

13.5.1 Options available

Most people need to withdraw money from their service companies to fund normal living costs. For a company within the personal services legislation, there are three possibilities, of which the first is inadvisable:

(a) Calculate the deemed Schedule E amount at the end of the fiscal year, pay over the tax and NICs, and then withdraw the net amount. This will cause further PAYE and NICs to arise, see **13.5.2** below;

(b) Pay sufficient salary during the year so that there is no deemed Schedule E amount at the year end, see **13.5.3** below;

(c) Pay out the profits of the company as a dividend. The legislation prevents double taxation of dividends covered by the deemed Schedule E payment, see **13.6**.

Of these three options, the first is clearly to be avoided. If there are no other factors, the tax cost of options (b) and (c) are the same, see Example 13H.

However there may be other issues, both practical and legal, which cause one route to be preferred over the other, for example the impact of the dividend route on Statutory Sick Pay and Statutory Maternity Pay (**22.5**).

13.5.2 Withdrawal of funds following deemed Schedule E calculation

Where funds have been subject to PAYE and NIC under the PSC rules, they will be taxed again if they are subsequently withdrawn as salary. This is because there is no 'franking' of an actual salary payment by the deemed Schedule E amount – tax has to be paid on all salary received by the individual. The consequences of this were summarised by Robert Maas in his article *Alice in Primarololand*, published in *Taxation* 17 August 2000.

Particular care should be taken over credits to the director's current account, which count as payment of salary under s202B(1)(c) ICTA 1988. If the deemed Schedule E amount is calculated, PAYE and NIC paid over, and the net amount transferred to the director's current account, it will be taxable as earnings received by the director, see Example 13D.

Example 13D

Olivia is a model with her own personal service company. In the year to 31 March 2001 she had taxable income of £30,000, and CT allowable expenses of £2,803. She paid herself a salary of £500 per month.

In the year to 31 March 2002 her income remained at £30,000 and her other (non-salary) expenses decreased to £2,621. She continued to pay herself £500 a month.

In 2000/01 one of her engagements was within the scope of the personal services regime, and she received £12,428 of relevant income. On 19 April 2001 she calculated that she had a deemed Schedule E amount of £5,000 in respect of this relevant engagement, and paid over the tax and NIC by the due date. After PAYE and employee NIC, the net deemed Schedule E amount was £3,600, and this was transferred to her director's current account.

Corporation Tax computation 31 March 2001

	Notes	£	£
Income			30,000
Expenses:			
General		2,803	
Salary (12 × 500)		6,000	
Employer's NIC paid	1	197	
Expenses	2		(9,000)
Net profit			21,000

Tax at 10% on £10,000		1,000
Tax at 22.5% on balance	3	2,475

Total tax paid	3,475

Profits remaining	17,525

Notes

1. NIC due on salary of £6,000 is (6000–4385) x 12.2% = 197

2. There is no relief against the profits of the year for the deemed Schedule E calculation, as it is not paid within the accounting period, see **13.3** above.

3. The marginal tax on profits between £10,000 and £50,000 is calculated at 22.5 per cent, see **3.2.2**.

Deemed Schedule E calculation 5 April 2001

	£
Step One: Relevant income	12,428
5% allowance	(621)
Step Six: NIC on salary paid	(197)
Step Seven: Salary paid	(6,000)
Step Eight: Employer's NIC on deemed payment	(610)
Step Nine: Deemed Schedule E amount	5,000

Corporation tax computation 31 March 2002

	Notes	£	£
Income			30,000
Deemed Schedule E payment 2000/01		(5,000)	
Employer's NIC on deemed payment		(610)	
Salary paid at £500 a month		(6,000)	
Employer's NIC on salary paid	1	(174)	
Transfer to current account	2	(5,000)	
Employer's NIC on salary paid		(595)	
Other expenses		(2,621)	
Total expenses			(20,000)
Net profit			10,000
Tax at 10% on £10,000			(1,000)
Profits remaining			9,000

Notes

1. Employer's NICs are (6,000 – 4,535) × 11.9% = 174. For simplicity the NIC free amount has been deducted from Olivia's monthly salary, rather partly from this and partly from the current account transfer.

2. The transfer of the balance remaining after tax and NIC to her current account amounts to a further salary payment, see 13.5.2. The gross salary is the £5,000 on which employer's NICs of £595 are due at the 2001/02 rate of 11.9%.

The key point here is that 'making' a deemed payment simply establishes the amount of tax and NIC to be paid by the company to the Revenue. It does not 'frank' any subsequent salary payment. If the net amount is paid as salary, further tax and NIC will be due. In Example 13D tax has thus been paid twice on what are essentially the same funds.

Relief for the extra tax will be obtained in the following year's deemed Schedule E computation, when the taxed salary will be deducted from that year's income, see Example 13E below.

Example 13E

The background is the same as in Example 13D above. In the year to 5 April 2002, Olivia receives a further £12,428 of relevant income. Her deemed Schedule E computation is as follows:

Deemed Schedule E calculation 5 April 2002

	Notes	£
Step One: relevant income		12,428
5% allowance		(621)
Step Six: NIC on salary paid (174 + 595)		(769)
Step Seven: Salary paid (6,000 + 5,000)		(11,000)
Step Eight: Employer's NIC on deemed payment		(4)
Step Nine: Deemed Schedule E amount	1	34

Notes

1. The difference of £34 has been caused by the change in the NIC rates and bands.

Example 13F

The background is again the same as in Example 13D above. However, in the year to 5 April 2002 Olivia received only £7,000 of relevant income. Her deemed Schedule E computation is as follows:

Deemed Schedule E calculation 5 April 2002

	£
Step One: relevant income	7,000
5% allowance	(350)
Step Six: NIC on salary paid (174 + 595)	(769)
Step Seven: Salary paid (6,000 + 5,000)	(11,000)
Excess	(5,119)

No deemed Schedule E payment

Example 13E shows that relief is obtained in the following year for the extra salary paid, so almost eliminating the deemed payment. However, if the relevant income in the second year is inadequate to cover the full salary paid, excess tax will be suffered, see Example 13F. This problem is explored further in Example 13G.

Thus, although the payment of the net amount as salary is deductible in the following year's deemed income calculation, this is only effective if the individual continues to have sufficient relevant income to absorb the deduction. It can be seen from Example 13F that by taking the net deemed payment as additional salary, Olivia has paid tax on £5,119 more than was required under the personal service rules.

13.5.3 Salary during the fiscal year

Paying the relevant income as salary over the course of the fiscal year has many advantages:

(a) The deemed Schedule E amount will be nil or negligible, and the corporation tax and income tax problems discussed in **13.3** and **13.5.2** above thus disappear;

(b) Paying salary is likely to be simpler than the dividend route, see **13.6** below;

(c) The lower the deemed Schedule E amount, the lower the risk of a large interest charge arising because of a delay in paying over the tax and NICs resulting from the deemed Schedule E calculation, see **16.4.2**.

It is sometimes thought that paying a salary reduces the income which forms the basis of the 5 per cent deduction. This is not the case: the deduction is 5 per cent of the gross amount received by the intermediary in respect of relevant engagements. It is thus immaterial, as far as the 5 per cent deduction is concerned, whether salary is paid during the year or whether there is a deemed Schedule E amount at the end of the year.

Problems with salary payments

(a) If the company's actual costs exceed the allowable Schedule E expenses, it may be unable to pay sufficient salary to reduce the deemed Schedule E amount to nil without risking insolvency, see **13.7.4** below. The balance would then be subject to PAYE and NIC, even though it could not be paid out. However, a similar situation would arise under the dividend alternative, as the excess costs reduce the dividend payable, see **13.6.3** below. If the company has adequate reserves brought forward this problem will not arise;

(b) The tax and NIC is due on 19 April following the deemed payment, rather than on 19 April following the month end, as is the position when salary is paid during the year. The deemed payment thus gives the company a slight cashflow advantage;

(c) If more salary is paid in the year than is required under the personal services rules, the excess cannot be carried forward or back into other years. Unfortunate timing of salary payments can thus cause an increased tax liability, see Example 13G. In comparison, dividends may be more flexible, see **13.6** below.

Example 13G

Wendy has her own service company that provides gardening and horticultural services. In 2000/01 she receives £10,000 from a relevant engagement with the local Council, plus £20,000 of other earnings. Expenses relating to the relevant engagement are £500 and those relating to other work are £4,000. She pays herself a salary of £1,500 a month.

In 2001/02 the Council increases her hours and responsibility, so she receives £30,000 from the relevant engagement and £16,000 from other work. The service company's expenses are £1,000 for the relevant engagement (deductible under s198 ICTA 1988) and £3,000 for the other work. She continues to pays herself a salary of £1,500 per month.

Her deemed Schedule E income calculation is as follows:

Fiscal year 2000/01

	£
Step 1: Relevant income received	10,000
5% allowance	(500)
Step 3: Expenses	(500)
Step 6: Employer's NIC on salary paid	
(18,000 – 4,385) × 12.2%	(1,661)
Step 6: Salary paid (12 × 1,500)	(18,000)
Excess	(10,661)

No deemed payment

Fiscal year 2001/02

	£
Step 1: Relevant income received	30,000
5% allowance	(1,500)
Step 3: Expenses	(1,000)

Step 6: Employer's NIC on salary paid		
(18,000 – 4,535) × 11.9%		(1,602)
		25,898
Step 7: Salary paid		(18,000)
		7,898
Step 8: NIC on deemed Schedule E payment		(840)
Step 9: Deemed Schedule E payment		7,058

No relief is available for the excess salary paid in the earlier year. As a result, more income is taxed than is strictly necessary under the PSC rules, see below:

	£
Total relevant income over the two year period: (10,000 + 30,000)	40,000
Total salary/deemed salary subject to PAYE and NICs	
([2 × 18,000] + 7,058)	43,058
Salary taxed in excess of relevant income	3,058

13.6 Dividends

13.6.1 Using dividends to extract profits

Where a deemed Schedule E payment has already occurred, a dividend is the only way to extract the money without suffering further tax. This is because Sch 12, para 13 FA 2000 operates to prevent a double charge to tax when there is both a dividend and a deemed payment, and the net dividend is no greater than the net deemed payment.

A simple example is the easiest way of understanding how the two interact. In order to demonstrate comparability between the salary route and the dividend route, all other factors have been simplified.

Example 13H

Caroline is a supply teacher of Russian and Polish, with her own personal service company. All her engagements fall within the scope of Schedule 12, FA 2000. In the year IR35 was introduced, she asked her accountant to work out whether she should pay herself via a salary or dividends. Her accounting year end is 5 April.

In the year to 5 April 2001 she has income from relevant engagements of £60,000. Her expenses are £3,000, exactly equal to 5 per cent of her income.

Option 1: Pay salary equal to deemed schedule E amount

Under this option Caroline works out what the deemed Schedule E amount would be, and then ensures it is paid as salary on or before 5 April 2001.

Deemed Schedule E calculation

	£	£
Step One : Relevant income	60,000	
5% allowance	(3,000)	
		57,000
Step Eight: NICs		(5,721)
Step Nine: Deemed Schedule E amount		51,279

This amount is paid as salary on or before 5 April 2001.

Income tax

	£ *Income*	£ *Tax*
Personal allowance	4,385	
Tax at 10%	1,520	152
Tax at 22%	26,880	5,830
Tax at 40%	18,494	7,398
	51,279	
Class 1 employee NICs (maximum)		2,387
Total tax	(15,767)	15,767
Take home pay (51,279 – 15,767)	35,512	

Corporation tax

	£
Income	60,000
Expenses:	
General	(3,000)
Salary	(51,279)
Employer's NICs	(5,721)
CT profits	nil

Option 2: Using dividends to extract profits

Caroline calculates the deemed Schedule E amount as in Option 1 above, but does not pay it as salary. Instead, she pays over the PAYE and NIC on the due date, and then uses dividends to extract the funds from the company.

Deemed Schedule E tax and employee NICs paid

	£	£
As per calculation in Option 1:		15,767

Corporation tax

	Notes	£
Income		60,000
Expenses:		
General		(3000)
Deemed Schedule E amount		(51,279)
Employer's NICs		(5,721)
Corporation tax profits		nil

Accounting profits

	Notes	£
Turnover		60,000
Employer's NICs on deemed payment		(5,721)
PAYE/employee NICs on deemed payment	1	(15,767)
Expenses		(3,000)
Profits distributed as a dividend	2	35,512

Notes

1. Although PAYE and employee NIC liabilities normally attach to the individual, in this case it is a liability of the service company and should be deducted in the accounts. It is of course not deductible in the corporation tax computation.

2. All the profits are distributed as a dividend. £35,512 equals the net after-tax deemed Schedule E amount, and so no further tax is due on the dividend.

Example 13H demonstrates that the salary and dividend routes are neutral in terms of tax suffered, if all other factors are held constant. In both cases Caroline will receive £35,512 in cash. However in practice a number of factors may influence a person to take one route or the other, see **13.5.3** above and **13.6.2** below, as well as **22.5**.

If there had been no relief under Sch 12, para 13 FA 2000, further tax would be payable of £1,951 as follows:

Example 131

Income tax (with no relief for deemed Schedule E payment)

	£ Income	£ Tax
Dividend income (grossed up by 10%)	39,458	
Covered by tax credits and personal allowances	(32,785)	
Higher rate tax due on balance @ 32.5%	6,673	2,168
Less: tax credits		(217)
Higher rate tax		1,951

This would be in addition to the £15,767 already paid via the deemed Schedule E calculation

13.6.2 Claiming relief for double taxation

In order to obtain the tax relief, there must be both a dividend and a deemed Schedule E amount. In addition, there must actually be double taxation. A claim is necessary to obtain the relief.

There must be both a dividend and a deemed Schedule E amount

(a) The company must have paid a dividend after 5 April 2000 and also made a deemed Schedule E payment (Sch 12, para 13(1) FA 2000);

(b) The dividend can be paid before the deemed payment, see Sch 12, para 13(1)(c), as long as it is in the same tax year. Dividends paid during the first year of the personal services legislation will therefore fall out of tax if they are subsequently followed by a deemed payment;

(c) Where part of the dividend is paid out of relevant income, and part out of other Schedule D income, the taxpayer does not have to identify the source of the dividends;

(d) In applying the relief, distributions made in earlier tax years (but after the commencement of the legislation) are taken before those made in later years. Where more than one distribution is made in a tax year, the earliest is taken first (Sch 12, para 13(5)(a) and (c) FA 2000).

There must be double taxation

(a) There must have been a double charge to tax as a result of the dividend and deemed payment (Sch 12, para 13(3) FA 2000);

(b) The relief operates to reduce or eliminate the tax paid on the dividend; it does not change the tax due on the deemed Schedule E payment (Sch 12, para 13(4) FA 2000);

(c) Where the dividend is received by a basic rate taxpayer, there will be no further taxation, and thus no need to claim tax relief;

(d) The relief is available to any recipient of the dividend; it is not restricted to dividends received by the worker who carried out the relevant engagements. Other shareholders may therefore receive an unexpected windfall, if appropriate care has not been taken to obtain effective waivers in advance of the declaration of the dividend;

(e) Where both the worker and another person have received the dividends, the tax relief is given first to the worker (Sch 12, para 13(5)(b) FA 2000).

Method of giving the relief

(a) The relief must be claimed by the intermediary in writing (Sch 12 para 13(4) FA 2000). The Revenue have given the following guidance about making a claim (*Tax Bulletin* February 2001):

'The company should make any claim to its own Inland Revenue office and tell us about any dividends it has paid which it wants to be exempted. We will need the following information:

- Name and tax reference of the company making the claim;

- Name(s) and tax reference(s) of the person(s) who received the dividend;

- Amount of the dividend paid to each person and the total amount paid;

- Date the dividend was paid;

- Amount of the deemed payment and date on which it was treated as paid.'

Where the recipient of the dividend is not the controlling shareholder, and wishes to claim the tax relief, he is thus dependant on the intermediary making a claim and passing on the information about the result of the claim;

(b) The draft IR35 legislation gave a time limit for the claim, stating that it had to be made before 31 January following the tax year in which the distribution is made. This has however been removed in the final legislation, and thus the normal self-assessment time limits will apply, see **15.2**;

(c) The legislation reads as follows:

'If, on a claim being made, the Inland Revenue are satisfied that relief should be given in order to avoid a double charge to tax, they shall give such relief

299

by way of amending any assessment, by discharge or repayment of tax, or otherwise, as appears to them appropriate.'

Considerable discretion thus rests with the Revenue as to their operation of the relief. In particular, the legislation suggests that the computations of both the service company and the worker will be subject to review in order to calculate the amount of any relief and the manner in which it should be given. The process is described at ESM 3273.

The TLRC, in their rewrite of Schedule 12, point out that it is incorrect to suggest that this relief is 'given' by the Revenue, saying that they are 'not *giving* the relief, but is empowering the claimant (the intermediary) to advise its shareholder(s) that relief is available'. The TLRC have thus reworded the draft legislation to read:

'If on a claim being made the Inland Revenue are satisfied that relief should be given in order to avoid a double charge to tax, they shall direct the giving of such relief.' [*ED12 – Draft Income Tax [Earnings and Pensions] Bill Part 2 Employment Income*]

(d) Where the amount of the dividend is reduced by a claim under this section, the tax credit is (as one would expect) proportionally reduced as well (Sch 12, para 13(6) FA 2000).

13.6.3 Restriction on dividends payable

Paying dividends which are unsupported by distributable profits is illegal, see **3.10.3**. Therefore, it will not always be possible to withdraw the full Schedule E amount from the company as a dividend if:

- Some expenses are disallowed in the Schedule E computation; and

- All the income is 'relevant'.

This is because the net profits in the company will be lower than the deemed Schedule E amount. Consequently, some part of the deemed payment will not be able to be withdrawn as a dividend.

This apparently unfair consequence arises because the legislation is attempting parity, so far as possible, with the tax position of employees. If the company's funds have been used to pay expenses which would not be allowed under Schedule E, then the operation of the legislation will ensure that part of the worker's taxed income is effectively used to cover these costs, so leaving a smaller amount to be withdrawn as a dividend. See also **13.5.3** for the similar situation under the salary route.

13.7 Corporation tax losses

13.7.1 Expenses exceed 5 per cent of income

If a personal service company's only income is from relevant engagements, and its corporation tax allowable expenses exceed 5 per cent of the income, there will be a corporation tax loss in the service company, see Example 13J.

Example 13J

Nick works in the music industry via his own personal service company. The company's accounting period ends on 5 April. In the fiscal year 2001/02, Nick takes up a relevant engagement with a London radio station, which produces relevant income of £100,000 in the fiscal year. The company has the following costs:

Expenses	Notes	£
Travel to London from Bristol each week		2,500
Accommodation in London		9,000
Training course		2,000
IT support provided by his brother Richard		2,000
Accountancy and tax advice costs		2,500
Public liability insurance		500
Total expenses		18,500

Capital costs		
Purchase of electronic keyboard		3,000
Purchase of computer		2,500

Deemed Schedule E payment		
Step One: Relevant income		100,000
5% allowance		(5,000)
Step Three : Schedule E expenses	1	(11,500)
		83,500
Step Eight: Employer's NIC	2	(8,398)
Step Nine: Deemed Schedule E amount		75,102

Notes

1. Allowable expenses are accommodation and travel only, see Chapter 11.

2. Calculated as $(83,500 - 4,535) \times (11.9/111.9)$ – see **12.5.2**.

Corporation tax calculation

	£
Income	100,000
Deductible expenses	(18,500)

Capital allowances – computer 100%	(2,500)
– keyboard 40%	(1,200)
Deemed Schedule E amount	(75,102)
Employer's NICs	(8,398)
Loss	(5,700)

A loss is likely to occur where a company has one or more of the following:

- Outstanding commitments, such as hire purchase costs or lease payments, which are not deductible under the Schedule E rules;

- Capital assets, for which allowances are not due under the rules for Schedule E, see **11.11**;

- Other Schedule E disallowable expenses which outweigh the 5 per cent allowance. Examples might include wages for administrative assistance; training costs borne by the company and not the client (**11.6.8**); accountancy and tax advice fees, or insurance obligations (**11.10**).

There is a risk that expenses previously accepted as allowable by the Revenue may now be challenged, see **11.3.6**. If the costs were disallowed, the corporation tax loss would of course evaporate.

13.7.2 Using corporation tax losses

The legislation allows relief for corporation tax losses as follows:

(a) Against other trading profits of the company arising in the same accounting period (s393A(1) ICTA 1988). The claim must be made within two years of the end of the accounting period;

(b) If losses still remain, the company can make a further claim against profits of the previous accounting period (s393A(1) ICTA 1988);

(c) Losses can also be surrendered against the profits of another group company. Companies are 'members of a group of companies' if one is the 75 per cent subsidiary of the other or both are 75 per cent subsidiaries of a third company (s413(3)(a) ICTA 1988). The company owning the shares in the subsidiary must also be beneficially entitled to at least 75 per cent of profits available for distribution and to 75 per cent of assets available in a winding-up (s413(7) ICTA 1988). The rules for groups are subject to substantial anti-avoidance legislation, see Sch 18, ICTA 1988;

(d) If no claim is made, any losses will be carried forward against future profits of the same trade under s393(1) ICTA 1988;

(e) Loss relief is available under s393A(2A) ICTA 1988 on cessation of the trade, see Example 13B above.

13.7.3 Management of corporation tax losses

No immediate relief for the loss may be possible, because there are:

- No other trades against which the loss can be offset;

- No profits in earlier years against which the loss can be carried back; and

- No other group companies.

In this situation, attention should be paid to trying to manage the loss. Possibilities include:

(a) Undertaking some non-IR35 engagements which fall outside the personal services rules;

(b) Introducing other taxable income, such as bank interest, into the company, to offset against the trading loss. The capacity for such offsets is however limited by the decisions in *Bank Line Ltd v IRC* [1974] 49 TC 307 and *Nuclear Electric plc v Bradley* [1996] 68 TC 670, when the offsetting of losses against surplus funds was disallowed. In *Nuclear Electric*, Lord Jauncey held that 'whether income from investments held by a business is trading income must ultimately depend upon the nature of the business and the purpose for which the fund is held';

(c) Developing other trades or businesses within the company, so as to offset the profits arising against the loss. Note that a loss *carried forward* can only be offset against profits of the same trade (s393 ICTA 1988);

(d) Forming a trading group, perhaps with a company belonging to another family member, and offsetting the losses against the other company's profits. There are, however, provisions to prevent group relief applying to profits arising before a company joins the group, see s403A ICTA 1988. Forming a group will also have commercial consequences, which must be evaluated alongside any tax benefits.

13.7.4 Insolvency

If there is an accounting as well as a tax loss, there is a danger the company might become insolvent. The consequences of insolvency are beyond the scope of this book, but in the context of the personal service legislation it could occur where:

- It has received only relevant income;
- A salary equal to the deemed Schedule E amount has been paid;
- Costs and financial commitments exceed the sum of (a) the 5 per cent allowance and (b) deductible Schedule E expenses; and
- Insufficient existing reserves are held within the business to cover the loss.

This may occur because the individual believes, incorrectly, that the net amount has to be paid out once it has been subject to PAYE and NICs, or because he has confused the accounting position with the tax position. This misunderstanding caused the Revenue to clarify the position in their FAQ Legislation 2:

> 'The IR35 legislation will force my company to trade insolvently – isn't this illegal?
>
> The legislation simply determines the amount of tax and National Insurance that has to be paid. The deemed payment and secondary NICs can be deducted in the calculation of a company's profits for corporation tax purposes. However, there is nothing in the legislation which obliges a company to pay an actual salary of any amount, and therefore nothing that forces any company to trade at a loss.'

Advance planning is needed to ensure that the legal and financial position, as well as the tax issues, are being correctly managed. It should also be noted that some contracts with clients become void if the service company becomes insolvent.

13.8 Cessation and liquidation

13.8.1 Options available

Following IR35, an individual may decide to:

- Retain his company;
- Close down his service company and become an employee in someone else's business; or
- Freelance as a self-employed individual.

There is no single answer as to which course of action is appropriate; the decision must be made in the light of the facts in each individual case. The interaction with the IR35 calculation on cessation of the company's trade should also be understood, see **16.3.3**.

13.8.2 Retaining the company

Reasons for keeping the company include:

(a) A personal service company still has some tax advantages when compared to an employment, notably the 5 per cent allowance (**11.2**) and the more generous travel rules (**11.6**);

(b) If a loss arises in the first year of IR35, it can be carried back to the previous year. Tax paid in that year will be refunded, see **13.7.2**;

(c) Some clients and agencies will only offer work to service companies. Continuing with the company may thus offer more extensive work opportunities;

(d) Rates of pay tend to be higher for contractors than for permanent staff, and this may outweigh the costs of IR35;

(e) Contracting is more flexible than employment;

(f) It may be possible to include some non-IR35 work within the company, and thus take advantage of the tax planning opportunities set out in Chapter 3;

(g) The company's shares will be business assets for taper relief purposes. However, for the shares to have any value the company must have real business assets, which could include goodwill; the impact of anti-avoidance rules should also be examined.

13.8.3 Closing down the company

Reasons for closing down the company could include the following:

(a) The significant tax benefits, notably the NIC saving, have largely evaporated;

(b) The administration involved in managing IR35 is complex. The worker is likely to require additional professional support, which will tend to increase costs;

(c) The worker may be able to negotiate a salary package which would not be accessible if he continued to operate via a service company. For example, an employer might offer him a non-contributory final salary pension scheme or share options.

13.8.4 Freelance

If the individual decides he would be self-employed if he was operating without the company, he may decide to close down the company and work as an individual freelancer. His Schedule E/Schedule D status would then be judged by the same tests, but if he had been classified as Schedule D but was in fact Schedule E, the costs would normally fall on his engager rather than on the service company, see **21.3.4**.

13.8.5 Travel costs

If, on cessation of the company, a worker has been engaged on a single contract which comprised 'all or almost all' of his employment with the intermediary, the travel expenses in respect of that engagement may not be allowable, see **11.6.3**.

13.9 Tax planning points

The interaction between corporation tax and income tax is complex and individual advice may be needed. The following is a general summary based on the points discussed in more detail elsewhere in this chapter.

(a) The company should decide whether to pay an amount approximately equal to the deemed Schedule E amount as salary during the year, or whether to pay the accounting profits as a dividend. Although here are advantages and disadvantages to both, see **13.5.3** and **13.6**, the salary route is simpler and easier to manage;

(b) If the company decides to use the dividend route, so that it will definitely have a deemed payment, it should change its accounting date to 5 April forthwith. This will allow corporation tax relief to be obtained in the same period and prevent the excessive taxation highlighted in **13.3**;

(c) If the company plans to use the salary route, the deemed payment will be nil or negligible. There is then less need to change the accounting date, though it may nevertheless represent a good insurance policy;

(d) A particular danger is paying the net deemed amount, i.e., after PAYE and NICs, to the director either directly as a bonus or by way of credit to his current account. This will constitute a further payment of salary on which further PAYE and NIC will be due, see **13.5.2**;

(e) A loss in the first year can be carried back against the company's profits for the previous year, see **13.7**;

(f) Injection of other income or another trade into a service company may help absorb other corporation tax losses; alternatively the company may be able to become part of a group and surrender its losses, see **13.7.2**;

(g) If the shares are held other than by the worker/director, the dividend route may be problematic, see **13.6.2**.

13.10 Value added tax

The fact that all or most of the income within a personal service company is taxed under Schedule E does not change the VAT position. The company is still providing the services of the worker to the client, and must therefore comply with VAT legislation and regulations, see FAQ General 8:

> 'The VAT position will be unaffected by the new legislation. Fees charged by a service company for the provision of personal services will remain subject to VAT, even when these services fall squarely within the proposed new rules. This is because it is still the intermediary company that is contracting to provide services to its clients and as such the supply remains within the VAT regime. VAT would be chargeable as appropriate on any supplies and input tax recovery would be subject to the normal rules.'

Some particular points to note are:

(a) Income taken into Step 1 of the deemed Schedule E calculation is net of any VAT on the invoice from the sub-contractor to the client, see **10.2.4**. The Revenue view is that expenses are also included net of VAT if the company is registered, see **11.3.8**;

(b) Some partially exempt clients, such as banks or other financial institutions, consider that the extra fees charged by contractors to compensate for IR35, together with the largely irrecoverable VAT on this fee increase, make service companies too expensive. A number have reverted to direct employment; others are using shared employment structures with agencies;

(c) Where companies are below the VAT registration threshold they may, as previously, wish to opt for voluntary registration, in order to recover the VAT suffered on purchases such as computer equipment.

(d) Following the introduction of the flat rate scheme for VAT in April 2002, contractors should consider whether they are within the scope of the scheme and if so, whether joining is advantageous.

13.11 Company accounts

A discussion of the accounting treatment for limited companies is beyond the scope of this book, but the following points should be noted.

(a) The deemed payment is a deduction for corporation tax purposes only. It is not deductible in the accounts unless it is actually paid out as salary, which has the adverse effects described at **13.5.2** above;

(b) If the deemed payment plus the tax and NICs gives rise to a loss for tax purposes, see **13.7**, there is not necessarily an accounting loss. This will only occur if the costs actually borne by the company (excluding any deemed amounts) exceed the income;

(c) Although a provision for the deemed payment is not an allowable expense for tax purposes (Sch 12, para 17(2) FA 2000), a provision may nevertheless be made in the accounts in respect of the PAYE and NICs in an earlier accounting period than that in which the deemed payment falls. The Revenue are alert to the possibility that a double deduction may be claimed, see ESM 3200.

14   Partnerships

14.1 General

Very few partnerships fall within the personal services legislation, but if they do, the effects are significant. The interaction of partnership taxation with Schedule E gives rise to considerable complexity, affecting expenses, income and the timing of tax payments.

The government has said that the aim of the personal services rules is not:

> 'To place unnecessary burdens on partnerships ... what they want to do is to distinguish between partnerships which can be used by a worker to control the form in which income from relevant engagements is passed on to him or her, and partnerships which are legitimate businesses but may occasionally second a partner to work for a client in circumstances which might otherwise be caught by our legislation.' (FAQ Partner 1)

It is easiest to look first at these exceptions and concessions, before reviewing the impact of the legislation on partnerships which are within IR35.

14.2 Exceptions

14.2.1 No relevant engagements

Partnerships are excluded from the personal services legislation provided:

- No partner supplies personal services for the business of another;
- In circumstances which would have been an employment if carried out as an individual without the 'wrapper' of the partnership (Sch 12, para 1 FA 2000).

This exclusion will cover many professional practices, such as veterinary surgeons, doctors, architects, accountants and lawyers. To the extent that these firms have small amounts of Schedule E income, they are likely to be covered by the concessions set out in **14.3** below.

14.2.2 The statutory exemptions

The legislation sets out a number of tests which have the effect of excluding most partnerships. They state that a partnership is outside the rules, even where personal services are provided, unless one or more of the following apply:

(a) The worker, alone or with one or more relatives, is entitled to 60 per cent or more of the profits of the partnership; or

(b) Most of the profits of the partnership derive from the provision of services under (relevant) engagements either:

    (i) to a single client; or
    (ii) to a single client together with associates of that client; or

(c) Under the profit sharing arrangements the income of any of the partners is based on the amount of income generated by that partner through the provision of services under (relevant) engagements (Sch 12, para 4 FA 2000).

These are discussed below.

The 60 per cent test

If a worker, alone or together with one or more relatives, is entitled to 60 per cent or more of the profits, then he will potentially be within IR35.

This catches most family partnerships. 'Relative' is interpreted as 'husband or wife, parent or remoter forebear, child or remoter issue, or brother or sister' (Sch 12, para 4(2) FA 2000). It should also be noted that 'a man and a woman living together as husband and wife are treated as if they are married to each other' (Sch 12, para 21(4) FA 2000).

This 60 per cent test was first outlined in the Revenue's Frequently Asked Questions, Series 4, where it referred to situations where 'an individual, or persons connected with him or her, is entitled to 60 per cent or more of the profits'. There have been two significant changes since this FAQ. The first is the narrowing down of the test so that the 60 per cent interest has to be held by the *worker* i.e., the person carrying out the relevant engagements. Secondly, the phrase 'persons connected with him or her' has been restricted to the more limited phrase, 'relatives'. Thus a number of people in partnerships, who believed they were caught by the rules when they reviewed the Revenue's website, now fall outside IR35.

A partnership that is caught by this rule could of course change its structure to take itself outside the legislation. Involving some more remote family members in the business, such as brothers-in-law and sisters-in-law, or uncles and aunts, so as to reduce the worker's interest to below 60 per cent, would be effective. However, care should then be taken not to stream profits to the worker, and so fall within (c) above. Attention should also be paid to the settlements legislation, which is briefly discussed in the context of companies at **3.4.3**.

Single clients

Where most of the profits of a partnership are derived from services to a single client, or a single client plus associates, the partnership is caught. There is no definition of 'most'; it is understood that the Revenue have preferred to leave it open for 'common sense' negotiation.

Where the client is a company, its associates include any person connected with the company as set out in s839 ICTA 1988. This broad definition states that a company is connected with another company if:

- The same person has control of both; or

- A person has control of one and persons connected with him have control of the other; or

- A person has control of one and, together with persons connected with him, also has control of the other; or

- A group of two or more persons has control of each company, and the groups either consist of the same persons or could be regarded as consisting of the same persons by treating (in one or more cases) a member of either group as replaced by a person with whom he is connected.

In addition, a company is connected with another *person* if that person has control of it or if that person and persons connected with him together have control of it.

Where the client is an individual in business as a sole trader, the definition of associate is discussed in **4.5.2**; where the client is another partnership, the definition of associate is 'any associate of a member of the partnership' (Sch 12, para 19(c) FA 2000).

Interestingly, this test is based on the *profits* of the partnership which *derive from* the relevant income. The link between profit and income may not necessarily be straightforward. The partnership's relevant engagements may be less profitable than its other engagements, and if this is the case, it should be taken into account in applying the test. Whether the legislation is referring to accounting profits or taxable profits is not specified, but the latter may be assumed.

Profit sharing arrangements

This subparagraph is somewhat strangely worded. It states that 'under the profit sharing arrangements the income of *any of the partners* is based on the amount of income generated *by that partner* by the provision of services under (relevant) engagements'. It is understood that the intention here is that where there is a streaming of income received from relevant engagements through to the worker who undertook those engagements, then the individual is within the legislation.

However, where the partnership profits are pooled and shared between the partners according to some agreed formula, the receipt of income from relevant engagements will not be within the legislation unless it falls within one of the other tests listed above.

14.3 Concession and practice

14.3.1 Introduction

The Revenue have confirmed that both Extra-Statutory Concession A37 and the administrative practice set out in SE 03001-3 have been retained in the context of personal service companies. These are discussed below.

14.3.2 ESC A37: 'Tax treatment of directors' fees received by partnerships and other companies'

The text of the concession is as follows:

'Where fees are received in respect of directorships held by members of a professional partnership, they are in strictness assessable on the individual partners under Schedule E. It is however the practice of the Revenue to accede to a request from the partnership for the inclusion of the fees in the Schedule D assessment provided that:

(a) the directorship is a normal incident of the profession and of the particular practice concerned;

(b) the fees are only a small part of the profits; and

(c) under the partnership agreement the fees are pooled for division among the partners.

Partnerships seeking such treatment are expected to provide the Revenue with a written undertaking that directors' fees received in full will be included in the gross income or receipts of the basis period, whether or not the directorship is still held in the year of assessment and whether or not the partner concerned is still a partner.'

It should be noted that the concession is not automatically applicable, but requires action from the partnership – firstly to request that the concession be applied, and secondly to supply the written undertaking.

14.3.3 Revenue practice

The Revenue practice set out in SE 03001-3 extends the scope of the above concession to cover not only directors' fees but other Schedule E income received by partners. It is slightly narrower in its application – for instance, it requires that the fee be 'small' in relation to the income of the individual partner, while the concession looks at the fee in the context of the firm's profits. It says that:

'There would be particular practical difficulties if Schedule E were applied to the fees received by certain taxpayers … For example, accountants acting as company auditors or secretaries and solicitors acting as company registrars or secretaries often hold numerous such offices concurrently as an integral part of their professional practice. Similar difficulties can arise where a partner holds an office or employment and the fees are to be included with partnership income and pooled amongst the partners (e.g., a Solicitor who is clerk to a body of commissioners or a GP with a part time NHS hospital appointment). The amount of tax payable under the rules of the different Schedules will often be similar in these types of situation.

In these circumstances it is permissible to allow such fees to be treated as ordinary professional receipts within Case II of Schedule D and to allow any expenses admissible under the rules of that Schedule. This treatment should however only be applied where all the following conditions are met:

- The duties of the office or employment (in terms of time taken) are small in relation to other practice work (of the individual or partner) which is clearly of a Schedule D nature;

- The office or employment is in a field related to the profession and particular practice concerned;

- In a case involving a partner, there is an agreement between the partners that the fees are included as income of the partnership and pooled for division amongst the partners – and that agreement is acted upon;

- The individual and any partners agree that the income be treated for tax purposes in this manner and agree to pay tax on the fees on that basis (where appropriate as part of the partnership profits) – written confirmation should be obtained from all concerned to this effect;

- The fees are not derived from the directorship of a company and are small in relation to the receipts of the practice generated by the individual or partner.'

One of the requirements for applying this practice is that the office or employment must be in a related field. In assessing this, the nature of the duties of the office or employment should be compared with those of the practice conducted by the partnership and the profession concerned. For example, a solicitor who takes up an appointment as Clerk to the Special Commissioners would be occupying an office in a related field but if he became the secretary of a cycling club he would not.

Where the partner is appointed to a public tribunal such as a Royal Commission, and income from the appointment is to be pooled amongst the partners, the Revenue accept that the appointment is in a related field, even where the partner is appointed because of general business acumen rather than to provide specific input in respect of his own profession.

Again it should be noted that application of this practice to a partnership is not automatic, and undertakings are required from all affected partners.

14.3.4 National Insurance

There is a similar, statutory, National Insurance relief for directors' fees received by partners where:

- Being a director of a company is a normal incident of membership of that profession;

- The director is required by the terms of his partnership to account to his firm for the payment; and

- The payment forms an insubstantial part of the gross returns of that firm (SI 2001/1004 reg 27).

It should be noted that the NIC relief is only applicable to director's fees, and not to small amounts of other Schedule E earnings, and it is thus narrower in scope than the tax rules.

However, as long as the partner can satisfy both the NIC requirements, and either SE 03001-3 or ESC A37, the engagement will not cause the partner to come within IR35 for either NIC or tax.

14.4 Workers within partnerships

As well as the partners themselves, the personal services legislation also includes employees in a partnership where a payment or benefit:

- Is not chargeable to tax under Schedule E;

- Is received or receivable by a worker;

- Directly from the intermediary;

- Can reasonably be taken to represent remuneration for services provided by the worker to the client (Sch 12, para 4(3) FA 2000).

These rules, discussed at **4.6.1**, apply to catch a worker in any partnership, even those where the partners themselves are excluded because of the exceptions set out above.

This is largely a 'backstop' anti-avoidance provision to prevent partnership-type structures which might otherwise have replaced service companies.

14.5 The deemed income calculation

14.5.1 Introduction

If a partnership is within IR35, it broadly follows the same steps as regards the deemed income calculation as a corporate intermediary. These are set out at Chapters 10 to 12. However, there are a number of points where the detailed legislation and the consequences for partners are different from those which affect companies, and these are discussed below.

14.5.2 Step One

Step One requires the inclusion in the calculation of all 'payments and other benefits received by the intermediary in that (fiscal) year in respect of relevant engagements'.

Receipts basis

The deemed income calculation is on a received basis. There will thus be a difference between this, and the amounts brought into the partnership accounts on an accruals basis (s42(1) FA 1998). It is necessary to track receipts and expenditure both on a cash basis and an accruals basis in order to satisfy both sets of rules.

Fiscal year basis

The deemed Schedule E calculation is on a fiscal year basis. However, few partnerships have a 5 April year end, because only nine months and 25 days remain until the following 31 January, when the related tax return, accounts and computations have to be filed, and any balance of income tax and Class 4 NICs for the year paid. A 5 April year end does have the advantage of eliminating any overlap profit arising from the opening years and simplifies the tax filing, but these are commonly thought to be less valuable than the extra time for submitting the return and paying the tax and NICs.

However, partnerships affected by the personal services rules may now need to review their year end date, see **14.6.4** below.

The 5 per cent allowance

Once all the income received by the partnership in the fiscal year has been calculated, a round sum allowance equal to 5 per cent of total income is deducted. A summary of the expenses which it will have to cover is at **11.2** above, along with a discussion of the following points:

- Profits will remain taxable in the partnership if there are insufficient actual expenses to utilise the 5 per cent; and

- The allowance is available only against income or benefits received by the partnership. In particular, there is no 5 per cent reduction of amounts brought into the calculation at Step Two, because they have been received directly by the partners from the clients rather than being paid to the partnership. It is thus more tax efficient for amounts to be received by the intermediary rather than being paid or provided directly to the partner.

14.5.3 Step Two

Step Two adds into the calculation all payments and benefits received by the worker:

> 'Otherwise than from the intermediary, which are not chargeable to income tax under Schedule E, and which would have been chargeable if the worker were an employee of the client.'

This step is of particular relevance to partners. This is because, where an individual provides personal services via a company, any payments or benefits received directly from the client will commonly be by reason of his employment with the service company, and thus fall into tax apart from these rules under s154(1) ICTA 1988. Benefits from the client to a PSC director or worker rarely come within Step Two, see **10.5.4**.

However the same is not true of partners. Partners do not have an employment, and thus benefits provided by the client cannot be provided by reason of the employment. This Step is thus the mechanism by which payments and benefits which pass directly from the client to the individual partner are brought into the deemed Schedule E calculation. Examples of benefits which might be so provided, and comments on any applicable reliefs and exemptions are discussed at **10.6**.

14.5.4 Step Three

Step Three allows relief for:

'Any expenses met in that year by the intermediary that would have been deductible from the emoluments of the employment if the worker had been employed by the client and the expenses had been met by the worker out of those emoluments.'

The deduction is for expenses met by the partnership. Until 2002/03 onwards, costs incurred directly by the partner did not come into the deemed Schedule E calculation. For 2002/03 and subsequent years, a new paragraph 7B was inserted in the tax legislation, with a similar amendment to the NICs regulations. This reads as follows:

'Where the intermediary is a partnership and the worker is a member of the partnership, expenses met by the worker for and on behalf of the intermediary shall be treated ... as expenses met by the worker and reimbursed by the intermediary.'

Relief for costs paid by the worker can be obtained in the Schedule D computation of the partnership, but only if the expenses are deductible under Step Three of the calculation (Sch 12, para 18(3) FA 2000). In other words, the expense must satisfy the Schedule E tests to be deductible in the partnership's Schedule D computation.

Expenses borne personally cannot be claimed by the individual partner in his self-assessment return, see **15.3.4**. For years before 2002/03 it was therefore essential that partners who incurred expenses while carrying out their relevant engagements ensured that these costs were either met by the intermediary (see **11.3.7**) or included in the partnership's SA return. It was more efficient if the expenses were met by the intermediary as NIC relief was then available. The same continues to apply to capital allowances, as this part of the legislation was not amended in FA 2002, see **14.5.5** below.

The general rules for Schedule E expenses are discussed at **11.4**, and the more generous travel and subsistence reliefs at **11.6**. Partnerships need to pay particular attention to both, because while service company workers have always fallen within ss198ff ICTA 1988, the Schedule E rules are new to partners.

14.5.5 Step Four

Step Four gives relief for capital allowances in the deemed income calculation, but only if the stringent Schedule E tests are met. These require that the item be 'necessarily provided for use in the performance of the duties' (s27(2)(a) CAA 1990). A less demanding test, excluding the word 'necessarily', applies to cars, motor bikes and bicycles, for which allowances are due, providing the asset is used 'in the performance of the duties' (s27(2A) CAA 1990). However see **11.6.9** for the new rules on authorised mileage rates from April 2002 which precludes the claiming of capital allowances.

Step Four only gives a deduction where the capital asset has been purchased by the partnership. Capital allowances on assets owned by the partners personally, but used in the business, are not allowable in the deemed Schedule E computation. Instead, they may be deductible against partnership profits (s65(1) CAA 1990), but subject to restrictions where the asset is used for relevant engagements, see **14.6.3** below.

Partners should ensure that assets used in relevant engagements are either:

(a) Owned by the partnership; or

(b) Owned by the partner but with the allowance claimed by the partnership (para 5.17 *SAT1 (1995)*).

Of these (a) is preferable as the inclusion of the allowance in the deemed income calculation reduces the NIC on the deemed payment, see **11.11**.

Cars are the partnership asset on which capital allowances have most commonly been claimed. They are generally used both for business and privately, and a private use proportion is usually agreed with the Revenue. For years before 2002/03 the business proportion must now be further split into the amount relating to relevant engagements.

The Revenue's answer to FAQ Computation 9 (Example 14A below) shows how this would operate in practice. However, it should be noted that this example relates to years before 2002/03, and the new rules on authorised mileage rates remove the right to claim capital allowances (for Schedule E purposes) on these assets from April 2002, see **11.6.9**.

Example 14A

John and Mary are married, and work in partnership providing art and design services. They each carry out relevant engagements during the year. 50 per cent of the partnership income arises from such engagements and 50 per cent from other sources. Profits are split equally. Each is provided with a car, both of which are provided as partnership assets. The private use proportion of the motoring expenses is 30 per cent.

Partnership accounts show the following results:

Year ended 5 April 2001

	£
Income	80,000
Expenses (includes motoring expenses of £3,000)	(17,000)
Profit	63,000
Depreciation, private expenses etc.	(2,000)
Tax adjusted profit	65,000

Notes

1. Payments from relevant engagements: $80,000 \times 50\% = 40,000$

2. Schedule E expenses allowed against deemed payment: $3,000 \times 70\% \times 50\% = 1,050$

   This apportionment depends on the facts. In this case relief is available for 50 per cent of the business expenses reflecting the use of the cars in the relevant engagements. A further apportionment has to be made between the expenses relating to each partner. Where a car is concerned this is likely to be based upon milege. The claim can be based upon the actual expenses incurred and capital allowances or, as an alternative, upon the Inland Revenue Authorised Mileage Rates, see **11.6.8**.

3. As a partnership, any pension contributions will be paid personally by the individual partners and relieved under the usual rules, see **14.5.6** below.

Calculation of deemed payment at 5 April 2001

	Mary £	John £
Step One: Payments from relevant engagements	25,000	15,000
5% allowance	(1,250)	(750)
Step Three: Schedule E expenses	(700)	(350)
Step Eight: Employer NIC on deemed payment	(2,031)	(1,036)
Step Nine: Deemed payment	21,019	12,864

Recalculation of partnership taxable profit

	£
Partnership profit	65,000
Plus: disallowed expenses (Note 1)	4,450
Less: employer's NIC	(3,067)
Less: deemed payments:	
John	(12,864)
Mary	(21,019)
Taxable profit	32,500

Recalculation of personal liability

	Mary £	John £
Partnership profit	16,250	16,250
Deemed payment	21,019	12,864
Total taxable income	37,359	29,114

Note 1

The expense restriction is calculated as follows:

	£
Total expenses	17,000
Disallowed under Sch D rules	(2,000)
	15,000
Relating to relevant engagements: 50%	7,500
Allowable: Car expenses	(1,050)
5% allowance	(2,000)
Expense restriction	4,450

14.5.6 Step Five

Step Five gives relief for pension contributions made by the employer. However, where the worker is a partner in a partnership, the contributions cannot be made by 'the employer' as there is no employment. It is thus not possible for the partners to use pension contributions to reduce the National Insurance charge on their deemed payment, as it is for workers and directors within service companies, see **12.2.2**. Where a worker is an employee of the partnership, however, contributions can be made and relief obtained.

14.5.7 Steps Six and Seven

Step Six deducts any employer NIC already paid for that tax year in respect of the worker, and Step Seven gives relief for 'any payments … in respect of which the worker is chargeable to income tax under Schedule E'.

Since a partner will not have had any Schedule E income or benefits, apart from under these provisions, these steps are redundant in the context of a partnership.

14.5.8 Steps Eight and Nine

Step Eight gives a deduction for the employer's NIC on the deemed payment. This is calculated by a formula, see **12.5.2**. For the interaction between the Class 1 NIC payable on this deemed payment, and any Class 2 and Class 4 liability, see **14.7.1** below.

Step Nine states simply that 'the result is the amount of the deemed Schedule E payment'.

14.6 Interaction of deemed payment and partnership tax position

14.6.1 Deemed payment a requirement

In the case of a company, salary can be paid to the worker before the end of the fiscal year in order to eliminate the deemed Schedule E amount. However, this option is not open to partnerships, see **12.4.1**. Where there is a relevant engagement, partnerships are thus forced to make a deemed payment and pay over the tax and NICs.

14.6.2 Timing of deemed payment

The deemed payment is normally treated as made on the last day of the fiscal year, see Sch 12, para 2(2) FA 2000. However, this date is accelerated as follows if a 'relevant event' occurs:

- Where the worker leaves the partnership, the day before he ceases to be a partner or employee;

- The dissolution of the partnership or it ceasing to trade, the day before the dissolution or cessation of trading (Sch 12, para 12(3) FA 2000).

14.6.3 Deduction in partnership computation for deemed payment

Once the deemed payment has been calculated, both the payment and the associated employer NIC 'must be taken into account for the period of account in which the deemed Schedule E payment is treated as made' (Sch 12, para 17(2) FA 2000).

However, the legislation applies two restrictions to the deductibility of a partnership deemed payment which do not apply to companies. These place limits on both loss relief and expenses. The reason for these restrictions was explained by Dawn Primarolo in the debate on IR35:

'The legislation contains the special rules for partnerships because, if a worker uses a company as an intermediary, any loss arising in the company can be used only to reduce the profits of that company. If a partnership is used, any loss by that partnership can be used to reduce the partner's own tax liability and can be set against the tax due under Schedule E.' (*Hansard*, 6 June 2000)

Loss restriction

The amount of the deduction for the deemed payment is limited to the amount that reduces the profits of the partnership to nil (Sch 12, para 18(2) FA 2000). This means that the deemed payment cannot create a loss, in contrast to the corporation tax position, see **13.7**.

Expense restrictions

Expenses relating to the relevant engagement can only be deducted from partnership profits if they are also deductible in the deemed Schedule E computation. In other words, there is no scope to deduct any excess expenses, which might otherwise be allowable under the more generous Schedule D rules, from partnership income, if these expenses relate to the relevant engagement (Sch 12, para 18(3) FA 2000). This restriction is demonstrated in Example 14A, Note 1.

As explained in **14.5.4** above, where an expense relating to a relevant engagement is borne by the partner personally, it can be deducted in the partnership computation only if it satisfies the Schedule E rules for expenses.

Capital allowances are now treated as expenses rather than 'allowances' for partnership computation purposes (s140 CAA 1990). Thus where a capital asset is used for the relevant engagement and no allowance is due under s27(2)(a) or s(2A) CAA 1990, there will also be no relief in the partnership computation.

14.6.4 Accounting dates

The deemed payment is regarded as paid on the last day of the tax year. In a continuing partnership, the basis period rules mean that tax relief for the PAYE and NIC on the deemed payment can be considerably delayed – perhaps until the following fiscal year, see Example 14B.

Example 14B

Carol and Richard are a married couple who work in partnership providing theatrical support services. From June to December 2000 Richard has a relevant engagement with the local theatre, and calculates that he has a deemed Schedule E payment of £10,000. Profits are split equally between the partners.

The partnership has a 31 December accounting date. Their profits, unadjusted for the deemed Schedule E payment are:

- Year to 31 December 2000: £35,000,

- Year to 31 December 2001: £45,000.

The deemed payment is deducted from the profits in the period of account in which it is made, namely the year to 31 December 2001. The adjusted partnership profit for that year is as follows:

	£
Profits before adjustment:	45,000
less: deemed payment	(10,000)
NIC on deemed payment	(1,220)
	33,780

> This period of account forms the basis period for tax year 2001/02, and the taxable income is split: Carol: £16,890; Richard £16,890.
>
> The tax will be due for payment on 31 January 2002 (interim), 31 July 2002 (2nd interim) and 31 January 2003. In addition, Richard has a PAYE and NIC liability payable on 19 April 2001. Richard thus has tax to pay in the calendar year 2001 as follows:
>
> 31/1/01 – tax relating to profits of £17,500 (50% of 2000/01 partnership profits of £35,000)
>
> 19/4/01 – tax relating to deemed Schedule E payment on 5 April 2000 for 2000/01
>
> 31/7/01 – tax relating to profits of £17,500 (50% of 2000/01 partnership profits of £35,000)

Example 14B demonstrates that a partner in Richard's situation will have to pay Schedule D tax in full for the year in which he also has earned the deemed payment. It cannot be reduced by deducting the deemed Schedule E amount because the payment date falls into the following period of account.

He is also unable to reduce the interim payments in January and July 2001, because they are correctly based on the profits of the year ended 31 December 2000. However, in the following year his payments on account will be based on the profits to 31 December 2001. These will be much lower because of the deemed Schedule E amount, and he can thus apply to reduce the interim payments in January and July 2001 (s59A(3) TMA 1970). However, in the meantime he has suffered a severe cashflow disadvantage.

Change of accounting date to 5 April

To ameliorate the cashflow disadvantage, partnerships may want to change their accounting date to 5 April. If the business commenced within the last three years this can be done without having to meet any statutory requirements. Otherwise, the partnership must fall within the rules contained in s62 and s62A ICTA 1988, as follows:

(a) The new accounting period must not exceed 18 months;

(b) The Revenue must be notified of the change of date; and

(c) There must have been no change of date within the last five years, *or*, if there has been such a change, this further change must be made for genuine commercial reasons. It is specifically stated in the legislation that 'obtaining a tax advantage will not be accepted as a genuine commercial reason for a change of accounting date' (s62A(9) ICTA 1988).

The Revenue guidance on self-assessment commented on this as follows:

> '"Tax advantage" is not defined in the legislation. But since income tax is a personal liability "tax advantage" will include any cash flow advantage arising from the deferral of tax, as well as an absolute reduction in profits or an absolute increase in losses.' (para 1.54 *(SAT1 1995)*)

Avoiding the cashflow problem caused by the interaction of the Schedule D and IR35 rules thus appears to be a 'tax advantage'. Therefore, unless a partnership can fall within the five year rule in condition (c) above, or began trading within the last three years, it will be unable to change its accounting date under these normal rules.

If a partnership can change its accounting date, it will then crystallise some or all of the overlap relief (s63A ICTA 1988).

Election for discontinuance

The Revenue recognised that the new rules would create a difficult cashflow position for partnerships, and realised that some would be unable to change their accounting date because of the restriction in (c) above. As a result, the personal services legislation contains a specific provision allowing partnerships to elect for discontinuance at the end of the 1999/00 year, so that a new business commenced on 6 April 2000 (Sch 12, para 23 FA 2000).

This allowed the 'new' partnership to deduct the deemed Schedule E payment against the profits of the same period, and so achieve a better cashflow position. The deemed discontinuance and recommencement did not affect the ability of the partnership to carry losses forward from the old partnership to the new one (Sch 12, para 23(3) FA 2000).

This was a transitional relief, and applies only where:

(a) A partnership is carrying on business at the beginning of the fiscal year 2000/01; and

(b) Is treated as making one or more deemed Schedule E payments in that year.

It therefore does not apply when a partnership in a future tax year makes a deemed payment for the first time.

If the partnership does elect for discontinuance, it will have the effect of changing the accounting date to 5 April, see **14.5.2** above, and crystallising the full overlap relief.

A partnership which can choose between the discontinuance option and the normal change of accounting date rules should compare the results of both options before making the decision. One possibility for a partnership which can use the s62A ICTA rules is to change its accounting date to 30 April. This will not give a complete match with the fiscal year, but the difference should be manageable. A 30 April year end gives a much longer period for filing accounts and returns, see **14.5.2** above.

A further point to consider is that the discontinuance option will use the full overlap relief against the profits of the final period, while a change of accounting date may utilise only part of the relief.

14.6.5 Effects of deemed Schedule E payment on other partners

The effect of the deemed Schedule E calculation is to increase the tax charge on the partner who has carried out the relevant engagement. There are also consequences for the other partners:

- The deemed Schedule E payment, including the Class 1 NIC, is deducted from total partnership profits, although the tax liability on this amount is the personal liability of the individual partner, see Sch 12, para 11(5) FA 2000;

- The allowable expenses deducted from the partnership's taxable profits may be restricted, see **14.6.3** above and Example 14A.

If the partnership profit shares remain unchanged, and are based on the gross earnings of the partnership before tax, then the take-home pay of each partner will be significantly affected by the existence of the deemed payment.

In example 14B, the profits would normally be shared equally, giving Carol and Richard £22,500 each. Under the new provisions Carol only pays tax on £16,890, but Richard pays tax on £26,890. Similarly, in Example 14A, Mary pays tax on £38,803, but John only pays tax on £30,648, even though profits were again shared equally. There are also NIC implications, see **14.7** below.

Thus, where one or more partners have relevant engagements, the partners may wish to review their profit sharing arrangements.

14.7 National Insurance

14.7.1 Interaction with Classes 2 and 4

A partner who is within the personal service rules is 'treated as employed in employed earner's employment' by the partnership. He or she thus has 'attributable earnings' which are assessable under Class 1. This has the consequential benefit of allowing the partner to claim jobseeker's allowance, statutory sick pay and statutory maternity pay.

These earnings are 'treated as received by him in his personal capacity and not as income of the partnership' (SI 2000/727 reg 8(3)).

Assuming that the individual also has Schedule D earnings from the partnership in the fiscal year, he will thus have paid Class 1, Class 2 and Class 4 contributions. In consequence he may have overpaid NIC in the year.

If the total Class 1, Class 2 and Class 4 paid in 2001/02 is more than £2,586.40, the partner can apply for a refund. If he anticipates the situation, he can apply for deferment of:

- Class 2 (if total contributions are expected to be more than the value given above); and/or

- Class 4 (if any Class 1 contributions at all are expected to be paid) with a 'catch-up' payment at a later date if total contributions prove inadequate.

In addition to the employee contributions, the partnership will have paid employer's NIC on the deemed payment. This is deducted from the taxable profits of the partnership, see Examples 14A and 14B above.

14.7.2 Small earnings exception

If, after deducting the attributable earnings from the deemed Schedule E computation, the Schedule D earnings of the individual from the partnership are within the 'small earnings exception', he will escape Class 2 (s11(4) SSCBA 1992). The partner must apply for this exception; it is not granted automatically (s11(5) SSCBA 1992). For 2001/02 the limit is £3,955. The exception can take effect up to 13 weeks before the application date and continues for the rest of the fiscal year.

Where exception has not been applied for in time, but would have been available had an application been made within the time limit, a repayment of contributions maybe obtained, less any amount paid by way of contributory benefits which would not have been received but for the Class 2 contributions which are now being repaid (SI 1979/591 reg 47).

A claim for repayment must:

- Be in writing to the Inland Revenue;

- Be supported by evidence of the earnings (i.e., profits) of the tax year in respect of which a repayment of Class 2 contributions is sought;

- Not be made before the beginning of the following tax year;

- Be made by 31 December in that following tax year (SI 1979/591 reg 47).

Thus partners who may be able to claim this relief should be aware of their overall NIC position before 31 December following the end of the fiscal year.

14.8 Payment of PAYE and NICs

The payment deadlines for the PAYE and Class 1 NIC on the deemed Schedule E amount are discussed in Chapter 16. There are a few points which particularly affect partners:

(a) The concession relating to penalties on late payment of the PAYE and NIC liability, discussed at **16.4.2**, is dependent upon the intermediary making a 'payment on 19 April of a lower amount on account of the tax and NICs due'. In the case of a company, payment of salary will often have been made at some point during the tax year. But where the worker is a partner, no salary can have been paid. Thus to obtain the benefit of the concession on PAYE penalties, *some* tax and National Insurance must be paid on or before 19 April – it is understood that 'payment of a lower amount' cannot be interpreted as a nil figure!

(b) The partnership has to submit Forms P14 and P35 in respect of the deemed Schedule E payment by the normal deadline of 19 May. This is because the intermediary is treated as the secondary contributor in respect of the worker's attributable personal service earnings (SI 2000/727 para 6(3)(b)). If the amount paid on 19 April is provisional, this should be indicated on the form, see **16.4.2**;

(c) A supplementary return including the correct final figure for the deemed payment should be sent in to the Revenue by 31 January following the end of the tax year.

15 Self-assessment and personal services

15.1 General

Individuals and companies are both within the UK self-assessment system. Under self-assessment it is each person's responsibility to consider whether there is tax to pay, and if so, to determine the amount of that that liability. If a person's self-assessment is incorrect, he is likely to suffer interest and penalties. This chapter does not cover all aspects of the self-assessment system, but considers how the rules impact upon personal service workers and their intermediaries.

Companies, partnerships and individuals within the personal services regime must self-assess their own liability based on whether or not they have relevant engagements. Although the Revenue have offered help in reviewing individual contracts, see **7.7**, at the end of the day the onus to get it right is on the taxpayer. In practice, however, most policing of the personal services regime is likely to occur via reviews of the intermediary's PAYE compliance, see **16.9**.

15.2 Outline of SA for individuals and partners

Everyone within the UK is potentially within the self-assessment (SA) system, but only some eight million people receive a return. If an individual has a liability to tax which has not been collected directly (e.g., via PAYE or by deduction from bank interest), but does not receive a return, he must notify the Revenue by 5 October following the end of the fiscal year.

The basic individual return covers interest, dividends (including those from a personal service company) allowances and reliefs. There are supplementary pages covering employment income (including any deemed Schedule E income the provision of personal services) self-employment, partnership income, foreign income and other special areas. It is the individual's responsibility to ask for the pages he needs. In addition to the form and any supplementary pages, the Revenue send each person a calculation guide, which helps to work out the tax liability.

If the completed return is received by the Revenue by 30 September following the end of the tax year, the Revenue will calculate the individual's tax. If the return is sent after this date, the taxpayer must work out his own liability using the calculation guide, and send it to the Revenue. Any return not received by 31 January following the end of the tax year will incur an automatic £100 penalty unless the individual has a 'reasonable excuse' (see **16.7.3**), the tax due is less than the penalty, or the filing deadline was extended.

The Revenue will process the return, and, based on the self-assessment, tell the individual if he has any tax to pay or whether he is due a refund. Any tax outstanding must be settled by 31 January following the end of the fiscal year, whether or not the return has been submitted, or there may be interest and penalties, see **16.5** and **16.6**.

Assuming the return was submitted on time, the Revenue have until the following 31 January to raise questions on the return. These might be on a single issue (an 'aspect enquiry') or a more general review (a 'full enquiry'), see **15.5.4** below. If the return is received late, the Revenue's enquiry deadlines are extended.

If the filing deadline was met, and the Revenue do not give notice of an enquiry by the following 31 January, the tax return becomes final and conclusive, subject to the rules for 'error and mistake' and 'discovery', see **15.5.3** and **15.5.5**.

If the return is issued but not sent back to the Revenue, they can determine the tax liability. If the return is subsequently submitted, the Revenue's determination will be superseded by the self-assessment.

The individual taxpayer has an obligation to keep the records on which his self-assessment is based until 31 January following the filing date (or later, if the filing deadline was missed). Partnerships must keep records for five years from the same date. There is a maximum penalty of £3,000 for failing to comply (s12A TMA 1970).

15.3 Reporting personal services income via self-assessment

15.3.1 Notifying chargeability

An individual who has carried out relevant engagements within the UK is within the scope of UK tax and thus both the personal services regime and self-assessment. However, because the liability to tax on a deemed payment is dealt with via PAYE, there may be no further tax to pay. Where this is the case, and no return has been received, there is no requirement to request or complete a return.

15.3.2 Salary and deemed Schedule E income

An individual within IR35 will have received salary, deemed Schedule E income, or both. Deemed Schedule E income arises on the last day of the tax year, and should be included on the self-assessment return along with any actual salary received. This applies both to partners who have relevant engagements just as it does to employees and directors of service companies.

There is no special box on the self-assessment form for the deemed income, but instead the Notes to the Employment Pages of the Return provide some assistance. Under 'Special rules' the Notes for 2000/01 say:

'Deemed Schedule E payment

If you provide your services to clients through a company or partnership you may have been treated as receiving a deemed Schedule E payment. The rules will only apply if you would have been an employee of your client, had it not been for the existence of your company or partnership. The deemed payment is treated as income from employment with the company or partnership. It should be included in the figure in box 1.8. If you have any other income from employment with the same company or partnership you should record the total amount, including the deemed payment. PAYE tax on the deemed payment should be included in the figure in box 1.11.'

This makes it clear that as well as requiring the salary and deemed income to be included, the return also asks for the PAYE suffered on both the actual earnings and the deemed Schedule E payment. In practice both should be combined on the worker's P60, and it should simply be a question of taking the number off the P60 and including it on the self-assessment return, see **16.2.3**.

The fact that the worker has not actually received the deemed Schedule E income does not change his tax liability. The legislation deems it to be his income, PAYE has been deducted by the service company, and the deemed earnings and the related tax should be included on his self-assessment return.

Where a worker is within IR35 for NICs but not for tax then an attributable earnings calculation, but not a deemed income calculation, has to be completed (see **12.7**). However, the result of the calculation is not earnings for tax purposes and thus does not have to be returned on the P14 nor on the worker's self-assessment form.

15.3.3 Benefits

Employees and directors

Where a benefit has been received from, or by arrangement with, a service company, its value should have been included on the individual's P11D, and he should enter it on his tax return. This will include most benefits from clients, see **10.5.4**.

If benefits have been received from the third party otherwise than by arrangement with the intermediary, the third party has to provide details of the benefits to the individual by 6 July following the end of the tax year (SI 1993/744 reg 46). These benefits should also be included on the individual's tax return.

Partners

Any benefits received by a partner from a client in respect of a relevant engagement are included within the deemed Schedule E calculation (**14.5.3**) and are not entered on the SA return.

15.3.4 Expenses and capital allowances

Employee or director

An employee is allowed to deduct certain expenses from his taxable income under ss198ff ICTA 1988, see **11.3.3**. Where these costs have been borne directly by the individual they should be claimed on his tax return. Any capital allowances on assets purchased by the worker which satisfy the narrow tests in s27 CAA 1990 are also included here, see **11.12**.

However, as explained at **11.12.1(c)** and **11.3.3** it is more efficient if:

- Assets on which capital allowances can be claimed are owned by the company rather than the worker; and

- Allowable expenses are met by the intermediary rather than the worker.

This gives both a cashflow advantage and a reduction in the Class 1 NIC on any deemed payment.

Partners

Before 2002/03 it was more efficient for partners' expenses relating to the carrying out of relevant engagements to be met by the intermediary so they could be deducted in the deemed Schedule E calculation, see **14.5.4**. Alternatively, but less tax-efficiently, they could be included in the partnership's SA return. From 2002/03 relief is available for amounts 'met by the worker for and on behalf of [the partnership]', and thus it is possible to obtain relief for expenses borne by the worker even if they are not met by the partnership.

The restriction on capital expenditure borne by individual partners remains, and was not amended by FA 2002, see **14.5.5**. Thus for years before 2002/03 for expenses, and for all captial expenditure, no relief is obtained for costs borne by partners personally because:

(a) Partners are not employees, and so could not claim a deduction under ss198ff ICTA 1988. As a result they could not offset expenses directly against their deemed Schedule E income;

(b) They cannot make a capital allowances claim under s27 CAA 1990 to deduct allowances from their deemed Schedule E income;

(c) Where a partner has met the expense or owns the asset personally, he cannot deduct the expense or claim the allowance on his SA Schedule D partnership return; it must be included in the partnership return. This point is explained in the Inland Revenue's booklet *The new current basis of self assessment* at paragraph 5.17 (SAT1 (1995)):

> 'Any expenditure incurred by a partner on behalf of the partnership must be included in the partnership return. It will not be possible for individual partners to make supplementary claims, whether to expenses or capital allowances, in their own tax returns.

> This is because revenue expenditure incurred by a partner only qualifies for relief if it is made 'wholly and exclusively' for the purposes of the partnership business. And the only legal basis for giving relief for any such expenditure is as a deduction in the calculation of the profits of the partnership business.

> Similarly the only legal basis for giving relief for expenditure qualifying for capital allowances is as a deduction in the calculation of the profits of the partnership business.

> However, this does not mean that expenditure incurred by a partner can only be relieved if it is included in the partnership accounts. The Inland Revenue will accept adjustments for such expenditure in the tax computations included in the partnership return providing the adjustments are made before apportionment of the net profit between the partners. But once the adjustments have been made the expenditure will be treated, for all practical purposes, as if it had been included in the partnership's accounts.'

15.3.5 Reliefs

If a pension contribution has been made by the individual, a claim for tax relief should be made on the tax return. Where the intermediary is a company it is more efficient for the pension contributions to be paid by the employer rather than by the individual, as this reduces the NIC due as well as producing a minor cashflow benefit, see **12.2.2**.

Where the intermediary is a partnership this is not possible, and relief for pension contributions must be claimed via the individual's SA tax return, see **14.5.6**. This may result in a repayment of tax already deducted under PAYE on the partner's deemed Schedule E income.

There is also relief for:

- Interest on a qualifying loan to buy into the partnership or to buy shares in the service company;

- Foreign tax suffered. The most efficient way to claim relief for foreign tax is as a deduction against the Schedule E *tax* using the Foreign Pages, see **15.3.8** below, rather than against the *income*. The Notes to the Foreign Pages explain the position in detail, see 'Foreign tax paid and tax credit relief'.

15.3.6 Dividends

Where a company has paid both a deemed Schedule E amount, and a dividend, the dividend may be outside the scope of tax, see **13.6.2**. Where this is the case, it does not have to be included on the tax return, see *Tax Bulletin* February 2001. ESM 3273 requires the Revenue office giving clearance to inform the tax districts of the individuals receiving the dividend, and to note the dividend on the individual's SA record.

It is surprising that there is no similar note in the Tax Return Guide, which deals generally with the inclusion of dividends on the Tax Return. It may thus be advisable to include an explanatory note in the 'Additional Information' section of the tax return explaining why the dividend has not been brought into tax. For dividends from an overseas company, see **15.3.8** below.

15.3.7 Student loan repayments

The 2000/01 tax return was the first to require an entry for student loan repayments. The interaction of student loan repayment amounts with the personal services rules, in particular with dividends and partnership income, is discussed at **22.4**.

15.3.8 Overseas income and residence status

The definitions of residence, ordinary residence, and domicile are discussed in Chapter 17. An individual who is resident, but either not ordinarily resident or not domiciled, will receive a tax return on the same basis as the rest of the population. A non-resident may receive a return, since the Revenue approach is that 'Income from employment will normally be taxed through PAYE, with a final settling up with the non-resident through Self Assessment where necessary' (*Tax Bulletin* 18, August 1995).

Non-resident, not ordinarily resident and/or not domiciled

If an individual is claiming that he is non-resident, not ordinarily resident and/or not domiciled for all or part of the tax year, he must complete the non-residence supplementary pages of the tax return. This is discussed at **17.7.3** and **17.11.5**. Use should be made of the additional information ('white space') if the individual considers that there are any particular facts concerning his residence status which he wishes to draw to the attention of the Inspector.

Overseas implications of personal services legislation

There are a number of possibilities here. If the individual:

- Is resident, ordinarily resident and domiciled in the UK, he is within the scope of the personal services regime even if his service company is non-resident (see **19.5.1**), or he has worked on relevant engagements overseas (see **17.10.1**);

- Is resident in the UK, but has suffered foreign tax on income earned overseas and wishes to claim double tax relief, this is deductible in the first instance against the corporation tax suffered by the company, see **17.10.2**. However, where there is insufficient corporation tax for relief to be obtained, the foreign tax may be deductible against the individual's Schedule E income. This should be claimed using the supplementary foreign pages of the tax return;

- Is resident, but either not ordinarily resident and/or not domiciled, his overseas personal services income may be on the remittance basis. See **17.11.5** for reporting obligations;

- Is non-resident but has carried out work here, he is within Schedule E for any earnings or deemed earnings on his relevant engagements, see **17.8**. However, he may be able to argue that the income is 'merely incidental' to his overseas work, see **17.8.2**, or that under the provisions of a double tax treaty no tax is due, see **17.8.3**.

Dividends from an overseas company

Many service companies, even those registered abroad, are in fact resident in the UK because they are managed and controlled here, see **19.2.3**.

If the company is not resident in the UK, any dividends will be Schedule D Case V income, and should be reported using the foreign pages of the SA return. However workers taxed on a remittance basis (see **17.13**) are only subject to UK tax on an overseas dividend if it is brought into the UK.

As with UK dividends, there will be no tax if the service company has made a deemed Schedule E payment which effectively covers the dividend, see **13.6.2** above.

15.3.9 Self-employed individuals

An employee or a director of a personal service company has to decide whether he is inside or outside IR35. To do this he has to consider whether he would be Schedule E or Schedule D in respect of his relevant engagements if he was working directly for the client. If he would have been Schedule D, he escapes IR35.

However this Schedule E/Schedule D test merely establishes whether he should be within the personal service rules; *it does not mean he is self-employed.* He remains an employee or director of his company. He can thus ignore the self-employment pages unless he has a separate Schedule D business.

15.3.10 Partners

A partner who has deemed Schedule E income from relevant engagements is required to:

- Complete the employment income part of the SA return as if he were an employee, see **15.3.2** above;
- Ignore any benefits received from the intermediary or a third party, as they will have been included in the deemed Schedule E calculation, see **14.5.3**.

In addition, partners have to complete the supplementary partnership pages, even if all the partnership income derives from relevant engagements and is thus taxable under the employment income section of the return. A partnership return is also required.

Expenses allowable against the partnership's trading income may need to be restricted, as explained in **14.6.3**. There may also be a limitation on the partnership losses. These adjustments should be made in the partnership return, and the partners should then be informed of the correct amount to include in the partnership pages of their own SA return.

Where the worker is a partner in a foreign partnership, a special tax return, Partnership Foreign, must be completed.

15.3.11 Repayments

If the amount of tax deducted by the service company from the individual's deemed payment is excessive, then the self-assessment form may trigger a repayment. This is discussed at **16.4.3**.

15.4 Disclosure

15.4.1 General

Where the taxpayer has additional facts which are relevant to his tax liability, it is usually recommended that he disclose these on the additional information or 'white space' area of his tax return. Once he has made this disclosure, then, providing no enquiry is received, his return will be closed from 31 January following the filing deadline, and cannot be re-opened (s9(6)(a) TMA 1970). If the return was submitted late, the enquiry window remains open for longer.

Disclosure thus gives the individual finality about his tax position. If there had been no disclosure, the Revenue have six years (longer if there has been fraud) to make a later 'discovery', see **15.5.5,** and to collect tax, interest and penalties. Thus the 'reward' for disclosure is that the assessment is closed after a relatively short time.

15.4.2 Personal services

The individual's tax liability under the personal services regime depends on whether he would have been self-employed in respect of his relevant engagements had he not been operating via an intermediary. Because of the complexity of the status tests, this may not be an easy decision to make.

The taxpayer can ask the Revenue to rule on a contract by contract basis as to whether each engagement is inside or outside IR35, see **7.7**. If he does this, and provides all relevant details to the Revenue, he should be able to rely on the ruling when completing his tax return, see **7.7.7**.

If he does not seek a ruling, he has to decide whether to disclose his reasons for considering that IR35 does not apply. However, it could be argued that disclosure via SA is not appropriate, because:

(a) Self-assessment is exactly that – the individual is supposed to work out whether he has a tax liability and if he has, to assess it. The rules for disclosure are not meant to cover issues where the tax payer has either given himself the benefit of the doubt, or is uncertain about the operation of the tax legislation. Whether an individual falls inside or outside IR35 could thus be said to be an inappropriate area for disclosure: the individual is either within the rules, in which case he should have received a deemed payment, or he is not;

(b) Liability to pay the tax and NICs in respect of a relevant engagement rests in the first instance with the intermediary. Once the service company or partnership has decided whether the worker has a liability to PAYE and NICs under IR35, it is required to pay over the tax and National Insurance. Details of the gross Schedule E deemed payment and the PAYE and employee's NIC are then provided to the individual via his P60. If the intermediary considers that there is no liability, there will be no deemed payment on the P60.

   If the intermediary is wrong, and the worker is within IR35, the Revenue will seek back PAYE and NICs, plus interest and possibly penalties, from the service company or partnership, see **16.5** and **16.6**. An employer compliance review will be the normal route by which compliance with the personal services legislation is enforced, see **16.9**;

(c) The usual time limit for a PAYE investigation is six years. Disclosure on the individual's SA return of the reasons why an individual believes he falls outside IR35 will not protect the company or partnership from a PAYE audit. Thus, while there may be 'finality' under self-assessment by 31 January following the filing date, this has little meaning given that the company can continue to be pursued for six years under the PAYE rules. If the company cannot meet the liability, the Revenue may seek to collect the PAYE from the worker, see **16.8.2**.

As mentioned in (b) above, investigations into the operation of the personal service legislation are likely to be carried out by employer compliance, rather than by targeted sampling of self-assessment returns, see **16.9**. However, like other taxpayers, the personal service worker may be selected for enquiry (see **15.5.4**) either on a random basis or because of some other question about his tax return. As part of the enquiry process the Revenue may ask why the individual considers the personal services legislation does not apply. This may then lead to a PAYE audit of the intermediary, and the collection of interest and possibly penalties by that route.

The individual thus has a vulnerability under the SA rules to interest and penalties if he has under-assessed his taxable employment income, although SA is not likely to be the normal route by which the Revenue will police the personal services legislation. Any back tax, interest and penalties are more likely to be collected from the service company under the PAYE regulations.

15.5 Changing the tax return

15.5.1 Methods of changing the return

Once the tax return has been submitted, it can be changed:

- By the taxpayer, using either the rules for 'amendment' or those for 'error or mistake', see **15.5.2** and **15.5.3**;

- By the Revenue, following an enquiry into the return, see **15.5.4**;

- By the Revenue, if they re-open the return under the 'discovery' provisions, see **15.5.5**.

If any of these changes causes the tax assessed to increase, there may be interest and/or penalties. Disclosure of the relevant facts on the return minimises the chances of 'discovery' and should prevent SA penalties.

15.5.2 Amendments

An individual may amend his return at any time within 12 months following the filing date, which is normally 31 January following the end of the fiscal year (s9A(4) TMA). A similar rule applies to partnerships (s12AB(2) TMA).

The taxpayer can thus change his mind about the tax position of his personal services income within this period. Clearly, an amendment to the SA return should not be considered in isolation from the PAYE/NIC position of the service company. If there is a change of view, so that IR35 is considered to have applied in that tax year, the individual should amend his self-assessment return, and the intermediary should make a late payment of PAYE and NICs. If the worker is a partner, the partnership return will also need amendment, and this will also affect the SA returns of the other partners.

An amendment may extend the period for which the Revenue can open an enquiry. Usually the extended period will relate only to the amended item, but 'there may be cases in which the amendment is so fundamental to the return that the whole return will be considered for enquiry'. (para 4.33 (SAT 2 1995)). No amendment can be made after the Revenue have notified the taxpayer that they are enquiring into the return. An amendment does not protect the taxpayer from penalties if he originally acted fraudulently or negligently, see *Tax Bulletin* September 1998.

15.5.3 Error or mistake

If the taxpayer has paid too much tax, so that for instance he and the intermediary have assumed that the IR35 provisions apply, but three years later he finds this is not the case, he can claim a refund of the tax overpaid. This 'error or mistake' claim can be made at any time during the five years after 31 January following the year of assessment (s33 TMA 1970). A similar claim can be made by partners, and this may also cause the assessment of the other partners to be adjusted (s33A TMA 1970).

A claim is not accepted, however, if the original SA return was made in accordance with the practice generally prevailing at the time – so if, for example, the law on status tests changed as a result of a House of Lords case, it would not be possible for taxpayers to go back six years and re-open their closed assessments (s33(2A) TMA 1970).

15.5.4 Enquiry

The Revenue have 12 months after 31 January following the filing date to open an enquiry (s9A TMA 1970). This deadline is extended if the return has been filed late. They do not have to give a reason for opening the enquiry and have said they will not do so.

The enquiry may be into one area of the return – an 'aspect' enquiry – or it may be more wide-ranging – a 'full enquiry'. A percentage of enquiries are random, generated by a computer programme, but most are not. The taxpayer will not be told if his is a random enquiry. In the Revenue's 1997 *Self-Assessment Tax Bulletin*, they said that:

'The vast majority of returns selected for enquiry will have been selected because of the potential risk that they are incorrect or incomplete. Selection for enquiry may be on the basis of a risk assessment of the information contained in the return, or on the basis of information from other sources, or a combination of both.

About one return in every thousand will be selected for full enquiry at random ... These cases are selected centrally and notified to local offices at the time of the bulk issue of returns in April each year. Selection of a small proportion of enquiries at random will mean that no one who is not complying with his or her obligations can feel safe from detection.

The depth and scope of all enquiries will be tailored to the circumstances of the individual case and proportionate to the risk of error or omission. We will not pursue risks that are trivial or remote, or seek information that can be verified from our own records.'

They also comment elsewhere that 'the 12 month time limit before finality is achieved will allow information from third parties – employers, contractors, financial institutions – to be used in the enquiry selection process' (para 4:32 (SAT2 1995)). See **21.2.4** and **21.3.3** for returns made by agents and clients to the Revenue.

If a return is selected for enquiry, the Revenue may ask for underlying records or other documents, and they may want to meet with the taxpayer. It is recommended that professional advice is sought if the Inspector enquires into the tax position of the individual's PSC income.

15.5.5 Discovery

The Revenue can re-open a tax return under the 'discovery' provisions if information subsequently becomes available which indicates that the self-assessment was too low, see SP8/91 and s29(3) TMA 1970. However, a discovery cannot be made unless either:

(a) The loss of tax is the result of fraudulent or negligent conduct by the taxpayer or any person acting on the taxpayer's behalf; or

(b) The Revenue could not have been reasonably expected to have identified the circumstances giving rise to the loss of tax, before the expiry of the normal enquiry period, or before the conclusion of any enquiry, using the information that had then been 'made available'.

Information will be treated as having been 'made available' if it is:

- Contained in the *SA return* for the relevant period (or the two preceding periods); or

- Contained in any *accounts, statements or documents supplied with the SA return*; or

- Contained in any *claim* made for the relevant period (or the two preceding periods), or in any of the accounts, statements or documents supplied with the claim; or

- Contained in any documents, accounts or particulars supplied in connection with an *enquiry* into a return or claim; or

- is information which could *reasonably be expected to be inferred* from any of the above; or

- It is information that was *notified to the Revenue officer in writing* by the taxpayer (s29 TMA 1970).

The Revenue have confirmed that 'a change of opinion on information that has previously been made available to the Revenue will not be grounds for a discovery' (para 4:99 (SAT2 1995)). However they have pointed out that:

> 'There is clearly an onus on the taxpayer to draw attention to any important information relevant to a tax liability, particularly if there is some doubt as to the interpretation that can be placed on that information. It is not sufficient just to provide that information if it is hidden away or obscure' (SAT2 1995 4:100).

Thus if information has been clearly disclosed in the tax return, there can be no discovery.

15.6 Interest and penalties

15.6.1 Alternatives

The Revenue have a range of penalty and interest legislation which can be used against the taxpayer if he submits late or incorrect SA returns. However, since the tax on the deemed Schedule E payment is primarily a PAYE liability, it is more likely that the penalty and interest provisions under that legislation will be used, see **16.5** and **16.6**, rather than those applicable to self-assessment. This is, however, their choice, and the SA provisions could be called upon if required.

15.6.2 Tax paid late

If tax is paid laid, interest runs from the due date to the date of payment. There is also a 5 per cent surcharge on any tax unpaid by 28 February following the year of assessment and a further 5 per cent surcharge on any tax unpaid by the following 31 July. If the surcharges are not paid within 30 days of the issue of the surcharge notice, interest begins to accrue on the surcharge itself.

If the taxpayer has a 'reasonable excuse' (see **16.7.3**) for paying the tax late, the interest will be waived or reduced. Where tax has been overpaid, interest runs from the due date (or date of payment if later) to the date of repayment. The rate of interest on tax overpaid is lower than that on overdue tax.

15.6.3 Late submission of returns

Penalties are also exacted where the return is not submitted by the due date, see **15.2**. These are:

- £100 if the return is not received by 31 January following the end of the fiscal year;

- A further £100 if it has still not been received by 31 July;

- In addition the Revenue can ask the Commissioners to impose a daily penalty of £60;

- If the return is outstanding a year after the due date, a penalty equal to any tax due can be imposed (s93 TMA 1970).

If the amount of tax due is less than the fixed £100 penalties, the penalty will be reduced (s93(7) TMA 1970; EH 640).

Partners are subject to similar rules, but without the tax-geared penalty; they are also unable to reduce the £100 fixed penalties (s93A TMA 1970).

15.6.4 For fraud or negligence

There are also tax-geared penalties for fraud or negligence (s95 TMA 1990). The maximum penalty equals the tax unpaid. The general law concerning fraud and negligence is discussed at **16.6.3**.

In the context of the personal services legislation, negligence could include understating the tax due because the worker was considered (incorrectly) to fall outside the personal services legislation. However in the period following the introduction of the regime, the government have promised that the Revenue will apply a 'light touch', and give individuals the benefit of the doubt, see **16.7.2**. However, this gentle approach will not apply:

> 'In the rare cases in which avoidance *(sic)* of tax and national insurance liability is deliberate and intended.' (Dawn Primarolo, House of Commons, 3 May 2000, *Hansard* Pt 24, Col. 26)

So if the worker knew he was within the new rules, but deliberately took steps to conceal his liability, for instance by using an offshore company to hide the profits, this could amount to fraud and the individual would be subject to the full rigours of the system.

15.7 Interim payments under self-assessment

If the tax due under self-assessment is more than a certain de minimis amount, it is collected by means of two interim payments of equal amounts, based normally on the liability for the previous year. These are due on 31 January in the year of assessment and the following 31 July, with a final balancing payment on the 31 January of the next year.

Interim payments are not collected if substantially all of a taxpayer's liability is covered by deduction of tax at source, including PAYE. Before IR35 a worker might have been within the interim payment regime because he received significant dividends from his service company or because he received his partnership income as Schedule D. If he is now within the personal services legislation, all or almost all of his income is likely to be taxed under PAYE.

He may therefore be able to apply to have his interim payments reduced or eliminated using Form SA 303. However, in some cases the interaction between interim payments and PAYE mean that there is still significant overlap. An example of the interim payment position in the context of a partner is at **14.6.4**.

15.8 Corporation tax self assessment

15.8.1 Outline of system

Corporation tax self assessment (CTSA) came into effect for accounting periods ending after 1 July 1999. As with individual self-assessment, responsibility for determining the tax due rests with the taxpayer, not the Inland

Revenue. When returns are received they are processed without checking, unless an amendment is necessary for the return to be processed. Any enquiries are carried out later, see (g) below.

(a) A company which does not receive a tax return but has a corporation tax liability must notify the Revenue of this within 12 months following the end of the accounting period. Failure to notify chargeability may lead to penalties (Sch 18, para 2 FA 1998);

(b) The return must generally be filed within 12 months following the end of the accounting period, together with supporting accounts, computations and any other relevant information. The return must include a declaration that the return is correct and complete to the best of the knowledge of the person making it (Sch 18, paras 3 and 14 FA 1998);

(c) Claims, such as for group relief, should be made as part of a return. If they are made later, they are technically an amendment to the return (see **15.8.2**). Group relief claims may be particularly relevant to a PSC because it is likely to make losses, see **13.7**; the rules for group relief are given in Sch 18, paras 66–77 FA 1998;

(d) Tax should be paid within nine months and one day following the company's year end (s59D TMA 1970), unless the company is 'large', when quarterly payments are required. This is unlikely to apply to a PSC;

(e) Losses should be included in the return in the same way as profits, and can equally be the subject of amendment and enquiry;

(f) There are penalties for submitting a late return (Sch 2, paras 17–19 FA 1998), for failing to keep documents (Sch 18, para 23 FA 1998), and for fraud or negligence, see **16.6.3** (Sch 18, para 89 FA 1998). Interest may also be charged (s87A TMA 1970);

(g) Enquiries can be made by the Revenue within 12 months following the filing date, unless the return was sent in late, in which case the enquiry deadline is extended (Sch 18, para 24 FA 1998). If there has been no enquiry within the time limit, the return will become final, subject to the rules for discovery, see **15.5.5** and Sch 18, para 42ff FA 1998;

(h) The usual time limit for an assessment is six years following the end of the accounting period, extended to 21 years in the case of fraud or negligence (Sch 18, para 46 FA 1998).

15.8.2 Implications for personal services

Interactions between the personal services legislation and CTSA occur in a number of areas, including amendments to the return, error or mistake claims, loss reliefs, changes of accounting date and double tax reliefs. In addition, the return may be selected for enquiry.

Amendments to the return

The company may amend its return within 12 months of the filing date. There is no official form for an amendment, and it is usually done by correspondence.

If the amendment is made after the normal filing date, the Revenue time limit for making an enquiry is extended. The new deadline is the quarter day following the first anniversary of the making of the amendment. The Revenue have confirmed that, in this situation, enquiries will be limited to the area of the return that was amended, see *Guide to Corporation Tax Self Assessment* paragraph 6.6.11.

A personal service company may need to amend its CTSA return if it realises that it should have taken account of IR35, but did not do so. This is because the deemed Schedule E payment is deducted for corporation tax purposes 'for the period of account in which (it) is treated as made' (Sch 12, para 17(2) FA 2000). If there was a unrecognised obligation to make a deemed payment in an earlier accounting period, which is later acknowledged, it is understood that the deduction attaches to the corporation tax period in which the payment should have been 'made'.

Error or mistake

If the assessment needs to be corrected outside the time limit for amendments, an error or mistake claim may be possible. Again, this may be necessary if a PSC has to make a late payment of PAYE on a deemed Schedule E amount following an employer compliance review. A claim must be made within six years of the end of the accounting period to which the error or mistake relates. This relief is not available in the case of an incorrect claim or election or where the original assessment was made in accordance with the practice generally prevailing at the time (Sch 18, para 51 FA 1998).

Loss reliefs

The PSC legislation may cause corporation tax losses, because the deemed Schedule E amount, together with any actual salary paid and the existing expenses, are likely to exceed the company's taxable profits, see **13.7**.

A claim to use these losses must be made within the appropriate time limits, see **13.7.2**. From the point of view of CTSA, a loss claim is regarded as an amendment to the return.

Change of accounting date

A company may wish to align its accounting date with the 5 April deemed payment date in order to ensure that tax relief is obtained, see **13.4.6**. A change of date:

- Will move the CTSA filing date and thus the date on which corporation tax is payable;
- May change the profits against which a later loss relief claim is carried back;
- Alters the time limits for claims and elections, so care is needed.

Double tax relief

Where work is carried out overseas, the service company may suffer foreign tax on its profits. A foreign tax authority may also withhold tax in respect of payments made to the company. Relief for any such foreign tax credits is normally given against the company's UK tax liability.

However, the Revenue have confirmed that:

> 'Where the company does not have sufficient UK tax liability to give full effect any such credit, but the worker does, then the balance may be allowed against the tax liability on the deemed payment. Relief can only be given where it is possible to directly link the work in the overseas country and the deemed payment.' (FAQ Foreign 5, see **17.10.2**)

Enquiries

Although it is anticipated that the enforcement of the company's PAYE requirements by the Revenue's Employer Compliance Unit is likely to be the main method by which personal service companies are investigated, see **16.9**, nevertheless CTSA enquiries may also lead to a review of the company's compliance with IR35.

Under CTSA the Revenue have 12 months from the company's filing date to open an enquiry into the return, and this date can be extended if the return is amended, see above. They do not have to justify an enquiry either by stating dissatisfaction with the return or by identifying particular aspects which have given cause for concern, and will not in fact give reasons for opening the enquiry, although they may identify particular areas of focus (*Guide to Corporation Tax Self Assessment*, paragraphs 6.1.12ff).

The Revenue's *Code of Practice into Company Tax Returns* (COP 14) says that:

> 'We carry out a comprehensive programme of checks. We look at information in the company's return and compare it with information we hold. Following these checks, if we think there is a risk the company return may be incorrect, or if we think something requires fuller explanation, we start enquiries. We also enquire into some returns at random.'

The return may be subject to an 'aspect' enquiry or a 'full' enquiry. An aspect enquiry may range from requests for clarification of particular entries, to detailed consideration of whether those entries have been treated correctly for tax purposes. In COP 14 the Revenue explain the scope of a full enquiry as follows:

> 'We may decide to conduct an extensive examination which considers all aspects of the company's tax affairs. Enquiries of this type will typically involve an in-depth review of the records on which the company's tax return was based. As part of this review we may ask for information relating to third parties, for example, directors or shareholders.'

The CTSA enquiry may thus lead into a separate Revenue investigation of the directors or shareholders. Conversely an SA enquiry may lead to a CTSA investigation. COP 14 says:

> 'We may need to keep enquiries into the company's tax return open where other enquiries (for example, into the directors' or shareholders' personal tax returns or tax returns of other companies) suggest that the company's tax return may not be correct. Where we need to do this we will tell you why we are not able to close the enquiry into the company's tax return.'

The Revenue's Investigation Handbook takes this one stage further, recommending that the CTSA inspectors 'arrange joint visits to business premises with Employer Compliance staff to examine business records' (IH 2334). This would allow the CT return to be checked along with the company's compliance with its PAYE and NIC obligations.

This indicates a high degree of connectivity between different Revenue investigating units. Inappropriate categorisation of personal services relevant income, or erroneous calculation of the deemed Schedule E amount could thus be unearthed by:

- CTSA enquiries into the company's returns;

- SA enquiries into the personal returns of the directors or shareholders;

- Section 16 TMA 1970 returns from a client or agency, see **21.2.4** and **21.3.3**; or

- An Employer Compliance Unit review of the PAYE, P11D, SLR and NIC returns.

16   Tax payments, penalties and investigations

16.1 Introduction

This chapter discusses the timing of tax and NIC payments on the deemed Schedule E amount. It also reviews the case law and legislation on penalties and interest, and discusses how penalties might be reduced or eliminated. It looks at whether, and to what extent, the Revenue may be able to pursue directors or workers for uncollected PAYE and NIC, and briefly covers Revenue investigations into intermediaries' compliance with the personal services rules.

16.2 PAYE, NIC and P11D administration

16.2.1 PAYE and NIC deductions

PAYE

The aim of the PAYE system is that the tax deducted during the year should be, as far as possible, equal to that due on the worker's Schedule E income. The system operates via coding notices, which take account of expected salary, benefits, reliefs and allowances.

However, where a deemed payment is treated as made to a worker who had no previous Schedule E income, he will have no coding notice. This scenario is most likely to arise with partners who are only within the Schedule E rules by virtue of the personal services legislation. In this situation, the employer is advised to operate code BR, see *Employer's Quick Guide to PAYE Card 5*. The BR code deducts basic rate tax from the worker's deemed payment, and any overpayment or underpayment of tax is collected via self-assessment.

If a worker is on a week one/month one basis, and receives a large deemed payment on 5 April, this may cause an over-deduction of tax. Although this will be recovered in due course, the cashflow effect may be significant.

It should be noted that there is no requirement to include the deemed income on payslips during the year. The only employee documents on which the deemed payments and the related tax/NICs should be included are the P45 and the P60, see FAQ Computation 22 and **16.2.3** below.

NICs

There are a number of points to bear in mind when considering NICs and IR35:

- The NIC regulations require the calculation of attributable earnings, which are normally the same as the deemed Schedule E (SI 2000/727);

- Where a worker is within IR35 for NICs but not for tax (see **12.7**) then the attributable earnings calculation has to be completed. However the result of the calculation is not earnings for tax purposes and thus does not have to be returned on the P14 nor on the worker's self-assessment form;

- Once the deemed income/attributable earnings have been calculated, there may be both employer and employee NICs to pay;

- Employer NICs payable as a result of attributable earnings calculation are deductible for corporation tax purposes, see **13.2.1**; since the full deemed payment is also allowable there is also CT relief for employee NICs;

- Personal service workers are on an annual earnings period, whether or not they are directors, and their attributable earnings are aggregated with any other earnings paid to them by the intermediary during the year, see **4.8.2** and **4.8.3**.

16.2.2 P11Ds

Most personal services workers other than partners will receive a P11D even when they have a deemed Schedule E payment. This is because amounts are excluded from the deemed Schedule E if they are otherwise taxable, either as:

- *A benefit provided by the employer.* Where the intermediary provides a benefit for the worker, this is removed from the deemed Schedule E calculation by Step Seven. It will then be included on the P11D in the normal way;

- *A benefit provided by the client by arrangement with the employer.* In the case of a one-man company, most benefits received from the client are commonly 'by arrangement with the employer' and thus fall to be taxed under the normal Schedule E rules. These amounts are not included in the deemed Schedule E calculation in the first place, see **10.5.4**. Instead, they are reported on the P11D.

Timing issues

The P11D deadline is 6 July following the end of the fiscal year. However, the tax and NIC on the deemed Schedule E calculation is due on or before 19

April. In order to calculate the deemed payment, the intermediary needs to know what amounts to exclude under Step Seven, i.e., items included on the individual's P11D. Similarly, the amount of Class 1A NIC on the P11D benefits is needed for Step Six.

Thus, if service companies wait until 6 July to determine the amounts to include on the P11D, they will delay completion of their deemed payment calculation; **16.4.2** below discusses the consequences of delay.

16.2.3 End of year returns, P60s and P45s

Form P14

Form P14 must be submitted by 19 May following the end of the tax year, but there is a seven day period of grace, see **16.6.2**. The P14 shows earnings and various Class 1 NIC liabilities for each 'employed earner'. If the tax and NICs shown on the P14 submitted on 19 May proves to be inadequate when the deemed income calculation is completed, then further P14s 'showing only the additional amount of the deemed payment and the tax and NICs on it should also be submitted.' (ESM 3182)

Form P35

The P35 must also be submitted by 19 May following the end of the tax year, the same seven day period of grace applies, see **16.6.2**. The P35 gives the total earnings and Class 1 NIC liabilities of the workforce. The deemed Schedule E amount should be included on this return: two new questions have been added at Box 6 which ask:

> 'Do the rules relating to payments for service provided through a service company or a partnership apply to any of your business income? If yes, is PAYE and NICs on the deemed remuneration included over the page or on any continuation sheets?'

The helpsheet for the P35 advises that 'if you tick the second box yes, but the amount is provisional, confirm on a separate sheet and send it with the P45'. For details of provisional payments see **16.4.2**.

Form P60

The P60 given to the employee should include the deemed payment, and the figures on the P60 are then used to complete his self-assessment return, see

15.3.2. However, as the Revenue point out in their February 2001 *Tax Bulletin*:

> 'If, however, only a provisional amount of tax had been paid by the time the P60 was issued, the worker may receive a revised one when the correct deemed payment is calculated and tax accounted for. In such a case, use the pay and tax figures on the revised P60.'

A more recent FAQ, issued in December 2001, said that where changes are needed after the original P60 has been issued, it is not necessary to issue a revised P60:

> 'So long as all pertinent details are included, the Inland Revenue will accept notification of changes to a P60 return by means of a letter. Other Inland Revenue forms affected by the change to the P60, such as a worker's self-assessment return, may need to be updated by means of submitting a revised return. Please contact your local tax office for advice.' (FAQ General 19)

Form P45

When an individual who is within the personal services legislation leaves the service company or partnership a P45 should be completed. This should include both the actual salary and the deemed salary. The latter should be calculated:

> 'Based on the fees received up to the date when the worker leaves the intermediary; once a P45 has been issued it cannot be amended. If additional fees are received after the P45 has been completed, the employer should account for tax at the basic rate on any additional amount of deemed payment and let the employee know of this.' (FAQ Computation 19).

More detail on procedures relating to post-P45 amounts can be found at ESM 3183 and in the *Employers' Further Guide to PAYE and NICs*; in the context of IR35 see also **16.3.2.**

16.3 Timing of deemed Schedule E payment

16.3.1 Relevant events

The deemed Schedule E payment is in normal circumstances 'treated as made at the end of the tax year' (Sch 12, para 2(2) FA 2000). However the date is brought forward in some circumstances, known as 'relevant events'. These occur in the following situations:

- If a worker leaves his personal service company, or ceases to be a director of the company, the deemed Schedule E payment is treated as made on the day before he departs or ceases to be a director;

- If the intermediary is a partnership, and the worker leaves the partnership, the deemed Schedule E payment is treated as made on the day before he ceases to be a partner or employee;

- If the intermediary is a partnership and it is either dissolved or ceases to trade, the deemed Schedule E payment is treated as made on the day before the dissolution or cessation of trading (Sch 12, para 12 FA 2000).

Note that until tax year 2002/03 there is no relevant event if a company ceases business, see **16.3.3.** If there is more than one relevant event in a tax year, the deemed payment is made on earliest of them.

This acceleration of the deemed payment date means that the due date for PAYE and NICs is brought forward, see Example 16A.

Example 16A

Mike is a partner in a partnership supplying actuarial services. He is entitled to 65 per cent of the profits, and works 4 days a week at the firm's major client. The partnership received relevant income of £50,000 in the six months to October 2001 relating to Mike's work. Mike leaves the partnership on 8 October and becomes an employee of his client.

His deemed schedule E payment is treated as made on 7 October 2000. The PAYE and Class 1 NIC relating to it must therefore be paid by 19 November 2000. The extended time limit (**16.4.2**) does not apply in this situation, see ESM 3182.

16.3.2 Receipt of income after relevant event

The acceleration of the deemed payment date does not allow amounts to escape the personal services rules, for example because they have been received after the deemed Schedule E amount has been calculated. The legislation says that:

'The fact that the deemed Schedule E payment is treated as made before the end of the tax year does not affect what receipts and other matters are taken into account in calculating its amount.' (Sch 12, para 12(2) FA 2000)

'Other matters' here is taken to mean expenses paid after the relevant event, for which relief will continue to be available in the calculation, despite it being on a cash basis (**11.3.2**).

However a late receipt may cause interest and penalties to arise, see **16.5, 16.6** and Example 16B. However in this situation it should be possible to argue that there was a reasonable excuse, see **16.7.3**, and that no penalty should be levied. Interest would however be due from 19 April. For the P45 position, see **16.2.3** above.

Example 16B

Mike's deemed schedule E payment of £16,000 was treated as made on 7 October 2000, and the PAYE and NIC relating to it was paid on 19 November 2000. However in May 2001 a further amount of £2,000 was received. The deemed Schedule E calculation is thus incorrect, and PAYE and NIC is

---

16.3.3 Cessation of business

Although there is a relevant event when a partnership ceases business (Sch 12, para 12(3)(a) FA 2000), the same did not apply to a company until the legislation was changed for 2002/03 by the addition of a new subparagraph (Sch 12, para 12(2)(za) FA 2000). For earlier years this could cause problems, see Example 16C.

Example 16C

Kevin is the only director of his personal service company. The company ceases to trade in December 2001 and is finally struck off in June 2002. Kevin's deemed payment of £50,000 arises on 5 April 2002. However this amount is not an allowable deduction for corporation tax purposes, because the company's trade ended three months earlier.

Kevin could have avoided this problem had he resigned as a director, and so precipitated a relevant event under Sch 12, para 12(2)(b) FA 2000. But someone would have had to take his place in order to arrange for the company's liquidation or winding up.

If Kevin was an employee as well as a director, then resigning from his employment would also have precipitated a relevant event. For years before 2002/03 the Revenue indicated in correspondence that, where IR35 applies to a cessation, they will accept that an individual has an employment as well as a directorship even where there is no explicit contract of employment. While helpful, it is unclear how this reconciles with their position on the minimum wage, see **22.2.2**.

Alternatively Kevin's company could have paid the net amount due as a salary before the end of the accounting period, or made a credit to the director's current account, see **13.4.4** and **13.5.2**.

For years before 2002/03, the Inland Revenue commented on cessations as follows:

'It is important to be aware that where the intermediary is a company the cessation of trade does not mean a deemed payment is treated as paid on that date unless one of the other events occurs at the same time. However, where someone working through their service company continues to work for the company as an employee or a director the Revenue will not normally seek to argue for this purpose that the trade has ceased at an earlier date.' (*Tax Bulletin* February 2001).

Thus, if the company was aware of this difficulty and did not precipitate a problem, the Revenue will not raise the issue.

16.4 Payment of PAYE and Class 1 NICs

16.4.1 19 April payment deadline

The PAYE and NICs legislation and regulations apply to the deemed Schedule E amount (Sch 12, para 11 FA 2000; SI 2000/727 reg 8). As a result, the PAYE and NIC relating to the deemed payment must be paid over by 19 April following the end of the tax year. However in practice this is an impossible deadline for most personal services businesses and their accountants – it is at best ten working days, and two of these are commonly Easter bank holidays.

The Revenue were asked to extend the payment deadline, either to 6 July in line with P11Ds, or to a date following each intermediary's accounting year end. Both were rejected on the grounds that they gave an additional cash flow advantage to those who worked via intermediaries rather than directly as employees of the client.

16.4.2 Concession on penalties

The Revenue did concede, however, that a provisional payment could be made some time on or before 19 April – either during the tax year or following it, and the balance paid later. Although interest will be charged, there will be no penalties on the shortfall.

The guidance is set out in the Revenue's February 2001 'Penalty Statement' as follows:

'Although the information needed should be available, the Inland Revenue appreciates that some employers may have difficulty calculating the correct amount of a payment deemed to arise at 5 April before the tax and NICs are due to be paid on 19 April. However, it should be possible to estimate the tax and NICs due and so make a payment on account by 19 April. As the employer, you should do this if you cannot calculate exactly the deemed payment by 19 April 2001; interest will be charged in the normal way on any tax and NICs paid after that date.

Some employers may find that they are not even able to calculate the correct amount before the Employer's Annual Return is due on 19 May. To enable you, as the employer, to file the return (P35) on time, you can submit a return and accompanying documents that include estimated amounts for the deemed payment, and tax and NICs due on it, using either the payment on account estimates, or newer more accurate estimates. Where this is done no penalty for an incorrect return will be sought provided all the following conditions are met:

- The return (P35) is submitted by 19 May 2001;

- It is stated on the return or in a covering letter that the service company legislation applies to the employer;

- An amount is included in the return for the tax and NICs due on the deemed payment;

- It is made clear in a covering letter that the amount is provisional pending finalisation of the deemed payment calculation;

- A correction to the return and accompanying documents, notifying the correct final amount for the deemed payment and the tax and NICs due, is made by 31 January 2002;

- Any additional tax and NICs due as a result of the correction to the return are paid by 31 January 2002.

To make it easier for employers to indicate that the service company legislation applies to them there is an additional question on the front of the Employer's Annual Return, but notification that the tax/NICs amounts relating to the deemed payment are provisional should be made in a separate letter.'

This is a very useful concession, but comes with a sting in the tail: there is no remission of interest for late payment. Accountants should thus warn their personal service company and partnership clients that an interest charge is likely on the shortfall. Clearly this can be minimised by paying roughly the correct amount of salary on a monthly basis, see **13.5.3**.

The penalty statement also contained a number of warnings:

- No extension will be given to the 19 May 2001 filing date;

- The service company legislation will not be accepted as a reasonable excuse for failing to file the return by 19 May;

- If the employer neither paid the correct amount on time, nor indicated that the amount paid was provisional, then the Inland Revenue will follow the normal approach set out in leaflet IR109 – *Employer compliance reviews and negotiations* – and may seek penalties. This will be the case even if the employer has indicated that it is within IR35.

When the penalty statement was published, the Revenue indicated that this arrangement would be reviewed after 2000/01. However confirmation was received in February 2002 that it will apply 'until Government Ministers announce a change' (FAQ Computation 28).

The normal procedure where an employer is relying on the penalty statement is that the local tax offices will keep a record of all cases where a P35 is sent in with figures marked as provisional; if the amended return has not been received by 31 January, it will issue reminders to the company concerned.

If the provisional amount does, in fact, turn out to be the correct number, no penalty can arise even if the employer does not file an amended return. However, it is only common sense to let the local tax office know. Otherwise the employer will receive Revenue reminders, and failure to respond may even trigger an investigation.

16.4.3 Repayments of PAYE and NICs

If too much tax is deducted by the service company from the individual's deemed payment, a repayment will be made. This may occur, for example, where the individual's coding notice is incorrect, or he is retrospectively treated as non-resident for part of the period.

The repayment will be made to the individual, even though the PAYE on the deemed income has been paid by the company. Where there is more than one shareholder, the service company may thus wish to provide, in its contracts with workers, that any such overpayments refunded by the Revenue can be recovered by the company.

Similarly, where the deemed income/attributable earnings calculation means that the total employee NICs deducted in respect of an individual exceeds the maximum for the tax year – perhaps because he has other employment – then the excess will be refunded. The regulations say that:

> 'Where there have been paid in error by a person or a secondary contributor (if any) any contributions (other than Class 4 contributions), or there has been any payment of contributions in excess of the amount specified in

regulation 21, such contributions shall be returned by the Board to that person or the secondary contributor, as the case may be.' (SI 2001/1004 reg 52(1))

The expectation here is that the overpaid amounts will be returned to the person who suffered the deduction – so employee contributions would normally be repaid to the individual and employer contributions to the company. Where the company has borne the cost of employee NICs on the deemed payment, these amounts may be repaid to the company, but only with the written permission of the worker, see FAQ General 16.

16.5 Interest

Where payment of the tax or NIC on the deemed payment is late, interest runs from 19 April (SI 1993/744 reg 51 and SI 2001/1004 Sch 4 para 17). As explained at **16.4.2** above, the late filing concession granted for the deemed payment extends only to penalties and not to interest.

Where the deemed payment has been accelerated because of a relevant event, see **16.3.1** above, there is no interest on late payment of PAYE or NICs until the 19 April following the relevant event.

16.6 Penalties

16.6.1 General

A range of penalties can be exacted for non-compliance with PAYE or NIC liabilities, from fixed monthly amounts to imprisonment and confiscation of assets. However a personal service intermediary will not be liable to penalties if it is within the concession discussed at **16.4.2** above.

In addition the intermediary may be able take advantage of the 'benefit of the doubt' approach described by Dawn Primarolo (see **16.7.2** below) or claim reasonable excuse (see **16.7.3**). If penalties are nevertheless due, mitigation may be possible (see **16.7.4**).

16.6.2 Fixed penalties

The deadline for filing the end of year return is 19 May, although by concession a period of grace of seven days is allowed before a penalty will be charged (ESC B46). This states that no penalty will be charged providing the return is:

'Received in [the Revenue's] hands on or before the last business day within seven days following the statutory filing date. A business day, for these purposes, is any day other than a Saturday, a Sunday, Christmas Eve, Good Friday or any bank or other public holiday.'

If the end of year return is not filed in time, the Revenue can levy a fine of £100 for each month or part month for which the return is not filed, up to a maximum of 12 months. The penalties are greater where there are more than 50 employees, but this will not normally be the case in a personal service company or partnership. The same legislation applies where the end of year NIC return has not been filed, but where (as is generally the case) the same return covers both, there is only one penalty (Sch 1, para 7(3) SSCBA 1992).

If the failure to file the return continues beyond 12 months, there is an additional penalty not exceeding the tax that was unpaid 14 days after the end of the year to which the return relates (s98A(2)(b) TMA 1970). Where both tax and NIC are overdue, the maximum penalty equals the sum of the total tax and NIC unpaid (Sch 1, para 7(5) SSCBA 1992). Similar provisions apply to the end of year return in relation to student loan repayments (SI 2000/944 reg 42(5)).

16.6.3 Fraud and negligence – generally

Fraud

The classic definition of fraud was given by Lord Herschell when he said that 'fraud is proven when it is shown that a false representation has been made knowingly, or without belief in its truth, or recklessly, careless whether it be true or false'. *Derry v Peek* [1889] 14 AC 337.

In their Investigations Handbook at paragraph 5010 the Revenue say:

'Fraud (in relation to the Revenue) includes, in its various forms, falsification with an intention to deceive and this may be present even as a mere conscious understatement in, or omission from, a return or accounts. Thus, the active intention to deceive may, on the one hand, be so slight that the falsification differs little from that resulting from carelessness or negligence. On the other hand, falsification may be deliberately planned with the clear intention of deceiving and cheating the Revenue by, for example, the omission, manipulation or invention of figures, or other records. This may require consideration by Special Compliance Office and even, possibly, the institution of criminal proceedings.'

Negligence

Negligence has been defined as 'the omission to do something which a prudent and reasonable man would do'(*Blyth v Birmingham Waterworks Co* [1856] 11 Ex 781). In the Revenue's view a reasonable man would, among other things:

- Comply with the requirements of the law by, for example, notifying his chargeability (see **15.2**);

- Make, promptly, a complete and correct return of his income and gains when required to do so under statutory authority;

- Keep such records as are necessary to enable him to make accurate returns or prepare accurate accounts;

- Read carefully the notes supplied with the return form, so far as they affect his own circumstances;

- Seek professional help with matters, such as the preparation of accounts, which he is unable to cope with satisfactorily himself. (IH 5050)

Establishing fraud or negligence

The onus is on the Revenue to establish the evidence for fraud or negligence, and in the recent case of *Rochester (UK) Ltd and another v Pickin* [1998] SSCD 138 it was held that:

- The standard of proof was the balance of probabilities; and

- The cogency of the evidence required to meet the standard of proof depends on the seriousness of the allegations.

However once the evidence has been established, the onus is on the taxpayer to prove his innocence. The earlier case of *Brady v Group Lotus Car Companies plc and Another* [1987] 60 TC 359 held that:

> 'The burden of proof, as distinct from the evidential burden, was through- out on Lotus to show that the assessments were wrong.'

The Revenue explain this as follows (where 'you' is a Revenue officer):

> 'Although the onus is always on you to demonstrate that there has been fraud or negligence, you will normally show that there has been an error or omission and that there is no known acceptable explanation. The onus will then be on the taxpayer to establish that the error was entirely innocent and involved neither fraud nor negligence: this is not an easy task.' (IH 5065)

16.6.4 Penalties for fraud or negligence

If an incorrect return has been submitted fraudulently or negligently, the maximum penalty is the difference between the amount payable under the return and the amount which would have been payable had the return been correct (s98A(4) TMA 1970).

Where NIC is unpaid as well as tax, a single penalty may be exacted up to the total of any tax and contributions remaining unpaid. This is because s98A TMA 1970 applies to NIC as it does to tax, by virtue of Sch 1, para 7 SSCBA 1992.

Finally, if student loan repayments have not been correctly deducted, the same penalty and interest provisions apply as for PAYE and NICs (SI 2000/944 regs 41 and 42, see **22.4**). The maximum penalty is £3,000 per employee per year. This applies where 'an employer fraudulently or negligently (a) makes incorrect deductions; or (b) makes or receives incorrect payments in a year of assessment' (SI 2000/944 reg 51).

If the service company incorrectly took the view that there had been no relevant engagements, this might be seen as negligent, leading to an assessment on the company for:

(a) Unpaid PAYE and NIC;

(b) A penalty which could equal the unpaid PAYE and NIC;

(c) Interest for late payment, see **16.5**;

(d) A fixed penalty for late payment, see **16.6.2** above;

(e) Any student loan repayments, plus interest and penalties.

The company may be able to reduce or eliminate any penalties, particularly in the early years of the personal service regime, see **16.7** below.

16.6.5 Criminal penalties for fraud or negligence

In addition to the specific fraud and negligence provisions in the Taxes Acts and the Social Security legislation, the Revenue can also call on sanctions within the criminal law. These are however rarely used: Statement of Practice 2/88 explains that the Revenue will usually seek a financial settlement and not a criminal prosecution. If a case does go to court, the standard of proof in a criminal case is much higher than where charges are brought under the civil law. It was held in *Hornal v Neuberger Products Ltd* [1957] 1 QB 247 that:

'A civil court, when considering a charge of fraud, will naturally require for itself a higher degree of probability than that which it would require when asking if negligence is established.'

The criminal sanctions are:

- 'Fraudulent evasion of income tax,' a new offence which was introduced by s144 FA 2000. The section can apply both to the taxpayer and any other individual who is 'knowingly concerned' in the fraudulent evasion, and took effect from 1 January 2001. The maximum penalty is seven year's imprisonment;

- Section 5 of the Perjury Act 1911, for 'knowingly and wilfully' making materially false statements or returns for tax purposes, see for example the accountant referred to in the case of *Tudor and Onions v Ducker* [1924] 8 TC 591 who perjured himself giving evidence that the accounts he had prepared for his clients were correct, and was prosecuted;

- The common law offence of cheat, used in *R v Cunningham, Charlton, Wheeler & Kitchen* [1996] STC 1418, and *R v Dimsey and Allen* [1999] STC 846, which centred on offshore companies;

- The Theft Act 1978, see *R v Hiscox* [1978] 52 TC 497, which concerned forged subcontractor certificates, and *R v Downes* [1983] CLR 819, also a subcontractor case;

- Conspiracy to defraud, which was discussed but not used in the *Dimsey* case, and rejected by the judge in *N Ltd v H M Inspector of Taxes* [1996] SSCD 346;

- Section 6, Forgery Act 1913 which was also used in the case of *R v Hiscox* above.

16.6.6 Third party penalties

The penalties discussed earlier in this chapter apply to the employer, although they may be transferable to the worker or director, see **16.8.2** below. Penalties can be imposed on third parties for non-compliance with s16 TMA requirements, see **21.2.4**, or under s99 TMA 1970. This states that:

'Any person who assists in or induces the preparation or delivery of any information, return, accounts or other document which (a) he knows will be, or is or are likely to be, used for any purpose of tax, and (b) he knows to be incorrect, shall be liable to a penalty not exceeding £3,000.'

Section 99 could be deployed against the administrator of a faulty composite company (see **23.4.4**) or against an agent, adviser or client involved in a flawed

IR35 scheme, see Chapters 21 and 23. However some comfort can be taken from the fact that this section is rarely used. The Revenue's Employer Compliance Manual gives the following advice:

> 'When considering penalties under TMA 1970 s99 bear in mind that the onus is on the Revenue to prove that the person concerned knew that the information/return was to be used for tax purposes [and that] the information/return was incorrect ... It is usually the nature of, and the participants in, the case, rather than the monetary value which will determine whether a penalty should be sought.' (ECM 21010)

The Revenue also say that 'the main use of TMA 1970 s99 is against accountants'(ECM 21018). Cases are dealt with via Special Compliance Office rather than by the local district. It should be noted that the time limit for an offence under this section is 20 years rather than the more normal six years.

16.7 Reducing the penalties

16.7.1 Summary

The intermediary can seek to reduce or eliminate the penalties by one or more of the following routes:

- Using the 'benefit of the doubt' concession explained by Dawn Primarolo and expanded by the Inland Revenue;

- Claiming 'reasonable excuse';

- Asking for the penalties to be mitigated.

These are explained below.

16.7.2 Benefit of the doubt and reasonable steps

In the House of Commons debate on IR35, Dawn Primarolo said that:

> 'Officials are to give the benefit of the doubt where businesses make genuine mistakes when trying to comply with the rules. This is only fair, given the change during this period. It is a light-touch approach. Of course, in the rare cases in which avoidance *(sic)* of tax and National Insurance liability is deliberate and intended, the same compliance regime and penalties will apply as exist in the tax system for trying to avoid paying tax and National Insurance.'(*Hansard* 3 May, pt 24 Col. 216)

The Minister's assurances are welcome. She has acknowledged that those struggling to come to terms with the complexity of the new regime need assistance rather than punishment. It is comforting to know that the full force of the interest and penalty regime will not be invoked against them.

It should be noted, however, that the Minster spoke of 'avoidance', not 'evasion'. Where the taxpayer has actively sought to escape the new regime, and has not succeeded – perhaps because the scheme he entered into was technically faulty, or because his substitution clause was a sham, then the normal penalty rules are likely to apply.

Dawn Primarolo's words were followed in February 2001 by the Revenue 'Penalty Statement' (see **16.4.2**) which said that

> 'If you, in your capacity as employer, act prudently by taking all reasonable steps to understand and ensure that your intermediary service company or partnership meets its obligations under the service company legislation, no penalty will be imposed should an incorrect return be submitted.'

The PCG subsequently published helpful guidance, following discussions with the Revenue, on what was meant by 'reasonable steps' in this context. This is set out more fully at **7.7.8** and includes:

- Taking appropriate professional advice; or

- Seeking Inland Revenue clearance; or

- Satisfying oneself by a review of the legislation and one's own position.

The case of *Pleasants v Atkinson* [1987] 60 TC 228 should, however, be noted. In this case an accountant submitted an incorrect computation on behalf of an architect, and the Revenue alleged that the latter was guilty of wilful default. The court held that while the architect had not been personally guilty, his accountant had committed wilful default on his behalf and he was thus liable for penalties. The concept of wilful default has now been subsumed into 'fraudulent and negligent conduct', see IH 4151.

If the individual has neither taken appropriate advice nor informed himself as to the true tax position, his last resort can be found in IH 50000. This says that if the area is highly technical (and the application of the personal services legislation may fall into this category) and the taxpayer is unrepresented by a professional adviser, he may succeed in claiming ignorance of the legislation.

16.7.3 Reasonable excuse

The reasonable excuse legislation is contained in s118(2) TMA 1970, a text which demonstrates the need for the Tax Law Rewrite:

> 'For the purposes of this Act, a person shall be deemed not to have failed to do anything required to be done within a limited time if he did it within such further time, if any, as the Board or the Commissioners or officer concerned may have allowed; and where a person had a reasonable excuse for not doing anything required to be done he shall be deemed not to have failed to do it unless the excuse ceased and, after the excuse ceased, he shall be deemed not to have failed to do it if he did it without unreasonable delay after the excuse had ceased.'

The Revenue consider that 'reasonable excuse' is not an absolute:

> 'There are no absolute standards by which the words 'reasonable excuse' can be defined. Generally, it can be said to be an excuse which sounds reasonable in the mouth of the person giving it, that is, the standard of reasonableness can vary according to the type, education, background etc. of the taxpayer concerned.' (IH 5062)

They accept that the following are reasonable excuses (*Tax Bulletin 34*, April 1998):

- Where a cheque is dishonoured solely through bank error (and payment is made immediately after the taxpayer learned of the bank's action);

- Where a cheque is lost in the post or by the Revenue (although evidence may be required to show that every effort was made to pay by the due date);

- Serious illness of the taxpayer or a close relative or domestic partner which began shortly before the due date; or

- The death of a close relative or domestic partner at or around the due date.

Excuses not considered reasonable by the Revenue include:

- Pressure of work;

- Failure by a tax agent (see *Nunn v Gray* [1997] SSCD 175);

- Not knowing how much to pay; or

- The absence of a reminder that the tax is due.

In the context of IR35 the Revenue have said that the personal services legislation will not be accepted as a reasonable excuse for filing an annual return late, given the extended payment concession, see **16.4.2**.

However, if the taxpayer disagrees with the Revenue's interpretation and considers he does have a reasonable excuse, he can go to the Commissioners. In this context it is interesting to note the following useful guidance published on the website of the National Association of Tax Commissioners in March 2002:

'It is for the Commissioners, not the Revenue, to decide what is a reasonable excuse in a particular case. Many bodies of Commissioners do not take kindly to the Revenue telling them how to exercise a discretion that Parliament has given to the Commissioners. Accordingly if the Revenue say they do not regard a particular thing as an excuse and that the Commissioners should bear in mind the need for consistency between taxpayers, do not be afraid to point out that Parliament has given the discretion to the Commissioners not the Revenue and that what is reasonable must depend on individual circumstances and it is not sensible to lay down some sort of rule of thumb divorced from the circumstances, so that consistency is not necessarily a laudable objective.'

In the case of *Akarimsons Ltd v Chapman* [1997] SSCD 140 the Commissioners cancelled a penalty and agreed that the taxpayer had a reasonable excuse for the late submission of a return because:

(a) The director and company secretary were seriously ill;

(b) 'The company secretary was confused by [the form] and … regarded its contents as ambiguous'; and

(c) As the judge said, 'the Revenue cannot escape responsibility for some of the muddle which occurred'.

In *Steeden v Carver* [1999] SSCD 283, the Commissioners accepted that a taxpayer who relied on the Revenue's advice concerning a time limit had 'as reasonable an excuse as could be found'.

16.7.4 Mitigation of penalties

The Revenue have complete discretion to mitigate or eliminate any penalty (s102 TMA 1970). However, for fixed penalties their normal practice is not to use these powers: if the taxpayer does not have a 'reasonable excuse' which takes him out of the penalty altogether, they will not mitigate.

In the case of tax-based penalties where a maximum penalty of 100 per cent could be exacted, their normal procedures are to start with the figure of 100 per cent and then take the following factors into account:

(a) *Disclosure.* A reduction of up to 20 per cent (or 30 per cent where there has been full voluntary disclosure), depending on how much information was provided, how soon, and how that contributed to settling the investigation;

(b) *Cooperation.* A reduction of up to 40 per cent, based upon a comparison of the cooperation actually given in the investigation with that which the inspector believes would have been possible. The Revenue view of cooperation in the context of a PAYE audit is as follows:

> 'If you supply information quickly, produce records when asked, answer questions honestly and accurately, and give all the relevant facts, you will get the maximum reduction for cooperation. If you put off supplying information or producing your records, give untrue answers to questions, do nothing until formal action is taken against you and generally obstruct the progress of the review you will get no reduction at all. Between these extremes, there is a wide range of possible circumstances.' (Revenue booklet 109)

(c) *Gravity.* A reduction of up to 40 per cent, depending upon the nature of the offence, how long it continued and the amounts involved (Revenue pamphlet IR 73).

16.8 Assessment and collection

16.8.1 Time limits for collection

In most cases there is a six-year time limit for collecting unpaid PAYE and NIC (s34 TMA 1970; SI 1993/744 reg 49(7)). However this can be extended in the case of fraud or negligence to 20 years from 31 January after the year of assessment in which the fraud or neglect occurred (s36 TMA).

It would, however, be unusual for an assessment to be made outside the six-year time limit unless there was a serious and culpable action or omission by the taxpayer. To extend the time limit the Revenue have to prove, on the balance of probabilities, that there was fraud or negligence, see *Rochester (UK) Ltd and Another v Pickin* [1998] SSCD 138 (**16.6.3** above) for a recent case in which they did not succeed.

16.8.2 Collection of unpaid tax and/or NICs from the worker or director

PAYE

If the company does not pay the amount assessed, for instance because it is insolvent, the Revenue may be able to pursue the individual worker or director for the uncollected tax under Regulations 42(3) and 49(5) of the Income Tax (Employments) Regulations 1993. These regulations allow the Revenue to collect the under-deduction from the employee, instead of from the employer. However they can only do this if they consider the employee received the payment of remuneration knowing that the employer's failure to operate the correct PAYE correctly was wilful.

However, at the time of writing it appears these regulations will not operate to catch underpayments of PAYE on deemed Schedule E amounts. Regulation 42 reads:

> '[Where] the Board are of the opinion that an employee has received his emoluments knowing that the employer has wilfully failed to deduct the amount of tax which he was liable to deduct under these Regulations from those emoluments, they may direct that the amount which they consider to constitute the excess ... shall be recovered from the employee.' (SI 1993/744 reg 42(3))

The wording of reg 49(5) is similar. However, in the case of a deemed Schedule E payment, the employee has not *received* any emoluments, and no tax could therefore have been deducted from the emoluments. To be effective, the regulations would need to be amended to cover the non-payment of tax on deemed payments.

Since the policing of the personal services legislation depends in part on having the full panoply of powers available under the PAYE Regulations, an amendment is likely.

National Insurance Contributions

The Revenue have powers to collect unpaid NICs from individuals as follows:

> '(Where) the body corporate has failed to pay the contributions at or within the time prescribed for the purpose; and the failure appears to the Inland Revenue to be attributable to fraud or neglect on the part of one or more individuals who, at the time of the fraud or neglect, were officers of the body corporate ("culpable officers"), the Inland Revenue may issue and serve on any culpable officer a notice ... specifying the amount of the contributions to which this section applies ... requiring the officer to pay ... a specified sum in respect of that amount; and specified interest on that sum.' (s121C SSAA 1992)

> 'Where an offence under this Act ... which has been committed by a body corporate is proved to have been committed with the consent or connivance of, or to be attributable to any neglect on the part of, a director, manager,

secretary or other similar officer of the body corporate, or any person who was purporting to act in any such capacity, he, as well as the body corporate, shall be guilty of that offence and be liable to be proceeded against accordingly.' (s115 SSAA 1992)

These sections operate differently from the PAYE regulations, in that:

- The liability can be transferred to individuals if they are responsible for an offence against the Act, and thus the legislation should be effective in a situation where a service company has failed to apply IR35;

- Under the PAYE regulations an individual worker who has received emoluments can be required to pay the tax. Under the NICs regulations the liability attaches to the directors or other managers of the company;

- The NIC regulations allow interest to be collected from the responsible individuals; this is not currently possible under the PAYE regulations.

Since the personal services legislation is largely aimed at avoidance of NICs, these powers are more important than the equivalent PAYE regulations, and it may matter less that the latter appear ineffective.

In addition, a new criminal offence of fraudulently evading NICs was introduced by the Social Security Act 1998 (s114A SSAA 1992) and took effect from 6 April 1999. The section is aimed at large scale and repeated evasion, and at directors of 'phoenix' companies, but it is wide enough to cover other situations. Directors caught under these provisions are liable not only for the debt outstanding, interest and penalties, but can also lose their homes and personal assets.

16.9 Investigations

It is understood that most of the responsibility for policing the personal services legislation will rest with the Revenue's employer compliance unit, see FAQ Compliance 1:

> 'What will happen if someone fails to follow the new rules?
>
> Where the Inland Revenue discover the new rules have not been followed, they will follow the normal approach to cases of PAYE/NICs failure set out in Inland Revenue leaflet IR109 – "Employer compliance reviews and negotiations".'

The Employer Compliance Unit is likely to target intermediaries that have not applied the personal services legislation, in order to establish whether they are genuinely outside IR35. An investigation might be triggered because:

- A review indicates that very little PAYE was paid on a relatively high turnover;

- The Revenue are aware from other information that the company is potentially within the personal services regime;

- Data gathered from clients and agencies under s16 TMA 1970 as to the identity of intermediaries and amounts paid to them has been cross-checked to PAYE returns, see **21.2.4**;

- A self-assessment enquiry into the worker's tax affairs, or a CTSA enquiry into the company's return, has led to questions about the company's compliance with the personal services regime, see **16.9**;

- The company is being checked as part of a regular cycle of audit visits.

The Revenue have given comfort that use of their contract clearance process will not be one of the triggers for an investigation, see FAQ Compliance 2.

In the context of IR35, it should be noted that the Revenue have access to the following information sources:

- The individual's own self-assessment return, see **15.2**;

- The company's corporation tax return, for which the period of enquiry is likely to be longer than that for the SA return, see **15.8**;

- Information under the s16 TMA from agencies and clients, see **21.2.4** and **21.3.5**. This has long been required from film and TV companies, see **20.10.2**;

- Information under the Oil Taxation Act from North Sea oil and gas operators, see **20.6.5**;

- Data received from overseas tax authorities under the exchange of information provisions within double tax treaties;

- Miscellaneous gossip supplied by neighbours and former friends.

In addition to the review work carried out by the Employer Compliance units, the Revenue have said that their Special Compliance Office may be involved in:

> 'Schemes that present themselves as a means to evade or avoid tax. It is likely that schemes advertised to "Avoid IR35" will consequently attract their attention, and may lead to an investigation.' (FAQ Compliance 4)

17 Overseas implications – tax

17.1 General

17.1.1 Introduction

In the House of Commons debate on IR35, Mr Trend asked:

> 'How do the government think British businesses are going to adapt to the
> e-commerce revolution when the consultants who put those systems in
> place have left the country?' (*Hansard* 3 November 1999, Col. 414)

In saying this he was merely reflecting an oft-repeated threat that the skilled
people caught by IR35 would go overseas to avoid its impact. However, as
Robert Maas has aptly remarked:

> 'Emigration is ... the ultimate form of tax avoidance ... As a form of tax
> planning it ought therefore to be looked on as a last resort.' (*Tolleys Tax
> Planning 1999*)

Parliament also highlighted the interaction between personal services and tax
residence. Richard Ottaway, speaking in the House on 3 May 2000, said:

> 'Would Laetitia Caster, the model chosen to represent the symbol of the
> French Republic, La Marianne, have come to the United Kingdom if she had
> known about IR35? She almost certainly works through a personal service
> company ... It comes as no surprise that when she arrived and saw what was
> going on, she quickly announced that she would not be resident in the UK
> for tax purposes.' (*Hansard*, Col.185–6)

17.1.2 Outline and scope

International tax is complex, and this chapter only outlines the main issues
from a UK tax perspective; detailed guidance should be sought in individual
circumstances.

Different residence rules apply for capital gains tax, and these are outside the
scope of this book. Special rules apply to EU officials and Crown servants, as
well as to mariners and oil workers (**20.6.3**), and these are also not covered in
this chapter. National Insurance is dealt with in Chapter 18.

This chapter looks first at the position of service company workers coming here from overseas, and then at the consequences for those leaving the UK to work abroad. It concludes with a brief note on partners.

17.2 Residence and personal services

If an individual is within the personal services rules, he is subject to Schedule E tax. However the rules for Schedule E differ depending on the individual's residence, ordinary residence and domicile. Thus it is necessary to understand these concepts to know to what extent an individual falls within the personal services legislation, and whether its impact can be avoided or reduced.

Schedule 12, para 11(3) FA 2000 makes this link with the Schedule E residence rules explicit. It specifically excludes individuals from the scope of the personal service legislation:

> 'If, or to the extent that, by reason of any combination of the following factors –
>
> (a) the worker being resident, ordinarily resident or domiciled outside the United Kingdom,
>
> (b) the client being resident or ordinarily resident outside the United Kingdom, or
>
> (c) the services in question being provided outside the United Kingdom,
>
> he would not be chargeable to tax under Schedule E if the client employed the worker, the worker performed the services in the course of that employment, and the deemed Schedule E payment were a payment by the client of emoluments from that employment.'

In other words, if the rules for residence and domicile would have allowed a worker to escape Schedule E tax had he been an employee of his client, then he will also escape from IR35. This has important implications for individuals who are non-resident or not ordinarily resident in the UK, or who have a foreign domicile.

17.3 Definitions

Despite the fact that residence, ordinary residence and domicile are fundamental to an individual's UK tax liability, they are not defined in statute. Indeed, over 70 years ago Viscount Sumner warned that:

> 'The words "resident in the United Kingdom", "ordinarily" or otherwise, and the words "leaving the United Kingdom for the purpose only of occasional

residence abroad", simple as they look, guide the subject remarkably little as to the limits within which he must pay and beyond which he is free. This is the more likely to be a subject of grievance and to provoke a sense of injustice when, as is now the case, the facility of communications, the fluid and restless character of social habits, and the pressure of taxation have made these intricate and doubtful questions of residence important and urgent.'
(*Levene v CIR* [1928] 13 TC 48)

As a result of this lack of definition, questions of residence and domicile are mostly decided using a mixture of case law and Revenue practice. On occasion, such as in the case of *Reed v Clark* [1986] 58 TC 528 (see **17.9.3**), the Revenue may seek tax even where an individual has relied on their published guidance. Workers seeking to avoid liability to IR35 by using an overseas residence or non-domiciliary route are thus advised to take great care and not to cut corners.

17.4 Outline of the rules

The legislative basis for the income tax treatment of residence, ordinary residence and domicile is found in s19(1) ICTA 1988. This divides Schedule E into three sub-categories, Case I, Case II and Case III.

If a worker is resident, ordinarily resident and domiciled in the UK, he will be taxed under Case I on all his earnings, whether the work was carried out in the UK or overseas. All his engagements are thus potentially within the personal services rules.

On the other hand, he will escape Schedule E, and therefore the personal services rules, either wholly or partly in the following situations. If he is:

- Non-resident in the UK, he is not taxed on earnings from work carried out overseas. He is taxable under Case II of Schedule E in respect of relevant engagements carried out in the UK, but may be able to escape tax by arguing that his UK work is 'merely incidental' to his overseas engagements, see **17.8.2** below. Alternatively, he may be excluded from UK tax by a double tax treaty, see **17.8.3**;

- Resident, but not ordinarily resident, he is not taxed on earnings from engagements carried out overseas, as long as the earnings are not remitted to the UK. He is taxable on earnings from any UK relevant engagements under Case II of Schedule E, and under Case III on any remitted monies from the overseas work;

- Resident and ordinarily resident here, but not domiciled, he is within an exception to Case I. He will escape the personal services rules for work carried out wholly overseas for an overseas client, as long as the money is not remitted here. Money earned for work carried out overseas by a non-domiciliary is known as 'foreign emoluments' (see **17.12.3**; s19(1) ICTA 1988; FAQ Foreign 5).

17.5 Coming to the UK from overseas

17.5.1 Residence

Outline

If an individual is non-resident he will be able to shelter all overseas earnings from the deemed income calculation; he may also be able to protect UK earnings by arguing that they are 'merely incidental' or covered by a double tax treaty, see **17.8.2** below. It is thus important that a personal services worker retain non-resident status for as long as possible, and does not accidentally become resident here.

This is possible because the residence position of an individual who has come to the UK from overseas depends not only on how long he spends in this country but also on what his plans are. Care is therefore needed, as it is possible to accelerate UK residence and ordinary residence by an expression of intention, or by certain actions, such as the purchase of a house.

A further issue is that some residence rules take retrospective effect from the beginning of a fiscal year, so a change of status may bring money already earned into the scope of IR35.

The tax position of non-residents is discussed in more detail at **17.8** below.

Residence rules

An individual will be tax resident in the UK for a fiscal year if:

- He spends more than 183 days here, when he will be tax resident from the beginning of that fiscal year. Inland Revenue booklet IR20 states sternly that 'there are no exceptions to this'. However, if an individual is tax resident in two countries, he may be in the UK for more than 183 days and still be regarded as resident in the other country by virtue of a 'tie-breaker' clause in a double tax treaty;

- He owns a property here, or takes a lease on a property which is for three years or more. He will then be tax resident and ordinarily resident from the beginning of the year in which he buys or leases the property. However, if accommodation is the only factor which causes him to be classified as resident and ordinarily resident, and he disposes of the property and leaves the UK within three years, the status ruling may be reversed (SP 3/81; IR20, para 3.12);

- He arrives in the UK to take up permanent residence or to spend at least two years here. He is then resident from the date of arrival to the date of departure, provided that:

  'Prior to his arrival he was ... not ordinarily resident in the UK. The concession would not apply, for example, where an individual who had been ordinarily resident in the UK left for intended permanent residence abroad but returned to reside here before the end of the tax year following the tax year of departure.' (ESC A11)

- He is in the UK for 90 days a year, on average, over a four-year period. He will then be both resident and ordinarily resident from the beginning of the fifth fiscal year. If he decides, before the end of the four year period, that he will spend an average of 90 days a year here, he will be resident and ordinarily resident from the beginning of the fiscal year in which he formed that intention, providing he carries it out. (*Reid v CIR* [1926] 10 TC 673; *Levene v CIR* [1928] 13 TC 48; IM 40)

These possibilities are summarised in Table 17.1. It should be noted that where an individual has been classified as resident and/or ordinarily resident on the basis of his intentions, and these change, his residence status can be reversed.

Table 17.1 *Residence in the UK*

Individual's position	Resident from	Other points
In UK for 183 days or more in a tax year.	Beginning of that tax year.	Double tax treaty may make him resident in another country under tie-breaker test.
Purchases a house or takes a lease for three years or more.	The beginning of the fiscal year in which the property was acquired.	Will also be ordinarily resident. Status may be reversed if disposes of the property and leaves UK within three years.
Plans to spend more than 90 days in UK over a four-year period.	From beginning of tax year when he made the decision.	Will also be ordinarily resident. Status can be reversed if doesn't stay in the UK as planned.

| Spends more than 90 days in the UK over a four-year period. | From beginning of fifth tax year. | Will also be ordinarily resident. |
| Plans to live in the UK for at least two years. | From date of arrival to date of departure, subject to meeting ESC A11 conditions. | |

17.5.2 Ordinary residence

Definition

In addition to residence, the legislation also contains a second concept: ordinary residence. This is also not defined in the Taxes Acts, but it suggests greater permanence than 'residence'. If an individual is resident year after year, he is ordinarily resident. In *Levene* Viscount Cave said that it 'connotes residence in a place with some degree of continuity and apart from accidental or temporary absences'. This was expanded by Lord Warrington in the same case, who held that:

> 'It is in my opinion impossible to restrict its connotation to its duration. A member of this House may well be said to be ordinarily resident in London during the Parliamentary session and in the country during the recess. If it has any definite meaning I should say it means according to the way in which a man's life is usually ordered.'

An individual may be resident but not ordinarily resident here in a fiscal year. The Revenue consider that the converse is possible, so a person may be ordinarily resident without being resident. This might be, for example, because he usually lives in the UK but is absent on an extended holiday throughout a tax year (IR20, para 1.3). However Viscount Cave in *Levene* expressed doubt about this, saying that 'I find it difficult to imagine a case in which a man while not resident here is yet ordinarily resident here'.

Importance of ordinary residence

If a worker can establish that he is not ordinarily resident in the UK, any earnings from work carried out overseas is not within Schedule E, unless it is remitted here. In the context of the personal services regime, this means that earnings received by a service company for work carried out wholly overseas will not be included in the deemed income computation, provided it is not brought into the UK.

For an explanation of the remittance basis, see **17.13** below. If the money is subsequently remitted, a deemed income calculation needs to be performed, see **17.13.5** below.

As with residence, it is possible to accelerate a determination of ordinary residence by behaviour (such as the acquisition of a property) or by declared intention, see below. A personal services worker with overseas engagements should endeavour to remain not ordinarily resident for as long as possible, in order to shelter his foreign income from IR35. Examples of residence and ordinary residence determinations are given at **17.5.3** below.

Determining ordinary residence

An individual will be regarded as ordinarily resident on the earliest of the following events:

- Buying a house here, or taking a lease of at least three years;

- Deciding to remain in the UK. The Revenue say that an individual remains in the UK if he is 'here on a continuing basis and any departures are for holidays or short business trips' (IR20 para 3.1);

- Making regular visits here averaging 90 days over a four-year period, or intending to make such visits.

This is set out in Table 17.2, which is based on SP 17/91 and IR20.

Table 17.2 Ordinary residence

Individual's position	Ordinarily resident from ...
Purchases a house or takes a lease for three years or more.	Beginning of the fiscal year in which the property was acquired. Residence status may be reversed if property is disposed of and the individual leaves within three years.
Decides to stay in the UK for at least three years, counting from date of arrival.	Beginning of the fiscal year in which the decision was made.
Stays in the UK for more than three years	Beginning of the fourth fiscal year.
Beginning of fiscal year in which the here each fiscal year, on average over a four year period.	Plans to spends more than 90 days decision was made.
Spends more than 90 days here each fiscal year, on average, over a four-year period.	Beginning of the fifth fiscal year.

17.5.3 Examples of residence and ordinary residence determinations

The following examples (based on IR20 paras 3.3, 3.5 and 3.10) show how these rules are applied:

Example 17A

(a) Mwangi first came to the UK during 1999-2000, and intended visiting regularly until at least 5 April 2003. His visits average at least 91 days a tax year. He is resident and ordinarily resident from 6 April 1999, assuming he carries out his intention;

(b) Svetlana came to the UK with no definite intentions, but visited regularly during the tax years 1999–2000 to 2002–2003 and her visits average at least 91 days a tax year. She is resident and ordinarily resident from 6 April 2003;

(c) Xiao Liu first came to the UK during 1999–2000 with no definite intentions; she came again in 2000–2001 and 2001–2002; during 2001–2002 she decides she will come regularly in future years, and her visits will average at least 91 days a tax year. She is resident and ordinarily resident from 6 April 2001, assuming that she carries out her intention;

(d) Duke came to the UK to work on 14 July 1999 on a two-year contract, but in December 2001 his contract was extended until after July 2002. He is resident and ordinarily resident from 6 April 2001.

17.6 Counting the days

In deciding whether an individual is resident or ordinarily resident, the number of days spent in this country are significant. The normal rule is that days of arrival in and departure from the UK are ignored (IM50; IR20 para 1.2). However:

- This is concessional: the legislation imposes a liability to tax if the individual is in the UK during the fiscal year, see *Mitchell v CIR* [1951] 33 TC 53 and *Neubergh v CIR* [1977] 52 TC 79;

- There is authority in case law for a stricter hourly basis (*Wilkie v CIR* [1951] 32 TC 495). It is thus prudent to ensure that the taxpayer is not dependent solely on carefully monitoring his days of arrival and departure to obtain non-resident or not ordinarily resident status;

- In the case of *R v Inspector of Taxes (ex p. Fulford-Dobson)* [1987] 60 TC 168 the taxpayer relied on the split year concession relating to capital gains tax

(ESC D2), but was defeated. This was because his admitted intention was to go overseas to avoid CGT, and (as stated inside the front cover of Revenue pamphlet IR1, which lists the Extra Statutory Concessions in operation), a 'concession will not be given in any case where an attempt is made to use it for tax avoidance'.

- This rule about days of arrival and departure is not relevant to the concessionary split year treatment under ESC A11, see **17.5.1**, **17.9.2** and **17.9.4**;

- Any days spent in the UK for exceptional circumstances beyond the taxpayer's control, for example because of illness, are not normally counted for the purpose of establishing the number of days in the United Kingdom (SP2/91; IR20 para 2.2).

Useful worked examples demonstrating how to calculate the days in the UK are given in IR20 at paragraphs 2.10 and 3.6.

17.7 Procedure for establishing residence status

17.7.1 Introduction

It is no longer possible to obtain a formal Revenue ruling on a worker's residence status. The UK has a self-assessment system, and individuals must now self-assess their status. It is recommended that those arriving in the UK also complete Form P86 – the Arrival Questionnaire.

Great care must be taken when completing either P86 or the self-assessment form, as statements made about the worker's intentions may be difficult to rebut at a later stage.

17.7.2 Form P86 – arrival questionnaire

Form P86 settles the individual's residence status at a practical level: when it is received by the Inland Revenue, they use the information provided to produce an accurate PAYE code. This may prevent overpayments of PAYE during the tax year of arrival.

Where worker is within the personal services regime, obtaining a correct code may be particularly important, as the PAYE on the deemed Schedule E amount will be due in one lump sum. An incorrect coding may thus cause cashflow issues.

However the P86 process does not amount to a ruling. Inspectors are advised that 'the information given on form P86 should therefore be taken at face value without further enquiry wherever possible. Speculative enquiries should be avoided' (EPM 8089).

17.7.3 Self-assessment form

Individuals certify their residence status and domicile as part of their self-assessment (SA) return. If an individual wants to claim he is non-resident, not ordinarily resident or not domiciled, and this affects the tax he has to pay, he will need to complete the non-residence pages and submit these as part of his SA tax return. Additionally, where double tax relief is sought, further forms are generated through the supplementary non-residence pages.

If, following receipt of a SA return submitted by a personal services worker, the Revenue open an enquiry into his residence status, it is recommended that he supplies the Revenue with a copy of his contract along with any other information from the client or agent which indicates the intended length of his UK assignment, or otherwise supports his position.

17.8 Non-residents

17.8.1 Outline

An individual will be non-resident in the UK if he is here for less than 183 days in the tax year, and doesn't fall within any of the other tests for residence set out at **17.5.1** above.

The fact that an individual is treated as non-resident for tax purposes does not, however, necessarily mean that he has no liability to tax (s19(1) ICTA 1988). A non-resident can be taxed on work carried out in the UK, unless either:

- The work is 'merely incidental' to the work done abroad (s132 ICTA 1988), see **17.8.2** below; or

- It is covered by a double tax treaty, see **17.8.3**.

If the work carried out in the UK by the worker is neither merely incidental, nor covered by a tax treaty, he will be within the scope of the personal services legislation for his UK-based work, assuming that the contract was a 'relevant engagement'.

17.8.2 'Merely incidental'

The words 'merely incidental' are not defined in the Taxes Acts, but it has been said:

> 'The words "merely incidental" are … apt to denote an activity … which does not serve any independent purpose but is carried out in order to further some other purpose.'(*Robson v Dixon* [1972] 48 TC 527)

The Revenue view of 'merely incidental' is as follows:

> 'To determine whether work done in the United Kingdom is "merely incidental", you need to know the nature of both that work and the work done overseas. If the work done in the United Kingdom is subservient or ancillary to that done overseas, or if it is of a subordinate nature, it should be taken as being "merely incidental". If, on the other hand, the work done in the United Kingdom is of *the same kind* as that done overseas, or *if not the same it is of equal importance*, it will not be "merely incidental".' (SE 40203, the author's italics)

In the *Robson v Dixon* case quoted above, a pilot flew aircraft from Amsterdam to various parts of the world, rarely taking off or landing in the United Kingdom. He failed in his claim that his visits to the UK were merely incidental because they were so few in number. The case proved that the test is one of quality, not quantity: it is the nature of the duties performed in the UK, not the time spent on them, which matters.

Having said this, the Revenue do not accept that work done here can be merely incidental if 'the employee works in the United Kingdom for more than three months in a year' (IR20 para 6.7). They also give the following examples of whether work done by a non-resident will be regarded as 'merely incidental':

(a) An overseas representative of a United Kingdom employer, while on visits to the United Kingdom, which total less than three months in a year, does nothing more than report on trade conditions and results in his area, consult his employer on questions of policy, or receive instructions, or collect samples in preparation for his next tour. The duties he performs in the United Kingdom should be regarded as merely incidental;

(b) An overseas employee visits the United Kingdom for periods of training which do not exceed three months in the year. If he does no productive work while he is in the United Kingdom, the duties performed here are regarded as merely incidental;

(c) A company director, although usually working abroad, attends directors' meetings in the United Kingdom. That activity is basic to the joint duty of a board of directors to manage the company and therefore cannot be incidental to work done overseas;

(d) A courier visits many countries in the course of his work. Visits to the United Kingdom, however few and however short, are of the same importance to his job as visits to other countries and therefore cannot be incidental.

Where an individual operates through his own service company, the same tests should be applied in relation to the work done for an overseas client. A personal service worker who is otherwise non-resident, and who would meet the 'merely incidental' test if he were employed by his client, will not be within the PSC regime.

Using the Revenue examples, a non-resident individual who is contracted to work for an overseas company, and is sent by the client to report on trade conditions in the UK, would fall into the same category as the employee in (a) above; a contractor sent here by his client only for training would fall within (b) above.

Example (c) demonstrates that it is difficult to argue that work done by a director is 'merely incidental'. However, where a director of a service company is in the UK to carry out work for a client, and the work would have been 'merely incidental' if carried out by an employee of that client, he will be outside IR35 in respect of that UK engagement.

17.8.3 Double tax treaties

The UK has over 100 double tax treaties with different territories. They are not identical, and the relevant treaty must be reviewed in order to see which provisions apply in any particular case.

Having said this, standard OECD articles are found in most treaties. The article relating to 'dependent personal services' is of most relevance to the personal services worker. It states that where work is carried out in the UK by an individual from a treaty state (other than an entertainer or sportsman, see **20.2** and **20.7**) he escapes taxation in the UK if he fulfils all four of the following conditions:

(a) He is not tax resident in the UK; and

(b) He is present in the UK for not more than 183 days in any continuous period of 12 months; and

(c)   His remuneration is paid by an employer who is not a resident of the UK; and

(d)   His remuneration is not borne by a permanent establishment or fixed base which the employer has in the UK.

In the context of the personal services legislation, the worker needs to establish that he would meet the four tests above, if he were an employee of his client. Note that the 'presence in the UK' test in (b) refers to any 12-month period, not a calendar year or a fiscal year.

It should usually be easy enough to decide whether tests (a) to (c) are satisfied; (d) may sometimes be more problematic. This applies where:

> 'A formal contract of employment remains with the overseas employer, but the employee works in the business of the United Kingdom company, which obtains the benefits and bears any risks in relation to the work undertaken by the employee. In economic terms this state of affairs is recognised by the overseas employer recharging the cost of the employee's remuneration to the United Kingdom and the UK company might be described as the "economic employer".' (*Tax Bulletin* 17, June 1995)

The Revenue have confirmed that they do not allow the treaty relief to operate where an employee's true 'economic' employer is in this country. It is thus important that the worker discovers whether his costs are being borne by the UK.

If his costs are recharged, he may still qualify for exemption from the PSC rules, as the Revenue have said that they will not apply the 'economic employer' test where:

- The employee is in the United Kingdom for less than 60 days in a tax year; and

- That period does not form part of a more substantial period of time for which the taxpayer is present in the United Kingdom. (*Tax Bulletin* October 1996)

It is thus more difficult for an overseas PSC worker to come within the treaty reliefs than he may have first thought. If he comes to the UK to work for a client here, and stays for more than 60 days in a tax year, then that assignment will be within IR35 for tax. However, it may be outside it for NICs, see Chapter 18.

17.8.4 Apportionment of income

Where a non-resident worker does not satisfy the merely incidental test, and cannot claim double tax relief, he will be taxable on earnings from his UK work. This means that he will fall partly within and partly outside the UK tax system.

Thus a non-resident personal services worker who takes up a contract with an overseas client involving some UK work may find that his service company is required to carry out a deemed income calculation in relation to that UK work. For the responsibility of the company in this respect, see Chapter 19.

When dividing earnings between those taxable here and those taxable abroad, the Revenue normally accept that this should be on a time-apportioned basis, see SP 5/84 and **17.13** below. This time-apportioned basis will, however, not be accepted if there are special facts, for instance where it is clear that more income relates to the UK work than to the work carried out overseas. Dual contracts are an alternative, see **17.8.5** below.

17.8.5 Dual contracts for non-residents

Dual contracts are an alternative to apportionment, and, as discussed at **17.12.4** below, also shelter overseas income when the apportionment option is not available. In the context of the personal services legislation, the existence of separate contracts for UK and overseas work may simplify the administration, and make it less likely that the amounts brought into the deemed Schedule E computation will be challenged.

However it is important that the contracts are sound. For example:

(a) The UK contract and the overseas contract should be with separate clients, such as the UK subsidiary and the French parent company;

(b) Separate invoices should be submitted for each engagement;

(c) Records of expenses and capital expenditure related to each contract should be kept;

(d) The duties to be carried out for each client should be distinguishable;

(e) The amount charged for each engagement should be commercially sustainable. Attempts to 'load' the overseas contract are likely to be carefully examined.

17.8.6 Tax allowances for non-residents

If a worker is non-resident, he is nevertheless entitled to a full UK personal allowance if he is a Commonwealth or EU citizen, or comes into another approved category, see IR20 para 7.3. He can thus reduce the UK tax liability on his personal services income (and other UK source income) by offsetting it against the personal allowance.

Non-residents who are not domiciled in the UK, and who meet certain other requirements, can obtain tax relief for travel to the UK by family members, see **17.12.4** below.

17.8.7 Tax treatment of dividends received by non-resident personal services worker

If an individual is non-resident, he is not normally entitled to recover the tax credit on any dividend paid to him by a UK based personal service company, unless this is permitted under the terms of a double tax treaty. However, he is also not subject to UK tax on the dividend (s233 ICTA 1988). Thus there should be no need to invoke the double tax clause in the personal services legislation, see **13.6.2**. There may, however, be foreign tax implications: overseas fiscal authorities may seek to tax the dividend even though the underlying income has already been included in the deemed Schedule E calculation. If this is the position, the worker should extract his money from the company by salary, not by a dividend, see Chapter 13. Any double taxation of the salary will need to be dealt with in the home state.

17.9 Working overseas

17.9.1 Introduction

Contractors are a mobile workforce, and many have always operated overseas. IR35 has now persuaded others who have lived in the UK all their life to move abroad and seek foreign engagements in order to avoid the deemed Schedule E charge.

To be non-resident in the UK a personal services worker must:

(a) Work abroad for a fiscal year; or

(b) Not set foot in the UK for a fiscal year; or

(c) Take up permanent residence abroad.

Each of these are discussed below at **17.9.2** to **17.9.4**.

The legislation in this area is brief: s334 ICTA 1988 states that 'Commonwealth citizens and citizens of the Republic of Ireland' who have been ordinarily resident in the UK, shall remain within Schedule E if they leave the UK 'for the purpose only of occasional residence abroad'. This section has received recent Revenue attention in the context of 'mobile workers' – people who continue to have their home here but who make frequent and regular trips overseas. This is discussed at **17.9.7**.

17.9.2 Full time contract of service abroad

Revenue practice is to accept that an individual has become non-resident if he goes abroad for full-time service under a contract of employment and:

- All the duties of his employment are performed abroad (or any he performs here are incidental to his duties abroad); and

- His absence from the UK in the employment is for a period which includes a complete tax year; and

- Interim visits to the UK do not amount to six months or more in any one tax year or three months or more on average.

The period of non-residence for income tax purposes begins the day following the date of his departure until the day preceding the date of his return, providing he was in the UK as a resident and not a short-term visitor (ESC A11; IR20, paras 1.6 and 2.2).

An individual who satisfies the 'full time service under a contract of employment' test can therefore achieve non-residence status if he is away for at least a complete tax year, and his return visits are kept within the specified limits.

Clearly personal service workers with their own companies can give themselves a contract of employment which requires them to be overseas for a fiscal year. However this is unlikely on its own to amount to 'full time service'. The Revenue gave guidance on what they see as 'full time' in *Revenue Interpretation (RI) 40*, as follows:

> 'There is no statutory definition of "full-time" in this context, nor any guidance from the courts. The phrase can only therefore be interpreted in accordance with its ordinary, non-technical meaning. Where an individual is working "full-time" in an employment will always depend upon the particular facts of the case.
>
> In general terms, where a job involves a standard pattern of hours and an individual is putting in what a layman would clearly recognise as a full

working week, [the Revenue] would accept it as full-time. There is no fixed minimum number of hours for this purpose, but 35–40 hours is obviously a typical UK working week.

Some jobs, however, do not have a straightforward structure. There may, for example, be a mixture of round-the-clock working followed by a rest period; or, in the case of sportsmen, days of playing and training interspersed. Some jobs may not have a formal structure with any fixed number of working days. In deciding whether such jobs are full-time employments, [the Revenue] would look at the nature of the job, and, where appropriate, would take account of local conditions and practices in that particular occupation. Someone who had several part-time jobs overseas concurrently might also be accepted as being in full-time employment. If, for example, they had several appointments with the same employer or group of companies, it might be reasonable to aggregate the total time spent on them for the purposes of the full-time test. This approach could also apply where an individual was simultaneously engaged in employment and self-employment abroad.

Where a person has a main employment abroad but also works in the UK in some unconnected occupation (for example, as director of a family company), [the Revenue] would need to consider whether the extent of the UK activities might cast any doubt on the full-time nature of the main employment outside the UK. Again, [the Revenue] would have to look at the facts of the particular case in reaching a decision.

In [the Revenue's] experience there is rarely in practice much difficulty in deciding whether an individual is working full-time. These notes indicate [their] general approach in the minority of cases at the margins where the position may be less clear.'

Thus if the personal service worker is carrying out a series of engagements overseas during a tax year, as the director/employee of his company, and these amount to working 'full time', then the criteria for non-UK residence will be satisfied. However, contractors should also be warned that:

'If there is a break in full-time employment, or some other change in your circumstances during the period you are overseas, [the Revenue] would have to review the position to decide whether you still meet the conditions in paragraph 2.2. If at the end of one employment you returned temporarily to the UK, planning to go abroad again after a very short stay in this country, [the Revenue] may review your residence status in the light of all the circumstances of your employment abroad and your return to the UK.' (IR20 para 2.3)

Thus a return to the UK between contracts could jeopardise non-residence status, and the personal services worker should take this into account when planning holidays back home.

Accompanying spouses

If an individual satisfies the criteria set out in ESC A11, see **17.9.2** above, his spouse will also be treated as not resident and not ordinarily resident on a split year basis, if:

- The purpose of the trip was to join, or to accompany, the husband or wife who was working overseas; and

- The spouse satisfies the other conditions of ESC A11, apart from the requirement to be in full time employment overseas (ESC A78).

17.9.3 Out of the UK for a whole tax year

The Revenue have accepted that 'an individual who is not in the United Kingdom *at any time* during a particular tax year is not normally regarded as resident for that year' (IM 36).

However in the case of *Reed v Clark* [1986] 58 TC 528 the Revenue argued that this did not apply – no doubt relying on the phrase 'normally'. Although the case was found in favour of the taxpayer, there remains some risk of attack where the individual cannot satisfy the 'full-time working abroad test'.

Having said this, the Revenue's internal guidance states that Inspectors are prepared to give a final non-residence decision where an individual has not been in the UK for a whole tax year, see **17.9.5** below, and this should give some further comfort.

17.9.4 Permanent residence abroad

Where an individual has been resident in the UK and leaves live abroad permanently, or for a period of at least three years, he will qualify for the split year concession, providing he is not ordinarily resident in the UK on his departure. He will thus be taxed as resident only up to the day he leaves the UK (ESC A11).

The same split year basis will apply if he can show that he has 'gone abroad for a settled purpose', has actually been out of the UK for a whole tax year, and has not visited the UK for more than 183 days in a tax year or 90 days on average (IR20 para 2.9).

In order to show that the individual has taken up permanent residence abroad, the following steps are helpful:

(a) Limiting visits to the UK, especially during the year of departure and the following three fiscal years. Ideally, there should be no visit at all in the tax year following departure. Visits in subsequent years should be as few as possible. It is unwise to return for the full 90 days each tax year, as the Revenue may (despite the guidance) may take the view that the individual has remained resident;

(b) When visits to the UK are made, a record should be kept of the reasons for these visits in order to demonstrate that they were not part of the individual's normal pattern of life. For example, a visit to the UK because of illness (either of the individual or another person) would be regarded as a temporary purpose;

(c) The Inland Revenue's internal guidance seeks to establish whether the individual has a home overseas, and whether their former home here has been either sold or let. In seeking to establish an overseas residence, it is thus important to rent or buy a property as soon as possible, and it is advisable to make the UK property inaccessible, either by selling it, or by letting it, preferably for four years. The Inspector is invited to ask the would-be émigré if he 'has a reason for having accommodation for use in the United Kingdom which is consistent with the aim of permanent residence abroad' (IM 41; IR20 para 2.8);

(d) If, for commercial reasons (such as the provisions of the Assured Tenancy legislation), a shorter let is recommended by the estate agency, there should be some evidence – perhaps a letter to the agency – setting out the intention to make the property available for at least a four year period.

17.9.5 Procedures for obtaining non-residence status

When an individual leaves the UK, it is recommended that he submit a form P85 to the Revenue together with details of the departure and his intentions. The Inspector will either accept the position, or ask for further details. Once it has been accepted, it should be possible to rely on this, as long as the individual's circumstances do not change for the next three years, although it is not a formal ruling.

The Revenue's own guidance states that the claim to be non-resident:

'May be admitted on a provisional basis at the outset, with effect as from the day following the date of departure, if the grounds on which it is based are adequately proved; but in no circumstances can a final decision be made until the individual's absence from the United Kingdom has extended over a period which includes a full tax year.

If adequate proof is not immediately available, a decision on the claim is postponed for up to three years from the date of departure, and the position is determined by reference to what has actually happened since the date of departure. During this period of up to three years, except for any complete year of absence, any claim in respect of allowances and reliefs due to a resident is granted provisionally.' (IM 41)

In addition to the P85 procedure, individuals may have to complete a self-assessment form. The procedures for this are discussed in Chapter 15.

17.9.6 Residence status abroad

When an individual goes to work abroad, he does not disappear, but enters another tax system. It is important that he receives proper advice on his tax liabilities and how they interact with UK taxes. This advice should be sought before he leaves the UK, as he could otherwise either miss some important planning points, or subject himself to double taxation.

17.9.7 Mobile workers

Mobile workers are those whose home continues to be in the UK, and their 'settled domestic life remains here' (*Tax Bulletin* 52, April 2001), but they make frequent and regular trips overseas. The classic mobile worker is a long-distance lorry driver working from a UK base and driving his vehicle to the continent most weeks. However, this mobile worker definition could also apply to an IT worker on a short-term project elsewhere in the EU who comes back to see his family at weekends.

The *Tax Bulletin* article makes it clear that the Revenue consider such workers to be UK resident, as they are 'unlikely to be able to show that they were absent for other than "occasional residence" abroad', and thus remain within the scope of Schedule E, see s334 ICTA 1988 and **17.9.1**.

However, this statement on mobile workers should not mean that contractors who satisfy the requirements set out at **17.9.2** will jeopardise their position if they retain a home and family here – they should be classified as non-resident if they have an overseas contract which extends over a complete tax year, and visits home are within the prescribed limits.

17.10 UK residents working abroad

17.10.1 Tax basis

If an individual is UK resident, ordinarily resident and domiciled, he will be within the UK tax system, and thus the deemed income calculation, in respect of all his earnings, whether the work was carried out in the UK or overseas. Where his overseas earnings have suffered foreign tax, he may be able to claim relief against the PAYE on his deemed income calculation, see **17.10.1**; a deduction may also be available for the costs of travel by family members, see **17.10.3**.

17.10.2 Relief for overseas tax suffered

Where a PSC worker is UK resident but works overseas, and the income received by his service company has suffered overseas tax, the normal rule is that this tax should be deducted from the UK corporation tax due on the service company's profits.

However, in many cases the PSC will have no corporation tax liability, since the personal services legislation will create losses, see **13.7**. The Revenue addressed this point as follows:

'Where work is carried out overseas then the company may suffer foreign tax on its profits. A foreign tax authority may also withhold tax in respect of payments made to the company. Relief for any such foreign tax credits is normally given against the company's UK tax liability.

However, where the company does not have sufficient UK tax liability to give full effect any such credit, but the worker does, then the balance may be allowed against the tax liability on the deemed payment. Relief can only be given where it is possible to directly link the work in the overseas country and the deemed payment. Relief cannot be given against the National Insurance liability.

Where it is considered that relief should be given in this way a claim should be made to the tax office dealing with the worker's tax affairs.' (FAQ Foreign 5)

This concession is welcome and will help minimise double taxation suffered by those who use personal services companies. It is an extension and development of the existing practice which applies to entertainers and sports people, see **20.2.6**.

According to the FAQ, tax relief is only available against the income tax on the deemed payment if it cannot be relieved against the company's corporation tax liability. This raises the following issues:

(a) It will be necessary to know what the company's tax position will be in respect of the accounting period in which the foreign tax could be claimed, before claiming a reduction in the individual's income tax;

(b) If a company pays a lower amount of PAYE because it believed it would be able to offset the overseas tax against the income tax arising on the deemed payment, but subsequently this proves not to be the case, an interest charge will arise, see **16.5**;

(c) If the overseas tax *can* be offset against the company's liability, the rate of tax suffered in the company may be lower than that borne on the foreign source income, resulting in irrecoverable overseas tax.

17.10.3 Travel expenses

Where an individual is resident and ordinarily resident in the UK, and works overseas for a continuous period of at least 60 days, in each tax year he can claim a deduction for the cost of two outward and return journeys by his spouse and any children under the age of 18 (ss193–4 ICTA 1988). The requirement that the 60 days be continuous is strictly enforced, unlike the more relaxed position taken for overseas workers in the UK (SE 34060; **17.12.4**). These sections also allow relief for the individual's travel costs, but these will generally escape tax under s198 ICTA 1988 in any event, see **11.6**.

In order to be allowable, the cost must actually borne by the intermediary, though reimbursement of the expenses by the service company is sufficient for this condition to be met. These travel costs will be deducted under Step Three of the deemed income calculation, see **11.3.1**.

Relief is not available if the earnings are foreign emoluments (see **17.12.3**), and unlike the normal Schedule E travel rules, see **11.6**, there is no relief for any associated accommodation and subsistence.

17.11 Domicile

17.11.1 Concept of domicile

Tax law also includes a third concept, domicile. A person's domicile is the place he considers to be 'home'. An individual may leave the UK and spend his working life overseas, yet intend to retire in Tiverton. He thus still considers the UK to be his home, and is domiciled here. Equally a Jamaican who has worked in Birmingham since he was 18, but who intends to go back to the West Indies once he retires, remains domiciled there.

17.11.2 Domicile of origin

Each person begins life with a domicile of origin, which is normally the country where his father was domiciled at the time of the child's birth. If a child is illegitimate, it acquires the domicile of its mother. Domicile of origin never changes, unless the child is adopted, when he obtains the domicile of his adoptive father.

This is important, because it means that a person born here may still have a foreign domicile if his father had not abandoned his domicile of origin, see Example 17B.

Example 17B

Divya, a tax adviser with her own personal service company based in North London, was born in Kenya to parents of Indian origin. She came to the UK when she was a child. Her father had Indian domicile when she was born, and he did not abandon that domicile. Divya will not be domiciled in the UK, despite having lived here most of her life, providing she does not make the UK a domicile of choice, see **17.11.4** below.

17.11.3 Married women

Women who were married before 1 January 1994 acquired their husband's domicile, and they will have retained this unless the position has changed by the acquisition of a further domicile, or a revival of a domicile of origin.

17.11.4 Domicile of choice

From the age of 16, or on marriage if earlier, an individual can change his domicile of origin and acquire a domicile of choice. In order to establish a change of domicile, the individual has to prove that he intends to reside permanently in the new country, see for example *Udny v Udny* [1869] LR 1 Sc and Div App 441, *Plummer v CIR* [1987] 60 TC 452 and the recent case of *Mrs F and S2 (Personal Representatives of F deceased) v CIR* [2000] SSCD 1.

A domicile of choice is not easily achieved – radical action, such as changing nationality, severing ties with the home country, and buying property in the new territory, including a grave plot, are all recommended if an individual is serious about changing his domicile. In *Henderson v Henderson* [1965] 1 All ER 179, Sir Jocelyn Simon said that:

> 'To displace the domicile of origin in favour of the domicile of choice, the standard of proof goes beyond a mere balance of probabilities.'

Domicile is not the same as nationality, as was reinforced in *Anderson (Anderson's Executor) v CIR* [1998] SSCD 43. The Special Commissioners held that there was:

> 'An inherent improbability in a 65-year-old Scotsman, who has lived in Scotland all his life, abandoning his roots and intending to acquire a domicile of choice in England.'

In contrast to residence and ordinary residence, an individual can only be domiciled in one territory at a time.

17.11.5 Procedure for establishing a change of domicile

It used to be possible for an individual to submit their arguments concerning a change of domicile, and ask the Revenue to rule on whether they had satisfied the tests. This is no longer the case.

Where an individual comes to the UK from overseas, he is advised to complete form P86 which also incorporates a section on domicile. Where domicile status is unclear from the information provided on the P86: for instance, if the individual was born in the UK but is claiming a domicile of choice elsewhere, he is likely to be sent a longer, more detailed form (DOM1). However, the fact that an individual has completed a P86 and a DOM 1 and sent it to the Revenue does not mean that they have accepted his claim, even if he has heard nothing further from them.

When the worker claiming to be non-domiciled comes to complete his self-assessment form, one of the questions is whether his domicile status has been examined in the last six years. If he answers 'no' to this question, the Revenue warn that this 'will prompt a review of an individual's domicile which may lead to the issue of a TMA 1970, s9A enquiry' (*Tax Bulletin* 29, June 1997).

However, if the claim to be non-domiciled does not affect the tax due, the Inspector will decline to examine the claim (IM 1635).

Non-domiciled status will be agreed without further investigation by the Revenue if *all* the following are satisfied:

- The claimant was born outside the United Kingdom;

- The claimant's father was domiciled outside the United Kingdom at the time of his/her birth;

- The claimant came to the United Kingdom for the purpose only of an employment and intends to resume residence abroad on the cessation of that employment (see the flowchart at RG 3.7).

17.12 Consequences of being non-domiciled

17.12.1 Tax advantages

Being non-domiciled in the UK has important income tax implications for those within the personal services regime. This is because a non-domiciliary is not taxed in the UK on work done overseas for an overseas employer unless he remits the money earned (the 'foreign emoluments') to the UK (s192(2) ICTA 1988).

Note that this is a narrower definition of the remittance basis than that which applies to those who are not ordinarily resident, see **17.5.2**. The non-domiciliary is only within the remittance basis if the work has been carried out abroad for an overseas employer; the individual who is not ordinarily resident is within the remittance basis in respect of all work carried out overseas, see **17.13** below.

In addition, being non-domiciled can have major inheritance tax advantages, but these are outside the scope of this book.

17.12.2 Personal services implications of being non-domiciled

The legislation, quoted in full at **17.2** above, indicates that a worker will not be taxed on his overseas earnings if he:

> 'Would not be chargeable to tax under Schedule E if the client employed the worker, the worker performed the services in the course of that employment, and the deemed Schedule E payment were a payment by the client of emoluments from that employment.'

Thus if a personal service worker can establish that he is not domiciled here, and is working wholly overseas for a client who is 'resident outside, and not resident in' the UK, he can exclude from IR35 money received by the service company as long as it is not remitted here. Considerable care is needed with regard to what constitutes a 'remittance', see **17.13** below. If the money is subsequently remitted, a deemed income calculation needs to be performed, see **17.13.5** below.

17.12.3 Foreign emoluments

The following points should be noted as regards the definition of foreign emoluments:

(a) To qualify for the exemption, the duties must be performed 'wholly' outside the UK, apart from duties which are 'incidental' to the work done overseas. The concept of merely incidental is discussed at **17.8.2**;

(b) If some of the work is to be performed in the UK and some overseas, then two separate contracts should be considered, see below;

(c) Earnings from the Republic of Ireland are not foreign emoluments (s192(1) ICTA 1988), see **17.13.6**;

(d) If the overseas client has a branch or agency in the UK, it could be argued that it does not satisfy the condition of being 'resident outside, and not resident in, the United Kingdom'. However the Revenue do not take this point, see SE 41010;

(e) Where the overseas client is a *branch or agency* of the UK company, the payment will be from a company which is resident in the UK. Amounts received from the branch or agency are thus not foreign emoluments. However, where the client is an overseas *subsidiary* of a UK company, the client is not resident here, and thus the emoluments qualify for the exemption;

(f) Where a worker is engaged by an overseas client, he should endeavour to establish the legal status of his engager in order to determine whether the amounts paid into his service company can escape the deemed Schedule E computation. Corporate tax residence is discussed at **19.2**;

(g) It is worth noting that Inspectors are instructed as follows:

> 'The benefit to the employee (of receiving foreign emoluments) is clear. There is likely to be a big reduction in the amount of emoluments chargeable to income tax in the United Kingdom. You should examine the facts closely before accepting that emoluments fall within this exception. In particular you should find out whether the employer has any place of business in the United Kingdom. If you

can trace an accounts file for the employer, ask the accounts Inspector for instructions on the employer's residence status.' (SE 40102)

Dual contracts

Where an individual works for a UK client partly here and partly abroad, apportionment will not protect the earnings for the work carried out overseas. It may be possible to have two contracts, so that one of them falls within the rules for foreign emoluments, see **17.12.3**. However if the engagements are 'associated', relief may be restricted to that which is:

> 'Reasonable having regard to the nature of and time devoted to the duties performed outside and in the United Kingdom respectively and to all other relevant circumstances.' (Sch 12, para 2 ICTA 1988)

'Associated' is defined in s416 ICTA 1988, and includes companies one of which controls the other, or where both are under common control. Thus an attempt to split a contract with, say, a multinational, so that the amounts charged to the overseas subsidiary are much higher than those charged to the UK company, are likely to fail. See SE 40104 for the Revenue's approach to dual contracts, and **17.8.5** above for dual contracts in the context of non-residence.

17.12.4 Travel expenses

If a worker within the scope of the personal services rules is non-domiciled, he may be able to claim travel expenses in relation to journeys to the UK under s195 ICTA 1988. From 6 April 2001 s195 was matched by an equivalent NICs provision (SI 2001/1004 Sch 3, para 5). Relief is available under these rules for a period of five years from the date of the employee's arrival in the United Kingdom, provided that:

(a) He was not resident in the United Kingdom in either of the two years of assessment immediately preceding the year of assessment in which he arrived; or

(b) He was not in the United Kingdom for any purpose at any time during the period of two years ending with the day immediately preceding the day of arrival. In practice the Revenue usually accept that attendance at interview in order to obtain the engagement does not disqualify the worker.

The main benefit of s195 is that it gives relief for travel by members of the individual's family, as well as for journeys made by the worker himself. The latter would be allowable in any event under the travel rules set out in **11.6**.

To qualify for the relief, the following conditions must exist:

- The worker must be non-domiciled;

- He must be taxable under Schedule E in respect of duties performed in the United Kingdom;

- The travel expenses must be borne by the intermediary, not by the individual.

The journeys relieved must meet the following conditions:

- Be a journey undertaken by the individual from his usual place of abode to any place in the United Kingdom in order to perform duties there, or to his usual place of abode from any place in the United Kingdom after performing such duties there; and/or

- Be journeys undertaken by his spouse or child (under 18) to accompany or visit him in the UK. This is limited to two outward and two return journeys for any one individual in any one tax year, and it only applies if the individual is in the United Kingdom for a continuous period of 60 days or more to perform duties. The requirement of a 'continuous period of 60 days or more' will be met if he spends at least two thirds of his working days in the UK over a period of 60 days or more and is present in the UK for the purpose of performing the duties of his employment both at the start and at the end of this period (*Tax Bulletin* 56).

Unlike the normal travel rules, see **11.6**, there is no relief for any associated accommodation and subsistence.

Thus a personal service worker who was in the UK for a relevant engagement of at least 60 days could deduct from his deemed income calculation the costs of his spouse or children accompanying him, or coming to visit him in the UK. The cost must actually be borne by the intermediary, though reimbursement by the service company is sufficient for this condition to be met. The expenses are deducted at Step Three of the deemed income calculation, see **11.3.1**.

17. 13 Remittance basis

17.13.1 Outline of issues

Workers with a foreign domicile, and those who are not ordinarily resident in the UK, are on the remittance basis. A number of issues arise:

(a) There is a difference between the remittance basis for those not ordinarily resident and that applied to non-domiciliaries, see **17.13.2**;

(b) Care is needed where money is remitted out of 'mixed funds', only part of which derive from overseas earnings, see **17.13.3**;

(c) Ensuring that earnings are not remitted is complex; it is relatively easy to transfer funds to the UK inadvertently, see **17.13.4**;

(d) The remittance basis also gives rise to certain calculation issues for corporation tax and partnership tax computations, see **17.13.5**;

(e) Work carried out in the Republic of Ireland is not regarded as overseas for the purpose of the remittance basis, see **17.13.6**.

17.13.2 Meaning of remittance

Although both non-domiciliaries and those who are not ordinarily resident in the UK are on a remittance basis, the rules are not the same.

The Schedule E earnings of non-domiciliaries only qualify for the remittance basis if they are 'foreign emoluments', see **17.12.3**. They must thus be from an overseas employer and relate to work carried out wholly overseas. In the personal services context, this means that the client must be overseas and the work wholly overseas.

In contrast, the personal services worker who is not ordinarily resident in the UK can protect foreign earnings whether or not they are paid by an overseas client, and there is no requirement for the work to be carried out wholly overseas: the part relating to the overseas work can be sheltered from IR35 as long as it is not remitted here.

17.13.3 Remittances out of mixed funds

'Mixed funds' in this context are sources such as bank accounts which contain both foreign emoluments and other money. The Revenue take a different approach to remittances out of mixed funds depending on whether the taxpayer is:

- Not ordinarily resident, and remitting money from a single engagement, part of which is carried out overseas; or

- On the remittance basis for another reason, such as because he is non-domiciled.

However this distinction in treatment is almost certainly unfounded, see below.

Not ordinarily resident with a single engagement

Where an individual who is not ordinarily resident has a single engagement, part of which is carried out overseas and part of which is carried out in the UK, it can be difficult to establish whether the former has been remitted to the UK.

The Revenue have a generous and relaxed attitude to this problem. SP5/84 states that where employees:

'(a) are resident but not ordinarily resident in the UK;

(b) perform duties of a single employment both in and outside the UK, so that they are potentially liable under both Schedule E Cases II and III, in respect of emoluments from that employment; and

(c) receive part of their emoluments in the UK and part abroad,

(then), provided the emoluments assessable under Case II are arrived at in a reasonable manner … the Revenue are prepared to accept that Case III liability will arise only where the aggregate of emoluments paid in, benefits enjoyed in, and emoluments remitted to, the UK exceeds the amount assessable under Case II for that year; and to restrict the Case III assessment to the excess of the aggregate over the Case II assessment.'

In other words, where the employee has a 'mixed' employment, he will be deemed to have remitted first his non-taxable income, and only be subject to UK tax on any balance. This is based on the decision in *Sterling Trust Ltd v IRC* [1925] 12 TC 868.

In the context of the personal services regime, this means that a worker who is not ordinarily resident will be deemed to have remitted taxed money before untaxed money, and can thus relatively easily protect his overseas earnings from the remittance basis, subject to the other tests at **17.13.4** below.

Other remittances

Where the ESC does not apply, the Revenue take a much stricter approach. This would therefore impact the earnings of non-domiciled personal services workers.

If earnings subject to the remittance basis are combined with other money, such as capital, within a 'mixed fund', the Revenue take the view that *taxable* amounts are remitted first, followed by any capital in the fund.

The Inspector's Manual explains the position as follows:

> 'Where a person maintains abroad a fund (for example, a bank account) containing income assessable on the remittance basis, a capital lodgement to the fund is normally considered to lose its identity in the fund. A subsequent remittance from such a mixed fund, therefore, represents income up to the full extent of the income content of the fund ... Only when the income content of the fund is exhausted will any balance remitted be regarded as capital. Where this is not accepted, the full facts of the case should be reported to International Division.' (IM 1566)

This view is based on the decision in *Scottish Provident Institution v Allan* [1901] 4 TC 409 where the judge held that 'no prudent man of business will encroach upon his capital for investment when he has income uninvested laying at his disposal'.

It is arguable that the Revenue view here is incorrect, and that the more correct view is that the taxpayer can choose whether to remit income or capital. The case for this was well made by David Williams and Gary Morris in *Taxation*, p422, 16 January 1997.

However it remains prudent, where the individual has capital overseas, to hold it separately from any income, whether interest or earnings. Having separate bank accounts for income and capital allows the latter to be remitted to the UK without having to dispute with the Revenue as to whether further tax should be paid.

Where the separate accounts approach has not been adopted, the arguments set out by Williams and Morris may be successful in protecting the individual from UK tax.

Further remittance problems arise where an overseas asset produces a capital gain, but these are beyond the scope of this book.

17.13.4 'Received in the United Kingdom'

Overseas earnings are treated as received in the United Kingdom if they are paid, used or enjoyed in, or in any manner or form transmitted or brought to, this country (s132(5) ICTA 1988). They remain earnings, even if they are subsequently invested in capital assets, see *Walsh v Randall* [1940] 23 TC 55.

The following therefore count as a remittance of Schedule E income into the UK:

- Payment abroad for goods or services supplied in the United Kingdom;

- Using a UK cheque or credit card to purchase goods or services, and the settlement of the debt out of overseas earnings, see IM 1569. A card issued by an overseas financial institution should thus be used in preference where it is intended to settle the bill out of unremitted funds;

- Purchasing an asset abroad out of overseas earnings, selling it, and then repatriating the proceeds;

- Bringing an asset into the UK which has been purchased abroad out of overseas earnings, and selling it here;

- Where money is borrowed overseas and brought to the UK and the loan is then repaid out of overseas earnings, this is a 'constructive remittance' (s65(6)–(9) ICTA 1988). This applies to non-domiciliaries but not to those who are not ordinarily resident.

However, where money is borrowed overseas and then brought to the UK, or alternatively used to purchase an asset here, and the *interest* on the loan is repaid out of overseas earnings, there is no remittance.

In addition, the mere transfer to the UK of assets purchased with overseas earnings does not itself constitute a remittance, see *Scottish Widows' Fund Life Assurance Society v Farmer* [1909] 5 TC 502.

17.13.5 Deemed income calculation issues arising from remittance basis

If an individual is on the remittance basis for services performed abroad he will not be chargeable under the rules of Schedule E. Thus he will not be within the personal services rules, see **17.2** above.

However, the calculation cannot be ignored, because if the amounts are remitted, they will become chargeable at that time (s19(1) ICTA 1988). Thus an individual could have a liability under the personal services rules several years after the work had been carried out, see Example 17C.

> **Example 17C**
>
> Marcin was born in Poland but moved to the UK several years ago. He has retained his Polish domicile. He has a personal service company providing IT services both in the UK and overseas. In 2000/01 he has income from relevant engagements of £50,000, of which £20,000 relate to engagements with overseas clients. His 2000/01 deemed income calculation was based on £30,000 of UK income.
>
> In May 2003 he and his wife buy a house, and he remits the £20,000 relating to his 2000/01 overseas work. This is then added to his other income from relevant engagements in that year, and included in his deemed Schedule E computation for 2003/04.

There is no deduction in the partnership or corporation tax computation for the deemed payment until it is 'treated as made' (Sch 12, para 17 FA 2000). Thus, if the sums are remitted at some future date, a deduction can then be claimed in the partnership or corporation tax computation.

17.13.6 Republic of Ireland

Where a UK resident individual is non-domiciled, or not ordinarily resident, income from the Republic of Ireland is taxable here, whether or not it is remitted. This is the case whether or not:

- The worker's domicile/place of ordinary residence is the Republic of Ireland, or whether it is a third country. (This may be particularly relevant for those working on IT projects in the Dublin Docks area);

- The income is from employment, self-employment, or other amounts such as interest (s68 and s192(1) ICTA 1988).

17.14 Partners

Where a partner carries on a relevant engagement, he will be taxed on the deemed Schedule E income received by the partnership from that engagement. He must thus determine his residence, ordinary residence and domicile status, and then follow the Schedule E rules for determining the taxation of his income, as follows:

- If he is resident, ordinary resident and domiciled, he will be taxed on the full amount calculated under Sch 12 FA 2000;

- If he is resident and ordinarily resident, but non-domiciled and the engagement is carried out wholly overseas for a foreign client, he will be taxed on the remittance basis;

- If he is resident and domiciled, but not ordinarily resident, earnings related to overseas work will be taxed on the remittance basis;

- If he is non-resident he will be taxed on work done here unless it is 'merely incidental', see **17.8.2** or is covered by a double tax treaty, see **17.8.3**.

The interaction between the taxation of partnerships generally, and the personal services rules, is covered in Chapter 14.

18 Overseas implications – National Insurance

18.1 Introduction

The basis of liability to social security contributions varies considerably across the world. It may depend on the individual's nationality, his employer's place of business, or his residence, ordinary residence and domicile. The rules of the country where he lives and those where he works both need to be considered, together with overriding laws such as those of the European Union.

The National Insurance implications of an overseas posting are therefore already complex. IR35 adds a further level of difficulty. NIC is due where a worker would have had a liability had he been an employee of the client. The interaction of this hypothesis with international social security treaties is far from straightforward, and it is clear that IR35 will prove particularly challenging for cross-border personal services workers.

This chapter looks first at the position of UK workers going abroad, and then at overseas workers taking up UK engagements. It does not consider the position of partners. It concludes that international social security treaties may sometimes override the PSC legislation to eliminate the IR35 NIC charge, so that there will be no attributable earnings. The worker may, however, still have a deemed income calculation, as the tax and NIC rules diverge. In other circumstances an individual may have an attributable earnings calculation but no deemed income.

18.2 Interaction with the personal services rules

Where a personal service worker carries out a relevant engagement abroad, or an overseas individual carries out a relevant engagement in the UK, the payments and benefits received by the intermediary from that engagement must be included in the attributable earnings calculation, and charged to UK employee NICs, if:

> 'The circumstances are such that, had the arrangements taken the form of a contract between the worker and the client, the worker would be regarded for the purposes of Parts I to V of the Contributions and Benefits Act as employed in employed earner's employment by the client.' (SI 2000/721 reg 6(1)(c))

In other words, it is necessary to imagine that the worker was an employee of the client, and then ask if he would have been 'employed in employed earner's employment' by the client. If the answer to that question is yes, then his attributable earnings will be subject to employee NICs.

Furthermore, where this occurs, the service company will be the secondary contributor in respect of those attributable earnings. The Regulations say that:

> 'The intermediary, whether or not he fulfils the conditions prescribed under section 1(6)(a) of the Contributions and Benefits Act for secondary contributors, is treated for those purposes as the secondary contributor in respect of the worker's attributable earnings.' (SI 2000/721, reg 6(3)(b))

This means that, where a liability for employer contributions exists, it falls upon the personal service company or partnership, whether or not it would have this responsibility under normal NIC rules.

18.3 NICs and individuals working abroad

18.3.1 Outline of existing NICs rules

The rules for deciding whether someone who is working overseas has a liability to UK NICs can be summarised as follows:

(a) The basic rule is that where all the work for a particular employer is performed overseas, the employee is not in 'employed earner's employment' because that requires at least some of the work to be performed in the UK (s2 SSCBA 1992), and thus no NICs are due;

(b) There is an exception to this rule, even where the work is carried out wholly overseas, if:

   (i)   The employer has a place of business in the UK; and
   (ii) The employee is ordinarily resident in the UK; and
   (iii) Immediately before the commencement of the employment, the employee was resident in the UK.

   In this case the employee is treated as in 'employed earner's employment' for the first 52 weeks of that employment (SI 2001/1004 reg 146). He is thus subject to Class 1 NICs, and his employer is a secondary contributor;

(c) The basic rule in (a) above is also overridden by various social security treaties, under which certain overseas employments are treated as if they had been carried out within the home country.

18.3.2 Personal service workers overseas

If the normal rules for working overseas are translated, so that they take account of the new regulations applicable to personal services, they read as follows:

(a) If all of the work for a particular *client* is performed overseas, then the *engagement* is not 'employed earner's employment' because that requires at least some of the work to be performed in the UK.

Since there can be no attributable earnings if there is no 'employed earner's employment', the PSC rules fall away. There is thus no attributable earnings calculation, and no liability to NICs. There might however be a deemed Schedule E liability because of the individual's tax residence status, see Chapter 17 and **18.4.5** below;

(b) There is an exception to the rule in (a), even where the work is carried out wholly overseas, if:

(i)   The *client* has a place of business in the UK; and
(ii) The *worker* is ordinarily resident in the UK; and
(iii) Immediately before the commencement of the *engagement* the *worker* was resident in the UK.

In this case, the *worker* is treated as in 'employed earner's employment' for the first 52 weeks of that employment. Under the personal services rules he will thus be subject to Class 1 NICs, and his service company will be the secondary contributor.

It is interesting to note that where a worker is not within (b) above, because the client has no place of business in the UK, there is no liability to NICs under the PSC rules. However, in the 'real world', the worker is employed by an employer who has a place of business in the UK – namely his service company. He is thus within Reg 120 and subject to UK NICs on his actual earnings, even though he has no attributable earnings.

The Revenue give examples of the situation in (a) and (b) above at ESM 3133:

'A worker was ordinarily resident in the United Kingdom and was also resident in the United Kingdom prior to posting to Angola by the intermediary. The client only has a place of business in Angola. The worker would be regarded as an employed earner for United Kingdom national insurance purposes by reason of the contractual arrangement between the intermediary, the worker and the client [i.e., the fact that he is employed by his service company]. The intermediaries legislation will not apply, for NICs purposes, because in deciding whether the legislation applies you consider what the situation would have been if the intermediary had not been involved.

However, a contract between a worker who was ordinarily resident in the United Kingdom and was resident in the United Kingdom prior to going to work for a client in Angola who has a place of business in the United Kingdom would be treated as an employed earner for the first 52 weeks. In these circumstances, the intermediaries legislation may apply. However there would be no NIC liability if the 52 week period had expired before the 5th April in the year of assessment.'

18.3.3 EEA treaty arrangements

General rule

The EEA countries are Austria, Belgium, Denmark, Republic of Ireland, Finland, France, Germany, Greece, Iceland, Italy, Liechtenstein, Luxembourg, Netherlands, Norway, Portugal, Spain, Sweden and the UK. These countries operate under the Social Security law of the European Union. Its fundamental principles are as follows:

(a) A person should not have to pay contributions in more than one Member State at the same time;

(b) He should normally be subject to the contribution law of the state where he is employed or self-employed;

(c) This is the case even if he resides in another state or his employer has a place of business or a registered office in another state (EC Reg 1408/71, Art 13).

Where a person leaves the UK to work for an employer in another EEA country, he will no longer be liable to UK NICs because he is not in 'employed earner's employment' in the UK. This is the case even if his employer has a place of business in the UK – it thus overrides Regulation 146 (see **18.3.2(b)** above).

Short-term posting

There is an exception to the general rule set out above, which covers short-term postings to other EEA states. Where a worker is employed in the UK, and is sent by his employer to work in an EEA state, he remains within UK NICs, provided that:

(a) The posting to the EEA state is not expected to last for a period in excess of 12 months; and

(b) He is not being sent to replace another person who has completed his term of posting (EC Reg 1408/71, Art 14(1)(a)).

If this short-term posting rule does apply, and the job overseas lasts longer than 12 months, although it was not expected to, the employee may remain in the UK scheme for a further 12 months, as long as the foreign social security authority agrees. Consent cannot, however, be given for an extension in excess of 12 months unless the two states have entered into a special agreement under Article 17 of the Treaty permitting longer extensions.

18.3.4 Application to personal services workers

General rule

Translating this to take account of the personal services regulations, the general rule would read as follows:

- A personal services worker who takes up a relevant engagement with a client in an EEA state would not have been an employed earner for UK NIC purposes if he had been an employee of the client. He will thus be outside the PSC rules;

- As a result he has no attributable earnings from his overseas engagement, no liability to employee NICs, and his service company has no secondary liability. However, he may still be within the scope of UK tax and have a deemed income calculation, see **18.4.5** below.

Once again, in the 'real world' he will still be employed by his service company, not the overseas client. He is thus subject to UK NICs on his actual salary and benefits as he was before IR35. This is confirmed by the Revenue at ESM 3131:

> 'The intermediary can obtain form E101 from NICO International Services and the worker is classed as a posted worker. He would be regarded as an employed earner for the purposes of the United Kingdom national insurance legislation by reason of the contractual arrangement between the intermediary, the worker and the client [i.e., the fact that he is employed by his service company]. However, the intermediaries legislation does not apply, for NICs purposes, because in deciding whether the legislation applies you consider what the situation would have been if the intermediary had not been involved.'

However, there may be a problem here with a rule known as AC162, issued by the EC Commission on social security for migrant workers in May 1996. This states that an individual with a service company can only remain in his home country scheme if he has a continuing link with the home country. This is understood to mean that there must be some continuing activity in the home country. With a one-man service company this will not always be the position – it is a question of fact in each case.

In the UK, for example, the Revenue have refused to give E101s to companies where, on inspection, the 'work force is substantially in another country and all that constitutes the UK employer is, say, a typist and fax machine' (CA Specialist Conference, 4 February 1997, quoted in *Tolleys National Insurance Contributions 2001*).

Thus an individual taking up a contract abroad will be outside IR35; if he wishes to remain within UK NICs in respect of his actual salary and benefits rather than falling into a foreign social security regime, he needs to convince the Revenue that he should be given an E101.

Short-term posting

The short-term posting rule, rewritten in the context of personal services, would be as follows:

> Where a worker has a relevant engagement with a client in the UK, and is sent by that client to work in an EEA state, he remains within UK NICs, provided that:
>
> (a) The posting to the EEA state is not expected to last for a period in excess of 12 months; and
>
> (b) He is not being sent to replace another person who has completed his term of posting.
>
> If the short-term posting rule does apply, and the engagement overseas lasts longer than 12 months, although it was not expected too, the *worker* may remain in the UK scheme for a further 12 months, if the foreign social security authority agrees.

A PSC worker sent overseas by a UK client whose posting met these conditions would have remained within UK NICs had he been an employee of the client. He will thus remain within the PSC rules. His earnings from the relevant engagement will be included in his attributable earnings calculation, and his service company will be the secondary contributor. Contractors who want to avoid IR35 should ensure that they are not within this rule.

In this situation contractors receive some help from AC162. If there is no continuing activity in the UK, the operation of AC162 may cause the Revenue to refuse to allow the individual to remain within UK NICs. This will take him out of IR35, but place him within the social security regime of the country to which he has been posted by the client.

Clearly, the ideal situation is to ensure that the contract is with the overseas engager in the first place, rather than taking out a UK contract and then having to deal with the complexities of the short-term posting rule and AC162.

Summary

One can attempt to summarise these complex rules by saying that:

- If a worker goes to work for an overseas client in an EEA country, he will be outside the PSC rules. He may, however, remain within UK NIC, which will then apply only to his actual salary and benefits, but this only applies if he can satisfy the requirements of AC162;

- If a worker is sent overseas by a UK client and the engagement meets the short-term posting requirements, he remains within the PSC rules, as well as being within UK NIC generally, unless AC162 applies. In the latter case, he will be within the social security regime of the overseas jurisdiction;

- Even if he falls outside the attributable earnings calculation for NICs, he may remain within the Schedule E tax rules.

It should be possible to structure arrangements so that a worker is not sent abroad by a UK client, but takes up a separate overseas engagement. This would prevent the short-term posting rule coming into effect.

18.3.5 Bilateral Social Security Treaty countries

The provisions of each social security treaty are not identical, but the following general points can be made:

- Many social security treaties allow UK employees to remain within UK NICs if they are working in the overseas country for a limited period of time. Where a worker would have remained within UK NICs had he been an employee of the client, he will remain within the personal services rules, and his income from the engagement will form part of the attributable earnings calculation;

- However it is not always the case that a person who takes up a job overseas will have remained within UK NICs – it depends on the treaty provisions. If a worker would not have remained within UK NICs had he been employed by the client, he will also be outside the PSC rules;

- He may, nevertheless, remain within the provisions of the treaty because he is legally an employee of his service company. He will then be within UK NICs in respect of his actual earnings, but will have no attributable earnings. There is a Revenue example of this scenario at ESM 3132.

18.4 NICs and individuals coming to the UK to work

18.4.1 Establishing whether the individual has a NIC liability

When an individual with a personal service company comes from overseas to take up a relevant engagement in the UK, the first question is whether there would have been a NICs liability had the worker been employed by the client. The answer to this question may be different depending on whether the individual has come from:

- An EEA country;

- A country with which the UK has a bilateral social security treaty; or

- From a country which is neither of these.

18.4.2 EEA countries

General rule

The basic EEA rules are set out at **18.3.3** above. Where a person comes to the UK from an EEA country to take up employment here, he is liable to UK NIC, unless he falls within the short-term posting exemption.

It should be noted that workers from other EEA countries are liable to pay UK Class 1 contributions from the outset under EC Reg 1408/71, Art 13(2)(a) provided they are EEA nationals. Unlike other overseas workers they are not exempt from liability for their first 52 weeks, because Article 13(2)(a) takes priority over SI 2000/721, reg 119(2).

Liability for secondary contributions follows the primary liability of the earner, irrespective of the fact that the secondary contributor may reside in a different state from that under which the earner's liabilities arise.

A personal services worker who lives in an EEA state, but takes up a relevant engagement with a client in the UK, remains employed by his overseas service company. As a question of fact he has not come from overseas to take up employment here, and so is not within Article 13. Thus he does not automatically fall within the personal services legislation, despite the fact that under IR35 he would have been regarded as an 'employed earner' had he been an employee of the client.

He may still, however, fall within UK NICs if AC162 applies, see **18.3.4** above. AC162 is applied in different ways by different member states, with some being much stricter than others. The UK is not part of the decision making process – all applications are handled only by the home country from which the worker comes.

If the home state considers that AC162 applies so that there is 'insufficient connection' between the individual and his home state, he must therefore transfer to UK NICs, and is thus potentially within IR35.

Short-term posting

This is also discussed at **18.3.3** above. When this rule is translated into 'personal services speak', in the context of someone leaving the UK to work in another EEA country, it reads as follows:

'Where a *worker* is engaged to carry out a relevant engagement by a *client* in an EEA state, and is sent by that *client* to work in the UK, he will not have to pay UK NICs, provided that:

(a) The posting to the UK is not expected to last for a period in excess of 12 months; and

(b) He is not being sent to replace another person who has completed his term of posting.

If this short-term posting rule does apply, and the engagement overseas lasts longer than 12 months, although it was not expected too, the *worker* may remain outside the UK scheme for a further 12 months, if NICO agrees.'

A PSC worker sent to the UK by an overseas client, whose posting met these conditions, would have remained outside UK NICs had he been an employee of the client. Thus he passes the test set out in the Regulations, and remains outside the PSC rules.

This is fine if he is sent by his client to work in the UK and he is within the short-term posting rule. But what happens if he 'sends himself' as an employee of his service company, to work for a UK client? The personal services legislation does not allow him relief – he would not have been entitled to the short-term posting rule had he been an employee of his UK client.

However, as a question of fact, he is an employee of his service company, and has been sent to the UK to take up an engagement with a client. Article 14 of the EC Regulations states that a worker on a short-term posting 'shall continue to be subject to the legislation of the first Member State'. This suggests that the PSC worker in this position will not fall within UK NIC laws at all, and thus will not come within the personal services regulations.

However, AC162 must also be considered, see **18.3.4** above. If the home state takes the view that there is 'insufficient connection' between the individual and his home state, he must transfer to UK NICs and may fall within IR35.

Where AC162 does not apply, a worker who is in the UK for a short time will not be within IR35 for NICs, whether he is posted here by a client (because of the short-term posting exemption) or by his own service company (because of Article 14). He will thus be exempt from NICs and outside IR35, but he may have tax liability, see Chapter 17 and **18.4.5** below.

18.4.3 Bilateral Social Security Treaties

If an individual is:

(a) Paying social security contributions in a country with which the UK has a bilateral Social Security Agreement covering NICs; and

(b) Sent by that employer to work temporarily in the UK;

he may exempted from UK NICs, depending on the terms of the treaty.

Translated into 'PSC-speak' this means that if a worker is:

(a) Paying social security contributions in a country with which the UK has a bilateral Social Security Agreement covering NICs; and

(b) Has a contract with a client there, who sends him to work temporarily in the UK;

then, assuming he would have been outside UK NICs if he had been employed by the client, he will also fall outside the personal services legislation.

As discussed in **18.4.2** above, if he is 'sent' by his own service company to work for a client in the UK, he is not within the same exemption. The terms of the treaty would have to be considered to see if they protect him from all UK NICs legislation (as does the EC Treaty) or not.

Where there is an exemption from UK NICs, the usual evidence is a certificate issued by the foreign social security institution, confirming that he continues to contribute to the overseas scheme. Again, although there is no NIC liability under the personal services rules, there may be a tax liability, see Chapter 17 and **18.4.5** below. The client may have a liability under existing NICs legislation, see **19.5.3**.

18.4.4 Other countries

If an employee is sent to work in the UK by an employer located overseas, then the provisions of SI 2001/1004 reg 145(2) apply. This applies where:

> 'A person is ordinarily neither resident nor employed in the United Kingdom and, in pursuance of employment which is mainly employment outside the United Kingdom by an employer whose place of business is outside the United Kingdom (whether or not he also has a place of business in the United Kingdom).'

The regulations state that such a person is not normally liable to UK NICs for the first 52 weeks while he is in the UK, although the position is complex, see *Tolleys National Insurance* 49.8.

Applying the personal services rules to this, if a worker is sent to work in the UK by an overseas client, he should likewise not have to pay NICs for the first 52 weeks.

This is, at least, what the regulations are probably intended to achieve. However, the PSC rules operate if an individual is an 'employed earner'. Regulation 119 does not say that the individuals cease to be employed earners for the first 52 weeks, merely that they do not have to pay NICs. Hopefully, the Revenue will take a purposive approach to this part of the Regulations, and treat the worker carrying out the engagement for the overseas client in the same way as if he had been employed by the client.

Assuming this is the case, there will be no attributable earnings calculation for the first 52 weeks, but there may be a deemed Schedule E payment, see Chapter 17 and **18.4.5**. Both employer and employee NICs will be payable from the 53rd week by the service company in respect of any attributable earnings. The client, however, remains the secondary contributor in respect of his actual salary and benefits, see **19.5.3**.

18.4.5 Consequences of being within the PSC rules for tax but not for NIC

Because the rules for establishing a NIC liability for overseas workers are different from those which determine the Schedule E tax liability, income can be included in the deemed Schedule E calculation for income tax purposes, but with no charge to NICs arising.

Despite the fact that no NIC is payable, it would appear that the deemed Schedule E calculation allows a notional deduction. Steps Eight and Nine of the deemed Schedule E calculation are as follows:

> 'Step Eight: Find the amount which, together with employer's national insurance contributions on it, is equal to the amount resulting from Step Seven …
>
> Step Nine: The result is the amount of the deemed Schedule E payment' (Sch 12, para 7 FA 2000).

Step Eight doesn't say 'together with employer's national insurance *payable* on it … '. This is in contrast to the NICs regulations, which read:

> 'Find the amount that, together with the amount of secondary Class 1 contributions *payable in respect of it* … '. (SI 2000/727 reg 7)

It is thus reasonable to assume that the difference is deliberate, and that the deemed income calculation will produce the same tax charge whether or not the worker is subject to UK NICs. This would be fair, since if he is exempt from UK social security taxes, this is almost certainly because he is paying the equivalent in another country.

That this is the correct interpretation of the law is suggested by the TLRC in their redraft of Schedule 12. They have rewritten Step Eight as follows:

> 'Step Eight: Assume that the result of Step Seven represents an amount together with Employer's national insurance contributions on it, and deduct what (on that assumption) would be the mount of those contributions.' (*ED12 – Draft Income Tax [Earnings and Pensions] Bill Part 2 Employment Income*)

The key additional phrase 'on that assumption' makes it clear that the number to be deducted in the IR35 tax calculation is the number generated from within that calculation, and is not the result of the separate IR35 NICs calculation. See 18B below for a worked example.

18.5 Worked examples

In example 18A the individual is within IR35 for NICs but not for tax; in Example 18B she is within the rules for tax but not for NICs.

Example 18A

Coletta works through her own limited company providing nursing services. She has been resident in the UK for many years, but during the whole of the year to 5 April 2002 she lived and worked in Zimbabwe and the Revenue have agreed that she is non-resident for tax purposes. However, she remains within UK NICs throughout the period. While she is in Zimbabwe her limited company receives £40,000 for the services she provides.

Coletta pays herself a salary of £20,000 during the course of the year, on which some tax is payable in Zimbabwe.

The limited company pays Coletta's travel to her clients, and this costs £500. It also pays £4,000 into her pension scheme.

		Notes	£
Step One	Total amounts from clients		40,000
	Less 5%		(2,000)
Step Three	Schedule E expenses		(500)
Step Five	Employer's pension contributions		(4,000)
Step Six	Employer's NICs on earnings paid	1	(1,840)
Step Seven	Salary paid in year on which NICs paid		(20,000)
Balance			11,660
Step Eight	Employer's NICs on deemed payment	2	(1,240)
Step Nine	Deemed payment		10,420
Employee NICs on deemed payment			990

Total amounts payable: £1,240 + £990 = £2,230

Notes

1. $(20,000 - 4,535) \times 11.9\% = £1,840$

2. $11,660 \times 11.9/111.9 = £1,240$

3. $(29,900 - 20,000) \times 10\% = £990$, where £29,900 is maximum earnings for employee NICs

---

Example 18B

Janine works through her own limited company providing environmental research services. She is normally resident in France, but during the whole of the year to 5 April 2002 she has lived and worked in the UK and is resident here for tax purposes. However, she remains within French National Insurance. While she is in the UK her limited company received £40,000 for the services she provides.

Janine pays herself a salary of £20,000 during the course of the year.

The limited company pays Janine's travel within the UK to reach her clients, and this costs £500. It also pays £4,000 into her pension scheme.

		Notes	£
Step One	Total amounts from clients		40,000
	Less 5%		(2,000)
Step Three	Schedule E expenses		(500)
Step Five	Employer's pension contributions		(4,000)
Step Six	Employer's NICs on earnings paid		–
Step Seven	Salary paid in year on which NICs paid		(20,000)
	Balance		13,500
Step Eight	Notional employer's NICs on deemed payment – see **18.4.5**	1	(953)
Step Nine	Deemed payment		12,547
	Tax on deemed payment	2	3,327

Notes

1. $(13,500 - 4535) \times (11.9/111.9) = £953$ Note that this assumes that no NICs have been paid on the salary already taken; as the author considers this would be stretching the words of Step Eight too far. It is also possible that no NIC deductions are allowable, see **18.4.5.**

2. Total taxable earnings: $20,000 + 12,547 = £32,547$.
   Tax has already been paid on £20,000 of earnings:
   $22\% \times (29,400 - 20,000) = £2,068$
   $40\% \times (32,547 - 29,400) = £1,259$

   £3,327

19 Offshore companies and partnerships

19.1 Introduction

Some of those affected by the personal services legislation have sought to distance themselves from it by setting up an offshore company. This chapter looks at what makes an intermediary 'offshore', and considers the implications of operating via an offshore service company or partnership within the context of IR35.

19.2 Corporate tax residence in the UK

19.2.1 Scope

A company which is tax resident here is subject to UK tax on its worldwide earnings. It is also required to operate PAYE and NIC in respect of employees who are themselves within the scope of UK tax. It was held in *ex parte Blain* [1879] 12 Ch D 522 that:

> 'All Acts of the United Kingdom Parliament must be construed as subject to territorial limitations, i.e., they operate only in regard to persons who are resident in the United Kingdom.'

Although the territorial limitations of some UK laws have since been stretched, the *Blain* case is respected authority for the fact that residence brings companies within UK laws, including those relating to the operation of tax and National Insurance. A UK resident company is thus required to deduct PAYE and NIC from a deemed Schedule E payment.

A company is tax resident in the UK if it is either incorporated here (s66 FA 1988), or is managed and controlled here (*Calcutta Jute Mills Co Ltd v Nicholson Ex D* [1876] 1 TC 83) However, double tax treaties may override this, so that if a company is resident in more than one jurisdiction, a tie-breaker clause in the treaty may determine that the company is tax resident in the other territory.

19.2.2 Management and control

The management and control test has been established by over a century of case law. In *De Beers Consolidated Mines v Howe* [1906] 5 TC 198 Lord Loreburn said that:

'A company resides, for the purposes of income tax, where its real business is carried on ... I regard that as the true rule; and the real business is carried on where the central management and control actually abides.'

It is therefore necessary to work out what is meant by the place of 'central management and control'. The courts have held that this is the location where the highest level of control is exercised over the business, which may or may not be the same as the place where the operations are carried out. The Commissioners' summary of the facts in the *De Beers* case provides a nice illustration of the concept:

'The head office is formally at Kimberley, and the general meetings have always been held there. Also, the profits have been made out of diamonds raised in South Africa, and sold under annual contracts to a Syndicate for delivery in South Africa upon terms of division of profits realised on re-sale between the Company and the Syndicate. And the annual contracts contain provisions for regulating the market, in order to realise the best profits on re-sale. Further, some of the Directors and Life Governors live in South Africa, and there are Directors Meetings at Kimberley as well as in London.

But it is clearly established that the majority of Directors and Life Governors live in England, that the Directors' Meetings in London are the meetings where the real control is always exercised in practically all the important business of the Company, except the mining operations. London has always controlled the negotiation of the contracts with the Diamond Syndicates, has determined policy in the disposal of diamonds and other assets, the working and development of mines, the application of profits, and the appointment of directors. London has, also, always controlled matters that require to be determined by the majority of all the Directors, which include all questions of expenditure except wages, materials, and such like at the mines, and a limited sum which may be spent by the Directors at Kimberley.'

The place of central management and control is thus often, but not invariably, the place where the directors meet. The Revenue say that:

'Where doubts arise about a particular company's residence status, the Revenue adopt the following approach–

(i)   they first try to ascertain whether the directors of the company in fact exercise central management and control;

(ii) if so, they seek to determine where the directors exercise this central management and control (which is not necessarily where they meet);

(iii) in cases where the directors apparently do not exercise central management and control of the company, the Revenue then look to establish where and by whom it is exercised.' (SP 1/90)

19.2.3 Application to personal service companies

In a one-man company, management and control rests with the single director. If he controls the company from the UK, the company will be resident here. Although in theory it is possible to control a company from overseas, even if the director is based in the UK, in practice it is very difficult. Business decisions cannot always be deferred until the director can reach a convenient offshore location.

In this context the Revenue say:

> 'Where ... it appears that a major objective underlying the existence of certain factors is the obtaining of tax benefits from residence or non-residence, the Revenue examine the facts particularly closely in order to see whether there has been an attempt to create the appearance of central management and control in a particular place without the reality.' (SP 1/90)

Thus purchasing an 'offshore' company from a jurisdiction such as Bermuda or one of the Channel Islands does not prevent it from being UK resident. If the director makes key decisions about the company from the UK, it will be managed, controlled and thus resident here.

19.3 Non-resident companies with a UK trading presence

The PAYE collection provisions, contained within s203ff ICTA 1988, state that:

> 'On the making of any payment of, or on account of, any income assessable to income tax under Schedule E, income tax shall ... be deducted or repaid by the person making the payment.'

In *Clark v Oceanic Contractors Incorporated* [1982] 56 TC 183 the Revenue argued that because this phrase included no territorial limitation, any employer could be required to deduct PAYE from his employees' emoluments, whether or not the employer was UK resident. However, the Lord Chancellor dismissed this:

> 'If the Crown is right, the garb of logicality which it claims for its submission conceals extraordinarily far-reaching and anomalous consequences. How can the PAYE duties be enforced? How can the system be made to work? How can it be supervised? How can the necessary documents be obtained for inspection by the Revenue, unless the foreign corporation is compliant? It all adds up to a practical impossibility of enforcing or monitoring the

system against an uncooperative employer outside the United Kingdom making payments outside the United Kingdom.'

Nevertheless, by a 3:2 majority the House of Lords held that, if they can be made effective, the PAYE tax collection provisions can be applied to a non-resident company. For that purpose a 'trading presence' of the company in the United Kingdom is sufficient.

Thus, even where a company is non-resident, it can be required to deduct PAYE from a Schedule E deemed payment if it has a trading presence here. Similar rules apply to NIC (SI 2001/1004 reg 145(1)(b))

This PAYE obligation does not depend on the company's residence, and so cannot be avoided by using the 'tie-breaker' provisions of a double tax treaty. These simply determine a company's residence for tax purposes, if it is resident in more than one country. The PAYE and NIC rules are determined by 'trading presence' not residence.

19.4 Non-residents with no trading presence in UK

19.4.1 PAYE

Where a company has no trading presence in the UK, it cannot be required to deduct PAYE from the Schedule E earnings of its workers under normal UK tax law. However, special rules have been introduced for deemed Schedule E payments, see **19.5** below.

The normal requirement, where a worker is assigned or seconded from an overseas employer to a UK-based business, is that the UK client becomes responsible for deducting the tax on the worker's emoluments (s203C ICTA 1988). This obligation applies automatically unless the overseas employer agrees voluntarily to deduct the PAYE.

The position is different if (a) the employer is non-resident, and (b) the worker is either non-resident, or not ordinarily resident. In this situation:

- The UK-based business is responsible for deducting PAYE on at least a proportion of the earnings (s203D ICTA 1988);

- But this only applies if a direction is given to the UK company by the Revenue;

- In practice the Revenue and the UK company will come to an agreement as to how much of the earnings should be taken into account.

19.4.2 National Insurance

The rules for National Insurance are similar. The UK client, or 'host employer' becomes the secondary contributor if a worker is employed by a foreign company and:

> 'In pursuance of that employment the personal service of the person employed is made available to a host employer; and the personal service is rendered for the purposes of the business of that host employer.' (s7(2)(b) SSCBA 1992, SI 1978/1689 Sch 3(9))

In other words, the UK client is responsible for the secondary contributions of the individual employed by the overseas company.

19.5 Special rules for offshore personal services companies

19.5.1 PAYE

Normally, the s203C provisions mean that where a worker operates from an offshore service company, but works in the UK for a client based here, responsibility for operating PAYE rests with the client, see **19.4**.

In the context of IR35, this would make the client responsible for deciding whether the engagement was 'relevant' within the meaning of Sch 12, FA 2000, and, if it was, require him to operate PAYE on the deemed Schedule E amount. This would have represented a reversion to the original personal services proposals set out in April 1999 (see **2.3.2**), under which the burden of complying with IR35 lay with the client.

In order to ensure that responsibility for IR35 rests with the intermediary and not the client, special deeming rules have been included in the personal services legislation. They apply where:

(a) The worker is resident in the United Kingdom;

(b) The services in question are provided in the United Kingdom; and

(c) The client or employer carries on business in the United Kingdom.

In these situations 'the intermediary is treated as having a place of business in the United Kingdom, whether or not it in fact does so'. (Sch 12, para 11(6) FA 2000)

The effect of this paragraph is that, providing the worker is resident here and provides services here to a UK client, the service company is deemed to have a trading presence here, whether or not this would otherwise be the case. The company is thus brought within the PAYE legislation.

19.5.2 Interaction with s203C ICTA 1988

The IR35 deeming provisions take priority over s203C ICTA 1988, because the latter are only operative if 'PAYE regulations do not apply (either) to the person making the payment … or to the employer'.

Thus, if a UK client engages a worker from an offshore service company, the obligation to deduct PAYE from the deemed Schedule E amount remains with the service company rather than with the client. However, this IR35 deemed trading presence rule has two important limitations:

(a) It applies only to the deemed Schedule E payment. Clients are still within the scope of s203C if the worker receives salary or benefits. The implications of this are discussed at **21.3.2**;

(b) It does not apply if the worker is non-resident, and thus section 203D ICTA 1988 remains in force, see **19.4.1**.

19.5.3 National Insurance

A similar approach has been taken for National Insurance. The service company rather than the client is responsible for the NIC on attributable earnings from relevant engagements. The regulations say that:

> 'The intermediary, whether or not he fulfils the conditions prescribed under section 1(6)(a) of the Contributions and Benefits Act for secondary contributors, is treated for those purposes as the secondary contributor in respect of the worker's attributable earnings.'

Thus the intermediary and not the client becomes the secondary contributor. However, once again this applies only to the IR35 attributable earnings and not to any salary or benefits.

19.6 Enforcement

19.6.1 Options

If the company is non-resident, and does not comply with its PAYE and NIC obligations in respect of the deemed payment, the Revenue have indicated that they will seek to enforce the liability at the UK address of the worker. They have also warned that:

'Action to recover employer's NICs not paid by an offshore company could also include action against any assets of that company located in the UK.' (IR175: *Supplying services through a limited company or partnership*)

The Revenue may also be able to make the worker personally liable for the outstanding tax and NICs, see **19.6.2** below. However, it has also been suggested that the IR35 deemed trading presence rules may be unenforceable and thus *ultra vires*, see **19.6.3**.

19.6.2 Transferring responsibility to the worker

If a company should have deducted tax and NICs, but has not fulfilled its obligations, the Revenue have general powers to collect the overdue amounts from the worker.

However, as discussed at **16.8.2**, these powers may be defective in the context of IR35, and thus the Revenue may be unable to transfer responsibility for the PAYE on the deemed Schedule E amount to the individual. However, the NIC regulations *are* effective, and collection of outstanding NICs can be therefore be enforced on the worker.

19.6.3 Is the legislation *ultra vires*?

If the intermediary has no trading presence in the UK, is the legislation unenforceable and thus *ultra vires*?

In *Clark v Oceanic* (**19.3**) the House of Lords held that the PAYE rules could be applied to the company because it had a trading presence in the UK. It was thus able, at a practical level, to make the required deductions from employees' salaries. The concept of *deeming* a trading presence therefore seems to contradict the logic of the court, which was based on practical capacity to comply with the legislation.

But the IR35 deeming provisions are effective only if the *worker* has a UK address. Given that in most cases there is substantial identity between the worker and the company, the presence of the worker in the UK could be considered as a practical equivalent to a 'trading presence', and thus the provisions are likely to be enforceable along the same lines as the decision in *Clark v Oceanic*.

Even if this were not the position, it is doubtful that they are *ultra vires*. Lord Wilberforce, speaking in the same case, said that 'an unenforceable obligation is still an obligation which may be onerous'.

19.6.4 Investigations and information

The Revenue's various sources of information are summarised at **16.9**, along with comments on the type of investigation which might take place. Deliberate use of a company registered offshore in order to disguise liability to IR35 is likely to be treated as at least avoidance and possibly evasion.

19.7 Partnerships

19.7.1 Residence

The official Revenue view is that because an English partnership is not a legal person, it has no residence. However they acknowledge that:

> 'There has been some nibbling away of the principle that a partnership does not have a residence (because) the concept of residence and partnerships appears in ... sections of the Taxes Acts.' (ITH 1609)

In practice they seem to accept that a partnership is resident where it is controlled and managed, and this approach was supported by *Padmore v CIR* [1989] 62 TC 352.

When considering where a partnership with both United Kingdom and overseas partners is controlled and managed, they say that:

> 'We would usually regard as significant such factors as the comparative seniority of the partners in age and experience (a simple head count will not do of course), the extent of their interests in the firm, the source and control of the finance, the places of decision on policy and major transactions, the places and locations of partners' meetings and what was done at those meetings. The place of meetings incidentally is not a conclusive factor any more than it is – or ought to be – for companies. So the nature of the business done at the meeting is important. Is it really about control and management or just part of a facade to mislead us about the place of actual control and management?' (ITH 1612)

If a partnership is controlled and managed wholly abroad, and the UK partner is either not domiciled or not ordinarily resident, he will be taxed on profits earned in the UK and only on overseas profits if they are remitted (s112 ICTA 1988), see **17.13**.

Where there is uncertainty as to whether or to what extent control and management is exercised in the UK, the position becomes complex and beyond the scope of this book. However, the Revenue's International Tax Handbook at paragraph 1617ff has an interesting discussion of the technical issues.

19.7.2 PAYE and NIC obligations

A partnership which is controlled and managed in the UK is regarded as within the UK Taxes Acts and so must apply PAYE and NIC to the deemed payment.

A partnership which is controlled and managed wholly overseas may still have a trading presence in the UK and thus be within ss203ff ICTA 1988, see **19.3** above. If there is no trading presence, the deeming provisions of Schedule 12, para 11(6) FA 2000 set out at **19.5** above come into play, as they apply to 'intermediaries' not simply to companies.

Thus a partner or employee of an overseas partnership, who is himself resident in the UK and carries on a relevant engagement here, will bring the partnership within the PAYE and NIC deduction rules as far as the deemed Schedule E payment is concerned.

The same issues regarding client responsibilities, and enforcement of the regulations, apply to partnerships as they do to companies, see **19.5.2**, **19.5.3** and **19.6** above.

19.8 Summary

The position of an overseas company in the context of IR35 can be summarised as follows:

(a) Most PSCs with UK resident directors will themselves be UK resident, because they are managed and controlled here, even if they are registered overseas. They will thus be legally required to operate PAYE and NICs on any salary and benefits as well as on the deemed payment;

(b) If the company is non-resident, but has a trading presence here, it is obliged to operate PAYE and NICs as if it were UK resident;

(c) If the company has no trading presence, it will be treated as having such a presence for the purposes of the PAYE and NICs on the deemed payment, but only if the client is in the UK and the worker is resident here;

(d) In any other situation responsibility for PAYE or NICs rests with the client.

20 Particular businesses

20.1 Introduction

Service companies are common throughout the economy. The Inland Revenue's February 2001 *Tax Bulletin* said:

> 'There is a common misconception that IR35 only applies to people working in the IT sector. This is not correct. Examples of occupations where people work through service companies run right across the board, including medical staff, chief executives of large pls, legal and accountancy staff, construction industry workers, clerical workers, press officers, night club bouncers and many others.'

This chapter summarises the key issues affecting the provision of personal services by some of these specialised businesses. It should be read in the context of the general rules discussed in the rest of this book.

20.2 Actors and entertainers

20.2.1 General

Personal service companies are widely used in the media and performing arts. However IR35 only applies to those who would be employees if they did not have the 'wrapper' of a company or partnership. Thus the first question is whether the actor or entertainer would have been self-employed had he operated as an individual rather than via an intermediary. The answer may not be the same for tax as it is for National Insurance, because of the existence of NIC provisions deeming certain actors to be employees.

20.2.2 Tax: employed or self-employed?

Actors and entertainers have for many years fought the Revenue on issues of status. The Revenue succeeded in the case of *Fall v Hitchen* [1972] 49 TC 433 and in *Warner Holidays v Secretary of State for Social Services* [1983] ICR 440, but the taxpayer won the right to be taxed as Schedule D in *Davies v Braithwaite* [1933] 18 TC 198.

In 1989 the Revenue announced that it was recategorising actors who had standard Equity contracts as employees, with an amnesty for those who had been Schedule D for the previous three years (ESC A75). This blanket recategorisation was successfully challenged by Alec McCowen and Sam West in 1993, who convinced the Special Commissioners they were self-employed.

After this defeat the Revenue retreated, and have now accepted that 'Schedule D assessment of a performer's/artist's earnings will normally be appropriate ... (they) will generally be assessable under Schedule D as a matter of law rather than concession' (IM 1810; ESM 4121-2). The Revenue have also accepted that the same treatment should be accorded to stage managers, who usually have Equity contracts, see ESM 4124. The terms of the standard Equity contract are interesting and are set out at **8.5.2**. In the author's view it is unlikely that a similar contract in another industry would be classed as outside IR35 by the Revenue, which leads one to wonder whether the current 'status tests' are being applied even-handedly across the population.

Because of the *McCowen and West* case, most actors and musicians should fall outside the personal services rules on first principles – they would not be employees if the intermediary did not exist.

However the Revenue have not completely abandoned the old case of *Fall v Hitchen*. They state that they continue to believe that Schedule E applies:

> 'Where a performer/artist is engaged for a regular salary to perform in a series of different productions over a period of time, in such roles as may be from time to time stipulated by the engager, with a minimum period of notice before termination of the contract, as was Mr Hitchen in *Fall v Hitchen*. This would apply for example to permanent members of some orchestras and permanent members of an opera, ballet or theatre company.' (ESM 4121)

If such individuals work via an intermediate company or partnership, they should consider whether they are within the personal services rules. In particular, where some members of a theatre company are paid via PAYE, and others operate through service companies, failure to apply the personal service rules is likely to be challenged.

20.2.3 National Insurance: employed or self-employed?

Historically, the DSS took a more aggressive line than the Revenue over the status of actors, and considered that almost all were 'employed earners'. However, after the case of *McCowen and West*, see **20.2.2** above, the DSS finally admitted in Press Release 98/202 (15 July 1998) that its view that actors and musicians are generally employees could not be sustained.

Despite this, under SI 1998/1728 (followed by SI 1999/3) actors who are paid 'wholly or mainly by salary' were deemed to be employees for the purposes of employee Class 1 contributions from 17 July 1998. The Revenue have emphasised that if:

> 'The entertainer is remunerated wholly or mainly by salary all payments derived from that engagement, including those which viewed in isolation would not amount to a salary, will be liable to National Insurance Contributions.' (*Film Industry Guidance Notes* 2001)

This begs the question of what is meant by 'salary', as the fees paid to many self-employed actors are commonly called 'salary'. However, this deemed status as employed earners for NICs has generally been welcomed by the acting profession as it allows them to continue to claim jobseeker's allowance when they are 'resting'.

Where an actor who uses a personal service company is not regarded as an employee for tax purposes, but is deemed to be an employed earner for National Insurance purposes because he receives a 'salary', he will have to carry out an attributable earnings calculation to work out the Class 1 employee NICs on those earnings. There will also be secondary contributions due from the intermediary. The service company will however be liable only for the NICs and not for any PAYE, see **12.7.2**. For simplicity, the attributable earnings calculation continues to be referred to in the following paragraphs as the deemed Schedule E calculation.

20.2.4 Expenses and other reliefs

The purpose of the personal services legislation is to subject the worker to tax and NICs on income from his relevant engagements broadly on the basis that it is employment income. As a result, the tax reliefs for employee expenses are applicable, rather than the more generous Schedule D legislation. Chapter 11 discusses the expenses and reliefs available under IR35.

Actors and entertainers who are used to the 'wholly and exclusively' corporation tax rules for expenses will find that some costs are not deductible against their earnings from relevant engagements. These will of course continue to qualify for relief in the corporation tax computation, but this will be small comfort, as profits are likely to be negligible and losses are possible, see **13.7**.

Because of the narrowness of the Schedule E expenses rules, it is much more tax efficient if the costs are borne by the theatre or other engager, rather than by the service company. This is on the assumption that they represent genuine business costs for the engager and do not constitute a benefit to the worker.

Allowable expenses

Expenses which qualify for tax relief include:

(a) *Genuine business expenses borne by the engager.* Business expenses borne by the theatre are likely to be allowable as wholly and exclusively for the purposes of the engager's business. Such costs might include make-up, clothes, props and laundry;

(b) *Agents' fees.* Where income is paid to the service company net of agents' fees, the fees are automatically excluded from the deemed Schedule E calculation, see **21.2.1**. Where they are paid by the worker, they must meet the criteria for tax relief set out in s201A ICTA 1988 that:

- They are paid to an employment agency under a contract with the worker, or to a co-operative society which acts as agent for its members;
- The fee is calculated as a percentage of the income from the engagement;
- It is deducted from earnings in the same fiscal year as those earnings are brought into tax;
- The maximum deduction is 17.5 per cent (inclusive of VAT) of the fees earned in the fiscal year;

(c) *Travel expenses.* Actors are often reimbursed their home to work travel, and this is likely to be allowable under the travel rules, see **11.6**. There may also be reliefs for travel abroad, or for overseas entertainers coming to the UK, see **17.10.3** and **17.12.4**;

(d) *Pensions.* The personal services rules allow a deduction from relevant income for employer contributions to an approved pension, see **12.2**. The deemed Schedule E amount qualifies as net relevant earnings for pension purposes.

20.2.5 Expenses disallowable in the deemed Schedule E computation

Expenses which actors could deduct in their service companies but which are not allowed against their deemed Schedule E income include:

- Make-up, hairdressing, wardrobe and props, though under standard Equity contracts these are generally provided by the engager;
- Costs of attending interviews and auditions;
- Advertising, photography and tuition;

- Laundry, gratuities and postage;

- Professional publications such as *The Stage*;

- Equity subscriptions;

- Scripts, theatre and cinema tickets;

- Compact discs and cassettes.

20.2.6 Overseas issues

General

Chapter 17 discusses the effect of IR35 on workers who come to the UK from abroad and the consequences of taking up overseas engagements. Actors and entertainers are, however, subject to special rules.

Most workers are taxed on the basis of their residence, and double tax treaties prevent them suffering tax in more than one jurisdiction at a time. However most agreements provide that income derived by entertainers may be taxed in the country where the activities are exercised, rather than in the country where they are tax resident (see OECD Model Agreement, Article 17). Because of the difficulty in assessing and collecting the tax, withholding regimes are commonplace.

Overseas entertainers working in the UK

In the UK a withholding regime deducts basic rate tax from any payments made to a non-resident entertainer for performance, recording or promotional purposes (ss555–7 ICTA 1988; SI 1987/530).

This withholding applies whether or not the payment is made to a self-employed individual or to a service company. The legislation requires the payer to withhold tax 'where a payment is made to whatever person' (s555(2) ICTA 1988).

Where an overseas entertainer is subject to this withholding regime, he is exempted from the personal services legislation (Sch 12, para 6 FA 2000).

UK entertainers working overseas

A withholding regime also operates in many overseas countries, and it is generally a final tax, so that it discharges any fiscal liability the individual may have in that territory. Where the actor operates via a service company, withholding taxes may still be levied, though this varies depending on the territory.

Any tax deducted relates to income which legally belongs to the service company, not to the individual. In the UK, credit for the foreign tax withheld is thus due against the corporation tax payable by the company on its profits, rather than against the income tax on the salary or on the individual's deemed Schedule E payment.

However, the Inland Revenue have agreed that relief may be given against the individual's Schedule E income, although a specific claim to Revenue Head Office is required. They say that this may apply where:

> 'The foreign tax is imposed in a personal capacity on the entertainer etc. notwithstanding that the performance payments are made to the service company ... If it is possible to directly link the performance in the overseas country and the income arising to the performer in the form of remuneration from the service company then it may be that the remuneration derived by the entertainer can be identified with the income taxed by the foreign tax authority.' (DTRM 905)

A version of this double tax relief is now available to all those with personal service companies, but it applies only where the service company has insufficient UK corporation tax to absorb the foreign tax withheld, see **17.10.2**. The DTRM was not amended following the introduction of IR35, and it therefore appears that entertainers can continue to take advantage of the more generous relief set out therein.

20.3 Directors

20.3.1 Social changes

In recent years the number of non-executive and temporary directors operating via service companies has grown considerably, in part as a result of corporate restructuring, 'delayering' and cost-cutting. More positively, there has also been a shift towards 'portfolio careers' where individuals combine a number of non-executive directorships with some consultancy work.

20.3.2 Employed or self-employed?

A director is an officeholder, and by definition chargeable under Schedule E (s19(1) ICTA 1988). However, the IR35 tax legislation only applies if 'the worker would be regarded for income tax purposes as an *employee* of the client' (Sch 12, para 1(c) FA 2000, the author's italics); it does not apply to officeholders as such.

It is thus necessary to look at the hypothetical contract between the individual and the client. If the individual would have been a director, but not an employee, if the intermediary did not exist, then he will not be within Schedule 12. This has been confirmed by the Revenue in FAQ Director 2. Thus someone who provides services as a non-executive director to a client will be within IR35 for NICs but not for tax. Other examples of this scenario are discussed in **12.7**.

However, the position is different for NICs. This is because the regulations apply where:

> 'The worker would be regarded for the purposes of Parts I to V of the Contributions and Benefits Act as employed in employed earner's employment by the client.' (SI 2000/727 reg 6).

Under s2(1)(a) SSCBA 1992 an 'employed earner' means a person who is 'gainfully employed in Great Britain either under a contract of service, or in an office with emoluments chargeable to income tax under Schedule E'. If the intermediary did not exist, the individual would thus clearly fall within Schedule E in respect of director's fees received. He is thus within IR35 for NICs, and an attributable earnings calculation must be carried out.

Non-executive directors are office holders and not employees, so they are within IR35 for NICs but not for tax. There is however an exception for certain fees received by professional partnerships, while in other cases it may be possible to split the contracts so that only part is subject to NICs. These are both discussed below.

The position for an executive director is more complex. He may of course be fully within IR35 for both tax and NICs. However he may be able to argue either that all the work is provided as a director, or that he is operating in a dual capacity.

All work carried out as a director

An individual may seek to argue that all his services are provided to the client in his capacity as a director, and not as a worker or employee. A similar approach has been accepted by the DTI in respect of the National Minimum Wage (NMW), see **22.2.2**. They have agreed that where a director does not have an explicit contract of employment he is not a worker, and is thus outside the NMW.

However, since IR35 is concerned with hypothetical contracts and not actual contracts, the NMW solution (i.e., not having an explicit contract) is not available. Each individual must thus consider whether he would have a hypothetical contract of employment with the client in addition to his directorship, if there was no intermediary. If there would have been such a contract, then IR35 will apply for both NICs and tax.

Dual capacity

If the individual's work for the client can be divided between his role as a director and that as a consultant, and he can show that he would be self-employed as a consultant if the company did not exist, then:

- IR35 does not subject the fees received as a director to PAYE because he has not received them as a worker;
- IR35 NICs will apply to the fees received as a director because he is a deemed employee for NICs;
- Neither NICs nor PAYE will apply to fees received in a consulting capacity.

For example, a professional adviser on supply chain management who is a non-executive director of a client company may also supply advice to that client on his specialist area and he would not be within IR35 in respect of the consultancy work.

Where this situation arises, it is recommended for simplicity that the consultancy work be severed from the directorship so that two contracts are set up between the service company and the client, one of which describes the director's duties and associated remuneration, while the second describes the other services to be provided, along with the fees to be charged.

Professional partnerships

Where directors' fees are received by partners, Extra-Statutory Concession A37 may allow them to be excluded from Schedule E. The concession applies where:

- The partners have received the fees as a normal incidence of their profession;
- The amounts are small in the context of the firm's business; and
- The fees are brought into the firm's profit pool.

This is discussed further at **14.3**. Exemption is also available from National Insurance on the same basis (SI 1979/591 reg 19B).

Although there is a Revenue practice (SE 03001-3, see **14.3**), which allows sole traders as well as partners to treat a small amount of employment income as if it were Schedule D, this concessionary treatment is specifically not extended to directors' fees. Only professional partnerships are accorded this particular privilege.

20.4 IT contractors

20.4.1 The Professional Contractors Group (PCG)

Led by Andy White, Kevin Miller and the Professional Contractors Group (PCG), IT contractors have been unrelenting in their attacks on IR35. Articulate, well-organised, independent and highly computer-literate, their campaign has been both formidable and unprecedented, culminating in the judicial review case, see *R v CIR (oao Professional Contractors Group Ltd)* [2001] STC 629 – see **2.4**. In the course of the judgment Mr Justice Burton said he was 'satisfied that the effect of the [IR35] legislation will be most heavily felt in those sectors which have substantially fed the membership of the PCG'.

Following the unsuccessful appeal against Mr Justice Burton's decision, the PCG are now considering one or more representative cases in the IT and 'knowledge based' area, in order to clarify the line between employment and self-employment (*PCG Press release 21 December 2001*). In the meantime a number of IR35 cases involving IT contractors have come before the courts, and these are discussed at **8.6**.

20.4.2 Employed or self-employed?

Some contractors, reviewing the status tests set out at Chapter 6, will find it difficult to avoid the conclusion that they fall within the new legislation. They work fixed hours over a long period with an open-ended contract under the direct control and management of the client's IT manager, and are generally indistinguishable from employees except for their higher rate of pay and lack of employment rights. An example of such a worker is Gordon, Example 1 in *Tax Bulletin* 45, see **25.2.2**.

At the other end of the scale are individuals with a business organisation, who work on a project basis, and have a highly marketable skill. They might be specialist designers of websites, or operate 'computer hacking' programs as part of a security review programme. They probably fall outside the personal services rules. Henry is the Revenue's model of a self-employed IT contractor, see **25.2.3**.

A third group of individuals are in the 'grey area' between employment and self-employment. An example is 'Charlotte' in *Tax Bulletin 45*, see **25.2.4**. Some have adjusted to IR35, while others have changed the way they work, so they fall outside the legislation. Ideas as to how this might be done are given in Chapter 9. Some particular points are highlighted below.

Standard contracts

The Revenue have reviewed the standard contracts used in the IT industry, and have concluded that those who work in the manner required by these contracts will usually be within IR35. See **7.6** above for further discussion of this issue.

Working as a professional

Some IT contractors may be able to argue for self-employment on the basis that they are professionals, exercising a skill, and moving from contract to contract as part of this profession. Despite the fact that they generally do not take financial risk, are employed on an hourly basis, are subject to some degree of control by the client, and provide little, if any equipment, they may still be within Schedule D, see **8.2** and **8.5** above.

Advice and solutions

It is recommended that individuals in the 'grey area' between Schedule D and Schedule E take advice on their status, either from the Revenue or from a tax adviser. The latter may also help the worker review ways of improving his position. An assumption that one is 'in the clear' may be dangerous, and prove costly if the company experiences an employer compliance review, with attendant interest and possibly penalties, see **16.9**. Individuals in this uncertain position may be able to insure themselves against the risk of a Revenue investigation into their status; as with all insurance, the exact terms and coverage should be closely studied.

20.4.3 Expenses

Where IT contractors fall within IR35, the expenses they can claim against their deemed Schedule E income are more restricted than those which are allowable in a company, see **11.3**. However, they remain entitled to a number of deductions and reliefs. These are discussed at **11.4** and are briefly summarised below.

Disallowable costs

Disallowable costs include:

(a) *Secretarial support.* Many contractors with service companies previously paid their spouse or partner a small salary for keeping the business records and taking client bookings. If the worker carries out only relevant engagements, and continues to pay his spouse, the salary will effectively be paid out of taxed income, see FAQ Employee 2. However, there may be minimum wage issues if the spouse is not paid, see **22.2.2**. If, on the other hand, the work involved in managing the contractor's work-flow, liaising with clients and dealing with invoicing/bad debts is significant, it may indicate that the contractor is in business on his own account, and can thus escape IR35;

(b) *Training.* This is only allowable if, improbably, it is borne by the client, see **11.8**;

(c) *Equipment.* This is discussed fully at **7.4.5** and **6.6.2**. The Revenue have set out their view on computer equipment owned by IT workers as follows:

'A deduction will only be given for capital allowances in working out the deemed payment where the plant or machinery is necessarily provided for use in the performance of the duties of the relevant engagement. This is a strict test and means that relief will only be given where the duties of the engagement meant that the company had to provide the equipment in question. If the company purchases the equipment out of choice then no deduction will be given. For example, where an IT contractor is required to use the client's computer equipment then no relief will be due for expenditure on computers owned by the service company. Neither will any relief be due where the client makes all the equipment necessary to do a job available but the worker uses his or her own computers, out of choice.' (FAQ Computation 7).

Note, however, that an IT consultant who 'must work exclusively at home using the worker's own computer equipment' may be self-employed and thus fall outside IR35 altogether' (*Tax Bulletin 45*, and see **11.12.2**);

(d) *Home as office costs.* Contractors have traditionally claimed part of the costs of heating, lighting and furnishing their homes on the grounds that their company is based there. These expenses are only allowable against their Schedule E earnings if they meet the stringent s198 ICTA 1988 test, see **11.11**. If the worker has only relevant engagements, the allowability of such costs in the corporation tax computation may also be questioned, see **11.3.6**.

Allowable costs

(a) *Travel.* Contractors' travel to the clients' sites is allowable for tax, assuming it meets the conditions described in **11.6**. This remains the case whether or not the expenses are reimbursed by the client.

However, the service company should reimburse the costs rather then them being borne by the worker personally, as this will allow them to be deducted in the deemed Schedule E computation and thus reduce the NIC due, see **11.3.3**;

(b) *Subsistence.* The tax treatment of subsistence follows that of travel. Where travel is allowable, so to is the cost of food, drink and accommodation taken during the journeys, see Example 20A (adapted from IR490 1:11).

Example 20A

Austin is an installation engineer who works at the premises of various clients throughout the United Kingdom. One week he travels between his home in Dover (where his service company is based) to a client's office in Gloucester, staying in a hotel for four nights and, then returning to Dover. The cost of the return journey is £130. The cost of subsistence (four nights in the hotel plus meals) is £300. Austin is entitled to relief for the full cost of his business travel, £430.

(c) *Overseas travel.* Where a UK resident and ordinary resident contractor goes overseas for an engagement lasting at least 60 consecutive days, tax relief is available not only for the costs of his travel and subsistence, but also for two return journeys made by his spouse and children, see **17.10**. This relief applies whether or not the family's journeys are reimbursed by the client. To be allowable the costs must be borne or reimbursed by the service company;

(d) *Call-out costs.* Where an IT specialist is on stand-by and he is reimbursed his travel costs when called out, this will be allowable on the same principle as other travel costs;

(e) *Professional indemnity insurance.* This is an allowable expense under s201AA ICTA 1988, see **11.10**;

(f) *Personal incidental expenses.* An amount of £5 a night (£10 for overseas engagements) when the individual is away from home overnight, is allowed to cover minor personal costs such as laundry and mini-bars. If reimbursed costs exceed this, they are however taxable in full, see **11.7**.

20.5 Musicians

20.5.1 General

Much of **20.2** above on actors applies also to musicians, who are equally likely to have personal service companies. In addition musical groups are sometimes considered to be a partnership for tax purposes, and these may also fall within the new rules.

20.5.2 Employed or self-employed?

The engagement may be under any of the following arrangements:

(a) Musicians engaged under 'first call' or 'guarantee' contracts. These give the orchestra the right to call on the musician's services, but then limit this demand so that they may undertake other work. The musicians are paid separately for each performance. These contracts are accepted by the Revenue as self-employment (ESM 4140);

This follows *Addison and others v The London Philharmonic Orchestra Society Limited* [1981] ICR 261 and *Midland Sinfonia Concert Society Limited v The Secretary of State for Social Services* [1981] ICR 454. In both cases the court held that the workers remained essentially freelance musicians pursuing their own professions as instrumentalists with individual reputations even when playing for an orchestra. They were thus self-employed even though they did not have their own business structure or risk their own capital, see **6.5.3**;

(b) Musicians who are shareholders in the major London orchestras are self-employed. This is because these orchestras are run by the members themselves, who are thus co-operating in the business;

(c) The Revenue accept that orchestral players who are paid separately for each performance and are not guaranteed a minimum amount of work by an orchestra are self-employed (ESM 4140);

(d) Musicians who are engaged under standard Musicians Union contracts to play at concerts, pantomimes and musicals are treated as self-employed, in the same way as actors under Equity contracts, see **20.2.2** above;

(e) Musicians who are permanent members of major orchestras are generally taxable under Schedule E on the authority of *Fall v Hitchen* [1972] 49 TC 433, see **20.2.2** above. See also *Warner Holidays Ltd v Secretary of State for Social Services* [1983] ICR 440, where two musicians were held to be employed earners because (in contrast to session musicians) Warner had full and exclusive control over them and paid them fixed salaries.

However it should be noted that, like actors, see **20.2.3**, musicians who are self-employed for tax purposes may be employed earners for NICs, as the regulations cover 'entertainers' and not merely actors. Thus a musician with a PSC who falls outside IR35 for tax purposes will nevertheless be required to carry out an attributable earnings calculation if he receives a 'salary' (SI 1978/1689 reg 1(2)). Having a liability for NICs but not for PAYE is discussed at **12.7.2**.

20.5.3 Royalty companies

Groups of musicians sometimes operate through a two tier structure, where each musician has his own PSC, and the PSCs jointly own a royalty/management company. All group engagements are obtained through the management company, which also collects and distributes royalties relating to the group's records. The PSC contracts with the royalty company to supply the services of the musicians.

If the services were being supplied by the PSCs directly to the end-users, the musicians would be self-employed. However, the interposition of the management company may create a technical problem:

(a) The musicians are supplying services to the management company via their PSCs, and there is thus an intermediary (the PSC) and a client (the management company);

(b) The contract between the PSC and the management company to supply the personal services of the musician is likely to contain elements which are characteristic of a contract of service. For instance, the musicians may work exclusively for the management company and be subject to its direction and control;

(c) It is thus arguable that the musicians are supplying services for the business of the management company, and are thus within the scope of Sch 12, FA 2000.

This would be an anomalous result, as the musicians are self-employed when they actually deliver their services to the end-user. It is hoped that the Revenue will not take this technical point. However, it is nevertheless recommended that the contractual arrangements between the PSCs and the management company should be reviewed to ensure they do not represent an 'employment' relationship.

20.5.4 Other points

The same issues concerning expenses and double tax reliefs apply to musicians as they do to actors, see **20.2**. For partnerships, see Chapter 14.

20.6 Oil and gas workers

20.6.1 General

Few North Sea oil and gas operators have many employees. Instead, they use flexible teams of workers each of whom has his own personal service company. Mr Doran MP described their position as follows:

> 'A large proportion of people now employed *(sic)* in the oil industry are contracted. The industry uses them to provide flexibility for the bad times. For example, at the beginning of last year, when the oil price almost halved overnight ... the redundancies were almost invisible because contractors were simply shaken out of the industry. Their contracts were terminated. All the contractors who stayed ... were forced to take substantial cuts, some as high as 20 per cent, which were imposed by the oil companies across the board with no questions asked. That was the requirement if people wanted to keep a contract. Contracts are written in a way that ensures oil companies have the power to do that. It gives the oil industry flexibility and that is the price that people who work in the oil industry have to pay.' (*Hansard* 3 May 2000, Col. 197)

20.6.2 Employed or self-employed?

Service companies became ubiquitous in the oil and gas industry after the Revenue won the case of *Clark v Oceanic Contractors Incorporated* [1982] 56 TC 183, in which the House of Lords held by a 3:2 majority that Oceanic had sufficient presence in the UK to be required to operate PAYE. This applied not only to the remuneration of employees working within the UK sector of the Continental Shelf, but also to employees working from barges in other non-UK sectors. As a result the operators' PAYE responsibilities were significantly extended.

Service companies were thus established at least in part to avoid PAYE, and many of the workers are therefore likely to fall within IR35. The standard contracts supplied by the operators or agencies have many elements which make them similar to employment contracts.

However, in some cases the standard industry contract has been accepted as a matter of convenience by the worker, and may not reflect the reality of the relationship between the service company and the client, see **7.6**. This is particularly the case where an individual is engaged for a relatively short period to carry out specialist skilled work.

Specifically, divers and diving supervisors are accepted by the Revenue as self-employed where they work as individuals (s314 ICTA 1988), and thus will fall outside the personal services legislation for tax purposes if they operate via a company. However, section 314 does not have effect for NICs, and thus to see whether an attributable earnings calculation is needed, the status of a diver should be established by applying the usual case law tests, see ESM 4050. Having an attributable earnings calculation but no deemed Schedule E is discussed at **12.7**.

20.6.3 Residence status and personal services rules

Outline of tax residence rules

The normal rules for tax residence are discussed in Chapter 17, and can be summarised as follows:

- *Resident and ordinarily resident*: taxed in the UK on all his earnings, wherever the work is performed;

- *Not resident*: taxed on work 'performed in the United Kingdom' (s19(1) ICTA 1988), but may be able to argue that it escapes tax either because it is 'merely incidental' to the overseas work, or because of a double tax treaty;

- *Resident but not ordinarily resident*: taxed on work carried out in the UK, but earnings from work done elsewhere are not within the scope of UK tax unless they are remitted here;

- *Resident and ordinarily resident but not domiciled*: taxed on all work carried out in the UK, and on work carried out overseas for a UK employer. Earnings from work carried out wholly overseas for a foreign employer are taxed on the remittance basis.

Extended boundary of UK for tax purposes

Most drilling work takes place outside the UK's territorial waters, and oil and gas workers operating in the North Sea are thus likely to be classified as not resident or not ordinarily resident. Under the normal rules for the taxation of earnings set out above, they would thus escape UK tax. To prevent this, s830(5) ICTA 1988 extends the boundary of the United Kingdom so that it covers any 'UK designated areas of the Continental Shelf'. The personal services worker is thus potentially within the scope of IR35 as respects tax on his earnings from a client located within a designated area.

The service company itself is also likely to be within the UK for tax purposes, if this would not otherwise be the case (s830(1) ICTA 1988, see Chapter 19); it is therefore responsible for PAYE in relation to the deemed income.

Interaction between extended boundary and tax residence rules

This extension operates only to tax the earnings of oil or gas contractors from work in the designated area as if they were resident and ordinarily resident in the UK. It does not actually change the workers' residence status. As a result the taxation of any other earnings, income, gains or assets is unaffected.

In particular the extended boundary rule does not affect the test of whether a person is absent from the UK. If he or she is outside the 12-mile limit at the end of a particular day that day is a day of absence (SE 33034). This is important because, in establishing whether an individual is resident, non-resident or not ordinarily resident, the number of days spent in the UK can be critical, see **17.6**.

In addition, following *Clark v Perks* [2001] STC 1254, the Revenue have accepted that, for years up to and including 17 March 1988, a jack-up rig was classed as a ship, and thus those working on it could take advantage of the more favourable Foreign Earnings Deduction rule to reduce their tax bills (Sch 12, para 3(2A) ICTA 1988 and s192A(3)(a) ICTA 1988).

Summary of tax position where worker has some non-UK income

Where workers have earnings from non-UK sources, they may be able to protect these earnings from UK tax in general, and the deemed income computation in particular, as follows:

- *Not ordinarily resident in the UK*: earnings from outside the designated areas which are not remitted to the UK will fall outside the deemed income computation;

- *Resident and ordinarily resident, but not domiciled*: can exclude his unremitted overseas earnings from his deemed income computation as long as his contract is with an overseas company and his work for that company is wholly outside the UK (including the designated areas). Where income is excluded from UK tax, however, it may be taxable in another territory, possibly at a higher rate;

- *Non-resident under normal rules, but operates in the designated areas*: may fall within UK tax because of the operation of s830. He may be able to claim the benefit of a double tax treaty, see **20.6.4** below; in addition any non-UK earnings which do not fall within s830 will be outside UK tax because he is not resident here;

- *Resident and ordinarily resident in UK but operates outside the designated areas*: may be taxed by a foreign government under the provisions of a double tax treaty, such as the UK/Norway treaty, see **20.6.4**. This would take those earnings out of the deemed income calculation but the worker may subsequently suffer foreign tax.

National Insurance

The rules for National Insurance are as follows:

- The 'designated area' rules apply to an individual's NIC position as they do for tax (SI 2001/1004 reg 114);

- The designated area rules only apply to treat a worker as an employee for NIC purposes; they do not deem the employer to be within Great Britain. In non-IR35 cases the employer may thus have no UK presence and not be required to operate National Insurance. However, if the *worker* is within UK NICs, the special rules for IR35 make the personal service company liable for secondary contributions, see SI 2000/721, reg 6(3)(b);

- Where a worker is outside the deemed income calculation for tax, for instance because he is operating outside a designated area, he does not necessarily escape the NIC charge, see Chapter 18. Where a worker is within IR35 for NICs but not for tax, an attributable earnings calculation will be required, see **18.5**;

- The operation of National Insurance differs depending on whether the individual is covered by EEA agreements or by a bilateral social security treaty, see Chapter 18. The UK has agreed with Norwegian and Dutch social security authorities that the designated areas are not classed as within the EEA, and thus workers in these areas are subject to the UK/Norway or UK/Netherlands reciprocal agreements rather than to EEA rules. However, the UK and Denmark have agreed to include the designated areas within the EEA. For the interaction with Norway, see **20.6.4**.

20.6.4 Foreign tax and double tax relief

A worker from overseas who operates both in UK territorial waters and in those of his home country may be exempted from UK tax because a double tax treaty deems him to be resident in his home country rather than in the UK. Where this is the case, he will also fall outside the Schedule E provisions of the personal services legislation, which say that:

> 'The worker is not chargeable to tax in respect of the deemed Schedule E payment if, or to the extent that the worker (is) resident, ordinarily resident or domiciled outside the United Kingdom.' (Sch 12, para 11(3) FA 2000)

However, care is needed. Some double tax treaties do not include the Continental Shelf in their definition of the UK, and thus the workers may remain within Schedule E because of the operation of s830, see **20.6.3** and SE 67125. For the NICs position, see **20.6.3** and Chapter 18.

Where foreign tax is suffered on income which is brought into the deemed Schedule E computation, the tax may be allowable against the PAYE on the deemed salary, see **17.10.2**.

Norway

Where a UK resident and ordinarily resident worker operates in Norwegian territorial waters, the UK/Norway double tax treaty provides that he is taxable only in Norway on earnings derived from that work. These earnings will thus be excluded from the deemed income calculation, but at the price of paying Norwegian taxes.

The UK resident worker may, however, not be within the Norwegian social security system but instead remain within UK NICs, see **18.3** and EPM 8231. Even where his Norwegian earnings are excluded from the deemed income calculation because of the double tax treaty, they need to be included when calculating his attributable earnings, see **18.3.5**.

Conversely, where a Norwegian is working in UK territorial waters, he is within the scope of UK tax, and thus the personal services regime applies to him. However, he is likely to remain within his home country social security system. Where this is the case he has a deemed Schedule E calculation, but no attributable earnings, see **18.4.5**.

20.6.5 Reporting requirements

The oil companies submit quarterly returns to the Revenue's Oil Taxation Office under Sch 15, para 2 FA 1973. The Revenue's *Oil Taxation Office Section 830 Manual* says, at paragraph 7.7.1, that:

> '(These) returns are the Oil Taxation Office's primary source of information about payments made to persons not resident in the United Kingdom which may give rise to a liability to corporation tax under ICTA 1988 s830.'

If it appears that there may be an undisclosed PAYE liability, relevant data from these returns is passed to Special Compliance Office. It is also likely to be used to help police IR35.

20.6.6 Travel expenses

Travel is a major cost for oil and gas workers, because their home base is often far from their place of work. A concession relieves them from tax on the cost of travel from the mainland to the rigs (ESC A65). It was expected that the travel rules introduced in 1998 (now included in s 198(1A)(b)(ii) and Sch 12A ICTA 1988) would ensure that workers obtained relief for their home to work travel for the part of their journey not covered by ESC A65, provided the standard two year/40 per cent tests were met, see **11.6.3** and *Tolleys Practical Tax* 29 July 1998. It was also accepted by the Revenue that if the rig itself moved, this amounted to a change of location, see *Tolleys Practical Tax* 23 September 1998.

However Sch 12A, para 5(3) ICTA 1988 says that there is no tax relief if a change in location 'does not have ... any substantial effect on the employee's journey, or expenses of travelling, to and from the place where the duties fall to be performed'.

Some inspectors have been reluctant to accept that a change of location from one rig to another, even one a hundred miles distant from the last, was 'substantial' in the context of the worker's total journey. This has been challenged by those affected, on the basis that:

- Substantial is an absolute as well as a relative term; and

- Tax relief is given for changes in location of other taxpayers, where the distances involved were tiny in comparison. Equity between taxpayers is a relevant factor here.

If the Revenue succeed, oil workers will be disadvantaged when compared to other personal service workers.

Where the worker travels to a rig outside the UK's continental shelf, he will however be going 'abroad' and thus may qualify for the reliefs set out in ss193–4 ICTA 1988, see **17.10**. He will then be able to claim the cost of all his travel from the UK to the rig, even if it is not allowed under normal rules, and this will be deductible at Step Three of his deemed Schedule E calculation.

Similarly, a non-domiciled worker from abroad who satisfies the requirements of s195 ICTA (**17.12.4**) may be allowed relief in his deemed Schedule E calculation for the costs of his travel to and from a rig in the Continental Shelf, as this is regarded as part of the UK for Schedule E purposes, see SE 35080.

Other expenses

The Revenue accept that protective clothing worn as a matter of physical necessity because of the nature of the job, such as oil workers' overalls, are allowable under s198 ICTA 1988, see **11.5**.

20.7 Sportspeople

20.7.1 General

From a tax perspective, sports men and women have much in common with actors and entertainers, see **20.2**, particularly when they work overseas. However, there are some significant differences. In particular, some cannot be employees of their service companies in respect of their main activity, because the regulations of their sport require them to have a contract of service with their club. They can thus only use a service company or partnership for sponsorship and similar activities.

20.7.2 Employed or self-employed?

Schedule E income

Professional footballers are required by Football League rules to sign a contract of personal service with their club, and the income from this contract is invariably Schedule E.

However, other amounts may be paid into the player's personal service company by the club for services provided in addition to those supplied under his employment contract. Before IR35 these payments were often challenged by the Revenue on the basis that they formed part of the player's remuneration. The Revenue are now likely to use the PSC rules.

Signing-on and transfer fees, payments for winning matches and loyalty bonuses all come within the scope of s19(1) ICTA 1988, see SE 64100ff. Benefit and testimonial matches may be outside the scope of Schedule E if they are not contractual (SE 64120). However if the testimonial or benefit match is 'expected or promised' the Revenue will hold that it is an implied term of the player's employment with the club and taxable under Schedule E. Monies from testimonials are not usually paid into a service company, as they are either outside the scope of tax, or taxable in any event under the player's employment contract.

Amateur players are not bound by the Football League rules, and thus are not required to have employment contracts with their clubs. The Revenue may nevertheless argue that they are employees. The Manual says:

> 'Where a payment or series of payments to a non-contract player appears to include a clear element of remuneration, for example appearance money, you should consider whether there is an oral or implied contract which makes the player an employee of the club ... You will also need to consider whether the terms of engagement of the player are similar to those applying to contract players. Other matters, such as the obligations imposed on keeping fit, training, availability for selection, times of reporting for matches, taking of instructions from managers and other officials, discipline and club rules and regulations generally may also be of relevance.' (SE 64145)

If a player had sought to protect himself from this sort of attack by using a service company, he will probably now fall within IR35, on the basis that he would have been an employee had he not operated via the company.

Professional cricketers and other sportspeople are also commonly under contract to their clubs, and their rewards from this contract are within Schedule E. Again, testimonials may be non-taxable, see SE 68400.

Sponsorship and promotional income

A sportsperson may have both an employment contract with his club, and an 'Image Contract' with his personal service company. The service company's objective is to exploit the player's name and likeness, and to collect fees for sponsorship and promotional activities. It may also own copyrights or trademarks relating to the player's activity.

In the context of IR35, the key question is whether the services provided under the Image Contract would be employments if the intermediary did not exist. In most cases the answer must be no. The service company is promoting the sports personality, not supplying quasi-employee services to a sponsor. Income received by the intermediary will therefore generally be outside the scope of the personal services legislation.

The recent case of *Sports Club v HM Inspector of Taxes (and related appeals)*, Sp C [2000] SSCD 443 provides support for this position. This has been anonymised but deals with a sports club (S) which recruited two international players (E and J), who had previously played for Southern European clubs. It was accepted that the players' salaries were emoluments of their employments, and were liable to PAYE. In addition, S entered into agreements with E and J's personal service companies Y and Z, under which the service companies agreed to provide certain promotional and consultancy services of the individuals.

In 1997 the Revenue challenged the payments to the service companies, and said that the sports club should have accounted for PAYE on these amounts. The Special Commissioners disagreed, holding that the promotional agreements were 'genuine commercial agreements' and not a 'smokescreen for the payment of additional remuneration'; the players were 'established stars ... capable of earning very substantial sums each year from commercial contracts'.

Rather surprisingly, this case was cited by *Tolleys Tax Cases 2001* as 'an example of the type of PAYE avoidance which the [IR35] provisions were designed to counter'. In fact IR35 would not change the decision, which was based on the fact that:

> 'The payments were made in return for promotional rights and consultancy services respectively and not in reference to the playing of games which was the service rendered by each player by virtue of his player's agreement with [the sports club].'

In other words, the individuals were not acting as employees or quasi-employees of the club when they carried out the promotional and consultancy services and thus would not have been within IR35 had it existed at the time.

However, this happy result is not always achievable. Where the worker supplies regular services via his PSC to a single client, such as spending three days a week coaching for a university team, this may be a relevant engagement and the income received may be within the scope of IR35.

20.7.3 Overseas issues

Most individuals are taxed on the basis of residence, and are protected by international treaties from suffering tax in more than one jurisdiction at a time. Sportspeople are however treated differently, and may be taxed in the country where the activities are exercised. In general, the rules applying to sportspeople are the same as those for actors, see **20.2.6** above. Relief is also available for foreign travel as described in **17.10.**

If an overseas sportsperson with a service company plays in the UK, he will be subject to the existing withholding tax rules under s555 ICTA 1988 and not to IR35 (Sch 12, para 6 FA 2000).

20.7.4 Pension schemes

As with other service companies brought within IR35, a deduction is available for pension contributions made by the intermediary in respect of the worker, see **12.2**. The contributions thus reduce the amount of PAYE and Class 1 NICs paid by the service company.

Many sportsmen and women are allowed to make an accelerated contributions into their pension scheme because their working life is shorter than that of the average person. In the context of the personal services legislation, the value of this may be substantial. The age at which retirement can be taken is as follows:

Age	Sport
30	Downhill skiers.
35	Athletes; badminton players; boxers; cyclists; dancers; footballers; National Hunt jockeys; real tennis players; Rugby League players; squash players; table tennis players; tennis players; wrestlers.
40	Cricketers; golfers; motorcycle riders (motocross or road racing); motor racing drivers; speedway riders; trapeze artistes.
45	Flat racing jockeys

20.8 Subcontractors

20.8.1 Introduction

Building industry subcontractors were previously treated as self-employed if they held a SC60 certificate allowing them to be paid gross by the main contractor. However, in the mid-1990s the Inland Revenue and the Contributions Agency launched a major assault on subcontractors, reclassifying many as employees. Some set up service companies in an effort to avoid recategorisation.

20.8.2 Recategorisation: the history

The first sign of an attack came with the publication in October 1995 of the booklet IR148/CA69: *Are your workers employed or self-employed? A Guide for Tax and National Insurance for contractors in the Construction Industry*. This was followed by new instructions to Inland Revenue and Contributions Agency auditors.

On a piecemeal basis, and subject to the randomness of the auditors' visits, many formerly 'self-employed' workers were recategorised as employees. However this scatter-gun approach was widely criticised, and the IR/CA finally announced that businesses would be given until 5 April 1997 to review the employment status of their workers (IRPR 19 November 1996). The Union of Construction, Allied Trades and Technicians (UCATT) have estimated that around 200,000 individuals were reclassified as employees as a result of this exercise.

An article in *Tax Bulletin 28* gave comfort by stating that, if properly managed, a service company would be an effective way of avoiding recategorisation. It confirmed that:

> 'A valid contract between two companies is not a contract of employment. However, IR and CA may want to check that the agreements are validly made, that they do in fact achieve the legal result that the parties intended and that the parties have acted in accordance with those agreements.'

In some cases clients and agencies, unsure of whether their subcontractors were inside or outside the rules for Schedule E, encouraged them to form limited companies. They thus avoided both responsibility for PAYE and the risks of a later recategorisation.

The final round: personal services?

The personal service legislation now catches those service companies established a few years ago in order to avoid Schedule E recategorisation. Those set up because of uncertainty about the worker's status can no longer avoid the issue.

Individuals with service companies should first review whether they would be employed or self-employed if they did not have a company, see Chapters 5 to 9. If they are within the personal services regime, they should become familiar with the interaction between the subcontractor rules and IR35, see **20.8.5**.

20.8.3 Employed or self-employed?

The tests to establish whether an individual is an employee are discussed in detail at Chapters 5 to 9. In particular, the case of *Lee Ting Sang v Chung Chi-Keung* [1990] 2 AC 374 should be reviewed, see **8.3.1**, in addition to the Revenue worked examples at **25.3**. The Employment Status Manual at para 4320ff further expands the Revenue position.

20.8.4 Use of partnerships

In their article on subcontractors the Revenue indicated that partnerships set up to avoid recategorisation could be ineffective:

> 'The existence of a contract between a contractor and a bona fide partnership will be a pointer towards self-employment. But the mere fact that a worker is a member of a partnership does not mean that he cannot be an employee. If the true nature of the contract between the worker and the contractor is one of employment, the contractor must account for PAYE and NICs on the remuneration paid. The fact that the worker may also be a member of a partnership is irrelevant.' (*Tax Bulletin 28*)

However where the contract is between the partnership and the client, rather than between the contractor and the client, the Revenue's legal advice is that it is not possible to redesignate the contract as one of employment. This type of arrangement would thus be effective in avoiding recategorisation as an employee.

Partnerships thus had to be brought within IR35, if only to prevent them replacing companies as the new tax-efficient vehicle – not only for subcontractors, but for all those who use personal service companies. The implications of IR35 for partnerships are discussed in Chapter 14.

20.8.5 Subcontractor tax deductions and the deemed income calculation

Subcontractors have their own tax arrangements under s559 ICTA 1988. In some cases they are paid net of tax by the main contractor, and this is then set against their tax liability for the year.

Where the subcontractor is a partnership or service company, the deduction is taken into account within the company's or partnership's computation. If too much tax has been deducted, this can be recovered once the computation for the year is final.

An individual working via a partnership or service company may be within both the personal services legislation and the subcontractor regime. However the tax already deducted under s559 ICTA 1988 is not taken into account when calculating the tax due on the Schedule E deemed payment:

> 'Where section 559 of the Taxes Act 1988 applies ... the intermediary is treated for the purposes of Step One of the calculation in paragraph 7 as receiving the amount that would have been received had no deduction been made under that section' (Sch 12, para 8 FA 2000).

Had nothing been done to change this position, subcontractors would have suffered a serious cashflow effect, as 18 per cent would have been deducted from their income before receipt, and both income tax and NICs would subsequently be deducted on the same money because of the personal services rules. After sustained pressure, a concession (ESC C32) was finally published by the Revenue on 4 April 2001, the day before the first IR35 deemed payment crystallised.

The effect of the concession is as follows. If a service company informs the Inland Revenue – when it sends in its end-of-year employer's return – that it wants to defer paying the tax due under the IR35 rules, it will be able to set the CIS repayment against the PAYE and NICs it owes. This means it will not have to pay two lots of tax.

Where such a claim is made (and accepted) then this extra statutory concession means that interest will not be charged on any late paid tax and NICs due under the IR35 rules. This is to the extent that the late paid tax and NICs are matched by the corporation tax repayment due to the company, up to the date of the repayment of the corporation tax.

Companies will need to include enough information in their claim to identify the amounts to be matched, including:

- Their accounting period(s);

- The amount of the CIS deductions to be matched;

- The serial numbers of the CIS25 vouchers, providing evidence of the dates and the deductions suffered;

- The date of the deemed payment calculation (if not 5 April); and

- The amount of PAYE and NICs to be matched.

Claims under this extra statutory concession in respect of tax and NICs due on 19 April 2001 under the IR35 rules must be made by 31 January 2002. For later tax years, at the time of writing it is understood that a similar effect will be achieved by a change in the legislation which will be included in Finance Act 2002.

There is, however, a problem with ESC C32 where the service company's year end is not co-terminous with the tax year. The difficulty is particularly acute with a 31 March year end, as follows:

- ESC C32 applies 'in respect of an accounting period which overlaps with a tax year for which a deemed payment is treated as made';

- The accounting period to 31 March 2001 overlaps with the tax year 2000/01 for which the first deemed payment is made;

- However, companies with a 31 March 2001 year end will not have their profits reduced by a deemed payment (it will be deducted in the following accounting period ending 31 March 2002, see **13.3**);

- Thus there may be no CIS repayment due to allow the ESC to run.

A change of accounting date, for instance to 5 April, has already been recommended to personal service companies for other reasons, see **13.4.6**, and this advice is doubly important for those in the subcontractor deduction scheme.

Example 20B shows the benefit of using the ESC, and the consequences if it is not claimed.

Example 20B

Dylan is a subcontractor working through his own limited company. His has two relevant engagements during the fiscal year 2001/02, and invoices his main contractor £100,000 in total, including materials of £6,000 and travel of £4,000.

He also has a further £5,000 in costs which are not allowable either under Schedule E or the subcontractor scheme, but are deductible for corporation tax.

Dylan is paid under deduction of tax by the main contractor. He has paid himself £18,000 in salary during the year. His corporation tax year end is 5 April. There is no difference between his accrued and received income or expenses.

His subcontractor position and deemed income calculation are as follows:

Part A: Subcontractor income

	Notes	£
Total invoiced		100,000
Less: materials	1	(6,000)
		94,000
Less 18%		(16,920)
Net receipt		77,080

Notes

1. Section 559 does not allow a deduction for travel.

Part B: Deemed Schedule E calculation

	Notes	£
Step One: Income received		100,000
5% allowance		(5,000)
Step Three: Allowable expenses	1	(10,000)
Step Six: Employer's NIC on salary paid	2	(1,602)
Step Seven: Salary paid		(18,000)
Income after expenses, salary and NIC on salary		65,398
Step Eight: NIC on deemed payment	3	(6,955)
Deemed Schedule E payment		58,443

Notes

1. It is assumed that the materials would be eligible for relief under s198 ICTA

2. £18,000 − 4,535 = 13,465 × 11.9% = 1,602

3. £65,398 × 11.9/111.9 = 6,955

Part C: Income tax and NIC calculation

	£	£	£
Salary			18,000
Deemed salary			58,443
Gross income			76,443
Personal allowance	4,535		
Tax at 10% on	1,880	188	
Tax at 22% on	27,520	6,054	
Tax at 40% on balance of	42,508	17,003	
	76,443		
Total tax due			23,245

Part D: Corporation tax computation

Turnover		100,000
Less: Travel	4,000	
Materials	6,000	
Employer's NIC (1,602 + 6,955)	8,557	
Other costs	5,000	
Salary and deemed salary	76,443	
		(100,000)
CT position		NIL

Part E: Tax and NIC suffered

Tax on subcontractor s559 deduction:	16,920
Tax on salary and deemed salary	23,245
Employer's NIC on salary and deemed salary	8,557
Employee's NIC on salary and deemed salary (maximum)	2,536
	51,258
Tax rate on net income after expenses of £85,000	60.3%
Tax recoverable when corporation tax computation agreed	16,920
True tax + NICs payable (23,245 + 8,557 + 2,536)	34,338
True tax + NICs rate	40.4%

If the benefit of the ESC is claimed, then Dylan will pay only £17,418 (£34,338 − £16,920) in respect of the tax and NICs arising from IR35; the balance will be met out of the subcontractor tax deductions.

Conclusion

The ESC, while not as good as a change to the legislation, does alleviate these hardships and subcontractors should ensure that they, or their advisers, complete the necessary paperwork to obtain the offset described above.

20.9 Teachers and lecturers

20.9.1 Introduction

Service companies have become increasingly common among teachers and lecturers, particularly where they are 'supply teachers'. As with all service companies, the key question is: what would their employment status be if they did not have a company? In answering this question the deeming provisions of the NICs regulations are relevant, as well as the normal employment/self-employment distinctions.

20.9.2 Employed or self-employed

A full time teacher or lecturer with a permanent position in a school or university is almost certainly an employee. However the position is less clear with part-time or supply teachers. A full discussion of contract law and the status tests is in Chapters 5 to 8, and the Revenue view is set out at ESM 4500ff. In the context of teachers and lecturers some factors to be considered include:

1. How much *control* the teacher has, for instance over the course content and the times the lessons are delivered. The more control, the more likely the worker is to be an employee. However, professionals are expected to have significant discretion over their own work, and little control may not prove self-employment, see **6.6.3**;

2. Does the teacher supply any necessary *equipment* at his own expense, such as a PowerPoint projector or photocopied handouts?

3. Whether the lecturer can send a *substitute*. This might be thought an easy condition to meet when a school is simply looking for a supply teacher – i.e., someone who broadly meets the requirements in order to fill a gap caused by absence. However in practice the educational establishment will revert to the agency to provide a substitute, not the lecturer. This will not satisfy the substitution test, because the right to send a replacement must rest with the worker, see **9.3.4**;

4. Does he satisfy the *Lorimer* test? In other words, does he have many short-term lecturing engagements with a variety of engagers; is there a common intention to create self employment as between the school/college and the lecturer; does he have a business-like approach to obtaining and organising his engagements? A more detailed discussion of the *Lorimer* case can be found at **8.2.1**.

5. What is the intention of the parties? The Revenue accept that this can be can be 'of fundamental importance in some instances' (ESM 4502).

Even where the worker can pass the self-employment test for tax purposes, he may not do so for NICs, see **20.9.3**.

Case law authority for Schedule D status

Teachers or lecturers have, on a number of occasions, succeeded in arguing that they are self-employed. Many were National Insurance cases decided before the special regulations were introduced in 1978. Teachers should assess their own position against the decided cases, both those in their own field and the other decisions discussed in Chapters 5 to 9.

In *Argent v Minister of Social Security* [1968] 3 AER 208, Argent was a teacher of acting. The DSS argued that his engagement with the Guildhall School of Music and Drama constituted an employment, but the court held that he was self-employed because he had significant other acting work, was given no guidance on his teaching methods, was paid by the session and had no administrative duties. The judge said:

> 'When one looks at all the facts found one has a picture of a man skilled and experienced in his own profession, of the services of whom the corporation, as the owners of the Guildhall School of Music, were anxious to obtain for the benefit of their students. They give him a fairly free choice of what he teaches and an entirely free choice how he teaches. They do not prescribe his syllabus. They leave to him the actual manner of his teaching as the expert in that field. They impose no administrative duties on him. They leave him free to pursue the artistic side of his work for the benefit of the students whom he is there to teach and train for their later careers on the stage. To say that in those circumstances when a man is so employed at a rate per hour or at a particular fee for a particular job that he is employed under a contract of service seems to me, with all respect, to be quite unreal.'

This followed a similar case involving a professional lawn tennis coach (M51 [1956]). He was held to be self-employed since he was not controlled as to his methods of teaching, was not obliged to accept engagements, and was remunerated by a fee for each session.

The more recent case of *St John's College School, Cambridge v Secretary of State for Social Security* [2000] unreported (ESM 7230) also confirmed the self-employed tax status of visiting instrumental teachers (VITs). Key factors here were that:

- The visiting instrumental teachers normally had additional teaching commitments at other establishments and would also give private tuition at home;

- They were not guaranteed work at St John's;

- They were hired at the instigation of parents and could not be dismissed by St John's, although the school found the VIT for the parents;

- No charge was made for the use of school premises;

- Lessons did not necessarily happen during normal school hours;

- The VITs 'work for the parents and are accountable to the parents for their performance. They report progress direct to the parents'. However, they liaise with the Director of Music at St John's over any problems with children or teaching matters;

- St John's was found to have 'no control over the VITs', and this was held to relate 'to the question of control as to the contract between the VIT and the individual parent and the VIT's conduct of the pupil's tuition'. It was likely that St John's could remove a VIT from the list of approved music teachers, if, for example, there was an incidence of gross misconduct;

- The VITs were paid by the lesson and claimed their fees at the end of each school term;

- St John's added the cost of the lessons to the children's termly bill and thus collected the fees from the parents and paid them on to the VITs. It was held that 'it was unlikely that any loss is passed on to the VITs'.

The Revenue accepted that the teachers had sufficient indicators of self-employment to be Schedule D for tax purposes; the point at issue was the NIC liability, see **20.9.3** below.

Case law authority for Schedule E status

The above cases should be contrasted with *Sidey v Phillips* [1987] STC 87. Mr Sidey was a barrister who lectured part-time for both Thames Polytechnic and the Inner London Education Authority. Although the arrangements for his engagements were exceedingly casual, Mr Sidey knew that there were standard terms and conditions for part-time teachers, and he was thus treated as having entered into contracts under those standard terms, and thus an employee. The same point was significant in the poorly argued case of *Fuge v McClelland* [1956] 36 TC 571.

Another case that went against the teacher involved was that of *Walls v Sinnett* [1987] STC 236. Mr Walls was a teacher of music who had a full-time post at a College of Further Education in Liverpool. Despite the fact that he had a number of other concurrent engagements, provided much of his own equipment, and was 'given a very wide degree of latitude in the organisation of his work and time', he was found to be an employee. The fact that he had signed a document called a 'contract of employment' was however not helpful!

In the Privy Council case of *Narich Pty Ltd v Commissioner of Payroll Tax* [1984] ICR 286, lecturers who were contracted to conduct weight watchers classes were held to be employees of Weight Watchers International Inc. because they were 'tied hand and foot' with regard to how they had to perform the work.

20.9.3 National Insurance

There are special NIC rules for teachers and lecturers, and these take precedence over the case law on employment/self-employment (SI 1978/1689 Sch 1, para 4). These rules state that anyone who is employed as a lecturer, teacher, instructor or in any similar capacity in an educational establishment by any person providing education, is to be treated as falling within the category of employed earner unless:

- The lectures are open to the public; or

- The number of days on which instruction is given has been limited, by prior agreement, to three days or less in three consecutive months; or

- Their earnings are paid by someone other than the body providing the education, such as directly by the students themselves; or

- The lecturers do not teach in the presence of those who are to receive the instruction, but do so by some 'distance learning' method, such as correspondence or videotapes. Open University teachers are an exception here – they have been brought within the NIC rules by special provisions (SI 1978/1689 Sch 1, para 4).

An attempt to argue that the definitions of 'educational establishment' and 'employed by' were narrow in scope were defeated in the *St John's College School* case, see **20.9.2**. The judge also held that the meaning of the word 'employed' in the context of the Regulations was not the case law definition of the term, but the dictionary meaning – namely it can include using:

> 'The services of (a person) in a professional capacity, or in the transaction of some special business ... to find work or occupation for (a person, his bodily or mental powers)'.

Fortunately the Revenue have not sought to use this decision to extend Class 1 NICs to all those who fall within this wider definition of employment.

The application of the NIC deeming regulations to service companies was confirmed in FAQ Status 4:

> '*I am a freelance teacher, working through a service company, and for tax purposes my work would qualify as self-employed. Does IR35 affect me?*

> Yes. Under IR35, your service company is responsible for Class 1 National Insurance contributions (NICs) if you would be regarded as employed in "employed earner's employment" if you provided your services under a

contract directly with your client, rather than through your service company (or other intermediary).'

Thus a teacher or lecturer could be regarded as self-employed for tax, but an employed earner for NICs. He would therefore have to carry out an attributable earnings calculation, but not a deemed income calculation, see **12.7.2.** The intermediary would be liable for secondary NICs.

20.9.4 Overseas issues

Visiting teachers or lecturers may qualify for special double tax reliefs. Most UK treaties exempt teachers from tax if they come here to work for two years or less. Since this applies to income subject to PAYE, it will also apply to deemed income calculated under the personal services rules and thus these teachers will be outside IR35 for tax. However some agreements only exempt the income if it is 'subject to tax' in the home country, and the Revenue may thus ask for proof that the personal services income has been taxed abroad, see DTRM 1936.

Teachers going overseas are subject to the same rules in reverse, so that their earnings may remain within Schedule E and the deemed income computation even though they are working overseas.

20.10 Temporary executives and interim managers

20.10.1 Introduction

'Interim management' has now become a career in its own right, with individuals moving from company to company supplying specialist skills or taking positions on a temporary basis. Where the interim manager is also a director of the client company, see **20.3** above.

20.10.2 Employed or self-employed

Some of those taking on short-term roles within an organisation are independent professionals, who see themselves as 'troubleshooting' a particular problem for a defined period of time. These individuals are more likely to fall outside IR35, in contrast to those who are simply covering a temporary vacancy following the unexpected departure of a senior employee.

The Revenue give an example of the consultant who falls outside IR35 in their discussion of 'profiting from sound management':

'A company may engage a consultant to thoroughly review a business process and report to the board with acceptable suggestions for improvements or a whole new process. The consultant agrees a fee of £20,000 and that the report has to be completed within three months. There may also be penalty clauses within the contract. Clearly the consultant might be able to complete the report well within the three-month deadline.' (ESM 518)

Even those interim managers who fall within IR35 are likely, because of the short-term nature of their assignments, to benefit from a service company structure. This situation arises because more generous travel and subsistence reliefs are available to those with PSCs, see **11.6** above. The pension deduction and the 5 per cent allowance, see **12.2.2** and **11.2**, are also useful.

20.11 TV and film industry workers

20.11.1 Background

Personal service companies are commonplace in the media. The Revenue Manual says somewhat testily:

'To avoid PAYE many film and video workers in Schedule E grades have set up limited companies. Normally the worker is the majority shareholder and a director. It is alleged that the service company supplies the services of the individual to a film or video production company. An examination of many such cases has shown that such arrangements often fail. The worker remains an employee of the production company. Tell the Film Industry Unit about any service companies of this kind that you find.' (ESM 4104)

This appears to suggest that the service company arrangements are a sham. However, the Revenue's guidance notes to companies engaging workers makes a different point, recommending that the film companies ensure that the service company arrangements are actually in place:

'It is not however sufficient that a service company exists; it is the duty of the production company to satisfy itself that there is in fact a *bona fide* contract **with the service company** for the provision of the worker's services. In a majority of such cases reviewed in recent years, no such contract was found to exist. If you have any doubt about the existence of a valid contract, payment should be made directly to the worker and the PAYE and NIC provisions should be applied in the normal way. If you fail to exercise reasonable care in this regard, you may be held liable for the deductions which ought to have been made' (*Film Industry Guidance Notes* 2001 edition).

Curiously, it then goes on to say that:

> 'If the worker's services are provided in circumstances such that if the worker
> had been employed directly you would have been able to make payment
> gross, you may make gross payments to the service company without
> further enquiry.'

This suggests that if the service company is within IR35, the client can make
the payment – but wrongly implies that if the service company is outside
IR35, there might be a problem. It also requires the client to decide whether
IR35 applies or not. One wonders if these guidance notes were written by
someone unaware of the changes made to IR35 between April and September
1999, see **2.3**.

20.11.2 Employed or self-employed?

In March 1983, the Inland Revenue announced that it had carried out a review
of workers within the film and allied industries and had concluded that:

> 'A number of workers engaged on "freelance" terms within the industry are
> engaged as employees under contracts of service, either written or oral.'

Re-categorisation of these workers began on 6 April 1983, and by the end of
1983 over 7,000 had been classified as employed earners (*Hansard* 16 January
1984, Vol. 52 Col. 14).

Following this exercise, the Revenue issued a list of the types of 'behind
camera' workers it considers to be self-employed, and this list is updated
annually. Workers who exercise a special skill on a production-by-production
basis, who work other than on premises provided by the engager, or who
provide substantial equipment, form most of the Revenue's Schedule D
group. A listing of jobs (or 'grades') which are accepted as Schedule D is
available on application from the Revenue's Film or TV and Radio Industry
Units.

In addition to the approved list, the Revenue may accept that an individual is
self-employed if he has very many short-term contracts with a number of
engagers, see **20.11.3**.

However, not being on the 'approved list' does not mean that a worker cannot
be self-employed; each case is decided on its own facts. Of interest are two
recent NIC appeals to the Secretary of State concerning set construction
workers. Services provided by set construction workers such as carpentry,

rigging and painting do not appear on the Revenue's Schedule D lists and income from such services is thus normally taxable under Schedule E. However in the cases of *Hamilton Heritage* [1997] and *Southbrooke Studios* [1997] it was held that the set construction workers were self-employed rather than employees (*Tax Bulletin 48*).

Despite losing these cases, the Revenue have said that they still regard set construction workers as being employed earners, because their contracts generally include clauses which are typical of a contract of service.

In summary, an individual's status is not necessarily as set out in the Revenue's listing; workers should take advice on their position. However, because film and TV companies will follow Revenue instructions, a personal service company may be preferable for those prepared to take a more independent line.

20.11.3 The seven day rule

The Revenue dispense employers in the film and TV industry from applying PAYE to engagements which are for less than seven consecutive days. The seven days includes rest days and weekends if these fall between the first and last days of the engagement, see *Film Industry Guidance Notes* 2001 edition.

The *Guidance Notes* make clear that this does not change the nature of the engagement and the worker remains an employee. However:

> 'Because many employed workers in the Film Industry have short engagements with a succession of different employers, the normal operation of PAYE is impractical and would in many cases result in excessive deductions of tax. The Seven Day Rule is intended to alleviate the hardship which might arise from such excessive deductions.'

This useful concessionary practice does not, however, extend to NICs, which must be 'accounted for in the normal way'.

If the contract was made between the film/TV company and the worker's service company, presumably this practice would not apply, as the risk of over-deduction would disappear. Thus it appears that the individual who works for a number of 'short engagements with a succession of different employers' may do better by remaining outside the service company structure.

However, this pattern of working is familiar. Mr Lorimer was found to be self-employed largely because he 'customarily worked for 20 or more production companies and that the vast majority of his assignments lasted only for a single day', and Lord Nolan considered that the key test to be applied in this sort of situation was 'the extent to which the individual is dependent upon, or independent of, a particular paymaster for the financial exploitation of his talents,' see *Hall v Lorimer* [1993] 66 TC 349. The film or TV worker whose working pattern is similar to Mr Lorimer's may also be self-employed both for tax and NICs, see ESM 4103, and thus the 'concessionary' Revenue treatment may actually reflect the individuals' true status.

It may thus be simpler for the individual in this situation to use a service company and so avoid having NIC deductions made by a succession of 'employers' as well as avoiding debates with payroll departments whenever an individual assignment stretches beyond the seven day point.

21 Agencies, clients and advisers

21.1 Introduction

Three groups of people stand on the periphery of IR35; they are not those at whom the legislation is aimed, but they are caught in the crossfire. These are the service company's agents, clients and advisers.

For both clients and agencies, the personal services legislation has significant legal and commercial consequences, some of which are still developing. For advisers, IR35 represents both a risk and an opportunity.

21.2 Agencies

21.2.1 Scope of the personal services legislation

Agency rules

Before IR35, s134 ICTA 1988 deemed individuals supplying personal services to clients via an agency to be employees of the agency for the purposes of both tax and NICs (SI 1978/1689 reg 2; Sch 1, para 2; Sch 3 para 2). These rules exclude services provided via companies.

IR35 made no change to the agency rules (Sch 12, para 24 FA 2000; SI 2000/727 reg 12). This is confirmed by FAQ Agency 1:

> 'Will the legislation for agency workers need to be rewritten?
>
> This measure will do nothing to disturb the existing agency legislation at s134 Income and Corporation Taxes Act 1988. This is because section 134 only applies to individuals. It does not apply to service companies.'

However, where the agency pays sums of money (other than a reimbursement of expenses) directly to an individual worker rather than to the service company, then these amounts may be within s134 ICTA 1988 and subject to PAYE and NICs. This is the case at present and IR35 has not changed this, see FAQ Agency 4 and **10.5.4 Note 1**.

Fees for agency services

The deemed Schedule E calculation is based on the income *received* by the intermediary. Fees deducted by agencies en route to the service company thus do not form part of the income included in the calculation.

If fees are paid to an agency by the worker or the intermediary, instead of being deducted en route, there is no relief for these payments in the deemed Schedule E calculation (other than as part of the 5 per cent allowance). The exception is for agency fees paid by actors, providing they fall within s201A ICTA 1988, see **20.2.4.**

Relevant intermediaries

The legislation is aimed at 'relevant intermediaries'. An agency, although clearly an intermediary, will not normally be a *relevant* intermediary because it does not come within the conditions set out in Schedule 12, paragraphs 3–5 FA 2000. As a result, it is not jointly and severally liable for the service company's PAYE and NIC liability: that responsibility only attaches to relevant intermediaries (Sch 12, para 16 FA 2000, see **4.5.5**).

21.2.2 Contracts

Soon after IR35 came into force, the Revenue reviewed the standard IT industry agency contracts, and concluded that they fell within IR35, see **7.6.** Although their blanket approach to these contracts was criticised by the judge in the judicial review case, it remains true that if these contracts reflect the reality of the engagement, the worker is likely to be within IR35. Since similar terms are generally included in other industries' standard contracts, they too are likely to fall within the personal services rules.

Agencies have been placed under considerable pressure to amend their contracts to help contractors escape IR35. How contracts may be changed is discussed in detail at Chapter 9. However, agencies should remember that:

- Liability under IR35 is based on the hypothetical contract between the worker and the client. If clauses are inserted in the contract between the service company and the agency, but not in the contract between the agency and the client, the Revenue (and ultimately the courts) will try and establish the actual arrangements, see **5.1.4.** A contractual term which contradicts that reality, or is unsupported by the facts, is likely to be ignored or set aside;

- If the clauses are a sham, the Revenue will look through them. If the insertion of such clauses was a deliberate policy on the agency's part, it might attract unwelcome Revenue attention. At an extreme, it could be investigated by Special Compliance Office and/or attacked under s99 TMA 1970, see **16.6.6**. This says that:

  'Any person who assists in or induces the preparation or delivery of any information, return, accounts or other document which (a) he knows will be, or is or are likely to be, used for any purpose of tax, and (b) he knows to be incorrect, shall be liable to a penalty not exceeding £3,000.'

- The introduction of certain clauses into client contracts, while increasing the likelihood that the worker will be treated as outside IR35, also increases the level of risk for the agency. If the worker can send a substitute (see **9.3**) and the substitute is unsatisfactory, the client's right of action is against the agency, not against the service company. Similarly, if the worker has moved to a project basis (see **9.4**) and does not complete the project on time, the agency may be held responsible. The commercial consequences of changing contracts must therefore be considered along with their tax effects;

- Having said this, agents who work with contractors and clients to adjust the working arrangements and devise IR35-proof contracts are likely to increase their business. Clients may be more willing to participate in this process if they are concerned about the employment law risk, see **21.3.1** below.

21.2.3 Other consequences of IR35

Workers who are within the personal services legislation may:

- Seek to put up their rates, to recover the extra costs of IR35, and this has consequences for agencies;

- Move to another agency which can offer more 'IR35 friendly' terms;

- Take up direct employment, either with the client or via an agency. The employer will have all the normal employment law obligations as well as the secondary NIC cost. In consequence the worker's remuneration is likely to be lower.

21.2.4 Reporting to the Revenue

The Revenue are using their existing powers to obtain from agencies details of service companies to which payments have been made, and the amount and nature of the payments (s16 TMA 1970). The legislation is as follows:

(a) A business can be required, by notice from the Revenue, to provide a return of payments made 'for services rendered by persons not employed in the trade or business' of the payer;

(b) The return can be for any period, but the period will be specified in the notice;

(c) The return must give the name and address of the person(s) to whom payments were made, and this may include 'any business name and any business or home address';

(d) It should state the amount of the payment, and payment includes 'the giving of any valuable consideration';

(e) Other particulars, such as the period over which services were rendered and the type of services which were provided, may also be required.

There are penalties of up to £300 if the return is late, and up to £3,000 for fraud or negligence (s98 TMA 1970). It is understood that letters have gone out to agencies under these provisions, requiring information about all payments to service companies of £1,000 or more.

Although the normal time limit for completion of the return is 30 days, agencies may be able to negotiate a longer period.

21.2.5 Does using an agency protect against IR35?

Using an agency may make it more difficult for mutuality of obligation to arise between the worker and the client, see **5.9**. However, the view that the legislation itself reduces or eliminates the impact of IR35 is not shared by all practitioners. The arguments, both for and against, are discussed in some detail at **23.2** and **23.3**.

21.3 Clients

21.3.1 Looking through the service company?

Background

The original personal services proposals made the client responsible for deducting PAYE and NIC from the earnings of personal service workers, see **2.3.2**. In response to representations, the government subsequently transferred responsibility for complying with IR35 to the intermediaries. This enabled many clients to take a more relaxed view of the proposals and they have since been inclined to ignore the legislation. However, this may be premature.

When IR35 was introduced, the government made it clear that the 'looking through' of the service company would take effect only for tax and NICs, and would not make the contractors employees of the client for employment law purposes, see for example Dawn Primarolo's comment in the Parliamentary debate on the Finance Bill:

> 'I am happy to confirm that nothing in the Bill alters the legal relationship between any worker and his or her client or employer … . One of the misleading rumours that is being spread about the Bill is that it deems that a service company worker will be an employee of his or her client. It has been suggested to clients that that would mean that they would be vulnerable to claims under employment law – for example, unfair dismissal. However, nothing in the Bill supports that claim.' *Hansard* 6 June 2000

Currently employment law does not look through the service company, except in respect of anti-discrimination legislation. In other areas the use of a PSC protects the client from having to comply with employment legislation in relation to contractors. Both these areas are dealt with below.

Anti-discrimination legislation

Ironically, on the very day that IR35 came into force, the Court of Appeal held that a limited company could be looked through in a disability discrimination case, *Tansell v Abbey Life* [2000] 1 All ER(D) 483. Mr Tansell supplied his services to Abbey Life via an agency (MHC) and through his own limited company. When he developed severe diabetes, Abbey Life terminated the contract with the agency and Mr Tansell claimed unfair dismissal. The Court of Appeal upheld his claim because the Disability Discrimination Act extends protection to 'contract workers' including those 'where there was no direct contract between the person making the work available and the employer of the individual who supplied that work'.

That the courts are taking a very wide view of their responsibilities in the area of discrimination is shown by *Harrods v Remick* [1998] 1 All ER 52. In this case Harrods was found liable for racially discriminating against workers employed by their concessionaires. Sir Richard Scott, giving the concluding judgment, said that in interpreting the Act:

> 'We should … give a construction to the statutory language that is not only consistent with the actual words used but also would achieve the statutory

purpose of providing a remedy to victims of discrimination who would otherwise be without one.'

The EAT took a similar line in the *Abbey Life* case, saying that:

'It would not be consistent with the legislative object to withhold protection from discrimination by a person to whom an employee, who was entitled to protection from his employer, had been supplied to do the same work.'

A succession of cases concerning Post Office workers have, however, made it clear that contract workers cannot claim under the discrimination legislation if they have no obligation to do the work personally and have the right of substitution, see *Sheehan v Post Office Counters Ltd* [1999] ICR 734; *Tanna v Post Office* [1981] ICR 374.

Other employment law

Most employment law does not give contractors such extensive protection, and recent cases suggest that the use of a service company does protect the client from claims such as redundancy and maternity rights. However, this position may not be sustained in the longer term.

In the decision of *Winter v Westward Television* [1977] EAT/589, Winter provided services to Westward via Samian Galleries Limited, a company controlled by Mr and Mrs Winter. In their judgment the EAT said that:

'It seems to us that it would be quite impossible to infer from the circumstances some relationship of employer and employee for a number or reasons, the principle one being that it is never right to infer a legal relationship when it is inconsistent with what the parties themselves have expressly agreed.'

This decision was based on findings of fact by the Industrial Tribunal, that the contract between Westward TV and Samian Galleries Limited was not a sham and had been genuinely entered into to achieve the object which those who put it forward had in mind.

This position was slightly eroded by the later case of *Catamaran Cruisers v Williams* [1994] IRLR 389, where an individual, previously an employee of Catamaran Cruisers, subsequently provided his services via a limited company. The court held that he was able to claim unfair dismissal because:

'There is no rule of law that the importation of a limited company into the relationship prevents the continuation of a contract of employment. If the true relationship is that of employer and employee, it cannot be changed by putting a different label on it.'

There is, however, a difference between 'importing' a company into an existing relationship and the company-to-company arrangement which normally applies from inception when a PSC is involved.

Then, in early March 2001, an Employment Tribunal sitting in Bristol held unanimously that an individual working through a PSC was an employee of his client. In a reserved decision (*O'Murphy v Hewlett Packard* [2001] Case Number 5300148/01) they found that the existence of the service company:

'Was no more than for administrative purposes and had no material impact on the relationship between the applicant and either the Agency or the respondent'.

However this decision was overturned on appeal because there was no contractual relationship between the worker and the client (*Hewlett Packard v O'Murphy* [2001] EAT/612). But the EAT judgment did not exhaustively explore all possibilities before coming to its conclusion, and others with service companies may seek to make a similar claim in the future, perhaps with more success.

Minimising employment risk

Because IR35 forces every contractor to consider the question: 'would I be an employee of my client if I wasn't working via my service company', contractors who fall within IR35 may consider making claims for employment rights. Mr Justice Burton, in his judicial review judgment, said that:

'There is no binding conclusion that [a contractor] is an employee simply because he is to be treated as if he were one for tax purposes, but if so advised he could seek to raise arguments to that effect.' *R v CIR (oao Professional Contractors Group Ltd* [2001] STC 629)

Clients may wish to pre-empt this, and instead of ignoring IR35, work with their contractors to change their working arrangements so they fall outside the personal services legislation as well as removing most of the employment law risks.

21.3.2 Overseas service companies

Where a worker is supplied to the client by an overseas employer, the client can be required to operate PAYE and NIC on any salary paid to the worker, see **19.5.2** (s203C ICTA 1988; s7(2)(b) SSCBA 1992; SI 1978/1689 Sch 3(9)).

However, if the employer is a personal services company within Sch 12 FA 2000, the obligation to deduct tax and NIC in respect of the *deemed Schedule E payment* rests with the service company. However, s203C continues to apply to payments of *salary actually paid* to the worker.

The client is thus in a difficult position, as he cannot know for sure what actual salary has been paid; he knows only what he has paid the service company. IR35 has not caused this problem, but has not made it disappear either. He has four options:

(a) To require the overseas company to supply the information. In practice he may only be prepared to rely on this if the overseas company is a connected party, such as a subsidiary or a joint venture partner;

(b) To deduct tax from the amount paid to the service company. This would, however, leave him open to an action from the worker, as this would be beyond his authority;

(c) Argue that although s203C is a legal obligation, it is unenforceable, as he does not have the information necessary to comply with the requirements. Since the overseas company is outside the scope of UK tax, it cannot be compelled to provide the client with the information. If the client takes this approach, the Revenue are likely to institute formal proceedings to obtain the PAYE (SI 1993/744 reg 42). This process is discussed in the Revenue Manual under the heading 'Corresponding with reluctant employers' (EPM 9178);

(d) Not use workers supplied by overseas service companies.

Option (d) is probably the most common response, unless the client can satisfy himself under (a). Many reputable agencies take the same approach, refusing to place workers operating via overseas service companies because of the s203C issues for their clients.

Although the personal services legislation has shifted some of the onus onto the service company, sufficient burden remains on the client to make the use of overseas service companies very unattractive.

21.3.3 Third-party reporting

Where cash or other benefits are paid or supplied directly to the worker by the client, there may be a PAYE or other reporting obligation on the client. The circumstances in which this can occur are discussed at **10.5.4(5)**.

21.3.4 Freelance consultants

Where a client uses freelance consultants, there is a risk that they could be recategorised as Schedule E by the Revenue's Employer Compliance Unit. The client may then be liable for up to six year's PAYE and NICs, as well as being vulnerable to expensive back claims for employment rights.

Where there is doubt about the Schedule D status of a freelance consultant, clients may wish to take advantage of the IR35 provisions and insisting that new contracts are only made with personal service companies and not with individual freelancers. By doing this the client will have transferred the compliance burden to the service company. If the freelancer is confident of his Schedule D status he will fall outside IR35, so using an intermediary will not significantly increase his tax liability.

21.3.5 Other issues

Many of the issues which are relevant to agencies also affect clients. In particular:

- Contractual changes and their implications for clients and agencies are discussed in Chapter 9 and **21.2.2** above. For example, if there is no notice period (**9.14**), there may be a danger that the project will grind to a halt while a replacement is found;

- If there is a dispute with the Revenue as to whether a contractual clause is valid, and thus what the true 'circumstances' of the arrangements are, the client is likely to be asked for his views and may be required to give evidence in court;

- The commercial issues concerning pricing and the PAYE alternative are similar to those for agencies, see **21.2.3** above;

- Clients, like agencies, may be asked for information from the Revenue under s16 TMA 1970 (**21.2.4**). At the time of writing, it is understood that requests under s16 have been made of most major banks and utilities. However, complying with s16 is likely be more difficult for a large multinational than it is for an agency. The agency is likely to be able to extract a list of payments made to service companies with relative ease; the client may have contractors working in many parts of its business, recorded under different headings. Their invoices may have been absorbed within an overall project cost and be difficult to identify. Where a s16 return is required, clients should thus seek to negotiate a reasonable time frame for its delivery to the Revenue;

- Clients who participate in artificial avoidance arrangements – for instance, hiving off their workers into a special purpose vehicle which has been designed to fall outside IR35 - may be attacked by Special Compliance Office under s99 TMA 1970, see **16.6.6**.

21.4 Tax advisers

21.4.1 Outline

When the revised Regulatory Impact Assessment (RIA) for IR35 was published in October 1999, it said that the introduction of IR35 would cost those affected around twenty million pounds in one-off costs, and up to nine million pounds per year thereafter. Most of this would be paid to tax consultants. Time has shown that the RIA was correct: there is a market for advice on IR35, and a clear financial incentive to provide that advice.

Tax advisers do however face some real difficulties. The main problems are those caused by the complexity of the legislation and case law relating to IR35, both of which are discussed elsewhere in this book. In addition there are consequential administrative and risk issues, which are outlined below.

21.4.2 Administration and risk management

IR35 is very wide-ranging, impacting on corporation tax, partnership tax and personal tax; the interaction with company accounts also needs to be understood. The IR35 client base is well-informed, and the Revenue are very interested. For individuals the tax and NIC costs of falling within IR35 are considerable, especially where more than one year is affected.

The combination of these factors means that the risk to advisers is significant. They should thus ensure that:

- They know how IR35 impacts upon their client base, including the employment/self-employment divide; the mechanics of the deemed income calculation, and its interaction with both accounts and corporation tax;

- Engagement letters make clear the scope of the adviser's remit – for instance, does it cover advice on status, contract review and redesign, taking a contested case to court, consideration of the corporation tax and accounting implications?

- Professional indemnity insurance is reviewed to ensure the level is commensurate with the risk;

- They are familiar with the Revenue's information powers, and are comfortable that s99 TMA cannot be used against them, see **16.6.4**. It should be noted that the Revenue's Employer Compliance Manual (at paragraph 21018) says that 'the main use of [this section] is against accountants';

- Any scheme they advocate is legal. In *R v Cunningham, Charlton, Wheeler & Kitchen* [1996] STC 1418, a barrister and three accountants were imprisoned for cheating the public revenue when a scheme they promoted was found to have been fraudulent. The judge said that the issue was 'whether [the barrister] was party to fraud on the one hand or that he was acting energetically in his clients' best interest on the other', and held that 'in our judgment, there was sufficient evidence of participation in the fraud ... to support his conviction'. As regards the accountants, he said that it was 'difficult to reconcile' their contention that they did not know that the schemes 'were applied dishonestly with the fact that all the schemes were misapplied in the same way'.

21.4.3 Managing the IR35 process

The adviser needs to consider numerous issues, some of which are summarised below:

- Has the client decided whether to use the dividend route or the salary route (**13.5.1**)?

- Does the client understand when his year end returns will be filed and whether there will be an interest charge for late payment (**16.4.2**)?

- Has the accounting year end issue been addressed (**13.4.6**)?

- Have the implications for partnerships been considered (Chapter 14)?

- Is the client seeking a Revenue opinion on his status (**7.7**)? How robust is any status opinion which the adviser provides? Is it backed up by current case law?

- Have the corporation tax and accounting interactions been explained (Chapter 13)?

- Has the adviser ensured that the records are supplied on a cash basis for the tax year, so he can calculate the deemed payment (**10.2** and **11.3.2**)?

- Has the adviser invested in, or designed, a model to calculate the deemed payment? Is he aware of the Revenue model (see **7.2.4**)? Spreadsheet models can compute 'shadow' deemed payments in order to work out the minimum salary, and may also calculate the pension on a net relevant earnings basis in time for the payment to be made (**12.2**).

Chapter 24 gives a series of checklists which the adviser might find useful. In addition, a timetable of events for each client showing what information is needed by when is likely to be of assistance.

22 National Minimum Wage, Working Families Tax Credits, Student Loans, SSP and SMP

22.1 Introduction

The National Minimum Wage (NMW) came into force on 1 April 1999. Its implementation is a matter of employment law rather than tax legislation, and this chapter will therefore only discuss the NMW in outline and consider how it affects the position of personal service workers.

The Working Families Tax Credit (WFTC) was first introduced in September 1999. It is a more generous replacement for family credit, awarded to low-paid workers with children. Despite its name, it is not a reduction in tax, but a government-provided earnings top-up. Entitlement to WFTC depends on the worker's income and assets, the number and age of any children, and childcare costs. From a personal services perspective, the key issues are how the deemed Schedule E payment, and any associated dividends, are treated for the purposes of WFTC.

There is also an interaction between student loans and IR35. Since 1 September 1998 students in England and Wales have been entitled to a student loan. After graduation the loan is recovered once income exceeds £10,000 a year. If the former student is employed, the student loan repayment (SLR) operates by way of deduction from salary. This chapter looks at how the deemed Schedule E amount and related distributions are regarded for SLR purposes.

Statutory Sick Pay (SSP) and Statutory Maternity Pay (SMP) are both paid by the employer to 'employed earners', including those within the deemed Schedule E calculation. However, those who rely entirely on the dividend/deemed Schedule E route will find that they do not obtain the same benefits as those who pay themselves a salary.

22.2 National Minimum Wage (NMW)

22.2.1 Outline

All workers are now entitled to the National Minimum Wage. The amount payable is £3.60 an hour until 1 October 2000, £3.70 until October 2001 and £4.10 from October 2001. Lower rates apply to workers under 21 and to those on accredited training.

Paying a worker the minimum wage is a legal obligation. There is no relief from the obligation simply because an individual chooses not to receive the money; and if the worker has an entitlement to the payment, then PAYE and NIC inevitably follow.

In the context of the personal services legislation, the key questions are:

(a) Who is a 'worker' for the purposes of the legislation?

(b) What is a 'wage' and does it include the deemed Schedule E payment?

(c) What is the position of a client or agency in the context of the NMW?

(d) How will it be enforced?

(e) What are the tax and NIC implications?

22.2.2 Definition of a worker for NMW purposes

A worker is anyone working under:

- A contract of employment, whether express or implied, and including an oral contract; or

- A 'worker's contract' under which the individual agrees to perform work personally for someone, but who is not an employee. (s54 NMWA 1998)

Directors

There has been considerable confusion as to whether a director falls within the definition of 'worker'. If he does, he would be obliged to pay himself a salary at least equal to the NMW. However, the DTI have confirmed to the ICAEW that their legal advice is as follows:

> 'If a person is a director and he does not have an explicit employment contract, then he will not be subject to the NMW legislation even when he carries out a wide variety of activities. These might include working in the company's shop: such duties will be done in his capacity as an office-holder (director) and not as an employee. Only if a director has an explicit employment contract as well as being a holder of the office of director will he be within the NMW.' (*TAXline*, April 2000)

A more detailed note was published by the ICAEW in September 2000 which confirmed this advice and said that:

'The DTI have told us that if there is no written employment contract or other evidence of an intention to create an employer/employee relationship they will not seek to contend that there is an unwritten or implied employment relationship between a director and his company. As the Inland Revenue administers the NMW as agents for the DTI, they will adopt this policy also.' *Taxguide 7/00*

This is of course the DTI's opinion and has not been tested by the courts. The *Taxguide* says that 'At the end of the day, in the event of a dispute, it is for the employment tribunals or Courts to decide.'

A number of court cases have already considered whether a controlling shareholder can be an employee. In *Parsons v Albert J Parsons & Sons Ltd* [1979] ICR 271, the Court of Appeal held that a director who worked full time in the family business:

- Was not an employee;

- Had no implied, oral or written contract of employment; and

- His remuneration wholly related to his fees as a director.

In a more recent case, *Secretary of State for Trade and Industry v Bottrill* [1999] EWCA case No 980132, Lord Woolf gave some guidance on how to decide the status of a controlling shareholder. He said that key factors included whether the individual has a controlling shareholding and whether there was a genuine contract of employment between the company and the shareholder.

In the context of a service company where the shareholder/directors have no explicit contract of employment it is thus unlikely that they are within the NMW. This means that directors do not have to pay themselves the minimum wage provided they have no formal employment contract with their companies.

Partners

Partners do not have a contract of employment with their partnership and the partnership cannot therefore be required to pay them the minimum wage.

Other family members

There is an exemption from the minimum wage for family members working in family businesses, but this is limited to workers in *unincorporated* businesses where the individual:

- Is a member of the employer's family;

- Resides in the family home of the employer; and either

- Participates in the running of the family business; or

- Shares in the tasks and activities of the family, and the work is done in that context (SI 1999/584 reg 2(b)).

There is a similar exemption for people who live in the family home and are treated as a member of the family 'in particular as regards to the provision of accommodation and meals and the sharing of tasks and leisure activities.'(SI 1999/584 reg 2(a))

Despite these exemptions, someone who works in a family business still has a right to make a claim for payment of the NMW. However, if there is no claim, the Revenue will not enforce the right.

This exemption clearly applies to family members working in partnership businesses, but does not extend to those working within limited companies. It is not possible for a family member working in a PSC to renounce entitlement to the minimum wage: there is no parallel in the NMW legislation to the Working Time Directive's opt-out clause, under which individuals can agree to work longer hours than the statutory maximum. Indeed the NMWA specifically provides that 'any provision in any agreement ... is void in so far as it purports to exclude or limit the operation of any provision of this Act' (s49 NMWA). Thus family members must be paid the NMW if they are not directors and the business is incorporated.

22.2.3 Pay for NMW purposes

Pay for minimum wage purposes is the worker's basic salary, plus items such as incentives and bonuses. Extra sums such as overtime or shift work premiums do not count. All benefits in kind except accommodation are also excluded (SI 1999/584 reg 5). Thus, if the company uses income from relevant engagements to provide benefits for the worker instead of paying him in cash, this will reduce the deemed Schedule E payment, see **12.4**, but will not meet the minimum wage requirements.

Status of deemed payment and associated dividends

Under IR35 a worker may have a deemed salary payment at the end of a tax year. This deemed salary is Schedule E for income tax purposes, and attributable earnings for NIC. The after-tax amount may be paid out as dividends.

However, neither the deemed Schedule E payment nor the associated dividends are wages for NMWA purposes. So workers who are within both the NMW and the personal services rules need to be paid an actual salary which is at least equal to the minimum wage.

Pay periods

The pay reference period for the NMW is the worker's actual pay period, *up to a maximum of one calendar month*. Workers who are paid less frequently than once a month will still have a pay reference period of one calendar month (SI 1999/584 reg 10). The employer should thus ensure that salary is paid at least monthly; it is not enough simply to pay a cash bonus once a year.

22.2.4 Position of the client

As discussed at **22.2.2** above, a director of a PSC is not a 'worker' as regards the services he provides to his company and a partner in a partnership is not a worker in the context of the services he provides to his partnership. However, what is the position of the client? Could the individual who is supplying services to the client, either directly or via an agency, be regarded as operating under a 'worker's contract' in respect of the services he provides to the client?

Exemption

There is an exemption from the NMWA where 'the individual undertakes to do or perform personally any work or services for another party to the contract' and the status of the individual performing the services is 'by virtue of the contract that of a client or customer of any profession or business undertaking carried on by the individual' (s54(3)(b) NMWA 1998).

The exemption is thus defined by reference to the contract between the parties, and the contract under which the services of the PSC worker is provided to a client will normally state that it is between supplier and customer. This should thus protect clients from having the NMWA applied to their relationship with personal services workers.

'Looking through' the contract

It could however be argued that the true relationship between the parties is not that of customer and supplier, but a quasi-employment relationship to which the NMWA does apply. A court might be encouraged towards this approach if the worker was within the personal services legislation, since IR35 identifies those relationships where the intermediary is a mere 'wrapper', and thus where the worker would be an employee of the client if he was contracting directly. The same issue is discussed in the wider context of employment rights at **21.3.1**.

However, if the contract were to be ignored in this way, one would also expect that payments made by the client/agency to the service company would be characterised as wages for NMWA purposes. It would be strange to look through the contractual arrangements in order to identify the status of the worker, and not also to recharacterise the payments made.

Conclusion

There is a slight risk that the NMWA could apply to payments made to PSC workers by the client or agency, and this risk may be increased by the tax legislation. The pragmatic solution is that amounts paid to contract workers should at least equal the minimum wage.

22.2.5 Enforcement

The Revenue, and not the DTI, enforce the minimum wage. Their guidance to employers states that:

> 'We may undertake an enquiry to check that you are paying at least the minimum hourly wage if one of your workers has contacted us, or as part of our programme of visits to employers to make sure you understand your obligations in relation to the National Minimum Wage.'

The service company or partnership could thus have its adherence to the NMW rules reviewed, even if no worker had made a complaint. Non-compliance can be a serious matter. The legislation makes it a criminal offence to:

- Refuse or wilfully neglect to pay the national minimum wage;

- Fail to keep adequate records;

- Keep false records; or

- Obstruct an enforcement officer.

If the NMW officers discover an underpayment, they can issue an enforcement notice. If this is not complied with, there may be a daily penalty of £7.20

in respect of each worker. The DTI's publication, *A Guide to the National Minimum Wage*, states comfortingly that 'Officers will give employers every chance to comply before considering any penalty.' However the maximum fine is £5,000, not to mention the criminal record.

PAYE and NIC implications

Non-payment of the minimum wage causes a further problem: unpaid tax and NIC. This is because, if there is a legal right to payment, the amount will be 'treated as received' and therefore within PAYE (s202B(1)(b) ICTA 1988).

Because of the pay period rules, see **22.2.3** above, entitlement to NMW subsists at the end of each month and interest will run from that date. The Revenue have confirmed to the ICAEW that arrears of tax will normally be sought from the employer by means of a settlement and interest will be due in the normal way. Penalties will not be sought. They have also pointed out that since the NICs legislation differs from that for tax, NICs should be accounted for in the normal way at the time of actual payment of the arrears.

Exchange of information

Finance Act 2000 introduced exchange of information provisions under which data collected for NMW purposes could be made available to other Inland Revenue departments (s143 FA 2000). Similar rights had already been given to NMW teams allowing them to access tax information (s39 Employment Relations Act 1999).

The Revenue have confirmed that if, during the course of an inspection a PAYE auditor had reason to believe that there was a failure to pay NMW, then the relevant information might be passed to a NMW enforcement officer. They have also said that an NMW officer might similarly pass information to a PAYE auditor.

22.2.6 Conclusion

Directors and partners are not normally within the scope of the NMW, and family members working for a partnership may also be exempted. Other employees *are* included, and neither the deemed Schedule E payment nor dividends counts as wages. A salary of at least the NMW must be paid to them on a monthly basis or more frequently. Otherwise the company or partnership may face overdue PAYE and NIC, plus interest and NMW penalties.

22.3 Working Families Tax Credit (WFTC)

22.3.1 Background

The government introduced the Working Families Tax Credit (WFTC) on 5 October 1999. It is an earnings top-up and, despite its name, effectively a rebadged social benefit. It replaced the earlier Family Credit but reaches more people. From 2003 the WFTC will be replaced by two new types of tax credit, the Child Tax Credit for those with children and the Working Tax Credit for those on low earnings.

WFTC can be claimed by low-income families with children, where at least one adult who is in paid work for at least 16 hours a week. The amount of the credit increases with each child, and is higher for older children. There is a further top-up if the adult works 30 hours a week or more.

Disabled Persons Tax Credit (DPTC) is similar to WFTC. A person is eligible for DPTC if he has an illness or disability which puts him at a disadvantage when getting a job.

Where someone qualifies for the WFTC or DPTC, a childcare tax credit (CTC) is also available. This covers 70 per cent of the cost of approved childcare, with the total spend capped at £100 a week for one child, and £150 a week for two or more children. For simplicity, in this chapter the WFTC, DPTC and CTC will normally be referred to as the WFTC.

Once a worker's earnings are above a given threshold, the WFTC is withdrawn at the rate of 55p for every pound earned. It is also tapered away where capital greater than £3,000 is held, see **23.3.3** below.

Most of the legislation dealing with WFTC has been pieced together out of the old Family Credit legislation, and is somewhat inaccessible. The tax credits are thus being administered using the Revenue's *Decision Maker's Guide for WFTC* (DMG) which is based on earlier guidance for Family Credit, and has no legal force. The rules are complex, and what follows is only an outline.

22.3.2 Earnings for WFTC

The main issue for personal service companies and partnerships is whether either the deemed Schedule E payment and/or dividends paid by the service company count as 'earnings' for WFTC purposes. If they do not, the worker may be entitled to WFTC.

Remuneration

Where a WFTC applicant is a director of his service company, the Revenue state that they will take into account as earnings both remuneration actually received and that 'to which a director is entitled but decides not to receive' (DMG 26027).

Surprisingly, the DMG does not yet deal explicitly with the deemed Schedule E payment and whether it is earnings 'which a director is entitled but decides not to receive'. But it looks at a similar issue when it considers whether amounts advanced to a director ahead of his legal entitlement are earnings:

> 'It is not uncommon for directors who are voted remuneration (at the annual general meeting) to draw from their own current or loan accounts during the accounting year in order to have an income. These drawings are neither earnings nor income other than earnings because the directors are drawing money from the company in anticipation of *future* earnings or income.' (DMG 26034, the author's italics)

This means that the tax legislation set out in s202B ICTA 1988 (**10.2**) on the recognition of earnings for tax purposes has no parallel for WFTC. On the contrary, even access to cash by the director does not accelerate recognition of the earnings. This would suggest that a deemed salary to which the director has no legal entitlement is not remuneration.

Whether a director would be 'entitled to receive' his deemed Schedule E payment is likely to be a matter of law. If the money has not been voted to him as remuneration, he will have no entitlement. Assuming that the board understands how the PSC legislation works, they will not vote him the net Schedule E amount remaining after deduction of PAYE and NICs, because this will simply be taxed again as an actual salary payment, see **13.5.2**. He will thus have no legal entitlement and the amount should thus not be taken into account as earnings for WFTC.

Dividends

Dividends received by a director are treated as capital for WFTC purposes. The DMG says that:

> 'The decision maker should disregard a share dividend because it is income from capital but take it into account as capital from the date it is normally due to be credited.' (DMG 26031)

Since in most cases the money that has been taxed as a deemed Schedule E payment will be withdrawn as a dividend, this suggests that neither the deemed payment nor the dividend will count as earnings for WFTC.

Notional earnings

The Revenue say that 'the decision maker may treat an applicant as having income that is not actually received' (DMG 25001). It instructs the decision maker to try and establish whether the applicant (or partner) has received less pay than is normal for the work done (DMG 25080). If the answer is yes, then the ability of the person to whom the services were provided to pay a higher amount should be considered. A person 'includes a limited company or other corporate employer as well as an individual' (DMG 25089).

It is thus possible that the decision maker could take the view that the service company should have paid a higher salary for the work done, and indeed the existence of a deemed Schedule E payment might support this contention.

If notional earnings are ascribed to the applicant, a deduction is allowed for income tax, employee's NIC, and 50 per cent of a pension contribution paid by the individual (DM 25106). Thus the worker will have a further deemed income calculation, on a different basis from that in the personal services legislation!

However, as the deemed payment will almost certainly be withdrawn as dividends, and these are specifically treated as capital by other provisions of the WFTC regulations, it is uncertain whether notional earnings would be ascribed to the worker.

Summary

Thus, from an earnings perspective it would appear that:

- The deemed Schedule E amount is not taken into account as remuneration;
- When dividends are withdrawn from the company they are treated as an addition to capital rather than as earnings;
- It is possible that 'notional earnings' would be ascribed to the worker on the basis that the salary paid by the company was lower than 'normal'.

22.3.3 Capital for WFTC

Even if a personal service worker's earnings are low enough to qualify him for WFTC, he may fail the capital test. The rules for recognition of capital are complicated, but in outline:

(a) To the extent that adults in the family have capital in excess of £3,000, the worker is credited with notional income of £1 a week for each £250 of capital. WFTC is withdrawn entirely once the family's capital reaches £8,000 (£16,000 for DPTC);

(b) 'Capital' for these purposes excludes the family's home, car, furnishings and certain other items, see DMG Chapter 44;

(c) Also disregarded are 'any assets of a business owned wholly or partly by the applicant or partner who is actively self-employed that business' (Sch 3, para 6 FCA (Gen) regs; DMG 44070). Thus a partner's share of his business is excluded from the capital assets which are taken into account for WFTC;

(d) Similar treatment is granted to the director of company 'if the shareholder's interest in the company is similar to that of a sole trader or partner' (DMG 43020).

Dividends

Because dividends are counted as capital (**22.3.2**), a worker will have no entitlement to WFTC if his dividends, plus other capital assets, come to £8,000 or more. If dividends plus other capital assets are less than £8,000 but more than £3,000, 'tariff income' of £1 a week is deemed to have been earned on every £250 of assets. A PSC worker who has a deemed Schedule E payment will generally have received dividends in excess of £8,000, and certainly in excess of £3,000, over the course of a year.

However entitlement to WFTC is based on the worker's position 'at the date of application' (DMG 11005). The Guide says: 'An award of WFTC or DPTC is payable for 26 weeks. It is not normally affected by any changes of circumstances during that period' (DMG 14063). The award may only be adjusted in limited circumstances, for example, if the applicant and/or his partner dies, a young person stops full-time education, or there has been a duplicate award (DMG 14071–14122).

Thus entitlement to WFTC may exist on a particular date even if the director expects to receive future dividends from the company (see DMG 26031).

22.3.4 Mechanism for receiving WFTC payments

Initially WFTC was paid by the Inland Revenue directly to recipients. From 6 April 2000 employed recipients have been paid their credits via their wage packets. Where one of the adults is not in employment, he or she can elect to receive the WFTC directly. However this option is not available where both parents are in employment or for employees who are single parents.

Where a worker is entitled to WFTC, it will normally be paid to him by his employer. This applies to personal service companies as it does to other companies. In most cases the credit is funded out of the tax and NIC deducted from the payroll. However, in the case of a service company, particularly one relying on dividends to extract funds, the payroll is likely to be small or non-existent. If the worker's entitlement to WFTC exceeds the company's expected PAYE and NIC deductions, the Revenue will fund the tax credits directly by making a credit transfer into the company's bank account (SI 1999/3219 reg 8).

22.3.5 Conclusion

The main assets owned by a personal services worker – his home, his car, and his company – fall outside the definition of capital for WFTC, and his dividend entitlement for the next period may not yet have crystallised. He may thus be able to pass the capital test. The decision maker may take the view that there are no notional earnings because the company's profits are being fully distributed as dividends, which are then taken into account as capital.

If the worker can satisfy the other conditions for WFTC entitlement, such as number and age of children and hours worked, the deemed Schedule E calculation and associated dividends may allow him to claim the tax credit while regular payments of salary might not. He may thus find, perhaps to his surprise, that he qualifies for the tax credits.

22.4 Student Loan Repayments (SLR)

22.4.1 Outline

The student loan system was introduced on 1 September 1998, and applies to all students starting full-time higher education or teacher training after that date. Interest is charged on the loan at no more than one per cent above base rate.

Student Loan Repayments (SLR) are made from the April following gradua-tion, or from April 2000 if later. No repayments are required if the individual's gross income is less than £10,000 a year. Unearned income of less than £2,000 per annum is ignored.

Where the individual has income of £10,000 or more, repayments equal to nine per cent of the excess is due annually. If the worker is employed, deductions are made via the payroll; if he is self-employed, they are collected by self-assessment.

An employer must deduct SLR from salary:

- Once he has received a 'start' notice from the Revenue to this effect; or

- If the employee has a 'Y' in the relevant box of his P45.

If no start notice has been received, and there is no indicator on the P45, there is no obligation to deduct.

SLR will be policed by the Revenue's employer compliance department, and thus will be audited along with PAYE and NIC, see **16.9**.

22.4.2 Interaction with personal services legislation

Deemed Schedule E amount

The SLR definition of earnings is the same as that for secondary Class 1 NICs. Benefits in kind and other non-cash payments are therefore not taken into account. The National Insurance aggregation rules apply for SLR as they do for personal services, see **4.8.3** (SI 2000/944 regs 27ff and SI 2000/727 reg 8(2))

Since the SLR obligation is based on the NIC definition of earnings, and the deemed Schedule E amount counts as earnings for NICs, see **10.1**, it will also be earnings for SLR purposes. If a worker with deemed Schedule E payment is within the SLR regime, the employer must pay over to the Revenue the SLR on the deemed Schedule E amount, along with PAYE and NICs, on 19 April following the end of the fiscal year.

There are penalties if the annual return is late, or if it is either fraudulent or negligent, on the same basis as for PAYE. The Revenue can also levy a maximum penalty on the employer of £3,000 per employee per year; this is greater than the amounts normally chargeable under the PAYE/NIC penalty legislation, see **16.6** (SI 2000/944 regs 21–26).

Dividends

Dividends in excess of £2,000 a year are unearned income for SLR purposes, and the worker is required to repay an amount equal to 9 per cent of the dividend using his self-assessment form.

However, where the dividends relate to the deemed Schedule E payment, a student loan repayment has already been made on what is effectively the same income. To the extent that the dividend is covered by the deemed Schedule E payment, it is ignored for tax purposes and will not need to be entered on the SA return (Sch 12, para 13 FA 2000 and **15.3.6**).

The Education (Student Loans) (Repayment) Regulations 2000 say that:

> 'In calculating a borrower's total income for the purposes of paragraph (1) there shall be excluded ... income on which the borrower could not become liable to tax under a self-assessment made under section 9 of the 1970 Act for that year.' (SI 2000/944 reg 15(5)(b))

Since it is understood that the dividend will not be included on the self-assessment return, it will also be ignored for SLR. This would be an equitable result, as otherwise two repayments will be required out of what is effectively the same funds.

Partners

Where the worker is a partner, the deemed Schedule E payment will likewise be earnings for SLR purposes. However, because partners are not employees, the partnership is unlikely to have received an SLR notice in respect of a partner with relevant engagements.

In most cases partners will therefore be required to deduct the SLR from income on their SA return, assuming this is more than £10,000 in total, and remembering that unearned income of less than £2,000 is ignored. The deemed Schedule E amount will be included as earnings on the self-assessment form, see **15.3.10**.

22.4.3 Conclusion

The deemed Schedule E amount will count as earnings for SLR purposes, but it is anticipated that any associated dividends will be ignored. Service company workers will have the amount deducted by their employer, partners will make the SLR via their self-assessment form.

22.5 SSP and SMP

22.5.1 Outline

Both Statutory Sick Pay (SSP) and Statutory Maternity Pay (SMP) depend on the level of earnings, and one would thus expect that, as the deemed Schedule E amount is treated as earnings for tax and NIC purposes, it would also give entitlement to both SSP and SMP. However this is not the case.

This may initially appear unimportant, since most PSC's have only one worker/director, and both SSP and SMP are benefits paid to the individual by the company. If there is no entitlement, this should simply mean that more funds are retained by the company. However:

- SSP is sometimes refunded by the government, and service companies may satisfy the conditions for a refund. Ninety-two per cent of SMP is always repayable, and 105 per cent of SMP is paid to small employers. Thus if there is no entitlement to SSP or SMP, there can be no repayment and the service company will be out of pocket as a result;

- SSP and SMP may be particularly relevant to service companies with more than one worker.

22.5.2 Statutory Sick Pay (SSP)

Statutory Sick Pay is paid to an 'employed earner' who:

- Is aged between 16 and 65:

- Is off sick for four or more calendar days in a row;

- Has average weekly earnings of not less than the Lower Earnings Limit (LEL), which is £72 from April 2001 and £75 from April 2002.

An employee is entitled to SSP if his average weekly earnings reach the LEL for NICs. However, it is only possible to take account of amounts actually paid to the individual – deemed salary does not count.

SSP is worth £62.20 per week in 2001/02. It is paid by the employer, but in some circumstances part or all of it can be reclaimed from the government under the Percentage Threshold Scheme (PTS). The PTS applies where 13 per cent of the total employer's and employee's NIC for the tax month is less than the SSP the company has had to pay. Example 22A shows the different consequences for individuals who take the deemed income/dividend path and those who pay themselves salary.

Example 22A

Lucus has his own service company and is within IR35. He has an 18-month contract with a client and works regular hours. His company receives £5,000 a month from the client. Lucus pays himself £3,000 in dividends each month. He knows that at the end of the year his service company will have to pay PAYE and NICs on his deemed salary, but he finds the calculation of a shadow deemed income difficult and has decided to wait until his accountant can help him after the end of the year.

He is in a relationship with Paul, who also has his own service company within IR35 and a long-term client contract. Paul pays himself a salary for each month he works of £3,500, on which tax and NICs is paid.

In December they both catch malaria while on holiday in India, and neither can work for three months. Paul is entitled to statutory sick pay for the months of January, February and March, totalling £812.50. This is itself subject to PAYE and NICs, and the NICs on these payments is £96.69. (Paul has already paid the maximum employee NICs because he is on an annual earnings period, see **4.8.2**). His company is due a refund of £715.81 as, in each of the three months for which he is sick, his company's NIC payments are less than the SSP payments.

However, the same is not true of Lucus. Despite the fact that he has deemed salary for the year well in excess of the LEL, he is not entitled to statutory sick pay. His company thus cannot obtain a refund.

It is clear that this problem can be solved if salary is paid rather the company suffering the deemed payment. But why should this be? The intention of IR35 was to use the deemed payment mechanism to equalise the position of those who paid salary with that of those who used the dividend route, but this clearly does not apply to SSP.

22.5.3 Statutory Maternity Pay (SMP)

Statutory Maternity Pay is payable where an 'employed earner':

- Has been continuously employed by her employer for at least 26 weeks continuing into the 15th week before the week the baby is due. This 15th week is known as the qualifying week;

- Has average weekly earnings of not less than the LEL;

- Is still pregnant at the 11th week before the week the baby is due or has had the baby by that time;

- Gives her employer medical evidence of the date her baby is due, or is born, within three weeks of the start of the Maternity Pay Period (the Maternity Pay Period is the period for which SMP is paid);

- Has stopped working for her employer wholly or partly because of her pregnancy; and

- Gives her employer notice of the date her maternity absence is due to start at least 21 days beforehand.

If a worker satisfies these conditions, she qualifies for SMP even if she does not intend to return to work after the baby is born.

Statutory Maternity Pay is payable for up to 18 weeks; the first six weeks are paid at the higher rate, which is 90 per cent of the employee's average weekly earnings. The lower rate is a set rate which is reviewed each year and is payable for the remaining weeks of the Maternity Pay Period. For 2000/01 the lower rate is £62.20.

All companies can recover 92 per cent of the SMP from the government; small employers can recover 100 per cent plus a further 5 per cent as compensation for the administration involved. To qualify for Small Employers' Relief the company must have paid, or been liable to pay, total Class 1 National Insurance Contributions of £20,000 or less in the qualifying tax year. This includes both employees' and employers' NICs.

Example 22B compares the consequences for SMP of the dividend route versus the salary route.

Example 22B

Kathleen has her own company providing nursing services; she is within IR35. She has an 18-month contract with a nursing home from which her company receives £2,000 a month. Kathleen's accountant arranges for her to receive £1,000 in dividends each month and has told her that at the end of the year he will sort out the tax and NICs on the deemed salary.

Kathleen's sister Deirdre also has her own service company and is also within IR35. In addition, Deirdre has a long-term client contract with the same nursing home. She pays herself a salary for each month she works of £250 a week on which tax and NICs is paid.

In May 2001 both sisters visit a pilgrimage site in the South of France and become pregnant. Deirdre's SMP is as follows:

For the first 6 weeks, £1,350 (250 × 6 × 90 per cent) plus 12 weeks at £62.20, totalling £2,096.

These payments are themselves subject to PAYE and NICs. However, Deirdre's company qualifies for small employer's relief and can thus recover 100 per cent of the SMP paid, plus a further 5 per cent compensation for the cost of the employer's NICs on the SMP. Thus the company receives £2,201 from the government.

However, the same is not true of Kathleen. Despite the fact that she has deemed salary for the year of the same amount as Deirdre, she is not entitled to SMP. Her company can thus not obtain a refund.

22.5.4 Conclusion

It is clear that this problem can be solved in both cases if salary is paid rather than the company suffering the deemed payment. But why should this be? The intention of IR35 was to use the deemed payment mechanism to equalise the position of those who paid salary with that of those who used the dividend route, but this clearly does not apply to SSP or SMP.

23　Solution shopping

23.1　Introduction

The best way of avoiding the personal services legislation is to restructure the way in which services are provided to the client so the individual would not have been an employee had there been no intermediary. This is discussed in detail in Chapter 9. However, this restructuring is sometimes not possible, and frequently requires a high level of knowledge and/or professional costs.

This chapter reviews some alternative solutions. They range from controversial analyses of the legislation through complex avoidance to outright evasion.

23.2　The single contract approach

23.2.1　Outline

For IR35 to apply, the services must be supplied:

> 'Not under a contract directly between the client and the worker, but under *arrangements* involving a third party (the intermediary)'. (Sch 12, para 1(1)(b) FA 2000)

Where an agency is interposed between the service company and the client, some advisers take the view that the only 'arrangement' to be considered is the contract between the service company and the agent. In other words, the contractual arrangements between the agent and the client are irrelevant.

The rationale for this interpretation is based partly on the wording of the legislation, and partly on the view that the service company and the worker cannot be bound by a contract they have not seen and to which they are not party. Both of these arguments are examined below.

If this argument were correct, it would mean that a service company could agree a contract with an agency which includes one or more 'get out of IR35 free' clauses, such as a right of substitution. The agency would not need to replicate, in its own contract with the client, these key provisions.

23.2.2 Legislative argument

The view that only the contract between the service company and the agency needs to be considered is based on the following analysis of the legislation:

- IR35 applies where 'the *circumstances* are such that, if the services were provided under a contract directly between the client and the worker, the worker would be regarded for income tax purposes as an employee of the client' (Sch 12, para 1(1)(c) FA 2000); and

- The 'circumstances' must have 'regard to the terms of the contracts *forming part of the arrangements* under which the services are provided (Sch 12, para 1(4) FA 2000); and

- The 'arrangements' for providing the services must *involve* the service company (Sch 12, para 1(1)(b) FA 2000).

The service company is not a party to the contract between the agency and the client, and it has therefore been argued that the 'arrangements' do not 'involve' the service company, and thus the 'circumstances' do not apply and IR35 is not in point.

23.2.3 Legislative counter-argument

The arguments set out in the previous section are highly debatable. 'Involve' is a wide term – it must be possible to hold that the provision of a service company worker via an agency 'involves' the service company – otherwise the agency contract would not exist in relation to that engagement.

This was confirmed by the Special Commissioner in the recent case of *FS Consulting Limited v McCaul* [2001] SpC 305, where she said:

> 'It seems to me that the phrase "arrangements involving an intermediary" is wide enough to include arrangements involving both an intermediary and a non-intermediary [e.g., an agent]; the phrase is not "arrangements with an intermediary" which would exclude arrangements with a non-intermediary.'

However, she also said this point was not 'free from ambiguity', but on consulting *Hansard* concluded that both contracts had to be considered (see **23.3.8** below).

A further argument is that Sch 12, para 1(4) FA 2000 begins by stating that the 'circumstances' to be considered '*include* the terms on which the services are provided, having regard to the terms of the contracts ... ' This is deliberately widely drafted, and is not narrowly focused on the actual contracts signed with the service company.

A better reading of the legislation is that one must consider the contract that *would have existed* between the worker and the client:

> 'Where the circumstances are such that, if the services were provided under a contract directly between the client and the worker, the worker would be regarded for income tax purposes as an employee of the client.' (Sch 12A, para 1(1)(c) FA 2000)

In other words, at the heart of IR35 is a hypothetical contract – one which does not actually exist – between the worker and the client. The same point was made by Mr Justice Burton in *R v CIR (oao Professional Contractors Group Ltd)* [2001] STC 629. Warning the Revenue not to put too much weight on standard contracts, he said:

> 'It appears to me clear that the Revenue must bear in mind that under IR35 they are not considering an actual contract between the service company and the client, but imagining or constructing a notional contract which does not in fact exist.'

The Special Commissioner in *FS Consulting Limited v McCaul* also referred to 'the notional contract between ... the worker and ... the client'.

To suggest that all the factors relevant to this hypothetical contract can be obtained by looking only at the actual contract signed by the agency and the service company is dangerous. It may of course be the case, in an individual situation, that the terms of the hypothetical contract mirror those of the agent/service company contract, but it cannot be relied upon as a general principle.

23.2.4 Privity of contract and 'common sense'

It has also been argued that the contractor cannot be bound by the agency/client contract because he has neither seen it, nor is he a party to it. Moreover, it runs counter to common sense for an individual's tax liability to be dependent on a document he has not seen.

But this is to miss the point. The individual whose tax and NIC liabilities are being determined under IR35 is *himself providing* the services in question to the client – he can therefore be expected to know the terms under which he is providing his own services. For instance, to what extent is he controlled by the client, is he able to hire an assistant, and will the client accept a substitute? These are the true 'circumstances' which form the terms of his hypothetical contract and on which the operation of IR35 depends. The contracts between him and the agency and between the agency and the client are pointers to the terms of the hypothetical contract, but are not in themselves determinative.

Of course, there may be situations where the client's view of the way the worker is to deliver the services is not the same as the worker's. This problem is exacerbated when a right (such as substitution) has not been exercised during the course of the engagement. But this is a practical difficulty and does not change the legal position, see **5.1.4**.

23.3 Agent as client

23.3.1 Outline

In order to come within the personal services rules the worker must:

> 'Personally perform, or [be] under an obligation personally to perform, services for the purposes of a business carried on by another person ("the client").' (Sch 12, para 1(a) FA 2000; SI 2000/727 reg 6)

If the agency is 'the client' in this paragraph, the question to be answered for IR35 purposes is 'would the worker be an employee of the *agency* if he had contracted directly with the agency rather than using a personal service company?'

23.3.2 Would the worker be an employee of the agency?

In *McMeechan v Secretary of State for Employment* [1997] IRLR 353, the Court of Appeal held that a worker was employed by the agency while he carried out an engagement for one of the agency's clients.

However, this decision is unusual, because it was based on specific contractual terms, including a clause which said:

> 'You are under no obligation to accept any offer ... but if you do so you are required to fulfil the normal common law duties which an employee would owe to an employer as far as they are applicable.'

The Revenue also takes the view that the scope of *McMeechan* is limited, saying:

'We do not think that many agency contracts will turn out to be contracts of employment but the possibility should not be overlooked' (ESM 2002).

Most other decisions go the other way:

(a) In *Wickens v Champion Employment* [1984] ICR 365; *Ironmonger v Movefield Ltd* [1988] IRLR 461 and *Construction Industry Training Board v Labour Force Ltd* [1970] 3 AER 220 it was held that there was no employment because there was insufficient mutuality of obligation between the two parties;

(b) In *Knights v Anglian Industrial Services* [1996] EAT 640 the court held that an individual was not an employee of the agency even though he had worked exclusively for one client over a three-year period;

(c) The views of Mr Justice Buckley in the recent case of *Montgomery*, see **5.9.2**, also suggests that while not impossible, it is difficult for a worker to be an employee of the agency.

Thus, if the agency is 'the client' in the legislation, the hypothetical contract between agency and worker is unlikely to be one of employment. Therefore, the personal services legislation would not apply to the services provided by the worker.

23.3.3 Could the agency be 'the client'?

Wording of Finance Act 2000

The legislation talks about performing 'services for the purposes of a business carried on by another person ("the client").' The individual is certainly providing services for the purposes of the agency's business, since the agency derives its profits from supplying contractor companies' services to third parties. Thus on a straightforward reading of the legislation, the agent could be the client for the purposes of IR35. The Revenue appear to accept this: their definition of 'client' at ESM 3015 is 'the person for whom the worker provides the services. This could be any third party in the contractual chain'.

There is also the view that the only contract to be considered for IR35 purposes is that with the agency. If this is the case, the agent must clearly be the client. This argument has been set out in detail in **23.2.2** above, and discussed at **23.2.3**.

Parallels with s134 ICTA

Although IR35 is new legislation, it has clear parallels with s134 ICTA 1988, commonly known as the agency legislation. Section 134 only applies if 'an individual ("the worker") renders or is under an obligation to render personal services to another person ("the client").

The following is an extract from a circular sent out to members of the Computing Services Association, which represents agencies supplying clients with computer staff. The circular was approved by the Revenue, although they say that 'it is intended only as guidance and is not binding on the Revenue or on members of the Association' (ESM 4020).

> '3. Personal services rendered to a client
>
> One difficulty which arises in interpreting the legislation is the determination of whether an individual is rendering services to a client *or to the member* [of the Computing Services Association]. The answer to that question will normally be found in terms of the contract between the individual and the member and whether, under those terms, be they in writing or otherwise, the individual or the member is taking legal responsibility for the services performed. In the event that the work for the client is negligent, or ineffective, who would take prime responsibility for putting it right – the individual or the member? If the member is the person primarily responsible, then the individual is unlikely to be rendering personal services to the client and Section 134 will not apply.' (the author's italics)

In the context of IR35 this would suggest that if the agency bore the legal consequences if the PSC worker did not deliver as expected, then the worker would be providing personal services to the agency, not to the client.

However, the guidance given in ESM 4020 is incorrect. Whether an individual is providing personal services cannot be answered by discovering who takes responsibility when things go wrong. Although this argument was put forward by the taxpayer in the agency case of *Brady v Hart (trading as Jaclyn Model Agency)* [1985] STC 498, the Revenue won that case on appeal to the High Court and the taxpayer was defeated.

Summary

Although neither ESM 4020 nor the arguments set out in **23.2.2** are persuasive, the clear fact that the services are provided for the purposes of the agency's business means that the agency could be the client. However, this is not the end of the story.

23.3.4 Is the end-user the 'client'?

The case of *Bhadra v Ellam* [1987] 60 TC 466 suggested that the 'client' is not the agency but the end-user. *Bhadra* concerned the application of s134 ICTA (the agency legislation). This is similar to IR35 in that it deems income received to be Schedule E if:

> 'An individual ("the worker") renders or is under an obligation to render personal services to another person ("the client") and … the worker is supplied to the client by or through a third person ("the agency") and renders or is under an obligation to render those services under the terms of a contract between the worker and the agency.' (s134 ICTA 1988 – previously s38(1) Finance (No. 2) Act 1975)

Dr Bhadra was placed in various locum hospital posts by an agency. He argued that:

> 'The statutory hypothesis … should be taken to its logical conclusion and that he should be regarded as having his place of employment situate where the agency was placed.'

In other words, he said he should be regarded as providing services to the agency. However, his argument was rejected by the judge, who took a somewhat purposive approach to the construction of the legislation, saying that:

> 'There is no question of any notional relationship of employment in connection with the agency, and I can see no basis, hypothetical or otherwise, for treating Dr Bhadra as rendering his services in any place other than that in which he did in fact render them, and in particular the place where the agency was situated.'

In other words, the judge held that the services were provided to the hospital, and the hospital was the client.

However, there are significant differences between s134 ICTA 1988 and the personal services legislation. Specifically:

- The agency legislation refers to personal services provided '*to* a person, the "client"'; FA 2000 talks of personal services 'provided *for the purposes of a business carried on by* another person'. It would be difficult to argue that a personal services worker is providing personal services *to* an agency, unless he is effectively employed by them, but plausible to hold that he is providing services for the agency's business;

- The agency legislation has three players – the worker, the client and the agency, all clearly identified. The personal services legislation has only two – the client and the worker. The status of the agency is thus unclear.

These differences may mean that the judge's words in the *Bhadra* case cannot be easily imported into a personal services context. However, that is not to say that a court may not take a similarly purposive approach to the interpretation of Sch 12, see **23.3.7** below.

23.3.5 Not mutually exclusive

Even if the worker is supplying personal services for the business of the agency, it is doubtful whether this makes any real difference to the application of IR35. Supplying services for the business of the agency does not prevent him also from supplying services to the client. In other words, the two are not alternatives.

Parallels for this view can be found in recent anti-discrimination cases. For example, in *Harrods v Remick* [1998] 1 All ER 52, an agency supplied a worker to Harrods (the client) and it was argued for Harrods that the worker was not providing services for the client because her only contract was with the agency. The court dismissed this, holding that the work was for both parties. In a recent case with similar facts, the EAT said that:

> 'We find nothing untoward in a temporary worker working both for the employment agency to whom she is contracted and the client to whom she is directed' (*Hanbury v EDS* [2001] EAT/369).

23.3.6 Revenue view

The Revenue view is set out in FAQ General 13. This clearly adopts the position that the arrangements with the agency and those with the client both need to be considered. It concludes by saying:

> 'In many cases, such as the commonly occurring worker–service company–agency–third party chain, *the worker will be providing services for the purposes of all of the businesses in the chain.* However, it is unlikely that the relationship between the worker and the agency would be employment. It is more likely that the relationship between the worker and the final client will be that of employment and therefore subject to the IR35 legislation.' (the author's italics)

23.3.7 Purposive approach

It is clear from Hansard, see **23.3.8** below, and from the various Revenue press releases, that IR35 is aimed at determining the nature of the relationship

508

between the worker and the end-user. Even if the literal wording of Sch 12 does support the interpretation that the agency can be the client, recent case law suggests that a court would take a purposive approach. Lord Justice Scott said in *Bibby v Prudential* [2000] STC 459 that:

'Ramsay v IRC makes clear that a literal construction of a taxing Act is not necessarily the correct one ... The warning against a literal construction that would permit the use of a taxing provision for a purpose never intended or contemplated by Parliament was directed at taxpayers, or their tax advisers.'

23.3.8 Intention of parliament

If a court felt that there was doubt as to whether the agency or with the end-user was 'the client', it would turn to the principle established in *Pepper v Hart* [1990] 65 TC 421. This allows Hansard to be consulted where:

'Legislation is ambiguous or obscure, or leads to an absurdity; the material relied upon consists of one or more statements by a Minister or other pro-moter of the Bill together if necessary with such other Parliamentary mate-rial as is necessary to understand such statements and their effect; and the statements relied upon are clear.'

In the case of *FS Consulting Limited v McCaul* [2001] SpC 305, the Special Commissioner used Hansard in order to understand what was meant by the 'arrangements', see **23.2.3** above. If it were necessary to consult Hansard to establish who was meant to be the client, it seems clear that the Paymaster General expected that the 'client' in the legislation would be the end-user. For example, on 6 June 1999 she said:

'A worker who is continuously employed by his service company and under-takes contracts for clients of the service company in different places, can claim the costs of travelling to and from those clients' premises.'

She also made the following relevant comment:

'Amendment number 13 [put forward by the Opposition] seeks to exempt from this provision any contract made through an agency. I can see no jus-tification for that. The involvement of the agency in setting up a relationship between a worker and a client will, in most cases, have no relevance to the nature of the relationship in relation to the employment test.'

23.3.9 Conclusion

It would seem to be unwise for a contractor to rely on the argument that the only 'arrangements' which need to be considered for IR35 are those between the agency and the service company, either for the reasons set out at **23.2** above or coupled with the 'agent as client' approach at **23.3**.

23.4 Umbrella companies

23.4.1 Umbrella companies before IR35

Before IR35 composite companies were structured as follows:

- The shares were held by the workers, with each having a separate class;
- The company's day-to-day business was carried out by an independent administrator;
- Earnings were subject to an administrative deduction which covered the costs of running the composite;
- Expenses relating to the engagements were commonly charged through to the company by the worker;
- Each shareholder earned a small salary, with the balance of his net earnings streamed through to him via the dividends on his personal class of shares.

Before IR35, these composite companies gave individuals the benefits of their own service company, without the administrative burdens. They also opened up the tax benefits of PSCs to a much wider group of workers, including secretaries, teachers and train drivers. The tax reliefs meant that running umbrella companies was profitable for the administrators, while the 'take-home pay' of the workers was higher than if they had remained employees.

It is understood that the growth of such companies was one of the main reasons for the introduction of the IR35 legislation. In answer to FAQ General 6: 'Will the new rules apply to people working for "composite" or "umbrella" companies?' the reply was a terse 'Yes'.

However, not all composites were set up for tax avoidance reasons. Some had as their primary aim the provision of administrative assistance to contractors who found the burdens of accounting and taxation too great. The complexity of IR35 means that there may still be a role for the umbrella company, but there are a number of risks involved, see below.

23.4.2 Umbrella companies after IR35

Outline

Since April 2000 administrators and accountants have continued to market composites, and these commonly fall into the following categories:

- Those which apply IR35 to all contracts and calculate the deemed payment for the worker;

- Those which seek to differentiate between workers' assignments, distinguishing those which 'pass' IR35 from those which fail. Sometimes the former are put into an old-style composite and the latter into a different company to which IR35 is applied;

- Those which only accept workers whose the assignments 'pass' IR35;

- Those which believe they can avoid IR35 even though the workers' assignments would normally be caught. One example of this type of avoidance structure is the use of 'independent' directors.

These implications of each are discussed below.

Within IR35

Workers who participated in umbrella companies before IR35 was introduced are potentially within the new legislation for the following reasons:

(a) The individual has a material interest in the intermediary, because he, and/or his associates, own five per cent or more of the shares, see **4.5.2**; or, more commonly,

(b) He receives from the company 'a payment or benefit ... that can reasonably be taken to represent remuneration for services provided by the worker to the client' (Sch 12, para 3 FA 2000); and

(c) He either receives, or is entitled to receive, a payment or benefit which is not taxable under Schedule E, or has rights which would entitle him to such a payment or benefit (Sch 12, para 2(b) FA 2000).

The Revenue give an example of an individual within a composite falling within IR35 at ESM 3107:

> 'Mr D works in the construction industry through a composite service company in which he holds four per cent of the ordinary share capital. The company receives £1,500 each month for his services. From this amount

Mr D pays himself a dividend of £1,150. The balance of £350 is paid as follows:

- £30 as an administration fee

- £50 to cover company running costs

- £120 to Mr D's wife and

- £150 to Mr D as a wage

Mr D performs no other services for the company other than to work for the client. The company has no other income derived from Mr D's services. Therefore, the amount he draws from the company can be linked to those services. The amount to be brought into account at Step One of the deemed payment is the full amount of £1,500 received by the service company.'

Contract review: Separating the sheep from the goats

Some of those who market composite companies divide their customers into those who 'pass' IR35 and those who fail. If this separation is carried out properly, the position for those who pass IR35 is the same as it was before April 2000.

Sometimes selection is on a self-certification basis, with the contractor confirming whether an assignment falls inside or outside the personal services legislation. Other providers analyse all contracts in order to identify which ones pass IR35.

Self-certification has obvious risks, but the contract review process may also come to the wrong conclusion. Deciding whether an engagement is inside or outside IR35 is not a simple matter. If the 'pass' designation is incorrect, the income from that engagement should have been brought within IR35.

Responsibility for carrying out the deemed income calculation and paying over the tax and NICs rests (at least in the first instance) with the directors of the composite. However the tax and NICs could be reclaimable from the worker, see **16.8.2**.

Individuals entering into these arrangements with composites should check:

- Whether the company can recover, from the individual, any PAYE, NICs, interest and penalties which may arise if an engagement is subsequently recategorised by the Revenue as within IR35;

- What information has to be provided, and by whom, in order to establish whether the Revenue's recategorisation of the engagement as 'relevant' is correct? Who will remain in control if there are negotiations with the Revenue? Who will provide, and who will pay for, any professional advice?

- If a worker's engagement is reclassified as within IR35, will other workers' income be used to settle the PAYE and NIC liability?

- The issues and risks identified at **23.4.3** and **23.4.4** below.

Avoiding IR35 by using 'independent directors'

Some composites aim to avoid IR35 by establishing the company with 'independent directors' who distribute money to the workers without there being any apparent link between the distribution and the amount brought into the company by each worker.

This 'solution' is, however, likely to fall within the widely drafted provision that brings workers within IR35 if they receive 'a payment or benefit ... which can reasonably be taken to be remuneration for services provided by the worker to the client' (Sch 12, para 3(1)(b)(ii) FA 2000). It will be difficult to argue that the money paid to the workers in one form or another from the 'independent directors' is not in fact the income received from the client, simply rebadged.

If, on the other hand, the distribution of monies *is* genuinely independent, workers may not actually receive their fair share – a result which could be more costly than paying higher tax and NICs!

23.4.3 Other issues with composites

Using the 5 per cent allowance

To the extent that the workers are carrying out relevant engagements, the composite can access the 5 per cent round sum allowance, see **11.2**. However, in many composites this is effectively used up in dealing with the company's administration. Since this is largely what the allowance was designed to cover, this may be a reasonable approach. But it bears more heavily on those who earn large sums than on those who are less productive.

Policing the expenses

The composite is also responsible for ensuring correct identification of Schedule E allowable expenses. In practice this is achieved by allowing only certain costs, such as travel to the client's site, to be passed directly through the company, with other expenses being claimed on the individual's self-assessment return.

However, excluding allowable costs from the deemed Schedule E calculation means that the PAYE and Class 1 NIC paid is higher than it need be. Although tax relief can be obtained via the self-assessment return, it is not possible to recover the NIC, see **11.3.3.**

Employment rights

Another area of risk is employment rights. Few umbrella companies provide the full range of benefits to which today's employees are entitled, such as maternity pay, statutory sick pay, paid holidays, and access to a stakeholder pension. Many composites operate a 'gentleman's agreement' under which these benefits are not claimed. But what would happen if an individual sued the directors of the umbrella for unfair dismissal following the client's termination of his engagement? Where would the funds come from to pay any benefits claimed? Would the umbrella have to close down?

23.4.4 Composites under attack

Likely areas of Revenue interest

The Revenue may attack composites which have been deliberately structured to avoid IR35, such as those purporting to provide 'independent directors' (**23.4.3**) and those which operate offshore (**23.7**); they are also likely to review those which seek to identify 'pass IR35' contracts to see if the composite has applied the correct tests. In addition, they may challenge the rate of corporation tax charged on composites, see below.

In the summer of 2001 it was widely reported that the Revenue's Special Compliance Office (SCO) was planning a swoop on umbrella companies, and firms running composites reported that they had received calls from an SCO office in Liverpool. These rumours received some support from a new Revenue FAQ: 'Why is the Special Compliance Office involved in IR35 cases', see **16.9.**

Corporation tax

Many administrators limit the number of workers who can be accepted into each composite. This keeps the turnover of the company within the small companies' rate of corporation tax, see **3.2.2.**

However it has been argued (by Gary Axe, *Taxation* 15 July 2001) that where the same administrator sets up a number of umbrella companies, they could be attacked under either or both of the following:

- The rules for associated companies contained in s416(6) ICTA 1988. The recent House of Lords case of *R v CIR (ex p. Newfields Developments Ltd)* [2001] STC 901 confirms the broad scope of this section;

- The rules for close investment holding companies, on the basis that composites are not companies formed to trade but for the purpose of gaining an unfair tax advantage. This would exclude them from small companies' relief under s13A ICTA 1988, see **3.2.2**.

The key question is whether composites can structure themselves so that they fall outside both s416(6) and s13A. However, s416(6) is very broad, defining control as including someone 'if he exercises, or is able to exercise or is entitled to acquire, direct or indirect control over the company's affairs'. The Revenue view of the application of s13A is given in some detail at paragraph 8160 of the Company Taxation Manual.

If a Revenue attack under either of these heads is successful, the composite company would be liable at the mainstream rate instead of suffering tax at the reduced corporation tax rates. Thus the NIC advantage achieved by receiving dividends instead of salary would be counterbalanced by the ten per cent additional corporation tax.

Whose responsibility?

If an umbrella company is successfully attacked, what happens? Most composites retain only one week's undistributed income and thus, if required to pay a large amount of back tax, NICs and interest, not to mention penalties, they would probably go into liquidation. The question is thus whether and to what extent the Revenue could seek the monies from the workers, the directors or the administrator.

The position of the workers and directors is discussed generally at **16.8.2**. The administrator may be liable for the tax and NICs if he is a director or shadow director. The latter is defined as 'a person in accordance with whose directions or instructions the directors of a company are accustomed to act' (s741(1) Companies Act 1985). This definition is also used for tax and NICs (s168(8) ICTA 1988 and SI 2001/1004 reg 1(2)).

At an extreme, the administrator could be investigated by Special Compliance Office or attacked under s99 TMA 1970. This states that:

'Any person who assists in or induces the preparation or delivery of any information, return, accounts or other document which (a) he knows will be, or is or are likely to be, used for any purpose of tax, and (b) he knows to be incorrect, shall be liable to a penalty not exceeding £3,000.'

The Revenue's Employer Compliance Manual at paragraph 21010 states that it might be appropriate to use this section against 'someone other than the employee [who] prepares a return (such as form P14/P35) knowing that it is to be used for tax purposes and knowing that it is incorrect.'

23.5 Employee benefit trusts

23.5.1 Background

Within the normal corporate environment, employee benefit trusts (EBTs) have long been part of remuneration planning. Money is placed into the trust and used at a future date as a reward for employees' performance and to act as a 'golden handcuff' in the meantime.

A full analysis of EBTs is beyond the scope of this book, but such trusts are commonly linked to share option schemes. Corporation tax relief is obtained when the monies are paid into the trust, and these funds are then used to buy the company's own shares. Assuming the trust is discretionary, no PAYE or NICs are due until the employees receive the benefit. The schemes thus defer tax, and when linked to a share scheme can bring other benefits.

23.5.2 EBTs and IR35

In the IR35 environment, offshore umbrella companies have been offering EBT structures linked to loans. The individual works in the UK and earns, say, £100,000, which is invoiced by and paid to the umbrella company. Out of this amount the worker receives £50,000 as salary, which is subject to tax and NICs in the normal way. The balance is placed within the EBT. Independent trustees decide when and how to pay out the profits of the EBT to the employees. In the meantime, the individuals can take loans equal to some or all of the money placed within the EBT. The loan is not a taxable benefit if it is granted at market value. In some cases, the loan is in a currency that is expected to devalue significantly against sterling, and in others it is made clear to the individual that the loan will never be recovered during his lifetime and will be written off on death.

EBT schemes appears to have a number of attractive elements:

- The worker gets access to the full £100,000 but only pays tax and NICs on the portion released to him as salary;

- Tax and NIC on the balance is deferred until the EBT 'pays out';

- Where the loan is in a depreciating currency, its value in ten years time may be negligible, so it can be 'repaid' rather than written off.

However, this structure has a number of problems:

(a) The independence of the trustees, and the supposition that the individual has no rights to the money placed within the EBT, are improbable and thus subject to challenge under anti-avoidance case law. Is the individual really going to risk his £50,000 being paid out to another worker in his stead?

(b) Schedule 12, para 3 FA 2000 states that amounts fall within IR35 where they are 'received or *receivable* by the worker *directly* from the intermediary, and can reasonably be taken to represent remuneration for services provided by the worker to the client'. The two key words here are in italics. It is likely that the money placed into the EBT is money 'receivable' by the worker – he will either access it via a loan, or by request, or on leaving the umbrella company. However, is it 'directly' receivable? If it comes from the EBT, it is not 'directly' from the intermediary. However, the EBT appears to have been 'inserted for the sole purpose of gaining a tax advantage' and thus breaches the basic principle established in *WT Ramsay Ltd v CIR* [1981] 54 TC 101. The Revenue may argue that its existence should be disregarded and a court may agree;

(c) When the employee leaves the umbrella company the loan will be written off and become taxable in full, irrespective of whether the individual is in the UK or overseas at the time of the write-off (s160(3) ICTA 1988, see SE 21745). Failure to report this write-off amounts to an under-declaration of tax;

(d) If the foreign currency loan route is taken so that the loan becomes worthless over time, the Revenue are likely to challenge this under anti-avoidance case law;

(e) Where it is clear that the loan will never be recovered, it is likely that a court would find that this amount is not a loan at all.

23.6 Off-the-peg contracts

23.6.1 Outline

As stated at **23.1** above, the best way of avoiding IR35 is to restructure the way in which services are provided to the client so that the individual would not have been an employee had there been no intermediary. In an attempt to reduce the time, knowledge and/or professional costs involved in carrying out this exercise, a number of contractors have been attracted by the idea of purchasing a ready-made 'escape IR35' contract.

23.6.2 Advantages

There is, of course, no point in everyone re-inventing the same IR35-proof contract. It is only common sense that those who have designed such a contract should make it more widely available in the market place, so that it can be used by service companies who do not want to pay for a bespoke product.

An off-the-peg contract solution works where the purchaser understands IR35 and is able either to adapt the contract to fit his circumstances without undermining its tax effectiveness, or where he can persuade the client to agree to the contract as it stands. However, in many cases obtaining the IR35-proof contract is only the beginning of the story.

23.6.3 Problems

Difficulties with off-the-peg contracts include the following:

- The contracts may not reflect the reality of the individual's working arrangements with the client. This is more likely to occur when the contract is one involving an agency, which, although prepared to sign the contract with the service company, agrees different contractual terms with the client;

- Some off-the-peg contracts contain so many get-out-of-IR35 clauses that they bear no resemblance to reality. They may include totally unfettered substitution and assignment, unlimited risk, complete freedom as to when, where and how the work is carried out and no notice period on either side. If challenged, this contract would be very hard to defend. At best, it would result in a costly debate with the Revenue, at worst it could leave the individual open to real commercial damage.

23.7 'Offshore' companies

Some of those affected by the personal services legislation work via foreign service companies. Chapter 19 looks at what makes an intermediary 'offshore', and considers the implications of operating via a non-resident service company or partnership within the context of IR35. Key issues include:

- A UK company is tax resident here if it is managed and controlled in the UK, irrespective of where it has been registered. A service company with a single worker/director is likely to be resident where the individual is based, see **19.2**;

- Even if a company is not resident here, it may have a 'trading presence' and thus come within the scope of PAYE and NICs, see **19.3**;

- There are special rules which apply for IR35, see **19.5**. These also cover the situation where a UK resident individual carries out work here for a UK client via an offshore umbrella company, even if the latter is not UK resident and has no trading presence.

In brief, it is not easy to avoid IR35 simply by using a company registered overseas; this may in fact amount to evasion and be subject to penalties, see **19.6**.

23.8 The 'Bill & Ben'

It is possible to structure an arrangement under which an individual agrees with an unconnected person to co-operate in avoiding IR35. Either:

- Each individual sets up a company of which they are the director; each company then employs the other. Since the two individuals are not 'associates' within Sch 12, para 19 FA 2000, and neither worker has a material interest in the company which pays him, IR35 does not apply;

- Alternatively, the two individuals go into partnership and agree to split profits 50:50, irrespective of the amounts each brings into the partnership. This avoids IR35 (Sch 12, para 4 FA 2000).

Both these routes have problems. Firstly, the company back-to-back arrangement is likely to be attacked under the 'Ramsay principle' as artificial (*CIR v Ramsay* [CA 1935] 20 TC 79 and subsequent cases). Secondly, the human element should not be ignored. In both these scenarios, each individual has to rely on the other. Will the director of company A pay over all the relevant monies to individual B? In the partnership, what happens if one individual falls sick, or malingers? Tax and NICs may then shrink into relative insignificance.

23.9 New schemes

This chapter cannot cover all IR35 avoidance schemes. New ones will be designed and offered to advisers, agents, contractors and clients. Before becoming involved in, or recommending, a scheme, the following points should be considered:

- Most schemes come with at least one legal opinion attached. An independent professional should be asked to review this opinion, including the 'Instructions' which set out the questions which were asked. Seek confirmation that the opinion is still valid – changes to law and practice may have caused it to be modified. Are there any questions which have not been raised in the Instructions? If so, ask the scheme promoters to raise these questions with their Counsel;

- How artificial is the scheme? In addition to the specific IR35 legislation, the Revenue can use anti-avoidance case law to attack schemes with little commercial substance. What comfort did Counsel give in this area? Would the contractor be prepared to fight the case in court? Does he have the funds to do this?

- Who controls the income of the worker? Many schemes involve an intermediate organisation, such as a partnership, company or trust, which takes all or some of the money earned by the contractor. What are the bona fides of the intermediate organisation? Who are its directors? What comfort has the worker that his money is safe? These questions become more relevant when part or all of the scheme is operating offshore;

- Does the scheme rely on the Revenue not seeing all or part of what is happening? If so, it could amount to illegal evasion rather than legal avoidance. If an individual is involved in avoidance, he can expect the Revenue to challenge his actions; evasion may bring with it criminal penalties, see **16.6.5**;

- What happens if it fails? Who will pay the costs of the investigation, and where will the funds to pay the back tax and NICs be found? Is there any risk that the individual's own money (perhaps held within the scheme company or other vehicle) will be used to settle liabilities relating to others?

- Even if the scheme succeeds, the individual may be the subject of detailed Revenue investigation. Is he comfortable with the rest of his tax affairs? Can he cope with the stress of detailed scrutiny?

- How much is withdrawn to cover the costs of the promoters? Schemes are not set up by altruists with philosophical objections to IR35;

- Lawyers, accountants or tax specialists should be comfortable that the schemes are legal: see *R v Cunningham, Charlton, Wheeler & Kitchen* [1996] STC 1418, discussed at **21.4.2**.

23.10 Conclusion

The best solution to IR35 is a robust, thorough approach to case law, combined (where necessary) with changes to the worker's operating methods, see Chapters 6 to 9. Many schemes are the modern equivalent of the philosopher's stone – magic solutions which seek to turn service companies back into gold mines. But alchemy does not exist, and belief is no substitute for tax analysis.

24 Tax planning after IR35

24.1 Introduction

Chapter 3 set out the tax advantages available to service companies in the halcyon days before IR35. It pointed out that these remain accessible to those companies which fall wholly or partly outside the personal services legislation.

This chapter identifies the opportunities which remain available to companies and partnerships within IR35, and summarises the risks and opportunities discussed at greater length elsewhere in this book.

24.2 Status and contracts

The fundamental tax planning requirement is a review of the worker's contractual arrangements. If the individual would not have been an employee of the client had there been no intermediary, IR35 does not apply. This issue is discussed in detail in Chapters 5 to 9. Particular questions to consider include:

- Is there mutuality of obligation? If there is no mutuality, there can be no employment (**5.3**);

- Can the worker argue, as in *Lorimer* (**8.2.1**), that he is providing his skills to a succession of engagers?

- What similarities are there between the worker's position and that of other taxpayers who have disputed their status in the courts (see Chapter 8)?

- Can a fundamental change be made to his contract, so that it includes substitution, the right to hire others to carry out the engagement, or significant risk (**6.5; 9.3-9.5**)? If he can, he is unlikely to be employed;

- Are other, more minor changes possible to his contractual arrangements that, taken together, would allow him to escape the personal services legislation (**9.6–9.14**)?

- Does the worker want the certainty of a Revenue ruling on his contract (**7.7**)?

- If not, has he taken other 'reasonable steps' to confirm his status (**7.7.8**)?

24.3 Managing the deemed income calculation

The complexities of the deemed income calculation, including the choice between salary and dividends, are discussed in Chapters 10 to 13.

24.3.1 Dividends versus salary

- The intermediary will normally choose between either (a) paying salary, or (b) paying the tax and NICs on the deemed income calculation, and then distributing the net amount as dividends, see **13.5.1**;

- Using solely the dividend route has an adverse effect on SSP and SMP, see **22.5**;

- If the company has a 31 March year end, and is planning to take the deemed income/dividend route, it should almost certainly change its year end, see **13.4.6**. Otherwise it may never obtain full tax relief for the deemed payment;

- Where some shareholders have no relevant income, dividend waivers may be needed so that the individual with the deemed payment receives the appropriate distribution, see **13.6.2**;

- A claim needs to be made to exempt the dividends from tax, see **13.6.2**;

- Those who receive a dividend which is 'covered' by a deemed payment should be made aware of the self-assessment treatment, see **15.3.6**.

24.3.2 Paying the tax and NICs

- PAYE and NIC on the deemed payment is due on the following 19 April. In order to reduce or eliminate the interest payable, the calculation should be completed as soon as possible after the end of the tax year, see **16.4.2**;

- Clearly, any interest cost will be reduced where the salary route has been taken, as the PAYE and NIC due on 19 April will be small;

- If the dividend route has been selected, a shadow deemed income calculation during the year on a monthly basis will allow the final calculation to be carried out relatively quickly.

24.3.3 Keeping appropriate records

Careful record keeping is essential, as the deemed Schedule E calculation is based on a cash rather than an accruals basis, and fiscal years rather than accounting periods. Specifically:

- The income in the deemed Schedule E calculation is on a received not an accruals basis, see **10.2**;

- Expenses, pension contributions and salary are all deductible when paid, rather on the accruals basis used for the accounts, see **11.3.2**, **12.2.3** and **12.4.2**;

- Where more than one worker carries out relevant engagements, the invoicing and record-keeping process should identify the income and expenses relating to each person's work. This is simpler than trying to apportion it later;

- Apportionments will also be required between relevant and non-relevant income, see **10.3**, if this hasn't been achieved via the invoicing process;

- The expenses deductible in the deemed calculation are those which relate to the relevant engagements. If the company has a mixture of relevant and non-relevant engagements, separate records will be needed on an engagement-by-engagement basis. A reasonable apportionment is probably acceptable as an alternative, although not specifically provided for in the legislation;

24.4 Expense reliefs

Although reliefs for expenses deductible in the deemed Schedule E calculation are much less generous than those available under the rules for corporation tax (**11.4**), nevertheless they should not be overlooked. They are discussed in detail in Chapter 11. Points to note include:

- Expenses should be borne by the intermediary rather than directly by the worker. They then reduce the deemed Schedule E amount and thus the NICs payable. If allowable expenses are borne by the worker, he obtains tax relief but no NICs relief, see **11.3.3**;

- The same is true of capital allowances – the assets should be owned by the intermediary, not the individual, see **11.12.1(c)**;

- Personal service workers should be fully conversant with the generous travel and subsistence reliefs, see **11.6**;

- Travel costs can be claimed in the deemed Schedule E computation even if they are not reimbursed by the client;

- Care should be taken when negotiating a contract of more than two years, or an extension to an existing contract which would take it beyond the two year point, as this will result in travel or subsistence expenses being disallowed from the date the contract *was expected* to exceed two years, see **11.6.3**;

- Taking a second contract which is geographically close to the first may cause the two year limit to be exceeded, if the change in location does not make a substantial difference to the travel costs, see **11.6.3**;

- The 5 per cent allowance may compensate for part or all of the intermediary's running costs. Since the allowance is related to income received, the higher the income within the intermediary, the greater the tax relief;

- The allowance is only effective for the purposes of the deemed Schedule E calculation. It has no effect on the corporation tax or partnership computation. If there are insufficient actual expenses to use up the allowance, a payment to a family member might be contemplated, see **3.4**, bearing in mind the caveat that this may be challenged by the Revenue if unsupported by work done;

- Relocation costs paid by the client are tax free providing they are within the limits set down by legislation, see **10.6.10**.

24.5 Losses

The combination of the deemed income calculation and the rules for corporation tax expenses means that corporation tax losses are likely, see **13.7**. Ways of using these losses are summarised at **13.7.2** and **13.7.3**. They include:

- Carrying them back against the previous year's profits so as to obtain a repayment of tax suffered;

- Group relieving them against the profits of another company;

- Introducing income into the company so as to shelter it from tax, though the Revenue may challenge this;

24.6 Pensions

Pension contributions paid by the employer are deducted from the deemed Schedule E amount. They thus reduce both the tax and the NICs payable.

Personal service companies are still in the privileged position of being able to use a Small Self Administered Scheme (SSAS) or an EPP (Executive Personal Pension) as the vehicle for their pension arrangements. As discussed in **3.6**, this type of pension often allows higher contributions than would be possible under a personal pension, as well as providing other tax planning opportunities.

Practical steps which should be taken in the context of pensions include:

- Reviewing the worker's current pension arrangements and taking advice on whether an EPP or SSAS should be considered;

- Working out what is the maximum in-year pension contribution which can be made. This probably requires the use of a model, and a shadow deemed income calculation, see **12.2**;

- Ensuring that, where possible, pension contributions are made by the company, not by the individual, as otherwise no NIC relief is obtained, see **12.2.2**;

- Considering whether there is scope to use earlier years' pension capacity under the carry-forward, carry-back rules (s625, s641 ICTA 1988). These contributions have to be made by the individual personally and will not therefore affect either the deemed income calculation or the NICs payable. Tax relief will however be obtained at the individual's marginal rate;

- Payments into a RAP are not allowed as a deduction in the deemed income calculation, and this should be taken into account when considering whether to switch to a personal pension, see **12.2.1**.

24.7 Overseas issues

The interaction between IR35 and concepts such as residence, ordinary residence and domicile is complex, see Chapters 17 to 19. A personal services worker going overseas or coming to the UK should obtain individual advice in relation to his specific position.

Planning points include:

- The rules for tax and NICs are not identical, and an individual can be non-resident (and outside the deemed income calculation) for tax, but remain an employed earner for NICs (and thus have to complete an attributable earnings calculation), or vice versa, see Chapter 18 and **12.7.2**;

- If an individual works overseas for a whole tax year, he will normally be non-resident and not within the scope of UK tax in respect of amounts earned that year, see **17.9.3**;

- It may be possible to establish or retain a foreign domicile (see **17.11**). This allows earnings from work carried out wholly abroad for an overseas client to escape UK tax in general, and the deemed income calculation in particular, provided they are not remitted to this country;

- A remittance basis also applies where the individual is resident but not ordinarily resident. This allows *all* earnings for work done overseas, not only that for an overseas client, to escape UK tax as long as it is not remitted here, see **17.5.2**;

- Workers coming to the UK should ensure that they retain their 'not resident and/or not ordinarily resident' status for as long as possible, to protect overseas earnings from the deemed income calculation. Care is needed, because intentions as well as actions can trigger both residence and ordinary residence, see **17.5.1**;

- Dual contracts should be considered by non-domiciliaries where engagements involve some overseas work, see **17.12.3**. Dual contracts may also be appropriate for those who are not ordinarily resident, see **17.8.5**;

- Workers may obtain relief for overseas tax suffered on their foreign earnings against the PAYE on their deemed income calculation, but only if the overseas tax cannot be offset against corporation tax on the company's profits, see **17.10.2**;

- A deduction may be available in the deemed income calculation for the cost of family members travelling to visit a PSC worker overseas. This is the case even if the client does not reimburse the costs, see **17.10.3**;

- Family travel expenses may also be allowable where an overseas worker is carrying out a relevant engagement in the UK, see **17.12.4**;

- If an individual is seeking to establish permanent residence abroad, but is not working there full-time, care is needed with the 90 day rule. It is possible to be outside the UK most of the time but still remain resident and ordinarily resident here and thus within IR35, see **17.9.4**;

- Where work is to be carried out in an EEA state other than the UK, it is better to have a separate engagement with an overseas client rather than being sent overseas by a UK client. This should prevent the short-term posting rule coming into effect, and ensure the worker escapes the PSC NICs charge and is liable only on his normal salary and benefits, see **18.3.4**;

- Where the director is working in the UK, his service company is likely to be tax resident here, even if it is registered overseas, see **19.2.3**. If the company *is* offshore, IR35 deems it to have a place of business here, providing the worker and the client are both resident in the UK, see **19.5**. In both cases the company is required to apply PAYE and NICs to the deemed payment, and failure to do so may incur penalties.

24.8 Partnerships

Although many of the problems and opportunities arising from the new legislation apply to all intermediaries, some points are particular to partnerships. They include:

- Partners should consider whether it is possible to escape IR35 altogether, by carefully reviewing the legislation and other exemptions, see **14.2** and **14.3**. It may be possible to exclude the partnership from the personal services legislation by taking in new partners, such as brothers-in-law or sisters-in-law, see **14.2.2**, although care should be taken with the settlements legislation, see **3.4**;

- For years before 2002/03, expenses should be borne by the partnership rather than by the partner directly, because this reduces the deemed Schedule E amount and thus the NICs payable. If allowable expenses are borne by the worker, tax relief can only be obtained via the partnership computation. There is also no Class 1 NICs relief, see **14.5.4**. Reimbursement of expenses by the partnership achieves the correct result;

- For capital allowances, assets should be owned by the partnership, not the partner, see **14.5.5**;

- There are strict rules for deducting expenses in the partnership return, and also for losses (see **14.6.3**). Partnerships need to be fully conversant with this part of the legislation to ensure that their self-assessment form is correct;

24.9 Clients and agencies

- Workers need the co-operation of clients and agencies if they are to restructure their contractual arrangements so as to fall outside IR35, see Chapter 9.

- In restructuring a contract, the risks for the agency and the client should not be ignored, see **21.2.2** and **21.3.5**;

- If the tax status of freelance consultants is uncertain, clients may wish to reduce their own PAYE and NIC exposure by engaging only service companies and not individuals, see **21.3.4**;

- If the service company is offshore, the client still has to deduct PAYE and NICs from any salary due to the worker, although responsibility for the deemed payment rests with the intermediary, see **21.3.2**;

- Engaging a worker supplied by an overseas service company can thus be administratively burdensome, and may create liabilities to PAYE and NICs which are not discovered until the client has a PAYE audit;

- Both clients and agencies may have to provide the Revenue with detailed information about payments made to service companies, see **21.2.4** and **21.3.5**. Establishing in advance how this data is to be collected will simplify the compliance process.

24.10 Penalties and investigations

- If the PAYE and NICs on the deemed payment are late, there will be an interest charge but no penalty, as long as the procedures set out at **16.4.2** are complied with;

- IR35 is likely to be policed by the Revenue's Employer Compliance Unit. If a company has misunderstood the rules, it should be able to rely on Dawn Primarolo's promise that the penalty regime will be applied with a light touch, see **16.7.2**;

- In other situations, the normal pleas for mitigation may be accepted, see **16.7.4**.

24.11 Other possibilities and risks

- It may be possible to retain surplus funds within the company in order to take advantage of the low corporate tax rates, see **3.8**;

- Capital gains tax planning, using taper relief rules and annual allowances, should be investigated where the intermediary has some intrinsic value;

- Tax reliefs are available against other income for interest on money borrowed and then invested in the company, see **3.7**;

- The deemed Schedule E payment does not count for minimum wage purposes, and workers other than partners or directors will thus need to be paid an appropriate salary, either on a monthly basis or more frequently, see **22.2.3**;

- IR35 does not apply to engagements with householders, so a service company could be used for domestic help, such as nannies or gardeners, see **4.3.1**;

- There may be an opportunity to claim WFTC, see **22.3**;

- The reasons for and against liquidating the service company are given in **13.8**.

25   Case studies

25.1 Introduction

The Revenue have provided six cases studies showing how the status tests apply to particular situations. *Tax Bulletin* 28, April 1997 covered subcontractors in detail, while the *Tax Bulletin* in February 2000 focused on IT contractors. But the general points in both are relevant to all personal service workers. The background to these case studies is discussed in Chapters 6 and 7.

25.2 Case studies for IT contractors with service companies

25.2.1 Outline

The Revenue's case studies show how the status tests apply to a worker who is:

(a)   Within the personal service rules (Gordon);

(b)   Outside the personal service rules (Henry); and

(c)   Balanced on the line between the two (Charlotte).

25.2.2 Example 1: Gordon, an IT contractor working through his own service company

Facts	Comments
Job description/Control	
Client is a large retail concern. The contract was obtained through an agency. The terms and conditions of the engagement are set out in the contracts between the client and the agency and the agency and Gordon's company.	The fact that the engagement has been obtained through an agency has no bearing on whether Gordon would have been an employee or not.
Gordon works as part of a support team for the client's payroll system. The team leader (another IT contractor) tells Gordon what work he is to carry out at any particular time (e.g., help-desk work, specific maintenance tasks, etc.).	The extensive right of control that exists here is a very strong pointer to employment. The more important features are the client's ability to shift Gordon from task to task and to specify how the work should be done – but in addition the client can control where and when the work is carried out.
The client has the right to tell Gordon 'how' the work should be carried out – although in practice such control is not normally necessary.	
Gordon must work a regular 40-hour week on the client's premises.	The company is paid an hourly rate for Gordon's services and the only financial risk comes from invoicing. There is no opportunity to profit from sound management of the work covered by the contract. Overall this points to employment.
Payment basis/risk	
Gordon's company is paid an hourly rate for Gordon's services. Any extra hours worked (by mutual agreement) are paid at 1.5 times the normal hourly rate. The client makes payment monthly following submission of an invoice by the agency. Gordon's service company invoices the agency.	The engagement runs for six months and holiday pay/sick pay might be expected had there been a direct engagement. But both parties see the actual company/client contract as a contract for services and this is probably why no such payments are made. A minor pointer to self-employment.

Holiday pay/sick pay

No sick pay or holiday pay paid under the terms of the inter-company contract.

Length of contract and personal factors

The contract is for six months.

Gordon uses a computer, telephone, fax, etc., at home to seek and negotiate contracts for his company.

Gordon's company has a limited 'business organisation' consisting of an office and associated equipment at his home. This is a pointer to self-employment – but not an overly important one in the context of a six-month contract of this sort.

Gordon has worked through his company for two other clients in the last two and a half years – one for three months and one for two years. Prior to that he was a direct employee of another engager.

Other points

Neither side can terminate the contract early.

Neutral factor (no right to terminate is common in engagements of this length – whether employment or self-employment).

There is no restriction imposed by the contract that prevents either Gordon or his company providing services to others during the engagement.

Mild pointer towards self-employment.

Both parties never intended Gordon to be an employee.

Pointer to self-employment, but will only be relevant if the other factors are neutral.

Overall picture

The engagement is fairly long term and there is an extensive right of control over Gordon. He must carry out the services personally. The client provides equipment and accommodation and there is no significant financial risk to the company.

The only pointers to self-employment are the minimal financial risk (from invoicing), the ability to work for others (again, a minor point) and the existence of a business organisation/work for other clients.

Standing back from the detail therefore the engagement is one which would have been an employment had it been direct between Gordon and the client. The common intention for self-employment does not alter that. Whilst it would have proved decisive in a 'borderline' situation a review of other factors points strongly to employment here. The new rules would apply to the engagement.

25.2.3 Example 2: Henry, a consultant engineer working through his own service company

Facts	Comments
Job description/Control	
Client is a large manufacturing company. Under a previous contract Henry has undertaken a broad review of a 15-year-old production line and established that significant improvements could be made to the line to increase productivity. Under the current contract Henry is to produce a further report with detailed and costed proposals on the improvements and how they might be carried out with minimum disruption to production.	A specific task has been agreed and the client cannot shift the worker to another task. Henry has the major say over how the work is carried out and when. The client does have some right to ongoing control over the work in that regular reports are required and changes in Henry's proposals can be sought.
Henry has a free hand over how his work is carried out and when (although there is a deadline of three months for completion). However, Henry is required to keep the client fully informed about progress and the client can require Henry to modify proposals if any aspect seems unsuitable to them.	Overall, control is limited.
Payment basis/risk/opportunity to profit	
Henry is paid £70 an hour but there is a ceiling of 300 hours on the work. If Henry takes longer than this he will only be paid extra if unforeseen difficulties arise or the client insists on unreasonable	Henry is being paid an hourly rate and there is no real prospect of his making a loss. Nevertheless he is subject to a ceiling and must complete the work in the

changes. If the work takes less than 300 hours Henry is only paid for the hours worked.

time allowed for otherwise he will have to finish the work in his own time without further payment. This is a mild pointer to self-employment.

Holiday pay/sick pay

No sick pay or holiday pay paid under the terms of the inter-company contract.

Pointer to self-employment.

Length of contract and personal factors

The contract has a deadline of three months.

Henry has worked through his company as an engineer for many years and it is accepted that the company is 'in business'. The company has had many engagements similar to the current one and is generally engaged to provide an 'expert' service by clients with little engineering expertise.

The company has a business organisation and many different clients. This is a significant pointer to self-employment.

Henry has an office and computer at home which he uses for work extensively.

Equipment

Henry visits the client's factory regularly to examine the production line and processes. The only significant equipment he uses is his own computer (to prepare the report).70 per cent of the work is done in his office.

Significant and fundamental equipment is provided by the company as is office accommodation. This points to self-employment.

Other factors

Engagement cannot be terminated 'early' other than following a breach of contract.

Neutral factor (no right to terminate is common in engagements of this length – whether employment or self-employment.)

There is no restriction imposed by the contract that prevents either Henry or his company providing services to others during the engagement.

Mild pointer towards self-employment.

| Both parties intend that the company is engaged to carry out the work and that Henry is not an employee of the client. | Pointer to self-employment, but will only be relevant if the other factors are neutral. |

Overall picture

Henry is a skilled worker who has been engaged to carry out a specific task and control over him is limited. He is paid based on an hourly rate but there is an over-riding limit within which the work agreed must be completed. There is a contract deadline of three months and the company has many other clients. Some important equipment is supplied by the company and the work is mainly carried out away from the client's premises.

Henry would have been self-employed if engaged directly by the client and the new rules will not apply. Even if the contract had been expected to last for a longer period – say, nine months – the other factors would still have led to a conclusion of self-employment.

25.2.4 Example 3: Charlotte, an IT consultant working through her own service company

Facts	Comments
Job description/Control	
Charlotte's client for this engagement is a software company. She has been engaged for her programming skills to work on a specific project as part of a team developing a new piece of software. She works to the client's project manager who allocates particular sub programs to Charlotte that she writes. The client expects the project to last for around three months.	There is an extensive right of control over Charlotte. The more important features are the client's ability to shift Charlotte from task to task and to specify how the work should be done. In addition the client can control to some extent where and when the work is carried out. But control is not total. Charlotte is engaged to work on a specific project so cannot be told to work on something completely different – and she cannot be required to work elsewhere. Overall, this is a strong pointer to employment.
The manager specifies the way in which the sub-program is to be structured and can require changes to be made to make the work fit in with other parts of the program as it is developed, to rectify overall design faults, etc.	

Charlotte works a set number of hours but actual working times are flexible in line with the company's flexitime arrangements for its employees. She is required to work at the client's premises.

Payment basis/risk/sick pay/ holiday pay

Charlotte is paid £3,600 every four weeks in return for working a 40-hour week. Extra payments are made at the equivalent hourly rate for any additional hours agreed. Payment is made 14 days after the company has invoiced the client.

It is the arrangements between the service company and the client that are important here. The company is paid the equivalent of a salary – with overtime payments – but no sick pay or holiday pay. Although the invoicing arrangements result in a small financial risk this is minor. Overall there is no significant financial risk and no opportunity to profit from sound management of the task. This points to employment.

No sick pay or holiday pay is paid, under the contract Charlotte has with her company. She is paid an on-going, but much lower, salary which includes provision for holiday pay and sick pay.

Length of contract and personal factors

The contract is for 12 weeks – but there is provision for an extension if the project over-runs and all parties agree to the extension.

Charlotte does some work for another client at weekends and has worked for various clients in the past – always through her company and often through employment agencies. Her contracts have usually lasted for between one and three months. Most have been similar to this one but some have involved her in specific tasks for a fixed fee using her own equipment and working at home.

Charlotte and her company have a 'business organisation' – including an office and associated equipment based at Charlotte's home. She has a variety of clients and all her contracts have been fairly short term.

Charlotte has an office at home and a computer and other office equipment that is used for some of her other work. These contribute to her company's business organisation – which she uses to obtain work, keep records, prepare invoices, etc.	This is a strong pointer to self-employment.

Other factors

The company is contracted to supply Charlotte to do the work personally.	Both point to employment.
All equipment is supplied by the client.	Both point to employment.
The engagement cannot be terminated 'early' other than following a breach of contract.	Neutral factor (no right to terminate is common in engagements of this length – whether employment or self-employment).
There is no restriction imposed by the contract that prevents either Charlotte or her company providing services to others during the engagement.	Pointer to self-employment.
All parties intended that the company/client engagement would be self-employment.	Pointer to self-employment, but will only be relevant if the other factors are neutral.

Overall picture

This is a borderline case. On balance, given all the facts, Charlotte would have been self-employed had she been engaged directly by the client. The new rules will not apply to the engagement.

The following point towards self-employment:

- Existing business and a variety of different engagements, some of which would clearly count as self-employed if she had been engaged directly by her client.

- Overall business organisation (office and equipment at home, businesslike approach to obtaining engagements and carrying them out, etc.). Charlotte would clearly be regarded as being 'in business on her own account' for those engagements where she carried out a specific task for a fixed fee using her own accommodation and equipment.

- Risk from invoicing.

- The lack of an exclusivity clause.

Other factors point to employment:

- There is fairly extensive control over Charlotte. The client can dictate 'what' work is carried out on the project and 'how' the work is done. But control is not total. Charlotte cannot be directed to work on another project or undertake some quite different work. Nor is there control in other areas (e.g., she is subject to the client's normal staff rules/disciplinary procedures).

- There is virtually no financial risk in the engagement and no opportunity to profit from sound management of the task.

- Charlotte must carry out the work herself.

- All equipment and accommodation is provided by the client.

What can then have more significance is the extent to which the individual is dependent upon, or independent of, a particular paymaster for the financial exploitation of his or her talents (see *Hall v Lorimer*). The fact that Charlotte's company is also engaged in contracts which involve carrying out a specific task for a fixed fee, using her own equipment, suggests that it is a genuine business and neither she nor her company rely on a single client for the exploitation of her talents. These factors balance the control and other employment factors that exist in this particular context and put the matter near the borderline where the mutual intention for self-employment becomes decisive.

However, the overall picture would have been rather different had the engagement been longer. For example, had the engagement been for twelve months the 'personal factors' would have been far less significant and the employment pointers would have predominated. Just because a person has an established business does not automatically make them self-employed for all engagements (see *Fall v Hitchen* (49 TC 433) – also referred to in *Hall v Lorimer*). Also, if she had not also had contracts of a type which would clearly have fallen within the definition of self-employment, employment pointers would have dominated and the contract at issue would have been one of employment. The same could apply to shorter contracts.

25.3 Case studies for subcontractors

25.3.1 Context

These were not aimed at subcontractors with service companies, as the publication of these case studies pre-dated the PSC rules. Instead they applied the status tests to individual subcontractors, asking whether they would be self-employed or employees. However, since the IR35 rules depend on the same status tests, these case studies remain highly relevant.

25.3.2 Example 1: General labourer

Facts	Comments
Job Description/Control	
Undertakes a variety of unskilled and semi-skilled work (e.g., digging footings, assisting craftsmen, etc.). Engager moves him from task to task as necessary. Can be told how to do a particular task but this is generally unnecessary in view of his experience.	Strong control exists here. The more important features are the engager's ability to move the worker from job to job as priorities change and to have the ultimate say in how the work should be carried out.
Payment basis/risk	
Paid a weekly wage plus overtime	No financial risk or opportunity to profit from sound management points to employment.
Holiday/sick pay	
No sick pay paid (has been sick twice over last 12 months). No holiday pay but has been allowed three weeks off (unpaid) for holidays during over the last the last 12 months.	The engagements run to some months and holiday pay/sick pay might be expected. But to take both parties think the engagement is self-employment and this is probably why no such payments are made. A minor pointer towards self-employment.
Length of engagement and personal factors	
Taken on for the expected duration of the engager's building project – usually weeks or months with the actual length depending on how	Not a 'permanent' employment, but a series of fairly lengthy separate engagements with one engager. No evidence of working for several

well the project progresses. Has worked for the same engager almost exclusively for three years – but with two periods of 'unemployment' of three weeks and two months during the same time.

engagers. Overall, the pattern of work suggests employment.

Does odd jobs for private householders at weekends with payment 'by the task'. Earned £600 from this over the last 12 months.

Is to this extent 'in business'. But small part-time earnings of this nature will not be the key factor when measured against a full time engagement running to weeks or months.

Worker keeps an 'office' at home. He has a home computer which he uses to record income and expenses. He also has a phone which he uses to arrange weekend work and new contracts.

Has an office and is fairly business-like in the way he organises and runs his engagements. This points towards self-employment.

Other factors

All equipment and materials provided by the engager except for working clothes and boots.

Points to employment

Hired personally to do the work.

Points to employment

Engagement can be terminated by either side on one week's notice.

Points to employment

Both parties clearly intend that the engagements amount to self-employment

Pointer towards self-employment and important in borderline situations. Not conclusive where – overall – other factors point to employment.

Overall picture

The picture which emerges is of a weekly paid worker carrying out unskilled and semi-skilled work with the engager having strong control. These are strong pointers towards employment. Other factors also point to employment (equipment, lack of financial risk, period of notice). Although some personal factors point to self-employment taking all factors into account the engagements amount to employment. The mutual intention for self-employment would only be decisive where the other factors were borderline – and here they point to employment.

The result would be similar even if personal factors were stronger (e.g., regular working for many engagers). Other factors (particularly the strong right of control) would outweigh such factors.

25.3.3 Example 2: Plasterer

Facts	Comments
Job Description/Control	
Contracted to plaster walls and ceilings of a two classroom school extension. Cannot be told 'how' to do the work but it must be completed satisfactorily. Work to be done during normal working hours at the site.	Little or no control over 'what' is to be done and 'where' (fixed by the contract) or how it is to be done. Limited control over when the work is to be done. Points to self-employment.
Substitution	
May choose to pay and send a substitute or use assistants. Engaged and used an assistant to help throughout the contract.	Strong pointer towards self-employment.
Equipment and materials	
Provides only equipment needed (hand tools and shovel/container for mixing). Materials supplied by engager.	No significant equipment required. The fact that the engager supplies materials points towards employment.
Payment basis/risk	
Paid per square metre plastered. Worker is responsible for completing entire job within time allotted.	There is opportunity to maximise profit from the sound management to the task. Worker must complete the contract so this is not pure piece work and there is real financial risk. E.g., were the worker to fall ill he would be responsible for hiring others to to complete the contract (even at a loss).
Three-week deadline for completion with a penalty of £100 per day for failure to complete the work on time.	Further risks arise from the penalty clause for failing to meet the deadline and the requirement to rectify work at his own cost (including materials).
Must rectify faulty work in own time and own cost (including supplying extra materials needed).	All pointers to self-employment.
Other factors	
Length of contract – three weeks	A minor pointer to self-employment.
Works for many engagers (20 in past 12 months). All contracts of	Has a pattern of working under short-term contracts for many different

less than six week duration. No holiday or sick pay. No right to end contract unless serious breach of terms.

engagers. Pointer to self-employment. Not significant in the context of a three week engagement.

No office at home. Prepares accounts from record book recording all receipts and expenditure. Has a phone which he uses to arrange new contracts.

Little in way of 'business organisation' (e.g., yard or office etc.). Not a significant pointer either way.

Both parties intend that the engagements amount to self-employment.

Pointer towards self-employment in borderline situations.

Overall picture

The picture painted is of a self-employed individual carrying out skilled work and genuinely accepting the risks of being in business on his own account. The worker.

- Is subject to little control.

- Faces real financial risk.

- Engages and pays an assistant to help perform the contract.

- Works for a variety of engagers on fairly short-term contracts.

25.3.4 Example 3: Bricklayer

Facts	Comments
Job Description/Control	
Engaged solely as a bricklayer. Engager moves him from task to task as necessary. He is provided with helpers who mix mortar, carry bricks, etc. Engager cannot tell him 'how' he wants the work done but expects competent workmanship and a reasonable level of output.	Control over 'what' is to be done – but limited to the extent of what bricks should be laid and cannot be diverted to quite different work. Little control over the manner in which the work is to be done. An employment pointer but not as strong as in Example 1.
Substitution	
Hired personally to do the work	Points towards employment
Equipment	
All provided by engager except for working clothes, boots and trowel.	Worker providing own 'small tools'. Engager supplies other equipment and all materials. Pointer to employment.

Payment basis/risk

Paid a weekly wage plus overtime.

No financial risk or opportunity to profit from sound management. Points to employment.

Length of contract

Taken on for the expected duration of the engager's building project (usually weeks or months at a time). Has worked for the same engager almost exclusively for three years but with three periods of 'unemployment' of one week, three weeks and one month during that time.

Not a 'permanent' employment but a series of fairly lengthy separate engagements with one engager. No evidence of working of several engagers. Overall, the pattern of working suggests employment.

Right of dismissal

Engagement can be terminated by either side on one week's notice.

Pointer towards employment.

Holiday/sick pay

No sick pay paid (has been sick once over last 12 months). No holiday pay but has been allowed to take a total of three weeks off for holidays (unpaid) during engagements over the last 12 months.

The engagements run to some months and holiday/sick pay might be expected. But both parties think the engagements are self-employment and this is probably why no such payments are made. A minor pointer towards self-employment.

Personal factors

No office at home. Records income and expenditure in a notebook. Has a phone which he uses to arrange weekend work and new contracts.

Little in the way of a 'business organisation' (e.g., yard or office, etc.) Not a significant pointer either way.

Does odd jobs for private householders at weekends with payment 'by the task' – earned £600 from this over the last 12 months.

Is to this extent 'in business'. But small part-time earnings of this nature will not be a key factor when measured against a full-time engagement running to weeks or months.

Prior to first working for this engager had been an apprentice bricklayer with another firm.

No evidence of existing full time business prior to working for this engager.

Has had a 714 certificate for the last three years – which expires in two years time.

Not a relevant factor.

Overall picture

The picture painted is of a skilled worker who is told what is to be done at any particular time but with little control over how it is to be done. 'Control' points towards employment but not as strongly as in Example 1. Other factors also point towards employment (e.g., weekly wage, lack of financial risk, period of notice).

Of those factors pointing to self-employment:

- Lack of holiday and sick pay are not conclusive.

- Mutual intention will only be decisive where other factors put the engagement near the borderline.

- There are no significant personal factors pointing to self-employment. There is not, for example, a clear pattern of regular working for many engagers or regular working under very short-term contracts. Further there is no evidence of an established pattern of working and business prior to the series of engagements with this engager.

Overall, the terms and conditions alone point towards employment and personal factors do not significantly affect this. The contracts are therefore considered to be contracts of employment. But the case is not far from the point where mutual intention would be decisive. If there had been a single ongoing contract or holiday pay/sick pay had been paid, the argument for employment would be much stronger.

On the other hand, if significant personal factors had existed (e.g., regular working for many engagers under short-term contracts), or there had been task based payment, the picture overall would probably be sufficiently borderline for mutual intention to decide that these SEPARATE engagements amounted to self-employment.

Index

References are to paragraph number.